The Ethics of Nonviolence

The Ethics of Nonviolence

Essays by Robert L. Holmes

Edited by
Predrag Cicovacki

B L O O M S B U R Y
NEW YORK • LONDON • NEW DELHI • SYDNEY

Bloomsbury Academic

An imprint of Bloomsbury Publishing Plc

1385 Broadway	50 Bedford Square
New York	London
NY 10018	WC1B 3DP
USA	UK

www.bloomsbury.com

First published 2013

Library of Congress Cataloging-in-Publication Data
A catalog record for this book is available from the Library of Congress

ISBN: HB: 978-1-6235-6642-5
PB: 978-1-6235-6805-4
ePub: 978-1-6235-6580-0
ePDF: 978-1-6235-6962-4

Typeset by Newgen Imaging Systems Pvt Ltd, Chennai, India
Printed and bound in the United States of America

No problem can be solved from the same level of consciousness that created it.
Albert Einstein

Contents

Introduction

I pictured to myself that instead of these national enmities which are instilled into us under the guise of love of one's country, and instead of those applauded slaughters called war, which from childhood are represented to us as the most heroic deeds, I imagined that we were imbued with horror at and contempt for all those activities, political, diplomatic, and military, which promote the separation of peoples; and that it was suggested to us that . . . to go to war—that is to say, to kill people, people virtually unknown to us, without any grounds—is the most horrible villainy, to which only a lost and perverted man, degraded to the level of a beast, can descend. I pictured to myself that all men believed this, and I asked: What would be the result?

Leo Tolstoy, *What I Believe*

The theme unifying this collection of Robert Holmes' essays can best be characterized as "the ethics of nonviolence." This introduction will offer a brief account of how such an ethical orientation differs from widely accepted ethical theories, and go on to explain the unique characteristics and implications of Holmes' conception of nonviolence.

For Holmes, "ethics is the study of morality," and "morality is a creative, cooperative enterprise whose end is the better world."[1] Philosophical ethics is focused on developing a systematic and rational account of good and evil, right and wrong; it usually centers around one principle—Utilitarianism and Kantianism are good examples—argued to be objective, universal, or even absolute.

I will not consider here the many controversies that such theories are familiar with. In the course of his fifty-year-long career of teaching and writing about ethics, Holmes dealt with them on numerous occasions. It is of more significance in this context to point out external problems that all mainstream ethical approaches hold in common. They (1) neglect the nonrational aspects of ethical evaluations and choices; (2) ignore the social, political, and cultural factors influencing our choices and behavior; and (3) leave unchallenged the basic structures of society.

An exaggerated emphasis on the "utilitarian calculus" and "practical reason" turns our attention away from the role of emotions and intuitions in our moral practice. To avoid usual misconceptions and prejudices against the role of nonrational elements, Holmes talks about "moral discernment," which he ties closely to conscience and personal experience. According to him, neither a rational calculus nor a categorical imperative provides a universal ground of morality. Whatever moral dilemmas encountered, the ultimate justification for our moral choices and judgments must be the conscience of an individual, with his or her personal moral experience.

---

[1] Robert L. Holmes, *Basic Moral Philosophy*, fourth edition (Belmont, CA: Wadsworth, 2007), quoting from pages 1 and 228.

In moral philosophy we mostly ignore conscience and personal experience, just as we tend to ignore various social and political aspects of the situations in which moral choices and behavior take place. This tendency is due to our expectation that there is an unchanging, universal, even absolute moral principle. Steeped in the pragmatist spirit of William James and John Dewey, Holmes rejects the absolutism of principles—and absolutism of any kind. This rejection leads him to a careful examination of the historical and cultural circumstances in which moral practice takes place. Proper knowledge of history and our recognition of various political, economic, and cultural trends are often the preconditions for a proper moral analysis. The influence of pragmatism also directs Holmes to develop his moral approach in terms of what he calls "moral contextualism." The core of this approach is the distinction between what is "actionably right" and what is "actually right." As life-experience teaches us, an action that we sincerely believe is right may fail to be actually right. Nevertheless, acts that are justifiably believed to be right are actionably right, and they are justifiably performed. Moral contextualism contends that we simply cannot know what is actually right most of the time. Hence we must make the best judgment from the perspective of our limited knowledge and understanding. And this means that each situation must be judged on its merits. Moral contextualism does not imply that our fundamental obligation is to change the world. It is rather "*to try* to do so, and to try as carefully and responsibly as possible; and to do so in the ways that are morally best."[2]

Because we cannot be certain about what is actually right and since we cannot foresee the consequences of our actions with any definiteness, moral contextualism emphasizes the role of the human individual in two ways. First, it underscores our responsibility as moral agents. We cannot merely follow some pregiven commandment as to how we should act, nor can we simply pursue a utilitarian calculus. A moral agent must try to be well-informed about a situation which he or she encounters, and also sensitive toward the needs, desires, and constraints of others. Morality is essentially an interactive, interpersonal enterprise. This includes the appreciation of the Other, as Levinas would say, or, in Kantian language, the treatment of other human beings as ends, and never as means only. Impressed by various Eastern outlooks (Taoism, Hinduism, and Buddhism), Holmes argues that morality also includes our relationship toward the cosmos as a whole.

And just as this cosmos has frequently been understood as an inert, inanimate object, in our contemporary world other human beings are often—in fact, too often—dehumanized and treated as objects. This realization brings us to Holmes' most important objection against the standard ethical theories: they leave largely unchallenged the basic structures of society and do not question sufficiently those structures mostly responsible for the dehumanization and mechanization of human life. Among these structures Holmes includes the police, courts, prisons, armies, and the technocratic infrastructure of the modern Hobbesian state. What he finds most objectionable about these structures is that they keep relying on violence, although the historical lesson we should all have learned is that such extensive use of violence

---

[2]   Ibid., 226, italics in the original.

simply does not work. What history teaches us is that, as Simone Weil expresses it poetically, "Violence obliterates anybody who feels its touch."[3] And by that Weil means that violence obliterates not just its victims but its perpetrators too. It poisons the entire society that so mindlessly relies on it.

Many authors have sufficiently documented the effects of violence during and after the periods of war. In the words of a veteran war correspondent, Chris Hedges,

> War breaks down long-established prohibitions against violence, destruction, and murder. And with this often comes the crumbling of sexual, social, and political norms as the domination and brutality of the battlefield is carried into personal life. Rape, mutilation, abuse, and theft are the natural outcome of a world in which force rules, in which human beings are objects. The infection is pervasive. Society in wartime becomes atomized. It rewards personal survival skills and very often leaves those with decency and compassion trampled under the rush. The pride one feels in a life devoted to the nation or to an institution or a career or an ideal is often replaced by shame and guilt. Those who have lived upright, socially productive lives are punished for their gullibility in the new social order.[4]

Wars do not break out randomly. Some countries are permanently war-oriented. Since World War II, for example, the United States has been at war with and/or bombed China (1945–6, 1950–3), Korea (1950–3); Guatemala (1954, 1967–9); Indonesia (1958); Cuba (1959–60); Vietnam (1961–73); Laos (1964–73); the Belgian Congo (1964); Peru (1965); Cambodia (1969–70); El Salvador (throughout the 1980s); Nicaragua (throughout the 1980s); Grenada (1983); Libya (1986, 2012); Panama (1989); Iraq (1991–9; 2003–11); Bosnia (1995); Sudan (1998); Yugoslavia (1999); and Afghanistan (2001–present). If we add to this mind-boggling list the so-called "war on terror"— ill-defined in terms of its objectives and spread throughout the whole world, ill-pursued in violation of numerous legal and humanitarian norms—there is little doubt that the military machine of the United States (and similarly oriented governments) represents the greatest threat for peace in the world. Despite the government's orchestrated propaganda against terrorism, Howard Zinn is right when he reminded us thus: "war is terrorism, magnified a hundred times."[5]

With its approximately 760 military bases currently maintained around the globe, a military budged that exceeds more than all other militaries on earth combined, and a permanent war economy at home, the US government has become a machine for manufacturing wars. As the main producer and exporter of weapons and military technology in the world, the US economy depends on new conflicts erupting all the time, for someone needs to be convinced to buy these weapons. And it is not just the international scene where weapons are omnipresent. The weapons industry and our permanent war economy are no less visibly present on the domestic scene, perhaps mostly thanks to the deeply entrenched conviction that the more weapons we have,

---

[3] Simone Weil, "The Iliad, or Poem of Force," trans. Mary McCarthy, *Politics*, Vol. 2, No. 11 (1943): 324.

[4] Chris Hedges, *War Is a Force That Gives Us Meaning* (New York: Random House, 2002), 103–4.

[5] Howard Zinn, *The Power of Nonviolence* (Boston: Beacon Press, 2012), ix.

the more secure and manly we are. Like an ostrich with its head deep in the sand, we refuse to see that this "popular wisdom" does not take us closer to our proclaimed goal of peaceful coexistence. With so many people equipped with weapons, why is it so surprising that domestic violence is also rampant? That the number of assaults has been exponentially growing in the past six decades? That our prisons are overcrowded and the government cannot build new "corrective institutions" quickly enough?

Holmes is a pacifist who believes that war is morally wrong, even absurd. He is also opposed to any other form of violent behavior. Yet Holmes' analysis focuses not so much on the facts illustrating this epidemic of violence as to its underlying causes and possible alternatives to violence. Following Tolstoy, Holmes criticizes the role that institutions play in the contemporary world. Tolstoy eyed primarily the role of the church and the state. Although Holmes looks at the irresponsible behavior of corporations in our world, his central target is the state—he is as much an anarchist as Tolstoy was. To be an anarchist means, minimally, to believe that the state (and its government) is unnecessary. It may also mean—more strongly—that the state with its structures of "legitimate" violence is a source of evil, perhaps even the most important source of evil.

The state derives its prerogative to use violence against other states and its own citizens because of the pessimistic outlook on human nature. St. Augustine, for example, thought of man's nature as sinful and eternally divided between the corrupt body and the pure soul. Luther and Calvin stretched further this view according to which most men are divinely preordained to be selfish and evil. Hobbes "secularized" it by claiming that man is a wolf to every other man. What is more, human beings are not just sinful, evil, and beastly; they are essentially powerless either to control their own harmful behavior, or that of others. When human beings are considered to be without dignity and humanity, then the human—and superhuman—characteristics are ascribed to institutions: to the church at first, and later (after the Treaty of Westphalia in 1648) to a sovereign state.[6] The best we can do, according to this view, is to put ourselves under the protection of the mighty, divine-like institutions, and pursue our selfish desires within the narrow bounds and laws they authorize.

One can react to this divinization of the state with civil disobedience, as Henry D. Thoreau did: "I think we should be men first, and subjects afterward. It is not desirable to cultivate a respect for the law, as much as for the right."[7] Martin Luther King, Jr, protested against the racial segregation, legitimized by the government, by distinguishing between "unjust laws" and "just laws"—"the laws of man" and "the laws of God."[8]

A range of protest can go far deeper than opposing unjust taxation, inhumane practices, or wars sanctioned by the government. One of Holmes' fundamental philosophical convictions and the key to his ethics of nonviolence is the refusal to accept the view

[6] In our time, such characteristics are ascribed to corporations and financial institutions.
[7] Henry D. Thoreau, "Civil Disobedience," quoted in *Nonviolence in Theory and Practice*, ed. R. Holmes and B. Gan, 3rd edn (Long Grove, IL: Waveland Press, 2012), 56.
[8] Martin Luther King, Jr, "Letter from a Birmingham Jail," quoted in *Nonviolence in Theory and Practice*, 108.

of the fallen—selfish and violent—nature of humanity: Is self-interest as important a motivator of human behavior as is generally believed (especially in the Anglo-Saxon world)? Are we so violent because of our allegedly fallen human nature? How then to account for the fact that, for the vast majority of human beings, nine out of any ten actions are nonviolent? And how to explain that so much human behavior is guided by far healthier and nobler impulses? According to Holmes' "thought experiment,"

> If a visitor from outer space were to come to know human beings on this earth, but to know them only in their personal lives, at work and play, and without knowledge of human history or international affairs, what would he conclude? No doubt that virtually everyone values friendship, peace and happiness; that most persons desire basic creature comforts, love their families, and seek neither to suffer nor to cause pain to others; that they rarely harm one another, and then do so mainly under duress or in fits of anger directed against friends or loved ones and regretted soon after; that while they all can be insensitive, and a few of them cruel, they for the most part treat those they know best with friendly feeling and others with civility; and that most of them wish nothing more than to be left alone to work out their life plans according to their lights, which they do with varying degrees of success when given the chance.
>
> If having observed all of this the visitor were then told that a scheme had been proposed by which to improve the world—not in the foreseeable future or in any future the proposer could identify—but which for the present would require that people pour their wealth into the production of weapons of destruction, organize vast authoritarian bureaucracies called armies, train their sons and daughters to kill and periodically send them off to slaughter and be slaughtered by other sons and daughters similarly organized by their governments, under conditions so brutal that even the survivors often return physically or emotionally incapacitated; if the visitor were told that humans could improve their lot provided only that they do all of these things, he would ridicule the scheme as having not the slightest chance of success, and even less of being accepted by rational beings.
>
> Yet this is precisely what humankind has been led to accept in the case of war.
>
> It has proven willing to abandon virtually everything worth living for, to do things all agree are abhorrent, for reasons few understand, and for ends (such as peace) that history shows cannot be secured by these means.[9]

Holmes does not believe in the existence of a demonic aspect of human nature. What he calls "the paradox of evil" consists in the realization that greatest evils in the world are performed by essentially good people; truly evil people, if there be such, are usually harmful only to a small number of persons in their immediate surroundings. People who commit evil deeds usually do so because they are misguided, not devilish; because of fear, not malice.

If that is really the case, then violent punishments the state inflicts on those who commit crimes do not constitute the proper response to evil. Vengeance and

---

[9] Robert Holmes, the opening paragraphs of his essay, "War, Power, and Nonviolence," reprinted in this volume, 143–4.

punishment do not address the source of evil; violence does not remove fear that leads to hatred and destruction. Violence only begets more violence.

Holmes the anarchist believes that governments have become increasingly cunning in creating and manipulating misinformation and fear among their citizens. He refuses to accept that positive human emotions and passions, such as the pursuit of comfort and happiness, endanger social life; he similarly denies the idea that coercion sanctioned by governments can preserve it. While refusing to accept that human nature is brutish, selfish, and evil, Holmes ascribes these vices to the state. It is the state that—in the name of our interest and security—leads to the perversion, dehumanization, and mechanization of our human dignity.

Just as war has to be exposed for what it is—organized murder and destruction—we need to remove the clouds of misconception around the nature of humanity. And just as the cry for peace is not only a protest against war but also a vision of a different world, the call for the restoration of human dignity is not only a protest against the degradation of humanity. More importantly, it is a reminder of the best and the noblest toward which human beings aspire, even under the worst possible circumstances. Victor Frankl, an Auschwitz survivor, testifies that those who had something to believe in found the strength to endure, to cope, and to hope, even in the most destructive atmosphere of concentration camps. While freezing in the blast of the Polish winter, he began to think about his wife, and the desire to survive in order to see her again became the source of his strength:

> A thought transfixed me: for the first time in my life I saw the truth as it is set into song by so many poets, proclaimed as the final wisdom by so many thinkers. The truth—that love is the ultimate and the highest goal to which man can aspire. Then I grasped the meaning of the greatest secret that human poetry and belief have to impart: The salvation of man is through love and in love.[10]

Vasily Grossman, who survived both a German concentration camp and Stalin's gulag, testifies in the similar vein about the power of human decency and kindness:

> I have seen that it is not man who is impotent in the struggle against evil, but the power of evil that is impotent in the struggle against man. The powerlessness of kindness, of senseless kindness, is the secret of its immortality. It can never be conquered. The more stupid, the more senseless, the more helpless it may seem, the vaster it is. Evil is impotent before it. The prophets, religious teachers, reformers, social and political leaders are impotent before it. This dumb, blind love is man's meaning.

> Human history is not the battle of good struggling to overcome evil. It is a battle fought by a great evil struggling to crush a small kernel of human kindness. But if what is human in human beings has not been destroyed even now, then evil will never conquer.[11]

---

[10]   Victor Frankl, *Man's Search for Meaning*, trans. Ilse Lasch (New York: Simon and Schuster, 1984), 48.
[11]   Vasily Grossman, *Life and Fate*, trans. Robert Chandler (New York: Harper and Row, 1985), 410. For a moving account of numerous acts of human kindness during the war in Bosnia (1992–5), see Svetlana Broz, *Good People in Evil Time*, trans. Ellen Elias-Bursać (Sarajevo: Grafičar promet, 2002).

Of all the proponents of nonviolence, perhaps no one has emphasized the role of love more than Martin Luther King, Jr. Following Jesus' "Sermon on the Mount," King's own sermons on nonviolence are rightly entitled "Strength to Love," and in them he repeatedly reminds us that love "is the highest good" and "the greatest of all virtues."[12]

Although Holmes also speaks of love, his ethics of nonviolence is based on a more generally understood faith in the power of human spirit. He finds his deepest inspiration in the ancient Buddhist classic, the *Dhammapada*: "Our life is shaped by our mind; we become what we think."[13] Gandhi was guided by the same insight: "A man is but the product of his thoughts; what he thinks, he becomes."[14] This is what Gandhi called *satyagraha*—the soul force.[15] As much as it was important for India to liberate herself from the British colonialism, it was even more important, insisted Gandhi, that India purified her soul and healed her wounds.

Holmes interprets this soul force in terms of courage and truthfulness. By courage, he does not have in mind physical bravery, associated with the behavior of soldiers on a battlefield. Plato considered courage to be that element of the soul that bridges the fissure between reason and desire, mind and heart. Likewise Holmes thinks primarily about spiritual courage: it is important to confront an adversary with pure intentions, with a benevolence based on our understanding of the sources of a conflict, and with our knowledge of the underlying similarities even between those who stand opposed in terms of their values, blood, or social status.

Perhaps even more than courage, Holmes values and emphasizes truthfulness as the key component of his ethics of nonviolence. In this point he also follows Gandhi, who famously changed his mind from believing that "God is Truth" to realizing that "Truth is God." The proclaimed revelations of God, or ancient sacred texts, must not be taken for granted and treated as an impervious dogma. Each one of us has a never-ceasing moral duty to keep reflecting, inquiring, and searching for truth on our own. The alternative is not only scary but unacceptable. As the recent world history testifies, "the sleep of reason brings forth monsters."[16] This is why in his consideration of violence and nonviolence, Holmes does not leave any monster unnamed, or any stone unturned. In his essays we find detailed examination of just war theory; of the irrationality of nuclear deterrence; of the impossibility of avoiding civilian casualties in technologically oriented wars; of physical and psychological violence; of individual and structural violence; of nonviolence as nonresistance, passive resistance, and nonviolent direct action; of unqualified and qualified nonviolence; of religious, metaphysical, and ethical grounds for nonviolence; of moral, social, and political objectives of nonviolence; of effectiveness of nonviolence as a tactic and as a way of life.

Holmes' emphasis on truthfulness—not only on speaking truly, but on living in truth and with truth—signals that he does not view his ethics of nonviolence as an

---

[12]   Martin Luther King Jr, *Strength to Love*, (Minneapolis, MN: Fortress Press, 2010), 152–3.
[13]   *Dhammapada*, trans. Eknath Easwaran (Peteluna, CA: Nilgiri Press, 1985), 72.
[14]   Mahatma Gandhi, *The Essential Gandhi*, ed. Louis Fischer (New York: Random House, 2002), 163.
[15]   This, of course, is not a literal translation of *satyagraha*, but it inspired the title of one of the most important books on nonviolence published in the past several decades: *A Force More Powerful: A Century of Nonviolent Conflict*, by Peter Ackerman and Robert DuVall (New York: Palgrave, 2000).
[16]   This quote refers to the title of "War, Power, and Nonviolence" in its earlier version.

ethics of conduct; it is first and foremost an ethics of virtue. The ethics of nonviolence deals not so much with what we have to do but with what we have to become. That is why Holmes does not treat nonviolence as our best tactic: nonviolence is far more than just a way of handling conflicts and reacting to violence. It is a generic name for a cluster of values and attitudes that we take toward our lives. Just as peace does not mean only the absence of fighting, nonviolence means far more than the mere lack of violence. Nonviolence directs us to a way of life in which means cannot be strictly separated from ends. We may never definitely know what is right, but we have to continually work on increasing our knowledge and understanding, courage and honesty. We are not striving toward some utopian peace-paradise but are involved in the process of living in which every step and every encounter with other human beings demands full attention and care. We understand the complexity of human nature and the variety of reasons for the presence of violence but have faith in the possibility of generating more trust and harmony in interpersonal relations.

Like the rest of us, Holmes gets frustrated with endless fabrications of ever-new enemies by our politicians, just as he is perturbed by devious manipulations conducted by mighty corporations for the sake of making ever more profit. Then he speaks about a nonviolent revolution that would bring about an urgently needed transition from the idolatry of violence to a culture of nonviolence. While Holmes does not offer any specific plan for such a revolution he points out its three center-pieces: nonviolent social defense, an economy of nonviolence, and education in nonviolence. Of these three, the last may be the most fundamental.

Holmes the educator justifiably wonders what would happen if we could relocate a good portion of the resources dedicated to the military training into an education for nonviolence. Instead of recording wars and violence, could our history books and our media focus on countless deeds of goodness among people? What if we start fostering trust among people and their faith in human goodness? Instead of further empowering an already too-mighty state (and corrupt corporations that control the state), what if we sincerely attempt to restore the dignity on an individual? What would happen if instead of paying just a lip service to peace we really give peace a chance? What if we seriously dedicate the next millennium to the promotion of nonviolence?

Like Lao Tzu, Holmes recognizes that "there is nothing softer and weaker than water, and yet there is nothing better for [transforming] hard and strong things."[17] More often than a nonviolent revolution, Holmes thinks of gradual evolution—an evolution that does not look for quick fix and flashy results but for a steady and genuine conversion of our outlooks, attitudes, and practices. This is how he has understood education and his own role as a teacher. In his role as a teacher, Holmes embodies three insights. The first of them can be expressed in a very simple way: education is not conveying knowledge and grading students for the short-term memorization of that knowledge. Education is like planting a seed. Don't worry too much about what will grow out of that seed and in what time. Just plant the right seed and let it grow on its own.

---

[17] "The Way of Lao Tzu," quoted in *Nonviolence in Theory and Practice*, 11.

The second insight is related, perhaps nothing but an illustration of the first one: people become trustworthy by being trusted. Trust is one of the most important seeds we can and must plant into other people, especially young people.

The third grain of wisdom is the most important and most difficult to achieve. Yet it is the most illustrative of Holmes' ethics of nonviolence. One must not expect anything from others; it is of oneself that one should demand too much. Only from oneself has one the right to ask for everything and anything. That way it is up to yourself, it is your own choice. What you get from others remains a present, a gift.

These, then, are the core views of Holmes' ethics of nonviolence. To those wondering whether this ethical approach could really "work," he answers in the following way:

[I]f one thinks of nonviolence as a way of life, then it works to the extent that one lives nonviolently and infuses everyday conduct with a nonviolent spirit. Effectiveness of this sort is not measurable in the same way as social and political changes. It cannot be quantified over a whole population. Nevertheless it is the relevant consideration in determining whether nonviolence is effective. Whether we are successful in bringing about certain consequences of our actions depends upon many circumstances beyond our control. It often depends also upon what others do. But whether we act nonviolently, considerately, and respectfully of others in all that we do is within our control. Nonviolence in that sense cannot fail to work if we resolve to see that it works.[18]

---

[18] *Nonviolence in Theory and Practice*, xx.

1

John Dewey's Moral Philosophy in Contemporary Perspective

Dewey never developed his ethical thought sufficiently. Holmes tries to remedy this shortcoming by showing first that Dewey's position is not that of naturalism, intuitionism, or noncognitivism (the positions many philosophers in the middle of the twentieth century believed to exhaust our viable choices). For Dewey, these accounts of moral judgments, while each containing a grain of truth, obscure for us a more important concern—our understanding of morality as a way of life. A judgment expresses a moral way of life if it is made with a view to promoting the good (individual and social), and if it is both warranted and verifiable from an empirical standpoint (rather than to be a result of mere habit or impulse). Holmes' interpretation of Dewey's ethics, which ties together moral practice and critical reasoning, as well as individual and social concerns, deviates from the traditional ethical approaches by looking away from a search for one universal principle of morality. Holmes' early essay on Dewey has two merits. First, it shows the vitality of a general approach to morality as a way of life, and, second, it prepares a ground for a context-based ethics of nonviolence, which Holmes himself developed in the later stages of his career.

It is regrettable that the ethical thought of so noted a philosopher as John Dewey should be as little understood as it is, particularly as it occupies such a central position in his philosophy as a whole. It would not be too much to say that his major contributions to philosophy, whether in metaphysics, logic or historical analysis, can only imperfectly be understood apart from his ethical writings. Dewey himself shares a measure of responsibility for this lack of understanding, however, inasmuch as he never states fully and unequivocally precisely where he stands on many of the principal questions of ethics. Thus those who read him tend to fix upon those few works which appear to have clear direction and, by extrapolation, try to develop an interpretation for his thought as a whole. This generally results in reading him as an ethical naturalist, an interpretation particularly tempting in view of his clear commitment to a metaphysical naturalism. This puts him, according to common accounts, in the tradition of Hume, Bentham, and Mill, and in the twentieth century on the side, notably, of R. B. Perry and (in his theory of value) C. I. Lewis. On this interpretation he would also be cross-classified as a cognitivist, which would align him with the intuitionists in regard to the possibility of attaining genuine knowledge in morals and against the emotivists and more recent anti-descriptivists, who deny that moral judgments are primarily informative. But though there is much to recommend this interpretation, and it certainly derives support from works which represent only a partial development of his views or selected aspects thereof, it does not survive closer examination in the light of his overall writings on ethics; writings which must be ferreted out from the whole voluminous body of unsystematic, difficult, and sometimes tedious writings of a long and productive lifetime. To take up the challenge posed by them, and to draw together the many relevant and often isolated strands of his thought, is to find in Dewey a timely, perceptive, and relatively coherent ethics of pragmatism, one which repays careful study by anyone interested in many of the problems in the forefront of contemporary ethical theory.

Cautioning in advance that summary treatment of any aspect of Dewey's thought, much less one as far-reaching in compass as his ethics, must of necessity be omissive, I shall in the following develop what I believe to be the most plausible rendering of his philosophy. In so doing I will confine myself principally to explicating his stand *vis-à-vis* contemporary metaethical positions, though I will expand upon this in the later sections and some of his normative, or substantive, views as well. In the final section I will outline a theory of morality as a whole which, though nowhere explicitly defended by Dewey, is consonant with various theses he does defend. The burden of my argument will be to show, first, that he is not holding the sort of position usually characterized as ethical naturalism, and secondly, that the position he does hold marks a significant departure from all three of the conventional metaethical positions, intuitionism, naturalism, and noncognitivism. Metaphorically he stands at the third point of a triangle, the other two points of which are naturalism and emotivism, for he adapts salient features of each of these positions to an orientation which fits the framework of his view of the nature of ethics, science and philosophy in general. Let us begin by assessing the chief arguments in support of a naturalistic interpretation, as these will provide a point of departure for clarifying his considered view.

Ethical naturalism

Since G. E. Moore's attempt to expose a fallacy in any theory which defines goodness in terms of natural properties, ethical naturalism has come to be associated with any view which holds that ethical terms in general can be defined in like fashion. By this view, ethical judgments are factual assertions, true or false, and capable of empirical verification in essentially the same manner as scientific statements. However, a naturalist need not hold quite all of what Moore ascribed to him, for he may deny the possibility or plausibility of defining moral terms in the way Moore criticized and yet hold that the judgments in which such terms occur are empirical. That is, we can distinguish the following two theses:

1. Ethical terms are definable by reference to non-normative terms.
2. Moral judgments are statements of empirical fact and are primarily intended to convey information.

Anyone holding both (1) and (2) we may call a naturalist in a strong sense; anyone holding just (2), either denying (1) or leaving it open, may be called a naturalist in a weak sense. Anyone who holds (1) presumably will also hold (2), though not necessarily vice versa.

It is obvious upon even a casual reading that Dewey makes no unequivocal commitment to naturalism in either of these senses. Indeed, it is doubtful that he was ever very much concerned with metaethics *per se*, for as he conceives it,

> the distinctive office, problems and subject-matter of philosophy grow out of stresses and strains in the community life in which a given form of philosophy arises, and . . . accordingly, its specific problems vary with the changes in human life that are always going on and that at times constitute a crisis and a turning point in human history.[1]

Although a concern with normative practical problems is not inconsistent with the holding of any given metaethical view, much less naturalism in particular, it is clear nonetheless throughout Dewey's writings that his main interest is with practical decision and the methodology by which it is reached, and that he is less concerned with linguistic distinctions than to see that intelligent thought provides the proper orientation for the handling of practical problems. No less than what he says on specifically ethical matters, his writings on politics, education and religion attest to this.

We may still ask, however, what stand he would have adopted on this issue had he been more keenly interested in it, and I believe that it is profitable to do so, for he certainly was concerned to distinguish normative and non-normative judgments and to see that the two are not confused.[2] And the naturalistic interpretation has initial plausibility in view of his emphasis upon the need of a scientific method for ethics, his insistence that judgments of value must make reference to verifiable consequences of action, and what is implicit throughout his writings, that moral judgments are capable of some kind of empirical confirmation. This has led many writers to the view expressed by Brand Blanshard when he asks: "Does Dewey mean that problems of value are *merely* problems of fact, that questions of duty, or right and wrong, of better and worse, are to be settled by observation in the same sense that the question can be so settled whether a chair has four legs?" and then concludes, "The answer is Yes, he does."[3] But important countervailing considerations have been given insufficient attention by those who interpret Dewey in this fashion, and it is these which I propose to discuss. They involve particularly the issues of the definability of moral terms and the cognitivity of moral judgments.

---

[1] Dewey, *Reconstruction in Philosophy* (New York: H. Holt, 1920), 8.
[2] Dewey, *The Quest for Certainty* (New York: G. P. Putnam's Sons, 1929), 260ff.
[3] Brand Blanshard, *Reason and Goodness* (New York: Macmillan, 1961), 184. However, most writers who interpret Dewey along these lines attribute to him a more sophisticated form of naturalism. See, for example, H. D. Aiken, *Reason and Conduct* (New York: Knopf, 1962), Chapters 1 and 2; C. L. Stevenson, *Ethics and Language* (New Haven, CN: Yale University Press, 1944), Chapter 12; and Morton White, "Value and Obligation in Dewey and Lewis," *Philosophical Review*, 58 (1949).

Meaning as function

The first point worth noticing is that Dewey nowhere explicitly defines moral terms, naturalistically or otherwise. This in itself should be noteworthy to those who read him as holding the sort of position described above, and it is evidence that even if he is subscribing to naturalism, it is unlikely that this is what we are calling the stronger form. It might be argued, of course, that he assumes some sort of definition along naturalistic lines, even though he never states clearly what it is. But the unlikelihood of this is clear from an important early essay which indicates, first, that he is more interested in judgments and propositions than in the terms which compose them, and secondly, that he is concerned to explicate meaning in terms of use and function rather than by definition. For, as he says of ethical judgment, "The work that it has to do gives it certain limiting or defining elements and properties. These constitute the ultimate Terms or Categories of all ethical science."[4] "Categories" here include the concepts operative in moral discourse, such as "right," "good," and "obligation." Just as science has its own categories which "define to us the limiting conditions under which . . . [intellectual or scientific judgments] do their work," so ethics is equipped with the tools "necessary to its task." To this extent ethics and science parallel one another.

It is upon closer examination of these "tools" of the respective disciplines that significant differences appear. In science, terms must be deliberately and precisely defined; prior to inquiry there must be agreement, for example, as to what conditions define a calorie of heat or a volt of electricity, with these and other concepts then entering into the formation of judgments. In this way they assist in the assimilation of factual data to the task of directing inquiry to a satisfactory conclusion. The reverse is the case with ethics, for although it is true that the terms enter into the construction of judgments, the meanings of judgments nonetheless in a sense precede the specific meanings of the terms they contain.

> An analysis of the make-up of [ethical judgments] . . . must reveal all the distinctions which have claim to the title of fundamental ethical categories. . . . *The differential meaning of any one of the terms is dependent upon the particular part it plays in the development and termination of judgments* of this sort.[5]

It is a mistake, in other words, to fix upon ethical terms in isolation from judgments in which they are used, and to suppose that they have some one meaning constant through all situations.

> Only reference to a situation within which the categories emerge and function can furnish the basis for estimation of their value and import. Otherwise the definition of basic ethical terms is left to argumentation based upon opinion, an opinion which snatches at some of the more obvious features of the situation (and thereby may always possess some measure of truth), and which, failing to grasp the situation as a whole, fails to grasp the exact significance of its characteristic terms.[6]

[4] Dewey, *Problems of Men* (New York: Philosophical Library, 1964), 233.
[5] Ibid., 235, italics added.
[6] Ibid., 234.

The point is that only by an analysis of the function of ethical *judgments* are we able to determine the meanings of their constituent terms. The approach to ethics which takes account of this would be what Dewey calls a "logic of conduct" and constitutes part of what he means by a science of ethics.[7]

This accords with his distinction between common sense and science, both of which constitute language systems but which differ in the character of the meanings which they embody. Common sense is the outgrowth of custom and convention, and its meanings have evolved slowly through the various demands for communication. Thus its language carries with it many of the beliefs and customs of the group within which it has evolved. In science, on the other hand, meanings have been deliberately fixed with a view to facilitating productive inquiry, and have been purposely divested of their subjective trappings.

> The primary meanings and associations of ideas and hypotheses are derived from their position and force in common sense situations of use-enjoyment. They are expressed in symbols developed for the sake of social communication rather than to serve the conditions of controlled inquiry. The symbols are loaded with meanings that are irrelevant to inquiry conducted for the sake of attaining knowledge as such. These meanings are familiar and influentially persuasive because of their established associations. The result is that the historic advance of science is marked and accompanied by deliberate elimination of such terms and institution in their stead of a new set of symbols constituting a new technical language.[8]

Hence the meanings of the terms of everyday discourse (the medium of moral discourse) are tied to the ways in which these words are used in judging, making statements, exhorting, advising, commanding, and so forth. To understand them requires examining the sorts of jobs they are used to perform, and it is in this sense that Dewey feels that understanding the nature of judgments and propositions and the way they function takes priority over questions of definition.[9]

It is clear that Dewey is not defining ethical terms, that is, is not asserting thesis (1) above, and hence is not holding ethical naturalism in the stronger sense. He would say that it is impossible to provide definitions which do justice to the variety and complexity of practical situations in which moral terms do their work,[10] and moreover, that in any event the quest for definitions runs the risk of overlooking what is really important in ethics, viz., to be concerned with the ways in which we ought to be judging.

---

7   Ibid., 248.
8   Dewey, *Logic: The Theory of Inquiry* (New York: Holt, Rinehart and Winston, 1938), 425.
9   Dewey even feels that a discussion of the nature of value can be undertaken without involvement in the problem of the definability of the term. See Dewey, "Value, Objective Reference and Criticism," *Philosophical Review*, 34 (1925), 314.
10 Here he bears an affinity to those recent philosophers who propose replacing questions about the meaning of moral terms with questions about their use. Interestingly, Dewey relies heavily upon the metaphors of "tools" and "instruments" which enter prominently into Wittgenstein's account of language.

What ought to count as a moral judgment?

The more difficult question is whether Dewey can plausibly be read as holding the weaker form of ethical naturalism, that which maintains that, though moral terms may be indefinable, moral judgments nonetheless are empirical statements primarily intended to convey information. This theory may take two forms, according to whether it asserts (a) that moral judgments are exclusively empirical, in the sense that their sole function is descriptive, or (b) that moral judgments have both descriptive and non-descriptive functions (such as expressive, commendatory, prescriptive, and so forth), but that qua moral their descriptive function is primary.

Now it is clear from his account of judgment that he believes that all practical judgments (of which moral judgments are a species) normally have a noncognitive function of expressing the dispositions and attitudes of the individual judging. Hence the strongest case for a naturalistic interpretation of his ethics lies in some form of the latter approach, one which takes an attitudinal reference to be ingredient in the nature of practical judgments. However, this approach in turn may assume different forms depending upon the kind of analysis offered of the descriptive function. For one might say either that moral judgments are about *existing* states of affairs, such as de facto approvals or likings, or that they are about possible *future* states of affairs, such as that the speaker or some person or group will or would approve of the act or object under certain conditions.

That Dewey does not hold the first position, at least in any form which makes essential reference to subjective states, is evident from his extended controversy with Philip Blair Rice,[11] whom he criticizes for holding that the immediate quality of an experience (e.g., its pleasantness) can constitute evidence for the truth of a judgment of value. If it were his view that value judgments asserted the existence of such experiences (or qualities of experience), especially if he held that it was their main function to do so, then the occurrence of such experiences in the appropriate circumstances would be expected to carry just such evidential weight. But by emphatically denying the latter, Dewey also denies to value judgments such a descriptive function.[12] The relevant question is whether he holds that moral judgments have some other descriptive function, e.g., one which has a forward-reference to consequences. It is not possible, of course, to assess individually all of the different variations which naturalistic theories might take, even those which have this prospective reference. But in any event it is unnecessary to do so, for it can plausibly be argued on other grounds that Dewey did not subscribe to *any* theory of this sort, whatever particular form it might take.

---

[11]   In a series of articles in the *Journal of Philosophy* in 1943. Dewey's contributions to the discussions are reprinted in *Problems of Man*.

[12]   With the qualification that for Dewey there is a sense in which values can be and often are reported by straightforward descriptive statements. This is with respect to what he calls "immediate values," where reference is simply to the fact *that* a certain liking or enjoyment is experienced. That is, sometimes a locution like "*x* is good" signifies only that the speaker likes *x* or that it pleases him, in which case it is a purely description assertion. But if it is merely reportive, then it fails to constitute a genuine *judgment* of value.

Before considering what these grounds are we should note one final point of importance in the way of clarifying our problem. It is that in the distinctive sense Dewey intends, what pass for moral judgments in everyday discourse are not often genuine moral judgments; if they were, there would be little need of the reconstruction he urges in moral philosophy. It is a central theme of his ethical thought that most people should be but are not reasoning and judging along the lines he proposes: "only deliberate action, conduct into which reflective choice enters, is distinctively moral."[13] Moreover,

> As far as de facto prizings rest upon current mores, plus the manipulations of those in positions of superior economic, political and/or ecclesiastical power, they are so perverting in effects as to provide whatever color or plausibility is possessed by the view that rational valuations are impossible. It is doubtful whether, at least for a long time to come, their operation can be wholly eliminated from the most reasonable evaluative judgments that can now be framed.[14]

Thus to the extent that judgments about conduct are either uncritical reflections of custom or unthinking responses to authority, they are not distinctively moral.[15] His account of moral judgments is not (primarily at least) descriptive of "ordinary" moral experience or language usage; it is, rather, a proposal concerning what *ought* to count as a moral judgment. Thus as a final qualification, the question we are considering must be reformulated along the following lines: If and when distinctively moral judgments are made, are they basically descriptive of matters of fact, intended to convey information? The answer to this, I submit, is that for Dewey they are not. This is supported principally by two considerations: the first involving the distinction Dewey draws between judgments and propositions; the second concerning the sense in which he maintains the moral judgments have cognitive status. For our purposes these two can be discussed together.

Practical judgments and propositions

Just as Dewey nowhere offers definitions of moral terms, he also never expressly defends the view that moral judgments are cognitive assertions. But he does say things which make it clear that he thought that there was a sense in which they have cognitive status. Because the mainstay of any naturalistic interpretation of his ethics must be the claim that he views moral judgments as cognitive assertions, it is important to see just what this sense is and to understand why it does not support a naturalistic reading.

---

[13]   Dewey, *Human Nature and Conduct* (New York: Random House, 1930), 279.
[14]   Dewey, "The Field of Value," in *Value: A Cooperative Inquiry*, ed. Ray Lepley (New York: Columbia University Press, 1949), 75.
[15]   This does not mean that what he calls "judgments" are not made in ordinary discourse. The point is, rather, that this form of judgment and the deliberative process that goes with it have not been sufficiently relied upon in the handling of moral problems.

The following passages give prima facie support to the view that moral judgments are cognitive in the same way as descriptive statements: "Valuations exist in fact and are capable of empirical observation so that propositions about them are empirically verifiable."[16]

And in his commentary upon C. L. Stevenson's *Ethics and Language*:

It is one thing to acknowledge (and insist) upon [the emotive] feature of ethical sentences as one demanded by their function or the use they are put to. It is quite another thing to hold that this subject-matter is not capable of and does not need *description*, and description of the kind belonging to sentences having "scientific" standing. I believe that examination of Stevenson's specific treatment of the "emotional" . . . will show that he takes the fact that factually grounded reasons are employed in genuinely ethical sentences in order to modify affective-motor attitudes which influence and direct conduct, to be equivalent to the presence of an extra-cognitive constituent in the sentences in question.[17]

Notice, however, that the first passage refers to the verifiability of propositions, not judgments. This is significant, because Dewey earlier makes an important distinction, developed most fully in his *Logic: The Theory of Inquiry*, between judgments and propositions, a distinction which recognizes that one of the two main species of proposition (viz., those which constitute what he calls the "material" means in inquiry, the other being "procedural" means) will consist of cognitive, empirical assertions. As such they may be *about* verifiable acts of valuation and hence in a sense be "value" propositions by virtue of their subject matter; in this capacity they play a key role in deliberation leading to a final judgment. But they are not to be confused with the *judgments* to which they are means. These latter are not descriptive statements at all, being expressive of the decisions, commitments, resolves, recommendations, etc., which form the terminus of deliberation. If we suppose that Dewey is adhering to this distinction, and it is likely that he is in view of the prominent place it occupies in the development of his thought,[18] then his remarks in the passage under consideration do not support a naturalistic interpretation.

How, then, are we to interpret the other passage, in which Dewey challenges the view that there is, as he puts it, an "extra-cognitive" constituent in moral judgments? The key to answering this question lies in the expressions "function" and "subject-matter," each of which he uses interchangeably with certain other locutions: these, in the case of "function," include "office," "use," "force," and "objective," all of which are associated with the notion of ends and ends-in-view, and in the case of "subject-matter" include "content" and "structure," both of which are associated with the notion of means.

The exact bearing of these distinctions upon the problem at hand becomes evident if we examine still another passage in which he quotes Stevenson's assertion that "ethical

[16]   Dewey, *Theory of Valuation* (Chicago: University of Chicago Press, 1939), 58.
[17]   Dewey, "Ethical Subject Matter and Language," *Journal of Philosophy*, Vol. 42, No. 26 (1945), 702.
[18]   On this subject, see my "The Development of John Dewey's Ethical Thought," *Monist*, 48 (July 1964), 392–406.

terms cannot be taken as fully comparable to scientific ones [because] they have a quasi-imperative function," and then observes that

> the point at issue does not concern the last of the two sentences quoted. Nor does it concern the correctness of the statement that "both imperative and ethical sentences are *used* more for encouraging, altering, or redirecting people's aims and conduct than for simply describing them." The point at issue is whether the facts of *use* and *function* render ethical terms and sentences not fully comparable with scientific ones as respects their subject matter and content. As far as concerns *use* it would not . . . be going too far to say the word "more" in the above passage is not strong enough. Of ethical sentences as ordinarily used, it may be said, I believe, that their *entire* use and function . . . is directive or "practical." The point at issue concerns another matter: It concerns how this end is to be accomplished if sentences are to possess distinctively and genuinely *ethical* properties.[19]

This indicates that when talking about use, function, objective, and so forth, Dewey is referring to the jobs moral judgments are used to perform; and he is in agreement with Stevenson that their jobs are practical, directive and action-guiding. Where he disagrees is with respect to the significance of the second group of terms, subject-matter, content and structure, i.e., about the *means* which are justified in effecting a redirection of attitudes in others. For Dewey, unlike for Stevenson, purely persuasive methods are ruled out.

> As far as noncognitive, extra-cognitive, factors enter into the matter or content of sentences purporting to be legitimately ethical, those sentences are by just that much deprived of the properties sentences should have in order to be genuinely *ethical*.[20]

That is, he is willing to sanction only what Stevenson calls *rational* methods of effecting changes in attitude.

> *Evaluative* statements concern or have reference to what ends are to-be-chosen, what lines of conduct are to-be-followed [their objective]. . . . But it is morally necessary to state grounds or reasons for the course advised and recommended [these constituting content or subject matter]. These consist of matter-of-fact sentences reporting what has been and now is, as conditions, and of estimates of consequences that will ensue if certain of them are used as means.[21]

Thus to be legitimately supported, moral judgments must be backed by factual reasons, and it is these which constitute their "subject-matter." To the extent that subject-matter is viewed as somehow "part" of the judgment, there is indeed a sense, however attenuated, in which moral judgments on Dewey's view have cognitive status. But this means only that they have their supporting reasons already built-in, as it were, a claim which accords with his other claim that only judgments arrived at through

[19] *Journal of Philosophy*, Vol. 42, No. 24 (1945), 709; quotation is from *Ethics and Language*, 36.
[20] Ibid.
[21] Ibid., 711.

deliberation (or intelligently formed habit) are genuinely moral. Although one cannot overemphasize the importance he attaches to descriptive statements in the formation of judgments, it is equally important to remember his insistence that moral judgments differ in kind from, and are irreducible to, such statements.[22]

We may conclude that, even granting that moral judgments are cognitive in this way, little support derives from this fact for the claim that Dewey is an ethical naturalist. Even the emotivist can (though, of course, need not) agree that judgments are cognitive in *this* sense. Thus not only is Dewey not defining moral terms in the required fashion, he is not even saying that moral judgments are primarily descriptive. This means that neither the weak nor the strong forms of ethical naturalism adequately characterize his position.

How, then, can his position best be characterized? To answer this brings us to the still larger question of his conception of the nature of morality as a whole, for these are so closely interrelated in Dewey's thought that wholly to sever one from the other is to distort the picture of morality as he conceives it. It will be profitable, therefore, to highlight the main points of his answer to the latter question in answering the former. Let us, however, draw out the implications of the preceding so as to focus more sharply his position relative to the prominent types of ethical theory today.

Dramatic rehearsal and final judgments

It will be considered a sufficient condition of a position's being called intuitionistic if it subscribes to either of the following propositions:

1. Moral terms refer to unanalyzable, non-natural properties.
2. Moral judgments are true or false and convey knowledge of a nonempirical sort.

And any theory which holds either of the following theses will be considered a form of ethical naturalism:

3. Moral terms refer to natural properties.
4. Moral judgments are true or false and convey empirical information.[23]

Common to both (1) and (3) is the assertion that moral terms are property-referring, and common to (2) and (4) is the assertion that moral judgments are cognitive. The noncognitivist's position can be stated negatively as the denial that moral terms are property-referring in either of the above ways. Dewey sides with the noncognitivist on both points; he denies that moral terms (at least qua moral) are property-referring and that the primary job of moral judgments is to convey knowledge (whether of

---

[22] Dewey, *Problems of Men*, 212f.
[23] I shall regard these as useful approximations to the intuitionist and naturalist positions. More exact formulations would require additional qualifications such as (a) that conditions (1) and (3) would be met if it is claimed only that *some* moral terms refer in the required sense; (b) that conditions (2) and (4) would be met by any view which maintains that at least some moral judgments are true or false, etc., as required; and (c) that conditions (2) and (4) would be considered met only if it is maintained that the direct or primary purpose of moral judgments is to convey information.

an empirical or an a priori sort). His view is, rather, that moral judgments express reflective approvals and disapprovals of persons, things, and courses of action.

This can be elaborated in the following way. The initial stage of the deliberative process leading to moral judgment consists of the various conative and affective phenomena (such as desires and aversions, approvals and disapprovals) which are part of man's socio-biological nature. Man cannot help having these, but he can avoid acting upon them impulsively. It is at this point that judgment comes into being, for it involves the working-out in the imagination of the full implications for future experience of the consequences of cultivating a present interest, satisfying an immediate desire, or acting upon a felt approval. The issue of this "dramatic rehearsal," as he sometimes calls it, is a final judgment as to the best course of action; a second order approval or disapproval, as it were, of the initial attitude, desire, liking, etc., and the course of action anticipated by it. As such, it too is rooted in man's affective nature; but it is reasoned and discerning rather than impulsive.

The closest Dewey comes to giving a summary statement of this is when he says that,

> Our immediate responses of approval and reprobation may well be termed intuitive. They are not based upon any thought-out reason or ground. We just admire and resent, are attracted and repelled. This attitude is not only original and primitive but it persists in acquired dispositions.[24]

> Unless there is a direct, mainly unreflective appreciation of persons and deeds, the data for subsequent thought will be lacking or distorted. A person must *feel* the qualities of acts as one feels with the hands the qualities of roughness and smoothness in objects, before he has an inducement to deliberate or material with which to deliberate.[25]

Finally, as to the deliberative process itself, he says:

> Deliberation is actually an imaginative rehearsal of various courses of conduct. We give way, *in our mind*, to some impulse; we try, *in our mind*, some plan. Following its career through various steps, we find ourselves in imagination in the presence of the consequences that would follow: *and as we then like and approve, or dislike and disapprove, these consequences, we find the original impulse or plan good or bad*.[26]

In these respects Dewey's stand is closest to that of the noncognitivist. But from this point on it differs importantly from the usual noncognitivist position, for as we have seen, there is a sense in which he says that moral judgments have a quasi-cognitive status and are capable of empirical confirmation. Although he never details for us the particulars of this latter claim, it is possible to construct the outlines of the account he most likely would have given.

[24] Dewey, *Theory of the Moral Life* (New York: Holt, Rinehart and Winston, 1960), 124. Originally published as part of Dewey-Tufts, James H., *Ethics*, rev. edn (New York: H. Holt, 1932).
[25] Ibid., 128.
[26] Ibid., 135; italics added in the last two lines.

Problematic situations

Dewey implicitly recognizes several levels of language, the characteristic expressions of which are subject to substantially unique criteria of truth, falsity, and verifiability. These include (1) material propositions, (2) procedural propositions, and (3) judgments. All of these are cognitive in Dewey's sense, and (2) and (3) are normative. Truth and falsity in a literal sense would apply only to expressions at level (1), and these would be subject to empirical verification in a strict sense. Expressions at (2) and (3), however, would not properly be said to be empirically true or false (at least not in the sense applicable to [1]), and they would neither be verifiable in the same way as expressions at (1) nor warranted under the same conditions. Empirical warrantedness at any one level would be establishable only by appeal to the findings at the lower levels (with the exception, of course, of level [1]). Likewise, verifiability would differ among the three levels and would be increasingly difficult to establish as one ascends from (1) to (3).

Propositions at level (2) are rules or directives to assist in the process of inquiry; in ethics these would include the moral rules and principles of one's society and would be warranted only if founded upon factual knowledge of the effects of various modes of conduct in the past. Verification would continually be forthcoming so long as adherence to them yielded satisfactory results in the guidance of conduct; so long, in other words, as they proved to be reliable guides to inquiry. Judgments at level (3) are warranted when born of careful deliberation in light of the available relevant factors, which include the data and directives expressed at (1) and (2). Thus the judgment: "This is the right thing to do," cannot be verified in precisely the same way as the proposition: "This table is brown," and neither of these can be confirmed in the same way as the procedural proposition: "One ought to keep promises."

In addition to the differences among these three levels, there are at least two distinguishable kinds of "verification" possible within (3) itself, one of which is commonsensical, the other of which is more refined and complex. The former is grounded in the fact that we often just *know* when an obstacle has been overcome and balance and harmony have been restored to a situation, just as we know after eating that we are no longer hungry, after a successful venture that we are pleased, or after a concert that we have enjoyed it. We are as confident of these things as, after observing it, that a certain table is brown, or after the appropriate tests, that metal x melts at a certain temperature. So with many of our ordinary judgments, which on Dewey's view are but the working-out of means by which to restore harmony to problematic situations, we often know with no less certainty that we have judged rightly or that we have judged wrongly. Not that we so much set out to verify these judgments; it is rather as though we wait for verification, keeping alert to the consequences of the resultant action and to the feelings and responses of others. Subsequent experience is always the test—or better, the testing ground—but there is never a neat formula for singling out just those features for which to look. On the other hand, between those cases where our judgments receive conclusive positive verification from experience and those cases in which they receive a conclusive negative verdict, are a whole range of decisions and choices concerning which there may always be uncertainty. Their verification must be sought at another level, and one must ask whether they are borne out by the *way of life* of which they are a part. Here we step into the virtually uncharitable land of personal ideals, in which only the most general guidelines are discernible; but these are important, for not just any way of life qualifies as moral. Let us consider, therefore, what conditions must expressly be met before one's life can be said to fall within the moral sphere.

The moral way of life

The main criteria in Dewey's scheme for guiding conduct fall into three categories: (1) personal preference (as I shall signify the grounds of one's choice of a way of life), (2) conventional moral rules, and (3) the greatest happiness standard. Dewey's emphasis upon personal choice of a way of life is brought out in his assertion that "the thing actually at stake in any serious deliberation is not a difference of quantity, but what kind of person one is to become, what sort of self is in the making, what sort of world is making."[27] This, he believes, is ultimately the underlying issue in all deliberation about conduct. But deliberate choice of this sort does not *by itself* constitute a sufficient condition for saying that conduct is moral. If it did, he would be committed to a forthright moral relativism; a Socrates and a Hitler would be equally justified in the adoption of their respective ways of life. But on Dewey's view limitations are imposed upon personal preference, first of all in the form of existing conventional rules. To see how this works, let us consider his conception of de facto rules.

In rejecting traditional moral theories with their conceptions of fixed ends, Dewey emphasizes that moral standards arise originally out of custom and that to recognize this is to remove the need to "deify" some one rule as *the* standard by which all conduct should be governed. As conditions change, rules may become outmoded and the conduct they prescribe no longer serve the needs of society. When this happens, their critical revision becomes imperative.

> Instead of being rigidly fixed, they would be treated as intellectual instruments to be tested and confirmed—and altered—through consequences effected by acting upon them. They would lose all pretense of finality—the ulterior source of dogmatism.[28]

> A moral law, like a law in physics, is not something to swear by and stick to at all hazards; it is a formula of the way to respond when specified conditions present themselves. Its soundness and pertinence are tested by what happens when it is acted upon. Its claim or authority rests finally upon the imperativeness of the situation that has to be dealt with, not upon its own intrinsic nature—as any tool achieves dignity in the measure of needs served by it.[29]

Rather than a given standard or set of standards being considered binding upon all men at all times, moral rules are relative to the needs and demands of the contexts in which they arise.

---

[27] Dewey, *Human Nature and Conduct*, 216f.
[28] Dewey, *The Quest for Certainty*, 277.
[29] Ibid., 278.

An obvious objection at this point is that Dewey invites moral anarchy by denying that moral rules are "absolute," and that license is thereby granted to any and all behavior so long as it conforms to some rule or other accepted by the agent. As the reply which he would give to such an objection has a bearing upon our discussion, let us pursue it a bit.

First, he would be quick to point out that, far from breeding chaos and laxity, the method he advocates would bring a greater strictness to morality. If one habitually depends upon ready-made rules to guide action, then in situations in which rules have no ready application he is ill-equipped to rely upon his own resources. Thus it is the supposedly rigid moral codes which in fact prove to be unexacting: "the only truly severe code is the one which foregoes codification, throwing responsibility for judging each case upon the agents concerned."[30] And in *The Theory of the Moral Life* he says that moral theory can help to clarify particular problems for us, and can generalize concerning different kinds of conflict and their resolutions in the past, and in this way assist us in the canvassing of relevant factors.

> But it does not offer a table of commandments in a catechism in which answers are as definite as are the questions which are asked. It can render personal choice more intelligent, but it cannot take the place of personal decision.[31]

To the contrary,

> What is desirable is that a person shall see for himself what he is doing and why he is doing it; shall be sensitive to results in fact and anticipation, and shall be able to analyze the forces which make him act as he does act.[32]

Thus he is saying that, by regarding ourselves as fully responsible for our actions, we will better check moral laxity than if we unquestioningly accept conventional standards.

This, of course, answers only part of the above objection. Even granting that the moral life may be more demanding under the view Dewey advocates, what happens when A's judgment conflicts with B's and both judgments have been arrived at by careful deliberation? On the one hand, Dewey suggests what may in the last analysis be the only answer from his point of view. It is tolerance. If we understand the real nature of moral principles, perhaps moral disagreements will take on a new light and we will not be so quick to condemn those who fail to see things as we do. This leaves the way open to mutual understanding—even amidst differences—in a way not often found when each side feels that it has all the forces of good, right and justice steadfastly on its side. Some such attitude as this is a prerequisite of good faith in moral discussion of any sort, whether between individuals or nations. And when neither side can win over the other, they may have to be content to agree to disagree.

On the other hand, another answer is suggested in Dewey's conviction that the use of intelligence will by and large *in fact* eventuate in a consensus of judgment among disputants—providing, of course, that the relevant factual information is forthcoming.

[30] Dewey, *Human Nature and Conduct*, 103.
[31] Dewey, *Theory of the Moral Life*, 7f.
[32] Ibid., 111.

This reply squarely meets the objection by undercutting one of its implicit premises, viz., that divergent moral judgments will result from the abandonment of fixed rules. For it may simply be that disagreements appear to be irreconcilable only because all of the facts are not yet in, and that further disclosures would resolve the differences. This, of course, presupposes faith, not only in the efficacy of intelligence but in the truly rational character of man; a faith which underlies much of Dewey's ethical thought. This conviction is closely allied with the attitude of tolerance, for without the latter, intelligent inquiry may never get started in the first place. For, as he says,

> [Tolerance] is positive willingness to permit reflection and inquiry to go on in the faith that the truly right will be rendered more secure through questioning and discussion, while things which have endured merely from custom will be amended or done away with.... Without freedom of thought and expression of ideas, moral progress can occur only accidentally and by stealth. Mankind still prefers upon the whole to rely upon force, not now exercised directly and physically as it was once, but upon covert and indirect force, rather than upon intelligence to discover and cling to what is right.[33]

Similarly, when speaking of conflicts between nations, he notes that,

> There is no common ground, no moral understanding.... Each appeals to its own standard of right, and each thinks the other the creature of personal desire, whim or obstinacy.... The demand of each side treats its opponent as a willful violator of moral principles, an expression of self-interest or superior might. Intelligence which is the only possible messenger of reconciliation dwells in a far land of abstractions or comes after the event to record accomplished facts.[34]

The point here is that irreconcilable conflicts arise, not in consequence of the approach he advocates, but precisely because it has not been implemented.

If these considerations represented the whole of Dewey's views on this topic, there would be considerable justification in one critic's remark that "by rendering intelligence in terms of method, questions of content are left pretty much to look out for themselves."[35] However sound the above might be as an approach to ethics, one nonetheless feels that concrete guidance in a specific direction is needed. And just such direction is revealed in the third line of reply, in which Dewey introduces a standard over and above conventional rules by which to guide conduct in particular situations. It is that we should be guided by considerations what will promote the greatest general welfare.

The question immediately arises as to the status and function of this standard, for it sounds as if Dewey is trying to work back into ethics just the sort of thing he has argued at length should not be allowed. His stressing of the responsibility of the individual, the uniqueness of moral situations and the need for reliance upon intelligence were all designed, it seemed, to remove the need for such a standard. What is its status, then, and how is it justified? Although Dewey's answers to these questions are not explicit, it is possible to reconstruct his thought along the following lines. Happiness, first of

33   Ibid., 84f.
34   Dewey, *Human Nature and Conduct*, 83.
35   A. K. Rogers, *Ethics and Moral Tolerance* (New York: Macmillan, 1934), 101.

all, is neither an end in the sense of a fixed goal nor a standard in the sense of a clearly defined formula testing particular cases. To construe it in either of these ways would be to contravene his critique of traditional ethics. What it does, rather, is to provide a *frame of reference* from which to approach moral problems, a *point of view* from which to evaluate the various demands upon the moral agent.

> If [happiness] were regarded as the direct end of acts, it might be taken to be something fixed and inflexible. As a standard it is rather a cautionary direction, saying that when we judge an act, accomplished or proposed, with reference to approval and disapproval, we should first consider its consequences in general, and then its special consequences with respect to whatever affects the well-being of others. As a standard it provides a consistent point of view to be taken in deliberation, but it does not pretend to determine in advance what constitutes the general welfare or common good. It leaves room open for discovery of new constituents of well-being, and for varying combinations of these constituents in different situations.[36]

Thus while men must individually cultivate their capacities for critical reflection, they do have, so to speak, a foothold from which to survey moral situations, one which reveals the guidelines of intelligent decision without attempting to detail particular answers.

A clue to the origin of this standard is found in a provocative passage from Dewey's early work, *Outline of a Critical Theory of Ethics*, in which, discussing justice, he asks,

> Would then justice cease to be a law for an individual if it were not observed at all in the society of which he is a member? Such a question is as contradictory as asking what would happen to a planet if the solar system went out of existence. It is the law of justice (with other such laws) that *makes* society; that is, it is those active relations which find expression in these laws that unify individuals so that they have a common end. . . . To imagine the abolition of these laws is to imagine the abolition of society; and to ask for the law of individual conduct apart from all relationship . . . to society is to ask in what morality consists when moral conditions are destroyed.[37]

This means that moral laws are woven into the very fabric of society; that they express relationships among individuals without which society could not exist. The existence of such relationships constitute conditions "which must be met in order that any form of human association may be maintained, whether it be simple or complex, low or high in the scale of cultures."[38] But Dewey does not enjoin support of the status quo, at least not without important qualifications; he is not saying, in other words, that the accepted rules of a society at any given time should be adhered to just *because* they are accepted. Some practices, for example, might well not be in the interests of progress; it is just this fact which makes reconstruction necessary. Its purpose is to distil-out, as it were, those standards and ideals which are implicit in a social structure.

[36] Dewey, *Theory of the Moral Life*, 142.
[37] Dewey, *Outlines of a Critical Theory of Ethics* (New York: Hillary House, 1957), 175.
[38] Dewey, "Anthropology and Ethics," in *The Social Sciences and Their Interrelationships*, ed. William Fielding Ogburn and Alexander Goldenweiser (New York: Houghton Mifflin, 1927), 34.

> Reflective intelligence cross-questions the existing morality; and extracts from it the ideal which it pretends to embody, and thus is able to criticize the existing morality in the light of its own ideal . . . and thus the new ideal proposed by the individual [the moral reformer] is not a product of his private opinions, but is the outcome of the ideal embodied in existing customs, ideas and institutions.[39]

The conditions under which social activities originate determine that certain ways of doing things are better than others. These modes of conduct become established as customs or conventions and acquire the status of rules governing the conduct of all members of the society, with sanctions against violators. Through various influences, including religion, prejudice, and superstition, they eventually become overgrown with other practices which are not in the interests of society but to which men nonetheless become directly responsive. Due largely to their origins and the authority they are deemed to possess, these latter become crystallized into fixed and inflexible rules, and it is they which need to be reexamined. The job of the moral critic, therefore, is to cut through what is superfluous and detrimental to the general interest, and to expose and clarify those rules of conduct demanded by conditions existing in society at the time. By providing the standard by which de facto rules are to be tested, the greatest happiness principle provides the very foundation of morality.

The standard itself is susceptible of no moral justification, since it is presupposed by such justification. But in a broader sense it has all the justification one can ask by providing the conditions under which men can live together and progress constructively as a social unit. The successes and failures of man as a civilized, social being are the only measure by which it can be evaluated. And although the standard has de facto acceptance to the extent that men live together harmoniously, what Dewey is urging is that we explicitly recognize and adopt it as the foundation of distinctively moral conduct.

These are the main points of the reply Dewey would likely give to the objection that his theory submits to a vicious ethical relativism, and they bring into sharper focus the prominent features of the moral way of life. The first of these, personal preference, exhibits a decidedly individualistic concern and indicates that the ultimate court of appeal in judgments of consequence—in determining what kind of self one is going to be—is the individual. The choice may not be rational or even in the best interests of the person making it; but a choice must be made—indeed *is* made in the ordinary course of life. And if we are to act in the moral sphere we must opt for a *certain* way of life, one which respects established moral rules but recognizes that the greatest happiness standard is overriding in affairs of conduct. From the moral standpoint, in short, the paramount concern is a social one.

The good and the right

Dewey speaks of the one real moral end as growth (he puts this at various times in terms of "freedom," "self-realization," "realization of specific function," etc.). Notice

---

[39] Dewey, *Outlines of a Critical Theory of Ethics*, 190.

that he does not take happiness to be the end. By growth or freedom he means the opportunity to seek happiness according to one's specific abilities; the proper aim is "to foster conditions that widen the horizon of others and give them command of their own powers, so that they can find their own happiness in their own fashion." The welfare of others, like our own,

> consists in a widening and deepening of the perceptions that give activity its meaning. . . . To "make others happy" except through liberating their powers and engaging them in activities that enlarge the meaning of life is to harm them and to indulge ourselves under cover of exercising a special virtue. Our moral measure for estimating any existing arrangement or any proposed reform is its effect upon impulse and habits. Does it liberate or suppress, ossify or render flexible, divide or unify interest? Is perception quickened or dulled? Is memory made apt and extensive or narrow and diffusely irrelevant? Is imagination diverted to fantasy and compensatory dreams, or does it add fertility to life? Is thought creative or pushed one side into pedantic specialisms?[40]

The free exercise of interests, as this might be called, may as a matter of fact secure happiness, and this, of course, is the ultimate point of growth and freedom. But no mere multiplication of units of pleasure guarantees success; happiness may assume as many different forms as there are moral ways of life. For the genius, it will be the life of creativity; for the common man, it will be the exercise of more prosaic interests. The point is that Dewey locates the end of conduct ultimately in the cultivation of personal dispositions, interests and attitudes, realizing nonetheless that a social concern for the growth and freedom of others (in effect, for their happiness) is, by the very nature of society the best way to effect the conditions which makes happiness for oneself possible.

In short, the Good has a dual nature: an individualistic side in the cultivation of freedom for oneself, and a social side in a concern for the welfare and happiness of others. In this, Dewey bridges the gap between utilitarianism and self-realization theories, relying upon a moral postulate which he thinks is in fact recognized by moral agents (if only implicitly) and which constitutes a presupposition of the moral way of life. It is that whatever promotes the good of the individual also promotes the good of the many, and vice versa.[41] "All moral conduct," he says, "is based upon such a faith; and *moral theory must recognize this as the postulate upon which it rests.*" Here, he believes, there is a parallel to science.

> All science rests upon the conviction of the thoroughgoing and permanent unity of the world of objects known . . . the "uniformity of nature." . . . Without this conviction . . . science would be an impossibility. Moral experience *makes for the world of practice* an assumption analogous in kind to that which intellectual experience makes for the world of knowledge. And just as it is not the affair of science, as such, or even of logic (the theory of science) to justify this presupposition . . . or to do more than show its presence in intellectual experience,

[40]   Dewey, *Human Nature and Conduct*, 293f.
[41]   Dewey, *Outlines of a Critical Theory of Ethics*, 127f.

so it is not the business of conduct or even of ethics (the theory of conduct) to justify what we have termed the "ethical postulate."[42]

Turning now to the concept of the Right, Dewey says of it that it "expresses the way in which the good of a number of persons, held together by intrinsic ties, becomes efficacious in the regulation of the members of a community."[43] That is, it represents the claims of a group as a whole upon the respective individuals in the group. These claims have overt expression in the de facto rules of a society and have their basis in the network of socio-economic, religious and other cultural ties which integrate into a society what otherwise would be a mere collection of individuals. These claims *may not* be justified and should never be honored just because they are made. But they do possess a presumptive claim to validity; unless acting upon any given rule can be shown to be detrimental to the good of the many, it should be obeyed. And what is for the genuine good of the community is, *ex hypothesi*, for the good of the individual.

The Good consists in the growth of the individual and the community (i.e., in the cultivation of interests, freedom, etc., of the two), and it is the function of morality to promote this end. The Right signifies broadly those modes of conduct which serve the function of ethics. It takes overt form in the de facto rules of a community, but is always subject to question, test, and revision in a direct appeal to the Good. To adopt the greatest general happiness as a standard, therefore, is to adopt the point of view which recognizes growth as the end of conduct, realizes that the Right can be justified only in terms of it, and finally, which makes the moral postulate.

Conclusions

Correlating our conclusions in summary form, we have the following picture of Dewey's account of moral judgments.

He views the meanings of ordinary evaluative expressions as rooted in the language system (common sense) of which they are a part. For this reason they are multifunctional and are used at various times to approve, commend, advise, exhort, and so forth. As such, they reveal in different ways and to different degrees the attitudes of the speaker, and hence in the long run disclose what kind of person he is. In this sense they have a quasi-cognitive function—conveying information obliquely rather than reporting it directly. But the fact that these expressions contain words like "good," "right," and "ought" and are used in the above ways does not in itself make them moral judgments. In this, Dewey departs both from ordinary usage and (in general) ordinary philosophical usage, for we do tend to think of the ordinary man's judgments of the sort "You ought to keep that promise," "He ought to repay that debt," etc., as moral. On his view further conditions must be met in the making of a judgment before it qualifies as genuinely moral, and it is at this point that his ethics as a methodology makes its

---

[42]   Ibid., 131f.
[43]   Dewey, *Theory of the Moral Life*, 81.

appeal. He urges that one rely entirely upon factual knowledge within the conceptual framework of the ethical system as a whole in arriving at his moral decisions.

The connection of these conditions with the structure of morality can be exhibited by means of the following theses:

1. A judgment is a moral judgment if and only if it serves the function of morality.

This indicates that there is some one function which morality serves and that it is a necessary and sufficient condition of a judgment's being moral that it serve this function. We can expand upon this by adding that,

2. A judgment serves the function of morality if and only if it expresses the moral way of life.

This emphasizes that personal choice is central in determining whether one's conduct falls within the moral sphere. This leaves the remaining question of what qualifies such a choice as moral, and this can be answered as follows:

3. A judgment expresses the moral way of life if and only if (a) it is made with a view to promoting the good, and (b) it is both warranted and verifiable from an empirical standpoint.

As we have seen, (a) refers to the promotion of growth in both its individual and social aspects; (b) requires that in addition to comporting with (a), the judgment must issue from a reflective survey of the facts, not from mere habit or impulse. It also means that once made it must be supportable by reasons of both a factual and conceptual nature, the relevance of which, qua moral, is determined by the context and nature of the problem. This does not mean that moral judgments are verifiable in the sense that they can be adjudged true or false on the basis of simple observations and calculations, or the performance of specific tests. It means, rather, that the action prescribed must have consequences assessable in the long run both from the standpoint of conduciveness to the Good and from the standpoint of the agent's personal ideals, so far as these are in keeping with the Good. And there is no formula which assures us in advance that an action and its consequences will meet these conditions, for this becomes known only in the living-out of a way of life.

On Dewey's view all moral judgments are, broadly speaking, judgments of value in the sense that their normative function sets them apart from factual assertions. But distinguishable among them are judgments of obligation and judgments of value in a narrower sense. The former arise when some claim has been made, either by the agent or upon him (by another person or society), or among others with respect to whom he is but a spectator. In each case, the judgment is an evaluation of the claim in light of the above requirements of morality. Whether one approves of a certain action in part determines what kind of person he is to be, and if he approves what promotes the Good he is opting for the moral way of life and his judgment is moral. But there is in this no guarantee that he will judge rightly; his judgment's being moral means only that it is guided in formulation by those considerations which best take account of the possible avenues by which he and others can pursue happiness. One's judgment is a value judgment in the narrower sense when it estimates the worth of some object, person or experience. These as a rule are not evaluations of claims or modes of conduct (although modes of conduct are involved, viz., pursuing pleasures, rejecting enjoyments, etc.), but are as Dewey says, about "immediately felt experiences." The boundary between these two sorts of judgment is not carefully drawn, and Dewey quite likely thought that there was no reason why it need be. Each is but a different aspect of the same deliberative process which is at the heart of reflective morality.

For Dewey, then, intuitionism, naturalism, and noncognitivism do not exhaust the possible interpretations of moral expressions, for there is a fourth alternative which views them as neither a priori, descriptive, nor emotive—nor as simply a combination of the latter two—but nonetheless as empirical, cognitive, and susceptible of verification in experience. For, as we have seen, he takes an expanded view of what it is for a judgment to be qualified in these latter ways. The upshot is that in moral judgment we have the integration into a reasoned and empirically grounded judgment of the emotional and intellectual aspects of life. As he expresses it in the *Theory of Valuation*:

> The hard-and-fast impassible line which is supposed by some to exist between "emotive" and "scientific" language is a reflex of the gap which now exists between the intellectual and the emotional in human relations and activities. . . . In fact and in net outcome, the previous discussion does not point in the least to supersession of the emotive by the intellectual. Its only and complete import is the need for their integration in behavior—behavior in which, according to common speech, the head and the heart work together, in which, to use more technical language, prizing and appraising unite in direction of action.[44]

The significance for ethics of Dewey's contention that engaging in inquiry is like engaging in a contract is here apparent;[45] for there is a basic commitment underlying any inquiry warranting the name ethical, viz., that it be conducted within the boundaries which define the moral way of life. Unless such a commitment is recognized and honored in practice, judgment does not fall within the moral sphere. This means that an ultimate pre-moral choice underlies distinctively moral conduct; and as only the individual can enter into the contract symbolized by such a choice, so only he can break it.[46]

[44] Dewey, *Theory of Valuation*, 64f.
[45] Dewey, *Logic: The Theory of Inquiry*, 16.
[46] Originally published in the *Review of Metaphysics*, Vol. 20, No. 1, September 1966, 42–70.

2

Consequentialism and its Consequences

There is an old proverb, often quoted by Tolstoy: "Do what is right, come what may." Holmes endorses it, but in order to do so, he makes a long detour which produces a devastating criticism of consequentialism. Holmes begins by quoting the words of William James, regarding "one unconditional commandment, which is that we should seek incessantly, with fear and trembling, so to vote and to act as to bring about the very largest total universe of good which we can see." While a view like this is often interpreted as favoring consequentialism, Holmes shows that the opposite is the case. After a detailed analysis of the relationship of means and ends, he demonstrates that our focus should be on means rather than on ends. The ancient wisdom of Taoism, Hinduism, and Buddhism, in modern times reaffirmed by Tolstoy and Gandhi, is that it is simply not given to us to know the consequences of our actions. If this is so, we must look to other grounds not only for our moral judgments but also for our attempts to realize the greatest "total universe of good"—projecting, measuring, and comparing consequences is not an adequate way to accomplish that.

Consequentialism, as commonly understood, tells us, in effect, always to do what is best. And how, one wants to ask, can that be improved upon? If it cannot, why bother with the categorical imperative, the divine command theory, natural law, and other pretenders to the throne of supreme moral principle? We know there are acts. We know they have consequences. And we know these consequences are good or bad in varying degrees. We do not know whether there is a God, or if there is one, exactly what he commands. Even less can we be sure what Kant meant, or what cognitively deprived rational beings would agree to in a cloistered original position. So why not simply cast our lot with William James when he says there is "but one unconditional commandment, which is that we should seek incessantly, with fear and trembling, so to vote and to act as to bring about the very largest total universe of good which we can see"?[1] And having done that, why not devote our energies to working together to achieve that end?

This oversimplifies, of course, but it contains the elements of a prima facie case in favor of consequentialism.

Two other claims reinforce this case. Both, if correct, have far-reaching implications. They bear in particular upon the relevance of moral philosophy to practical affairs, especially in light of the growing conviction—not shared by all, by any means, but

---

[1] William James, "Moral Philosopher and the Moral Life," in William James, *The Essential Writings*, ed. Bruce Wilshire (New York: Harper Torchbooks, 1971), 297.

nonetheless widespread—that moral philosophy *ought*, in some sense, to concern itself with the problems of people in what social scientists like to call the "real world."

The first claim is that, whether philosophers intend it or not, ethical theory over time works its way into the thinking of ordinary persons, where it exerts a subtle and largely unnoticed influence. So that while it may be debated whether philosophers should expressly tackle problems like poverty, discrimination, euthanasia, and war, philosophy is already having its influence in the way of spinning the perspectival web within which those problems are located and understood. Dewey captured the spirit of this outlook early in his career, when he observed:

> Not even customary morality, that of respectability and convention, is freed from dependence upon theory; it simply lives off the funded results of some once-moving examination of life.

> [Ethical theories] filter into the average consciousness, and their truth becomes, wholly unaware to the average consciousness, a part of the ordinary insight into life—a part of the meaning of the world of practice in which we live. Life looks different today to the man to whom Bentham and Kant are not even names, because of the formulae of the greatest good, the autonomy of the will, and the categorical imperative.[2]

The second claim is more specific. It assigns a privileged position to utilitarianism. Thus, for example, Sidgwick sees utilitarianism as underlying common sense morality, though not consciously so in people's minds. "It is there," he says, "not as the mode of regulating conduct with which mankind began, but rather, as that to which we can now see that human development has been always tending, that Utilitarianism may most reasonably claim the acceptance of Common Sense."[3] The thought here is that an evolutionary process is at work in which one substantive moral outlook, that of utilitarianism—the preeminent form of consequentialism—is gradually emerging as dominant.

Not only does consequentialism have a strong, precritical intuitive appeal, if Sidgwick is correct, it also has achieved—or, at any rate, is well on its way to achieving—a *fait accompli* in the workaday world of practical ethics. It is becoming the dominant moral outlook in human affairs. While philosophers debate the merits of different theories, humankind is issuing the only verdict that really counts. And for better or worse, on his view, that verdict is in favor of consequentialism.

---

[2] John Dewey, "Moral Theory and Practice," in John Dewey, *The Early Works, 1882–1898* (Carbondale, IL: Southern Illinois University Press), pages 96 and 102.

[3] Henry Sidgwick, *The Methods of Ethics*, seventh ed. (Chicago: University of Chicago Press, 1962), 456f. Bentham had, of course, in 1789 made the even stronger claim on behalf of the principle of utility that "[b]y the natural constitution of the human frame, on most occasions of their lives men in general embrace this principle, without thinking of it: if not for the ordering of their own actions, yet for the trying of their own actions, as well as of those of other men"; *An Introduction to the Principles of Morals and Legislation* (New York: Hafner, 1789), 4. An opposing appraisal was made by William E. H. Lecky in 1869 when he wrote that "our first question is naturally how far this theory agrees with the feelings and with the language of mankind. But if tested by this criterion, there never was a doctrine more emphatically condemned than utilitarianism. In all its stages, and in all its assertions, it is in direct opposition to common language and to common sentiments"; *History of European Morals from Augustus to Charlemagne*, Vol. 1 (London: Longmans, Green, 1882), 34.

Here serious problems surface. For some who agree that a particular moral outlook has come to dominate much of common sense thinking, and who agree that this outlook is consequentialist, part company with Sidgwick in his approval of this state of affairs. They think, rather, this development is regrettable and represents a trend that should be reversed.

Stuart Hampshire, for example, contends that, especially since World War I, the prevailing morality, particularly in governmental thinking, has been utilitarian—what he labels, disparagingly, "computational morality." He contends that this "utilitarian habit of the mind," as he calls it, "has brought with it a new abstract cruelty in politics, a dull destructive political righteousness: mechanical, quantitative thinking, leaden academic minds setting out their moral calculations in leaden abstract prose."[4] Just as Dewey argued that the quest for certainty in philosophy has had bad consequences throughout the centuries, the thought here is that the consequentialism embodied in the thinking of experts has likewise had bad consequences. Nor, among those who advance this objection, are consequentialism's bad consequences limited to those that issue from the thinking of Western quantitative analysts. Arthur Koestler, in a related criticism, sees utilitarianism as having taken hold in a whole ideology, namely Marxism, with similar consequences. Where Hampshire speaks disparagingly of "computational morality," Koestler does the same of what he calls "Commissar-Ethics":

> The transfer from the physical to the ethical level of the principles of quantitative measurement has probably produced the most disastrous results. The implied paradoxa of this kind of "Commissar-Ethics" are less obvious to us than those of the biological ethics of fascism because we have been so thoroughly trained to think in quantitative terms that the application of mathematical criteria to ethical method appears to us simply as an act of common sense. . . . We accept the argument of Soviet apologists that it is better to keep a thousand innocents in jail than to let one spy go free whose activity might endanger the lives of tens of thousands. And we do not notice the hitch in the argument, namely, that we have no physical instruments to measure the exact amount of harm caused by the detention of the thousand innocents and to compare it with the amount of harm to be expected from the hypothetical spy.[5]

Though neither Hampshire nor Koestler claims that consequentialism represents the mature morality of common sense, as Sidgwick suggests, each alleges that it has taken over important areas of thought and action, with unfortunate, if not disastrous, consequences.

What shall we make of such an objection? Can it be met, and can the promise of consequentialism be realized?

So stated, the objection obviously needs qualifying. Consequentialism itself has no consequences, good or bad (other, perhaps, than logical ones), so we must understand the objection to mean that the *holding* of consequentialism—its acceptance or following—has bad consequences. In order for its presumed bad consequences to be of the magnitude alleged by Hampshire and Koestler, one would have to assume that

---

[4] Stuart Hampshire, *Morality and Pessimism* (London: Cambridge University Press, 1972), 7.
[5] Arthur Koestler, *The Yogi and the Commissar and Other Essays* (New York: Macmillan, 1945), 242f.

consequentialism is, if not the dominant view of commonsense morality, at least the dominant view of some significant portion thereof—at the very least, of a significant number of persons, particularly those who wield power and influence. I shall not try to assess that claim, though a case could be made for it with regard to industrial, technocratic society. Let us consider, rather, some general considerations relevant to assessing the objection.

Before turning to these questions, let me indicate what I shall take consequentialism to be. For it has come to stand for a variety of different things in recent literature.

Consequentialism defined

I have spoken as though consequentialism were more or less identical to utilitarianism, and it is often understood in this way, particularly when contrasted with deontological ethical theories. At other times, however, it is identified more or less with teleological ethics in general (which itself is sometimes used more or less interchangeably with utilitarianism). Used in either of these ways the term represents an unnecessary proliferation of "isms," since it fails to mark out any distinctions not already covered by utilitarianism and moral teleology.

Consequentialism can, however, be understood in a way not covered by either utilitarianism or teleologism, and a way that is helpful in defining those other positions. In this sense it is simply the thesis:

C: Rightness and wrongness are determined solely by the consequences of actions.

Left open is what it is about consequences that is relevant. This means that consequentialism may take axiological or deontological forms, depending upon whether the comparative value of consequences is their relevant feature or putatively non-value considerations, such as whether they occasion rights violations, and if so, in what comparative measure (the latter type theory sometimes being called a "utilitarianism of rights"). Utilitarianism can then be understood as a consequentialist theory with a typically axiological orientation.[6] But it is not the only such theory. Ethical egoism is a consequentialist theory with an axiological orientation, as are various forms of what I call macro ethics—theories that take the relevant beneficiary of the consequences to be collective or abstract entities like the community, nation, or state. All such theories—theories, that is, that are consequentialist and take the resultant comparative value of consequences to determine right and wrong—may then be understood to be teleological (in the sense that they implicitly or explicitly identify an end to moral conduct, the maximization of value for the relevant entity). As such, they can be contrasted with the various deontological theories.

The assessment of the foregoing objection in the next section will apply primarily to utilitarianism, as that is the specific consequentialist theory Hampshire and Koestler

---

[6] I shall, for the sake of simplicity, ignore the many possible permutations of utilitarianism, such as those which appeal to preference satisfaction.

attack. Thereafter, in presenting a different objection to consequentialism, I shall take consequentialism to stand for any theory that affirms C, whether it be utilitarian or not.

Understanding the Hampshire/Koestler objection

Let us now return to the objection cited earlier. Does consequentialism have the alleged bad consequences, and if so, should it be rejected on those grounds?

I do not think this objection as it stands is sustainable, and for the following reason.

Let us begin by distinguishing among *accepting, following*, and *conforming* to a principle. On the face of it, one might accept a principle, in the sense of believing that it is the correct principle, without trying to live by it or doing so consistently.[7] Arguably, many Christians accept Christ's teaching in the Sermon on the Mount in this way, as do many Marxists the teachings of Marx. One might even concede that a certain principle is the correct principle of conduct and yet resolve not to act in accordance with it. To *follow* a principle, on the other hand, is not only to accept it, but to try to implement it as well—not necessarily invariably, but by and large and for the most part. It is to incorporate it in some significant way in the guidance of one's conduct. To follow a principle, in this sense, however, guarantees nothing about one's success in trying to implement it. *Conforming to* a principle, on the other hand, signifies acting in accordance with it—that is, actually doing as it prescribes. Normally that would imply accepting and following it, but it need not. Somewhat improbably, one could in fact do as a particular principle prescribes purely by chance, without consciously following any at all. Somewhat more plausibly, one might conform to one principle while following another. This could happen if the two principles were extensionally equivalent in the sense of yielding the same prescriptions (it has sometimes been thought, for example, notably by Plato, that prudence and morality coincide in just this way). One might even conform to a principle without in fact knowing that he was conforming to it, but one could not accept or follow a principle without knowing that he was doing so. We may say, then, that accepting a principle does not entail following or conforming to it; following a principle entails accepting and at least trying to conform to it. And conforming to a principle, while it probably normally involves accepting and trying to conform to it, does not strictly imply either accepting or following it.

If we assume that consequentialism is generally accepted, or accepted by a significant number of persons, and if the conditions in the society in which this is true are deemed bad, the Hampshire-Koestler objection might mean that this unfortunate state of affairs is a consequence of the fact that consequentialism is held as widely as it is. But if this is how the objection is understood, the consequentialist has a reply to it. It is that this unfortunate state of affairs is not due to the holding of consequentialism, but rather

---

[7] I say "on the face of it," mindful of the controversy over internalism and externalism on the question of the relationship between obligation—or recognition of obligation—and motivation, and of the complexities in spelling-out the relationship between motivation and conduct.

to the fact that there are so many who do not hold it. So long as the *acceptance* of the principle is significantly less than universal for the community in question, it may be that the bad consequences are the result of the conduct of those who do not accept consequentialism, not a result of the conduct of those who do, even if the latter are in positions of power. One can hardly hold against consequentialism the conduct of those who do not subscribe to it. It is, after all, the point of advocating consequentialism as a moral principle to encourage people to follow it, presumably in the conviction that their so doing will have the best consequences. If *not* following it has consequences that are less than ideal or even comparatively bad, that is precisely what one should expect. Indeed, the consequentialist might even cite the critic's facts as tending to support the case for consequentialism.

The objection cannot mean that conforming to consequentialism has bad consequences, since the principle (in its utilitarian form, as we are understanding it) calls upon us to do what is best. If everyone does that, we cannot improve upon what we have done.[8] If not everyone does that, then the consequentialist can revert to the previous reply and lay the alleged "bad consequences" at the feet of those who do not conform to consequentialism, whether their nonconformity is intentional or not.

I suggest, for these reasons, that the most plausible way to understand the objection is as saying that *following* the principle of consequentialism has bad consequences.

How can following consequentialism have bad consequences? It can if those who follow it fail to implement it correctly—fail, that is, to do precisely what its central principle prescribes. This can happen if those who follow it are weakly committed to it or weak of will. It can also happen if the principle is difficult to apply, as arguably it often is because of the difficulty of projecting the consequences of alternative actions. People with the best of intentions may often fail to do as consequentialism prescribes because what that is often is simply too difficult to ascertain. The temptation, then, is to do whatever one is predisposed to do, for whatever reasons, and to rationalize to oneself that this is what will have the best consequences.

This is a serious objection. The problems in trying to project consequences over an indefinite future were detailed by Moore,[9] himself usually considered a utilitarian, and they have never been convincingly resolved. Those problems certainly make it tempting to convince oneself that the course one prefers for other reasons is the course called for by consequentialism.

Still, consequentialists might well argue that just as the consequences of the actions of those who do not accept consequentialism cannot reasonably be calculated among consequentialism's consequences, so the consequences of the acts of those who carelessly apply it—or worse yet, willfully misapply it—cannot fairly be reckoned among those consequences either. Advocates of any principle are entitled to presume, in advancing it for everyone alike, which arguably is a condition of a principle's qualifying as moral, that any reckoning of the consequences of its adoption will include

---

[8] Deontologists will maintain that it may nonetheless have bad consequences *morally*. Maximizing value, on their view, does not ensure that all other morally relevant considerations are given their due.

[9] G. E. Moore, *Principia Ethica* (Cambridge: Cambridge University Press, 1903), Chapter 5.

only the consequences of its both being adopted and being correctly applied. Absent the satisfaction of this condition, the consequentialist can turn back against his critics the charge that, in alleging the bad consequences of consequentialism, they are tacitly presupposing consequentialism itself. Bentham had anticipated this response when he said:

> When a man attempts to combat the principle of utility, it is with reasons drawn, without his being aware of it, from that very principle itself. His arguments, if they prove any thing, prove not that the principle is *wrong*, but that, according to the applications he supposes to be made of it, it is *misapplied.*[10]

Seen in one light this reply seems decisive. For if consequentialism directs us—all of us, not just some of us—always to do what is best, and if conformity with that principle entails doing what is best, then the consequences of such conformity can never be bad, at least by comparison with available alternatives. If so, consequentialism seems impervious to any other than a frontal deontological challenge to the very idea that it can never be right to prefer a worse state of affairs to a better, even all things considered. (The deontologist, of course, can always say that producing the best consequences may fail to bring about what is *morally* best because it disregards other morally relevant considerations.)

But seen in a different light, this reply comes up short. True, one wants to say, if consequentialism tells us always to do what is best, then if we in fact do that, those consequences cannot be improved upon. But that simply reaffirms the original intuition with which we began. Consequentialists understandably want to disqualify from consequentialism's assessment the consequences of misapplying it. Nonetheless if there is something about the principle that systematically prevents it from being applied correctly, or makes it impossible to state precisely what a correct application would be, then that weighs against the principle, whether or not the failure is counted among consequentialism's consequences. Consequentialism, we should remember, represents advocacy of a particular principle, no less than does, say, Kantianism. We can all see the difficulties in applying a principle like the categorical imperative and properly consider it a failure of Kantianism if solutions to those problems cannot be found. So we should be prepared to acknowledge that if there are equally formidable difficulties in applying consequentialism's principle, that should be accounted a failure of consequentialism as well—not necessarily of the principle *per se*, but of consequentialism as a theory of ethics that presumes to guide moral conduct.

It is just such a difficulty that I now want to explore. It is concerned with consequentialism's consequences, now not in the sense of the consequences of following the principle, but in the sense of the consequences to which the theory would have us appeal in attempting to determine what is right and wrong. I shall henceforth take consequentialism in the broader sense characterized earlier, as standing for any theory which affirms C, not merely for axiological theories, and not merely for utilitarian theories.

---

[10]   Bentham, *An Introduction to the Principles of Morals and Legislation,* 5.

An act's consequences and the responses of others to it

Consider the following passage from Elizabeth Anscombe's essay "War and Murder":

> The distinction between the intended, and the merely foreseen, effects of a
> voluntary action is indeed absolutely essential to Christian ethics. For Christianity
> forbids a number of things as being bad in themselves. But if I am answerable for
> the foreseen consequences of an action or refusal, as much as for the action itself,
> then these prohibitions will break down. If someone innocent will die unless I do
> a wicked thing, then on this view I am his murderer in refusing. So all that is left
> to me is to weigh up evils.[11]

My interest here is not with the principle of double effect, which one can see lying
just beneath the surface of these remarks. It is with the implicit conception of what
is properly includable among an act's consequences. In disavowing answerability for
unintended though foreseen consequences in the sort of case she cites, it is clear that
Anscombe is allowing that the actions of others are sometimes among the consequences
of our own actions (the death of the innocent of which she speaks is a death at the
hands of someone else). It is just that when they are, and when they are unintended,
those consequences are not, in Anscombe's view, morally accountable to us, hence do
not bear upon the rightness of what we do.

Two issues emerge here. The first is whether the free and deliberate actions of others
are ever properly reckoned among the consequences of our own actions. The second
is whether, if they are, they should be placed on the scales when it comes to moral
calculations, and if so, with what weight.

Why is this a problem? It will be helpful to answer this by placing the issue in a
broader perspective by looking more closely at the nature of consequences.

Mediated and unmediated consequences

Everything that happens prior to a given action is a temporal antecedent of that action;
everything that happens after, a temporal consequent (things that happen concurrently
may be called temporal concomitants, but I shall for the sake of simplicity ignore
them for present purposes). In these terms an action's consequences are among its
consequents. But not just any consequent counts as a consequence; indeed, most
do not. If I move my arm and an apple falls from a tree in Shanghai, that happening
(along with every other event throughout the remaining history of the universe) is
a consequent of my action. But it surely is not a consequence.[12] On the other hand,

---

[11] Quoted from Richard Wasserstrom, ed., *War and Morality* (Belmont, CA: Wadsworth, 1970), 50.
[12] Not that with enough philosophical ingenuity one could not contrive hypothetical cases in
      which there were sufficient interconnections between the two events to warrant calling the one a
      consequence of the other; only that, in the normal course of affairs, this would be an inaccurate
      characterization. And by no plausible stretch of even the philosophical imagination could all
      of the subsequent happenings throughout the remaining history of the universe be called the
      consequences of my action.

if in moving my arm I knock over a glass of water, the water's spilling clearly *is* a consequence of my action.

Let us call any consequent of an act that would not have occurred but for the act an *outcome* of that act. Any consequent that is not an outcome let us call a *subsequence* of that act. Consequences clearly are among an action's outcomes. Along with effects and results, I suspect that they exhaust those outcomes. The relations among these notions are represented as in figure.

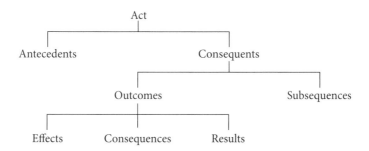

The differences among effects, consequences, and results resist precise delineation; ordinary language often uses them loosely and sometimes interchangeably. But arguably effects are the narrowest of the three, depending, as they do (by definition), upon a causal connection between the action and its outcome; and results the broadest, encompassing both effects and consequences and including some outcomes that do not fit so readily into either of the other categories (we might post the results of an exam, for example, but we could not post its effects or consequences; just as we announce the results of an election but, again, not its effects or consequences). Consequences include effects, and sometimes the two notions are used interchangeably (as in the Anscombe quotation above, and as in Moore's analysis in Chapter Five of *Principia Ethica*). But there are some candidates for consequences to which the notion of effects is inappropriate; notably, for our purpose, those outcomes that involve the actions of others.

Suppose that, rather than the apple falling after I move my arm, someone picks the apple. Barring an extraordinary configuration of circumstances, that action would not be an outcome of my own. If not, it is a mere subsequence of my action, not a consequence. But suppose terrorists threaten to execute hostages if their demands aren't met and carry out the threat when the deadline passes. Are the hostages' deaths a consequence of the refusal? Or, to take a concrete case, when President Bush threatened military action against Iraq unless President Hussein withdrew Iraqi troops from Kuwait, was the subsequent U.S. attack, and the casualties it entailed, a consequence of President Hussein's refusal to withdraw; that is, was Bush's order to attack and its execution by thousands of military personnel a consequence of Hussein's act?

Why are these cases troublesome? It is because some decision or choice of someone else has entered the picture.

If I shout "Hello!" from Echo Mountain, no cognitive response by anyone need intervene before my call echoes back to me. I shout, and the laws of physics do the rest. But if I cry "Fire!" in the proverbial crowded theater, cognitive responses on the part of others must intervene before panic ensues. Consequences, it seems clear, fall into one or the other of two kinds: those that are mediated by some thought, choice, decision—some mental operation, if you like—before they come about, and those that are not.[13] The echo is an unmediated consequence of my shouting; the panic is a mediated consequence.

The picking of the Shanghai apple, of course, presupposes some mental act on the part of the picker. So, many subsequences as well as consequences are mediated (every deliberate act by anyone throughout the future is, in fact, a mediated subsequence of the act of which it is a subsequence). But this raises no distinctive problems. The problems arise when consequents of a particular act are both mediated and outcomes of that act, that is, such that they would not have come about but for the act. Not all such cases give rise to the problem I want to focus upon, however. Every deliberate act by everyone living today is an outcome of many acts performed by their ancestors thousands of years ago (procreating just when they did, if nothing else), and the outcomes of every such act are mediated outcomes of those acts. Likewise, the outcomes of every free and deliberate act I perform today are mediated outcomes of many acts performed in the past (choosing to shop at a particular market is a mediated outcome of having chosen years before to reside in the city containing that market). There are, of courses, questions of ability that arise in at least some of these cases. If I give five dollars to a street person who promptly retires to the nearest bar with it, his subsequent consumption of alcohol is a mediated consequence of what I did. And it is mediated not only by his decision to go to the bar, but also by the bartender's serving him. This raises the question of where and how moral responsibility for his inebriation should be distributed (whether principally to him for asking for money then heading for the bar, or to me for granting his request, or to the bartender for serving him, or to all three in varying proportions).

The problem that interests me here concerns those cases in which mediated outcomes are *responses* to what someone else has done. For often these are considered consequences of the original act. The door's closing is a consequence of my having asked you to close it; the platoon's lurching forward is a consequence of the sergeant's order to march; and, of course, the calamitous panic in the crowded theater is consequence of someone's shouting "Fire!" Children often hear that punishment will be a consequence of misbehavior; governments often threaten that adversaries will suffer the consequences if they do or fail to do some particular thing.[14]

---

[13] More broadly, consequents in general—whether outcomes or subsequences—break down into mediated and unmediated. I shall focus upon outcomes, and among outcomes, upon those that are plausibly regarded as consequences. This is partly to keep the focus upon the concept that is central to consequentialism as an ethical theory (we do not yet have Outcomism as such a theory), but also partly because the notion of consequences is more at home in our everyday discussion of issues than is that of outcomes.

[14] The mirror image of many of these issues is found in tort law in the attempt to clarify causation, where, most generally, an act or omission is said to be the cause in fact of an injury if but for the act or omission the injury would not have occurred (thus making the injury an outcome of the act, as I have defined these notions). This leaves the proximate cause to be determined by further refinement of the contributing and determining factors in the injury (rendering it, in the preceding terms, an effect, consequence, or result of the act).

Are all of an act's consequences relevant to its moral assessment? Or only some? And if only some, which ones? And why?

By "all" here I do not mean the problem Moore dealt with, of where to draw the line in the unfolding of consequences into an indefinite future beyond which you may assume that the appraisal of their value won't be reversed. I mean, rather, are all *kinds* of an act's consequences morally relevant—specifically, both mediated and unmediated?

There is no problem (theoretically, at least) with unmediated consequences, particularly when they are effects of the acts in question. They unquestionably belong on the scales for any consequentialist trying to determine an act's rightness. But what of mediated consequences? Particularly those mediated by responses to the original action? Are they to be weighed as well?[15]

Clearly not everything others do in response to an act of mine—much less everything they would not have done but for my act—can plausibly be considered a consequence of that act, at least for purposes of moral assessment. That would lead to a proliferation of consequences so great as to compound immeasurably the already seemingly intractable problem of projecting and assessing consequences. Equally importantly, it would enable persons to determine many of the consequences of others' actions simply by the way they respond to them. From a consequentialist standpoint (as well as from non-consequentialist standpoints that allow a significant role to consequences), this would enable those appropriately situated, and possessing enough power, to make what others do morally right or wrong by seeing to it that the consequences of what they do are good or bad in the appropriate proportions. This is implied by Moore, with regard to judicial punishment:

> One of the chief reasons why an action should not be done in any particular state of society is that it will be punished; since the punishment is in general itself a greater evil than would have been caused by the omission of the action punished. Thus the existence of a punishment may be an adequate reason for regarding an action as generally wrong, even though it has no other bad effects but even slightly good ones. The fact that an action will be punished is a condition of exactly the same kind as others of more or less permanence, which must be taken into account in discussing the general utility or disutility of an action in a particular state of society.[16]

Although Moore does not expressly recognize the distinction between what I am calling mediated and unmediated consequences, his reasoning presupposes it. And the extension of such reasoning provides a foundation for a kind of moral totalitarianism. Any government with the power to determine the "consequences" of failure to do as it says—or of doing what it forbids—would not only be able to make disobedience imprudent, as governments regularly try to do anyway, but would make it morally

---

[15] One could expand the notion of mediated consequences to include responses by nonhumans as well—such as the outcomes of throwing rocks at a hornet's nest or not letting a sleeping dog lie. While these raise important conceptual and ethical issues on their own, I shall, for the sake of simplicity, limit mediated consequences to those involving cognitive acts of humans only.

[16] Moore, *Principia Ethica*, 159.

wrong as well. The same would apply to any person or persons with sufficient power. They could render the actions of others right or wrong, after the performance of those actions, and even without the foreknowledge of those performing them. Nudged only slightly to the extreme, this way of thinking would enable one to determine the moral character of the acts of persons long deceased.

At the same time, some mediated consequences seem incontrovertibly to be properly regarded as consequences of prior actions of others. If Kasparov places Karpov's king in check, and Karpov subsequently moves the king, it is natural to say that he did so as a consequence of the check. The same holds when one says that FDR's call for a declaration of war was a consequence of the Japanese attack upon Pearl Harbor, or President Bush's mobilization of U.S. troops was a consequence of Iraq's invasion of Kuwait. Moreover, the notion of coercion is sometimes understood as threatened intervention in the consequences of an action (or omission) by the performance of an act that the actor would find undesirable with a view to dissuading him from performing that action. And the very idea of deterrence (nuclear or otherwise) is that of leading others to refrain from acts they otherwise would perform by making it known to them that the consequences of those acts would be unacceptable to them—unacceptable because those issuing the threats will make them unacceptable. More philosophically, the Prisoner's Dilemma gets off the ground only because the responses of others (those controlling the hypothetical situation) are factored among the outcomes of the options available to the prisoners.

So how does one determine which mediated consequences should be counted for purposes of moral assessment, and which not?

There is no apparent way to answer this in morally neutral terms. The flow of events of which our doings are a part does not admit of a sharp and indisputable individuation of consequences—and perhaps not even of acts either—when the conduct of others is sluiced into them, as invariably it is in interpersonal, social, and international affairs of greatest moral interest. This, indeed, may be what most significantly distinguishes our assessment of human affairs from that of the physical world by science, and casts doubt upon the possibility of anything like a science of ethics, or perhaps even a value-neutral social science.

This opens the way to bias in the judgment of controversial cases in the guise of making neutral consequentialist calculations. This is a problem that would remain even if Koestler's concern about quantificational calculations could be allayed. If a woman is assaulted walking down an inner city street at night, her rape is a mediated consequence of what she did. But should it be considered a consequence for purposes of moral assessment? If it should, it would, *ceteris paribus*, make her walking down that street at night—supposedly something anyone has a right to do—morally wrong from a consequentialist standpoint, with all that implies about further judgments of responsibility. Those who contend that women in such circumstances are asking for trouble tend to count such consequences, to the point of saying in such cases that women act wrongly. Those who contend that to say that is just another way of blaming the victim insist that her victimization was an act of the rapist, pure and simple. If two gays walk down the street holding hands in an area known for attacks by homophobic gangs, is their subsequent victimization a consequence of their action for purposes of moral assessment? Again, predispositions reflecting underlying biases are likely to determine the answers to this question.

The problem is not simply that people often give way to temptation to tailor their estimates of consequences to support what they are predisposed to believe—where, with enough care and conscientiousness, they could get matters straight. Here the problem is that there is no objective non-normative fact of the matter to be ascertained. One must make the determination in some sense a matter of decision. The question is: Which among an action's consequences in situations of this sort *ought* to be counted for purposes of moral assessment? This is a moral question itself, nested inside what to appearances is a neutral determination of facts. And the answers to it often presuppose moral judgments. We are judging more than just an act in these cases; we are judging broader contextual wholes containing acts and various candidates for their consequences.

If this is correct, it means that a rather simple model of what is involved in the making of moral judgments is inadequate. According to that model, there are "facts" and there are "values" (taking this broadly to include norms and principles), and to judge the latter you must first ascertain the former, which is an objective, quasi-scientific undertaking. Having established the facts, you then apply the appropriate principle and arrive at a moral judgment. But this will not do if the preceding account is correct. For on that account one is involved in the making of moral judgments in the very determination of what the facts are (where what the consequences of an act will be are among the preeminent "facts").

It is beyond the scope of my present concerns to try to spell out what enters into the making of these judgments. But these considerations highlight the importance of recognizing the non-neutrality of many so-called "facts" in social affairs and suggest that, to a considerable extent, our understanding of the social world may be constituted by evaluations. Whereas early epistemological idealists recognized an egocentric predicament that led them to conceptualize the world as constituted by perceptions (strictly, the ideas or data of perception), and Kant argued that nature cannot be understood apart from the order and coherence our mind brings to it, perhaps we need to recognize a kind of moral-centric predicament, in which we cannot fully determine our world independently of moral evaluations—a world in which, as Plato thought, the notion of the good (or perhaps some other normative concept) is as essential to our basic understanding of human affairs and institutions as the sun is to our understanding of the processes of the natural order. Having conceptualized the natural order in a way which from the start excludes values, much of ethical theory has puzzled over how to derive value from fact, or "ought" from "is." Perhaps the problem, rather—at least where the consequences of acts are concerned—is how to derive facts from values.

The inadequacy of consequentialism

What implications does this have for consequentialism? They are, I believe, that it fails as an ethical theory.

The problem is more serious than just one of overcoming difficulties in applying correctly whatever consequentialist principle one might take to be authoritative. It is that there is no correct way to apply it in the sense intended. There is no morally neutral determination of consequences that enables us to say what the principle prescribes in particular situations. Put another way, insofar as consequences are regarded as properties of actions, and insofar as morally neutral determination of the properties of alternative actions is a precondition of being able to apply a consequentialist principle correctly, that condition cannot be met when at least some of the consequences are mediated.

For all of this, I believe we should cling to the sentiment that it can never be right to prefer a worse state of affairs to a better; or, at least, we should cling to it until forced to relinquish it by compelling reasons. It is just that I do not think this sentiment supports consequentialism. But it does support a non-consequentialist axiological position, as, I believe, does the earlier quotation from William James. The particulars of such an outlook I am not able to detail here; but I would suggest that adumbrations of them may be found, not so much in Western philosophy (though, in different form, they may be found in Stoicism and Kantianism) as in Eastern thought, particularly in Taoism and some of the classics of Hinduism and early Buddhism, and more recently in the philosophy of Gandhi. This is an outlook which stresses that, in important respects, it simply is not given to us to know the consequences of actions. Hence we must look to other grounds for our moral judgments (or leave off making them altogether, as Zen Buddhism would sometimes have it). This does not mean that we should not have ends and pursue them with dedication. It means, rather, that our primary emphasis should be upon the means to adopt rather than upon ends, in the faith that if they are good, whatever they lead to in the way of consequences will stand the best chance of also being good.

So, in a sense, we might in the end agree with William James that the best we can do is to try to realize the greatest total universe of good that we can. It is just that projecting, measuring, and comparing consequences may not be the best way to do that.[17]

---

[17]   Originally published in *Kant's Legacy: Essays in Honor of Lewis White Beck,* ed. Predrag Cicovacki (Rochester, NY: University of Rochester Press, 2001), 227–44.

3

The Limited Relevance of Analytical Ethics to the Problems of Bioethics

In this essay Holmes clarifies a number of fundamental ethical distinctions, important for our understanding of his ethics of nonviolence. Besides the standard division of ethics into normative, metaethics, and applied ethics, he draws a sharp line between "legalism" and "particularism." Legalism is a widely held view that particular moral judgments must be justifiable by reference to rules or principles, or that the rightness of particular acts is derivative from fundamental moral rules or principles. In the spirit of pragmatism, particularism counters that the correctness of moral judgments is nonderivative; it stresses context-priority over rule-priority. Particularism opposes all attempts toward a value-neutral ethical analysis, for no such value-neutral position is possible. Instead, particularism stresses the role of a broader social, cultural, and historical context in which moral issues arise and in which they must be addressed. In Holmes' words, "the cultivation of a morally sensitive, caring, and compassionate character probably counts for more in the end than these analytical skills. Those who have such sensibilities will do about as well as humanly possible when confronting such problems." This viewpoint is important irrespective of whether we discuss problems in bioethics, or any other moral problem. Theoretical analysis is an insufficient substitute for practical moral wisdom.

I've now alas! Philosophy,
Med'cine and Jurisprudence too,
And to my cost Theology,
With ardent Labor studied through.
And here I stand, with all my lore,
Poor fool, no wiser than before.
Goethe, *Faust*

Introduction

Aristotle was the first major Western philosopher to criticize another philosopher's ethical theory as having no practical relevance, when he leveled this charge against

Plato's Idea of the Good.[1] But the charge has recurred in the twentieth century, and has often been directed against mainstream Anglo-American analytic ethics.

The tone of that approach to ethics was set by the Platonist G. E. Moore with his *Principia Ethica* in 1903. Moore urged ethicists to get their questions straight. After that, they could proceed systematically to provide answers that would put ethics on a scientific footing. Although the metaphysics that underlay his own theory, and the intuitionism of his account of moral judgments, were sloughed off by later philosophers, Moore's analytical and polemical style came to characterize much of subsequent philosophical ethics. His emphasis upon the importance of conceptual analysis as the starting point for ethics became central to the concerns of what has come to be called metaethics; the spirit and much of the style of that approach has found its way into normative and applied ethics as well.

For better or worse, the spirit of this approach, and the categories and distinctions it has spawned, provide the background for much of the current writing on bioethics as well. I say for better or worse, because I want to suggest that much of the analytically inspired work on bioethics has as little practical value for the answering of the basic moral questions of bioethics as Aristotle thought Plato's account of the good to have for conduct in general. This is not to disparage such ethics or to deny its intrinsic theoretical interest; it is only to suggest that more should not be expected of it than it is capable of delivering.

The question, in the last analysis, is what we are to ask of philosophical ethics. Should it try to provide solutions to practical moral problems, and if so, can it do so by means of the same techniques of reasoning and analysis that it brings to bear on the problems of analytical ethics? Or should it go about its business in the rarified air of conceptual analysis? And if its results do not move us closer to such solutions, what is the point of taking it so seriously, and of making so much of teaching it to young people in our universities?

There is, notice, a temptingly simple answer to this question. It is that however abstract and narrowly focused ethics may be, *any* elucidation of the issues in philosophical ethics (theoretical or applied) cannot help but advance our understanding of practical problems. In that way it contributes, if only infinitesimally, to the eventual solution of those problems.

It is hard to deny this claim; certainly one wants to believe that something like it is correct. But it is relatively unhelpful. If there were a consensus as to which developments represent progress in ethics, then the practical moralist might be able to seize upon these for what they are worth and give them their due in his practical deliberations. But this is rarely the case. The abstract analyses of philosophers are as hotly contested at the theoretical level as many of the practical problems they are supposed to illuminate at the practical level. After centuries of theoretical analysis, there is little agreement over whether deontological or consequentialist theories are more nearly correct, over whether rights-based theories are fundamental to ethics, or over whether we should be emphasizing the virtues as opposed to rules and principles. There is not even agreement on many such highly technical issues as whether one can derive an "ought" from an "is," and if so, in what sense. So while such a claim may provide some solace to philosophers who are uneasy about not contributing more to the ameliorization of contemporary problems, it is doubtful that much more can be claimed for it.

---

[1] Aristotle, *Nicomachean Ethics*, I, 6.

We need, rather, to look more closely at the different approaches philosophy has taken to the understanding of morality in recent Anglo-American philosophy. I am referring here to metaethics (or moral epistemology, as it is coming increasingly to be called), normative ethics and applied ethics. I shall assume an understanding of what is practiced under each of these headings. Suffice it to say that theories of the nature and analysis of moral judgments (like emotivism or ethical naturalism) represent metaethical theories; theories about the correct principles of rightness like utilitarianism or Kantianism illustrate normative theories; and analyses of specific moral problems like abortion or animal rights represent examples of applied ethics. All three may be distinguished from what I shall call substantive morality, the ongoing process of making moral judgments that all of us engage in during the course of living. I take bioethics to be a branch of applied ethics in this sense. But the problems bioethics is primarily concerned with are *moral* problems, and as such bioethics belong to substantive morality. Solutions to these problems may be thought to require the findings of any or all of the other three areas of philosophical ethics.

I shall not presume to prescribe what the proper function of ethical philosophy as a whole is; in fact, I believe it has many functions, some of them practical, others theoretical. But I want to say enough about the problems involved in trying to specify what those functions are to enable us to clarify their value to bioethics. In so doing I shall consider as much of metaethics and normative ethics as is necessary to illuminate the full dimension of the problem.

Metaethics and normative ethics

The question of the relevance of ethics (by which I shall henceforth mean philosophical ethics of the sorts indicated) to substantive morality conceals three separate questions. One can ask this question separately of metaethics, normative ethics, or applied ethics. While it would be logically tidy to take up each of these in turn, the issues are so complex and interrelated as to make that unfeasible. I shall instead focus upon what I take to be key issues in connection with each of these three dimensions of ethics.

Does metaethics have priority over normative and applied ethics? Moore, following Socrates and Plato, thought that it did (at least where normative ethics is concerned). He thought that unless we have correct answers to questions concerning the analysis of concepts like those of goodness and rightness, there is little headway to be made in establishing general propositions about what is good and right, the aim of normative ethics. Although he does not speak of applied ethics, and has little to say about substantive moral issues as specific as those that occupy bioethicists, he very likely would have said the same about it. In short, ethics as a science (albeit an a priori one, given his understanding of the nature of judgments of intrinsic goodness) presupposes correct answers to metaethical questions.

Much of twentieth-century ethics has departed from Moore in this belief that the question of metaethics (particularly with regard to the meanings of ethical concepts) must be answered before one can effectively tackle the questions of normative ethics. Thus one finds that many discussions of utilitarianism or of theories of justice or rights proceed without presuming to have resolved the specific issues dividing cognitivists and non-cognitivists with regard to the definability of ethical terms or the analysis of moral judgments (though some of these issues are beginning to reappear in the debate over ethical realism). And among those doing applied ethics it is uncommon to find sustained attention to metaethics of the sort that occupied Moore, even where it is believed that normative theories are presupposed by applied ethics. Carried further, and extended to substantive morality as well, this outlook virtually severs the connection between metaethics and the making of moral judgments. As some contemporary writers put it:

> True, this academic discipline [ethical philosophy] has an intense interest in action and decisions, since the concepts "right" and "good" are used to approve of actions, decisions and the states-of-affairs resulting from them. However, it is a long step from consideration of the characteristics which justify calling any action "right" to recommendations about what particular action is right in this situation. It is a step that ethicists as such are not better prepared to take than any other morally sensitive person.[2]

The assumption here seems to be that expertise in metaethical analysis provides one with no particular warrant for presuming to be able to make better moral judgments in particular situations than anyone else. My contention is that the same is true of normative ethics and applied ethics as well.

There are, however, some discussions of metaethical issues among contemporary philosophers that would seem to have momentous consequences not only for normative ethics, but also for applied ethics and substantive morality; it is just that it is not claimed that one must resolve these issues before doing normative ethics or defending substantive moral judgments. For example, of contemporary concern is the proper analysis of moral dilemmas, where the question is in part whether there even are such things. Any casual survey of the literature on bioethics shows that it is replete with what are represented as moral dilemmas. If it should turn out that there are no such things (at least in any sense approximating what is meant by them in bioethics), that would suggest that it is pointless to agonize over what one falsely takes to be moral dilemmas, or over what are in fact moral dilemmas but are in principle incapable of solution. On the other hand, R. M. Hare—who has made contributions in metaethics, normative ethics, and applied ethics—has expressly argued for the relevance of certain positions in metaethics to the problems of conduct, even though he does not believe that ethical terms can properly be analyzed in ways that logically commit one to any particular moral judgments. The relevance is established through the principle of universalizability, which requires that one be prepared to make similar moral judgments in relevantly similar situations. Exploitation of the implications of this

---

[2] A. R. Jonsen and L. H. Butler, "Public Ethics and Policy Making," *Hastings Center Report*, 5:1975, 24.

principle, he believes, reveals how rational moral argument is possible over substantive moral issues.

Normative ethics and applied ethics

If there is sharp disagreement over the relevance of metaethics to normative ethics, the practice of contemporary ethicists suggests there is little such disagreement over the relevance of normative ethics to applied ethics. This is true of bioethics as well. A standard anthology in bioethics will often have a section detailing the main types of normative ethical theory—Kantianism, consequentialism, egoism, and the like— followed by readings on specific problems. The clear impression students get is that you "apply" normative ethical theories to arrive at specific moral judgments about the permissibility of abortion, euthanasia, and so on. It is as though this is the way one should go about making moral judgments.

There is something troubling about this, however. If, for example, utilitarianism and Kantianism yield different conclusions about the morality of particular types of action (like abortion or euthanasia), then learning that fact is of little help in resolving the question of whether these types of action are right unless one knows which of those theories is correct. And to ask which theory is correct is to ask a metaethical question, the answering of which would require going beyond the very enterprise of applied ethics one intends to be engaged in. If one contends that they do not lead to different conclusions, that itself is a metaethical claim (namely, that there is a kind of extensional equivalence among normative ethical theories) that is highly controversial and needs explicit defense. Certainly, the debates between Kantians and consequentialists, and among consequentialists between utilitarians and ethical egoists, make clear that they do not believe that their theories all lead to the same substantive moral conclusions.

If, by contrast, one defends answers to the problems of bioethics without first resolving the problems of normative ethics, he is likely to end up justifying precisely the positions he was antecedently disposed to take on those issues in the first place. If Kantianism leads to one conclusion on a particular issue and consequentialism to another, then one need only choose the theory that yields one's favored solution, "apply" it to the problem at hand, and produce the desired outcome. It is not as though one *finds* a solution to the problem by applying a normative theory to it. The theory and the solution come as a package. One simply chooses the package that gives the desired solution.

One could, of course, have an antecedent commitment to a particular normative theory, "apply" that theory to a problem in bioethics, then accept the result even if that meant abandoning the initially firmly held conviction. One wonders, however, how often this happens. One need not be unduly skeptical to suspect that philosophers rarely change their views about issues like abortion and euthanasia because they become convinced that as Kantians, consequentialists, or whatever, they cannot consistently hold that position. Even if one remains committed to the initial normative theory, a little philosophical ingenuity can almost always make it yield the desired outcome when it is applied. If one is pro-choice, but feels as a Kantian that treating persons as ends points to the conclusion that one ought not to practice abortion, he can argue that the fetus is not a person. Or if, as a pro-lifer but an equally committed utilitarian, one believes that the socially beneficial consequences of allowing abortions clearly outweigh the detrimental consequences, he can find some other consequences to weigh into the scales (like violation of the rights to life of the unborn—which, *if* there are rights to life, and *if* the unborn have them, are unquestionably consequences of abortion), which arguably offset the documentably good consequences. In any event, if one simply *assumes* the correctness of a particular normative theory before arguing, by means of it, for the correctness of a particular position in bioethics, this is no better than simply assuming the correctness of one's position on the initial practical problem in the first place. Given enough assumptions, any of the standard normative theories can be interpreted so as to support either side on most controversial issues in bioethics. To detail the particulars of how that theory "applies" in some specific case may be interesting and of some theoretical value, but it cannot claim any greater objective warrant than simply committing oneself to one side or the other on the initial problem at the outset.

One may well wonder, then, whether ethicists hold the particular positions they do on issues of bioethics because those positions follow from the application of what they consider to be the correct normative theories, or whether what they take to be the correct normative theories (along with the philosophical scaffolding that goes into interpreting and applying them) is determined by what supports their pre-critical convictions on specific moral issues.

Applied ethics and moral expertise

To be sure, applied ethics should be contrasted with ethical theory (normative or metaethical), so that even if expertise in ethical theory provides no expertise in making particular moral judgments, it might nonetheless be that expertise in applied ethics does so.

The prevailing assumption of most practitioners of applied ethics, in fact, seems to be that those who are well versed in it have a kind of expertise that sets them apart from others when it comes to dealing with practical moral problems, and a marketable expertise at that. Thus there are now scores of so-called "bio-philosophers" employed in medical centers, consulting with and advising medical personnel on the range of moral problems they and their patients regularly face. And there are those who advocate that government and business employ philosophers as well. This way of thinking fits well with much of the medical profession, because most of them *are* experts in what they do. One suspects that at least part of the success of philosophers in making inroads into medical institutions owes to the fact that they have come to be viewed as having a similar expertise, only in something called bioethics, that uniquely qualifies them to make moral assessments of practical problems.

Moreover, the question of whether applied ethics is relevant to the resolution of the problems of substantive morality is, in one sense, easier to answer than in the case of metaethics and normative ethics. If one can show that certain practices or *types* of action (e.g., abortion or euthanasia) are permissible (and it is generally with types of action rather than with specific acts that applied ethics is concerned), then it follows that particular *instances* of those types will be permissible. What more direct practical relevance could ethics have?

The problem, of course, is that, if the previously mentioned assumption should be correct, that most practitioners of applied ethics think their analyses must be supported by an underlying normative theory, then exactly the same problems arise here as in connection with normative theories themselves, viz., that one can always choose the normative theory that supports the conclusion in applied ethics that yields the desired outcomes for substantive morality.

Not all of those who work in applied ethics seem to think that the solutions of the problems of applied ethics require all of the theoretical baggage of normative and metaethical theory. Some of them proceed as though they think that it is not so much ethical *theory* that needs applying as it is ethical *analysis*, and that the techniques of analytical philosophy applied rigorously will yield solutions to those problems. On this view, one need not approach the problems of bioethics with express and extensive metaethical or normative commitments; the problems of bioethics can be analyzed in a way that is largely neutral with regard to such commitments.

Applied ethics as analysis

Two influential analyses that fit into this mold are those of Jonathan Bennett and Judith Jarvis Thomson. Let us consider them in turn.

Bennett's argument is a critique of a moral absolutism that defends the principle:

(P) "It would always be wrong to kill an innocent human, whatever the consequences of not doing so."[3]

He claims that anyone who holds this sincerely and really understands it must either have "delivered himself over to authority or must have opted out of moral thinking altogether."

The principle has obvious relevance to abortion and euthanasia, both of which arguably involve killing the innocent. The case Bennett uses as the focus for his discussion is an obstetrical one:

A woman in labor will certainly die unless an operation is performed in which the head of her unborn child is crushed or dissected; while if it is not performed the child can be delivered, alive, by postmortem Caesarian section. This presents a straight choice between the woman's life and the child's.[4]

---

[3] J. Bennett, "Whatever the Consequences," *Analysis*, 26:1966, 83–102.
[4] Ibid., 83.

He sees the problem as involving the distinction between killing and letting die, which enters into the factual premise of an argument with (P) as its major premise:

(1) It would always be wrong to kill an innocent human, whatever the consequences of not doing so.

(2) In this case, operating would be killing an innocent human, while not operating would involve the death of an innocent human only as a consequence.

(3) Therefore, in this case operating would be wrong.

Bennett's strategy is to argue that, unless the defender of (P) (which he calls the "conservative," but I shall refer to as the "absolutist") is to accept (P) uncritically and on authority, he must maintain that premise (2), apart from (1) "gives *some* reason for the conclusion." He then says: "I shall argue that it gives no reason at all: once the muddles have been cleared away, it is just not humanly possible to see the premise as supporting the conclusion, however weakly, except by accepting the principle 'It would always be wrong etc.' as an unquestionable *donee*."[5] There follows a detailed analysis of the distinction between action and consequences as it pertains to the distinction between killing and letting die in the second premise. Bennett concludes that ways of making the distinction that could conceivably support a moral conclusion do not apply to all possible instances of the obstetrical example, and those that do apply could not possibly support a moral conclusion.

We need not go through the details of that portion of Bennett's argument. What I want to examine are the implications of his insistence that it is damaging to the absolutist if he cannot show that (2) provides a reason for (3) independently of an appeal to (P). For these reveal, I believe, that Bennett's argument, which on the surface appears to be a neutral piece of philosophical analysis, actually involves a tacit commitment to highly problematic positions on certain issues in metaethics and normative ethics.

First consider the implications of saying that, if (P) is to be held on grounds other than those of authority, (2) must, by itself (independently of (P)), provide some reason for the conclusion (3). This is an odd requirement. For (1) and (2) purportedly constitute the premises of an argument for (3). Since both are presumably necessary for the conclusion, one wonders why it should be thought that (2) alone must provide some reason for (3) (and by "reason" I take Bennett to mean a reason having some justificatory force, not an explanatory or motivating reason). Since (2) is to all appearances purely factual and (3) is unquestionably moral, to suppose that (2) provides a reason for (3) is to place a demand upon the absolutist that is virtually impossible to satisfy. In order for any factual statement to provide a moral reason for a particular act, one needs *some* rule or principle establishing the relevance of that consideration to the moral situation at hand. Normally this takes the form of a moral rule or principle, as in the absolutist's argument; sometimes it takes the form of a rule of inference. No fact constitutes a reason for a moral judgment in the absence of some warrant for the transition from fact to value or is to ought.

The one arguable exception to this is in the case of what we may call particularist as opposed to legalist moral theories. By a legalist position I mean one that holds that

5   Ibid., 85f.

particular moral judgments must be justifiable by reference to rules or principles (or, if you like, that the rightness of particular acts is derivative from moral rules or principles). Particularism, on the other hand, takes the correctness of particular moral judgments (or the rightness of specific acts) to be non-derivative. The first are rule-priority theories, the second act-priority.

Now if the absolutist were holding a particularist theory, then (P) would at best be a generalization from the wrongness of killing the innocent in particular cases. In that case one would need some basis for making the determinations of wrongness in the cases that provide the basis for the generalization. It would then make sense to ask *why* (2) provides some reason for (3), since the correctness of (3) would derive from the intrinsic wrongness of the act to which it refers. There would have to be something about that act, as characterized in (2), that would be morally relevant to (3), hence that arguably would provide some reason for (3) (though even here it is far from clear whether such reasons would be justificatory, as Bennett's objection requires, or explanatory).

Why would the absolutist maintain this? Absolutists typically take the moral assessment of particular acts to be determined *by* the appropriate principle rather than the other way around. That is, they are legalists. The point of making (P) the major premise of the argument leading to (3) in the first place would presumably reflect just that understanding of the position. Indeed, if (P) were simply a generalization from particular cases, it would be odd to speak of it as absolute, since however many confirming instances had been encountered in the past, there would always be the possibility that the future would yield one that would invalidate the principle.

Moreover, implicitly to assume that the absolutist must be operating with a particularist moral theory precludes him from holding his position on about the only ground that renders it even remotely plausible, and that is a rule-deontological ground. It also, for that matter, pretty much excludes its being defended on utilitarian grounds as well. That is, the defense of (P) becomes implausible if one takes its underlying justification to be utilitarian, since one can readily hypothesize circumstances in which killing an innocent person would have better consequences than letting an innocent person die. Utilitarian and consequentialist theories can only be stated in terms of a principle. And typically the principles are understood to determine the rightness or wrongness of particular acts. In any event, to insist that the absolutist must be a particularist would be to commit him to accepting certain moral judgments about particular cases every bit as unquestioningly as Bennett alleges him to accept with regard to (P). The absolutist cannot win either way.

If the aim is to show the implausibility of (P) as an absolute prohibition, there is a much simpler and more direct route to that end. It is to produce counterexamples. This is the course represented by the analysis we want to consider next in connection with the problem of abortion.

In her now classic essay, "A Defense of Abortion," Judith Jarvis Thomson concedes for the sake of argument that the fetus is a person.[6] She then proceeds to argue that despite that, and assuming that persons have a right to life, it can still be shown that

---

[6]   J. J. Thomson, "A Defense of Abortion," *Philosophy & Public Affairs,* 1:1971, 47–66.

abortion is permissible. It is not always and absolutely wrong to kill the innocent, as she puts it in one of several related ways closely resembling Bennett's formulation of (P). A woman also has a right to decide what happens in and to her body, Thomson contends, and sometimes this overrides the right to life.

Thomson raises counter-exampling to a new level in her attempt to show this. Her best known example is that of the violinist, hooked up to you for life-support (by the Society of Music Lovers), for a nine-month period. Under these circumstances, we are to conclude, you cannot reasonably be expected to remain intimately linked to this stranger, who has been connected to you without your consent, simply because so doing is necessary to preserve his life; the right to decide what shall happen to your body in this case overrides the right to life of the unfortunate violinist. Should the analogy of an adult stranger to your own unborn child (and remember that Thomson is conceding for the sake of argument that the fetus is a person) in your womb seem too strained, Thomson has another example. It is that of being trapped inside a house with an expanding child whom you must kill or let kill you as it expands beyond the capacity of the structure to hold it. The point here is that in cases in which (as in the Bennett example) an abortion is necessary in order to save the woman's life, defense of one's self overrides the right to life of the innocent. And if it should be objected that pregnant women usually become so through voluntary activities of their own, she has a third example. We are to imagine that there are such things as "people seeds" that float through the air, lodging in furniture or carpets, there to grow eventually into full-fledged persons. Should one be required to allow them to develop in one's home simply because he has chosen not to keep the windows shut tightly year round? Our intuitions are supposed to lead us to shake our heads [to] no. Reasonable precautions are enough, we are to conclude, and we are under no requirement to nurture these developing persons if we prefer not to.

I have abstracted these examples from the full context of the argument in which they play a role, so one should be mindful that full justice has not been done to the subtleties of that argument. But some observations can, I think, fairly be made. The first is that if one interprets principles—such as that it is always wrong to kill an innocent person—as absolutistic in a sense that precludes there being even any *conceivable* cases in which the act in question would be permissible, then such principles readily admit of refutation. For a little imagination can always generate hypothetical cases, however fantastic, in which no one in his right mind would cling to the principle rather than to admit the counterexample to it. There is nothing easier than to invalidate virtually any moral principle in this way.

The second point, closely related to this, is that probably no one but philosophers (and even among them, usually only those who are imputing positions to others) ever understands absolute prohibitions in such a maximalist sense. Most people do not, I suspect, take principles they might call absolutistic as holding for all logically conceivable circumstances, or if you like, for all possible worlds. They would not even understand these notions.

They mean, rather, something more like this: that they cannot imagine any situations of a sort one is ever likely to encounter in the course of ordinary life in which this prohibition would not hold. This is a far weaker claim, though one that is still strong enough in practical terms. And it is one that is left untouched by far-fetched counterexamples that may crushingly refute the principle if it is understood to be absolute in the philosopher's sense. The philosopher's refutation of the philosopher's interpretation of the principle becomes conspicuously irrelevant to the issues in which ordinary people find themselves caught up.

Moreover, the putative counterexamples on which our intuitions are supposed to converge presuppose a particularist, act-priority metaethics in much the same way as Bennett's analysis. If we are supposed just to "see" the correctness of the desired judgment in the case that is supposed to constitute the counterexample, and to see it independently of any antecedently specified normative theory, then the assumption must be that the rightness of particular acts can somehow be seen in the character of the acts themselves, independently of any principles from which that rightness is derived. Either that, or it is assumed that readers will all have in mind the same unarticulated theory that leads them to agree to the same moral assessment in the case at hand (or that they have in mind different theories that somehow lead to the same judgment). This, no less than in Bennett's case, indicates that either certain normative theories are being tacitly assumed in the argument to the bioethical conclusion, or that the correctness of one side or the other on the particularist-legalist metaethical issue is being assumed.

Conclusion

If I am correct that there is no more compelling reason to accept a proposed answer to a problem in applied ethics on the ground that it follows from an undefended normative theory than there is to accept an undefended affirmation of that position at the outset, the possibility emerges that personal moral convictions, as well as class, gender, racial and other biases, may govern the philosophical treatment of problems in bioethics more than an unvarnished dedication to the truth. Most of us do not turn to our philosophizing in applied ethics from a position of neutrality on the issues we examine. We come predisposed to be for or against abortion, euthanasia, surrogate motherhood and the like. If these predispositions can enter significantly into one's choice of a normative ethical theory when it comes to applying normative ethics to practical problems, it can do so even more directly in any attempt to analyze the problems of applied ethics without presuming to derive them from a background normative theory.

Although at first blush Bennett and Thomson's analyses seem to proceed from normatively and meta-ethically neutral positions, they are in fact as closely tied up with controversial positions in metaethics and normative ethics as those that expressly hold that one must first deal with the relevant normative and metaethical issues before arriving at solutions to the problems in applied ethics. The attempt to engage in neutral ethical *analysis* only obscures, rather than avoids, the problems in trying to apply ethical *theory* to practice. And by the nature of most such approaches the broader social, cultural and historical context in which these problems emerge is ignored. It is as though the problems can be abstracted from the situations in which they develop, analyzed as one might in a laboratory, and then the findings presented in detached, neutral terms. All of this, I suggest, is among the ways in which much of Anglo-American ethics has since the time the logical positivists suffered from its emulation of science. It is as though, not being a science, ethics aspires to be the next best thing, and that is scientific. But just as science cannot by itself yield answers to moral problems, ethical analysis that looks to science for its model cannot do so either.

So what relevance does philosophical ethics have to solving the problems of bioethics? Some, I suggest, but not much. It can provide conceptual clarity (such as by elucidating the idea of informed consent, or highlighting some of the considerations relevant to trying to determine whether a fetus is a person); it can provide the categories by which to discuss the problems theoretically; it can sometimes show that, *if* a certain theory or analysis is accepted, that has certain implications for substantive morality, and it can produce valid arguments and tell people when theirs are not, and why. But, while these are useful undertakings, they are insufficient to resolve the problems of bioethics or of applied ethics in general. They are not, I suspect, even necessary conditions of resolving those problems. The cultivation of a morally sensitive, caring, and compassionate character probably counts for more in the end than these analytical skills. Those who have such sensibilities will do about as well as humanly possible when confronting such problems. Those who do not will not, whether or not they have a Ph.D. in philosophy.

This is not intended to be subversive of philosophy or of philosophical ethics in particular. It is meant to suggest that expertise in philosophical ethics should be viewed with rather more humility than one often finds among bio-philosophers (and applied ethicists generally). While philosophical ethicists perhaps need not lament with Faust that all of their philosophical training has left them standing "no wiser than before," they might reflect seriously on the possibility that professional academic training as it is provided by most philosophy departments today is no guarantee of—and a poor substitute for—moral wisdom.[7]

---

[7]   Originally published in the *Journal of Medicine and Philosophy*, 15:1990, 143–59.

4

The Concept of Corporate Responsibility

Is the sole obligation of corporations to maximize profit? If so, as conservatives argue, then corporations ought not to assume social responsibilities. Or is it the case that corporations may, but are not obliged to, assume some social responsibilities? Or should we decisively affirm that corporations—insofar as they are to be treated as moral agents—ought to assume social responsibilities? Liberals argue in favor of this last claim and add that this is so even when assuming social responsibilities occurs at the expense of profit maximization. After discussing a spectrum of opinions—from Adam Smith to most contemporary voices—Holmes argues that the debate over whether corporations have social responsibilities should be put to rest. They certainly have such responsibilities, at least in the negative sense: they have a moral obligation not to harm anyone, and if they do, they owe reparations proportionate to the harm caused. This conclusion, Holmes believes, does not close the discussion regarding the moral status of corporations but only prepares a ground for more relevant issues: Which social responsibilities do corporations have, and which responsibilities should take precedence in cases of conflict?

Both sides in the debate over corporate responsibility agree that corporations have responsibilities. They disagree only over what those responsibilities are—specifically over whether they are purely economic, that is, to maximize profits,[1] or include social responsibilities as well—and if the latter, over how far corporations should go in meeting them.

But this issue is more complex than it at first appears, and it raises a number of difficult ethical and metaethical issues. Much of the debate, for example, isn't primarily over whether corporations have social responsibilities at all, but over whether they have social responsibilities which conflict with and sometimes override the responsibility to maximize profits.[2] Many who oppose the idea of corporate social responsibility do so because they see it as a threat to the successful performance of the corporation's central economic functions, and they would not object otherwise. I say many wouldn't, but

---

[1] Within the limits of the law it is usually assumed, though not always stated, that the responsibilities of a corporation are purely economic.

[2] Milton Friedman virtually defines "social responsibility" in such a way that it must conflict with the interests of a corporation. See his "The Social Responsibility of Business Is to Increase Its Profits," *New York Times Magazine,* September 13, 1970. For other statements of his views on this general topic, see also his *Capitalism and Freedom* (Chicago: University of Chicago Press, 1962), Chapter 8; and "Milton Friedman Responds," *Business and Society,* No. 1, Spring 1972, 5–17.

some would.[3] And this distinction marks an important difference among opponents of social responsibility. Some hold only that corporations have no obligation to assume responsibilities, but leave it open that they *may* do so provided it doesn't jeopardize profits. Others hold the stronger position that corporations not only have no social responsibilities but would be acting wrongly to assume such responsibilities.[4]

Positions on corporations and social responsibility

Let us make this clearer by formulating three principles in terms of which the Liberal and Conservative positions (as I shall respectively label those which favor and those which oppose corporate responsibility) can be stated.

1. Corporations ought not to assume social responsibilities.
2. Corporations may (but aren't obligated to) assume social responsibilities:
   a. when doing so is consistent with profit maximization; or
   b. even at the expense of profit maximization.
3. Corporations ought to assume social responsibilities:
   a. when doing so is consistent with, or in the interest of, profit maximization; or
   b. even at the expense of profit maximization.

What we may call the Pure Conservative position can then be defined as the acceptance of (1) and the Pure Liberal position at the acceptance of 3(b). Qualified Conservatism will be the acceptance of 2(a) and Qualified Liberalism the acceptance of either 2(b) or 3(a).

Now it is often assumed that the Liberal in this debate is arguing from a moral position and the Conservative from a nonmoral position. But this needn't be so. Each of the above can be held on either moral or nonmoral grounds (whether defensibly or not we shall consider in Part II). Each says only what corporations should (or may) do, not why they should do it, or what the justification is of their doing it. For the latter we need to look to more basic positions.

These can be broken down into two, each resting upon a specific claim regarding obligation. The first, which we may call the classical view,[5] in deference to the common but misleading belief that it is the unqualified view of classical economists, is as follows:

C: The sole obligation of corporations is to maximize profits.

On the relatively unproblematic assumption that the maximization of profits *simpliciter* isn't a moral end, this doesn't express a moral obligation, and, in fact, in light of the

---

[3] Theodore Levitt, for example, says that business involvement in social issues yields the frightening spectacle of "a powerful economic functional group whose future and perception are shaped in a tight materialistic context of money and things but which imposes its narrow ideas about a broad spectrum of unrelated noneconomic subjects on the mass of man and society"; in "The Dangers of Social Responsibility," *Harvard Business Review*, September–October 1958, 44. See also his "Business Should Stay out of Politics," *Business Horizons*, No. 3 (1960), 45–51.

[4] We have used "responsibilities" ambiguously here, as it is often used in discussions of this topic. In the first occurrence it is roughly synonymous with "obligations"; in the second, with "voluntarily undertaken commitments."

[5] Following Clarence C. Walton, *Corporate Social Responsibilities* (Belmont, CA: Wadsworth, 1967), 54.

word "sole," it entails that corporations have no moral obligations. It is compatible with both the Conservative principle (1) and with the Qualified Conservative principle 2(a). It would even be compatible with the Liberal principle 3(a) if the latter weren't taken (as it is here intended) to imply an obligation. Aside from that, it rules out only 2(b) and 3(b). It means—in line with the Kantian precept[6] that to will an end is to will the indispensable means to its attainment—that corporations ought to do whatever is necessary to maximize profits. The reason this is compatible with some forms of Liberal position is that it is conceivable, and in fact argued by some contemporary writers, that the most effective means to that end in the long run is through the assumption of social responsibilities, even at risk of a short-term diminution of profits.[7]

A convenient way of formulating the second basic position, which we may call the Moralist's view, is as follows:

M: The basic obligation of corporations is always to act morally.

This leaves open what morality specifically requires and whether it be teleological or deontological in character. But it would sanction any of the Liberal and Conservative positions if they could be shown to be justified by the basic principle(s) of morality. It could even support C if C were amended to read: The sole derivative obligation of corporations is to maximize profits. Such a possibility is suggested by Adam Smith when he says:

> Every individual is continuously exerting himself to find the most advantageous employment for whatever capital he can command. It is his own advantage, indeed, and not that of the society, which he has in view. But the study of his own advantage naturally, or rather necessarily, leads him to prefer that employment which is most advantageous to the society.. . . In this, as in many other cases, he is led by an invisible hand to promote an end which was no part of his intention.[8]

Though it is unclear whether Smith takes the interest of society to be the end which ultimately justifies the pursuit of self-interest (and by extension to our present concern, the pursuit of profit maximization by corporations), one very well might, in which case the justification of self-interest would be a putatively moral one. It is perfectly consistent to hold that people should promote the greatest good, or the general happiness, or some such putative moral end, but that the most effective means to that end is the pursuit by each person of his or her own interest. All that is required is the assumption—though a large one—that morality and self-interest coincide. The invisible hand, on this view, would then be a moral hand, perhaps a utilitarian one,

---

[6] Widely accepted in one form or another as a principle of rationality in much of contemporary social science.
[7] See, for example, Melvin Anshen, "The Socially Responsible Corporation: From Concept to Implementation," in *Managing the Socially Responsible Corporation* (New York: Macmillan, 1974), 6; and George Steiner, *Business and Society* (New York: Random House, 1971), 144. This outlook is explicit in an advertisement by the Eastman Kodak Company in which, after describing their various efforts at socially responsible action, they say: "In short, it's simply good business. And we're in business to make a profit. But in furthering our business interests, we also further society's interests." Reprinted in Robert Baum, ed., *Ethical Arguments for Analysis,* second edn (New York: Holt, Rinehart & Winston, 1976), 210.
[8] Adam Smith, *The Wealth of Nations*, Book V, Chapter 2.

as suggested by the quote. Whether the basic principles of morality be teleological or deontological, it is conceivable that human conduct will more nearly accord with them if people act upon some other principle(s) rather than attempting to implement them directly.[9]

Objections to the view that corporations have moral responsibilities

Both sides, I've said, assume that corporations have responsibilities. But, strictly speaking, this assumption isn't warranted. Corporations aren't living, rational beings and accordingly can't have obligations and responsibilities or be proper objects of moral praise or blame.[10] Even if they were, there would be no considerations, moral or otherwise, bearing upon their conduct which wouldn't bear equally upon the conduct of individuals who stand in the appropriate relationships to them (e.g., as directors, managers, stockholders) so that any obligations corporations had would devolve ultimately upon persons. Thus there is no advantage to hypostatizing corporations. They have life only through the choices and decisions of individual persons. We nevertheless do speak of corporations as acting and making decisions as though they were persons, and there is no harm in this so long as it is understood that such talk must be transposable into statements about the conduct of individuals—not necessarily without remainder, but with sufficient completeness to enable us to formulate the appropriate moral judgments about the latter.

Bearing this in mind, let us ask whether corporations, understood now in the manner indicated, have moral responsibilities, as the moralist affirms and the classicist denies. It might seem evident that they do, but there are two lines of argument by which this view might be challenged.

The first is to contend that morality has no application to corporations at all, and for that reason that the imputation to corporations of moral responsibilities makes no sense. The second is to allow that corporations are governed by morality but to maintain that it is a morality of a different type than applies to individuals—a collective as opposed to a personal morality—so that although corporations can have responsibilities of the former sort, they can't of the latter.

The first view can be handled with dispatch. The reply to it is implicit in what we said above about the relationship between corporate and individual conduct. Corporations can fail to have moral responsibilities only if corporate managers can fail to have moral responsibilities. And this the latter cannot do. No conduct is immune from moral assessment. Behavior sometimes is, as when it is deranged or psychotic. But self-directed, un-coerced action—conduct in the fullest sense of the term—is always appraisable as right or wrong. Morality isn't a compartment of human affairs which

---

[9] This view gains in credibility if one thinks, with Dewey, for example, that the end, say, of utilitarianism is just too remote to be an effective guide to practical conduct, and that more accessible ends—ends-in-view—are a better guide to the realization of social good.
[10] As Friedman maintains. See "The Social Responsibility of Corporations Is to Increase Its Profits" and "Milton Friedman Responds."

we step out of by passing through the door of an executive suite, or assuming public office, or putting on a military uniform. It constrains us in all that we do. To suppose otherwise is to indicate a misunderstanding of what it is all about.

The second, and more challenging, position is suggested by the following passage:

> The individual cannot be moral in independence. The modern business collectives force a collective morality. Just as the individual cannot resist the combination, so individual morality must give place to a more robust or social type.[11]

By "individual" here, the authors mean primarily the shareholder; their concern is with whether he can invest in a morally responsible way. But we can adapt the point to the case of corporate executives and ask whether they, qua corporate executives, are forced into a different morality than that which governs them in their capacity as ordinary persons—whether, if you like, corporations as collectivities unavoidably operate within a different moral framework than individuals.

Notice that the first sentence of the quotation may be taken in a number of ways. It may mean that individuals in independence (1) cannot act morally as opposed to immorally (i.e., cannot do what is morally right), or (2) cannot act morally as opposed to nonmorally (i.e., cannot bring their conduct even within the scope of morality), or (3) cannot be morally effective in changing things. Now (3) is often true of individuals with limited power in large institutions or in society at large. But the problem it highlights is that of how to render right action effective, not that of whether right action is possible. (1) and (2), on the other hand, bear upon our present concern, so let us take them in turn.

The first, adapted to the case of corporate managers, suggests that there is something about the circumstances in which they carry on their work which makes moral conduct impossible. It might be said, for example, that the business system itself is inherently immoral, and that for that reason individuals within it cannot act morally.[12] And if they cannot, it might be added, then corporations, whose actions their constitute, cannot act morally, hence cannot have moral responsibilities. But this involves confusion. It isn't conceptually possible for a person to be in a situation in which all of the alternatives are immoral. It is possible to be in a situation in which all of the alternatives are bad; depending upon one's outlook on life that happens rather often. But we're here concerned with right and wrong, not good and bad. The most that follows from the fact that one is in a situation in which all of the alternatives are bad is that all of the alternatives are right or permissible.[13] If "ought" implies "can," and one cannot avoid doing what has bad consequences, then one cannot be obligated to avoid doing what has bad consequences. But if, by hypothesis, all alternatives are immoral, then it should be permissible to do some immoral act, that is, it should be right to do what is wrong—and this is unintelligible. So given that "ought" implies "can," we cannot make sense of saying that one must ever act immorally.

---

[11]   John Dewey and James H. Tufts, *Ethics* (New York: Henry Holt, 1908), 519.
[12]   This view is suggested by Robert Freedman, Jr, in "The Challenge of Business Ethics," in *Issues in Business and Society*, ed. William T. Greenwood (Boston: Houghton Mifflin, 1964), 307.
[13]   And even this follows only if the alternatives are equally bad and if there are no further overriding moral considerations.

Let us look therefore at interpretation (2). The position it represents would be of little interest, of course, if it held that the imperatives of the two alleged moralities coincide; what it implies is that the morality to which corporations are beholden sanctions conduct that is wrong according to personal morality, and that when there is such a conflict it supersedes the latter. This is a common outlook on the conduct of nations and is equally applicable to that of corporations.

Consider a possible line of reasoning in support of this position. It runs as follows: The ordinary person isn't the architect of the socio-economic system in which he finds himself, or of the institutions that system comprises. These are given. And unless he dedicates himself to a life of reform or revolution—which, if justified at all, is supererogatory—he can only accept them. The most he can reasonably be expected to do is to conduct himself responsibly in the working out of whatever plan of life he chooses within that framework. A part of that plan may call for a career with a corporation, either because he likes the money, or finds the work rewarding, or simply believes in the value of the institution and of the capitalist system as a whole. Be that as it may, he is no more the creator of the duties and responsibilities attaching to the role he finds himself playing within such an institution than he is of the broader system of which it is a part. He may certainly be able to modify the former to a greater extent than he can the latter, but by and large they are fixed, and he either accepts them or finds another job. If, moreover—in the course, let us say, of managing a corporation or of implementing the decisions of those who do—those duties call for some conduct which in some of his other capacities (citizen, neighbor, Christian, Jew, etc.) would be adjudged wrong, he should allow the former to override the latter. Only in that way can he avoid obstructing the relatively smooth operation of the system which provides the setting for these other roles and makes the quality of life associated with them possible. Thus he cannot but recognize two different, and at some points incongruent, moralities, and to allow the higher, the collective, to override the lower, the personal.

This is a sketch of *an* argument, I say, for the recognition of two moralities. It's oversimplified, of course, but one can see the direction in which it moves and feel some of its force. It's true that it would commit us to an extreme form of moral relativism. If what the individual is permitted or even obligated to do from the standpoint of one morality is prohibited by the other, then one and the same act would be both right and wrong. One then either does whatever he pleases, which is tantamount to disregarding morality from the start, or he allows one of these moralities to supersede the other, as the argument intends. Despite this problem, it's the only line of reasoning in support of this conclusion that I find remotely plausible. Yet it is unsatisfactory for two reasons.

The first is that it is difficult to render fully intelligible the judgment that one morality ought to override the other, much less to provide a basis for that judgment. For the "ought" it contains is either moral or nonmoral. If it is moral, and set in one of the competing moralities itself, then there is no more reason to accede to it than to its counterpart in the opposing morality. If, on the other hand, it is nonmoral, then it must represent a point of view from which one can judge the imperatives of morality— and not only judge them (which one can do in any event from such points of view as self-interest, economics, national interest, and so on) but judge them with authority.

And there is no such point of view. There is no higher appeal than to morality—certainly not to the point of view of business or economics, since that already has representation in the collective morality and it is the latter's claim to supremacy over the individual morality that is at issue. What is needed is a vantage point outside of both moralities from which to choose between them with authority. And there is no such vantage point.

It is tempting to respond at this point that the collective morality should supersede the personal because there is a greater good to be achieved by it, and that that good (principal parts of which would be social cohesion and stability) is a precondition of whatever is of value in the personal morality. People simply cannot maintain the quality of life they enjoy, or carry out the responsibilities and obligations of personal morality, apart from the broader social context made possible by the collective morality.[14]

The thought behind this argument—that the best lives are possible only within a social context—may be granted. Philosophers from Plato to the present have made that same point in various ways (differing, of course, over what kind of social context is required). But this doesn't establish the existence of two moralities, much less the supremacy of one over the other. This can be shown by turning to the second reason why the main argument is unsatisfactory.

The second and principal reason why the main argument is unsatisfactory is that its conclusion is a *non sequitur*. One might grant virtually all of its premises without conceding the conclusion. Whatever concrete moral judgments one holds with regard to the priorities of business and economic conduct *vis-à-vis* interpersonal conduct can be defended without the assumption of different moralities. One need only say that there are within morality conflicting prima facie obligations, and that these often confront the corporate executive. The problems they pose may be vexing. Indeed, one cannot overstate the complexity of some of the dilemmas corporate managers face when confronted with the interests of shareholders on one side, and those of employees and society (and perhaps other societies as well in the case of multinationals) on the other. But it doesn't advance our understanding of these dilemmas, or aid in their resolution, to think that they arise because of competing moralities.

The response to our first objection, which stated that collective morality should supersede personal morality, can now be dealt with by saying that if it is indeed true (and we're not now challenging the correctness of this claim, though one well might) that, when they conflict, the prima facie social imperative to preserve a certain kind of status quo in society outweighs the more immediate prima facie obligations of personal life, this means only that what morality dictates on balance is that our obligation lies ultimately on the side of society. Nothing in this requires the postulation of two moralities. Whatever we may want to say on either side of this issue can be accommodated within the framework of a single morality. This doesn't, of course,

---

[14] Robert L. Heilbroner acknowledges the force behind some of this reasoning even while sharply attacking corporations: "Thus when corporations rape the environment or abuse us as guinea pigs, suddenly we awaken to the realities of our individual powerlessness *and of our dependence on their smooth and presumably benign functioning*." In Heilbroner and others, *In the Name of Profit* (New York: Doubleday, 1972), 235f.

prevent one from assuming that there are two moralities nonetheless, but it shows that assumption to be otiose.

Duties of nonmaleficence and reparation

If what we have said is correct, then although both the Liberal and Conservative positions can be held on either moral or nonmoral grounds, only the moral can justify either position. This means that corporations do indeed have moral responsibilities. But what those responsibilities are, and specifically whether they include social responsibilities in the sense under consideration, remains open.

We can nevertheless answer this latter question, at least in part, on the basis of our findings thus far.

To do this, let us consider what social responsibilities corporations might be alleged to have. These break down,[15] first, into internal and external responsibilities: the internal being to employees, and pertaining to such matters as working conditions, benefits, job training, and the like; the external being all those which are not internal, and pertaining to such things as racial and sexual discrimination, pollution, depletion of natural resources, and urban decay. Though often neglected by both sides to the debate, there are also possible external responsibilities of the same sort as those just characterized, but extending beyond our own society. These are particularly relevant in assessing problems raised by multinational corporations, whose operations have direct consequences for persons in foreign countries.[16] Additionally, there are those responsibilities related to social costs and those which are not. Social costs have been characterized in different ways, but we may follow Kapp in taking them to cover

> all direct and indirect losses suffered by third persons or the general public as a result of private economic activities . . . all those harmful consequences and damages which third persons or the community sustain as a result of the productive process.[17]

Social costs would include losses resulting from pollution, destruction of wildlife habitats, relocation of corporations, and so forth. Non social cost related responsibilities would include obligations to support charities, to contribute to universities, or to open facilities to the public for recreational use. Possible social responsibilities thus break down as follows:

---

[15]   Following Steiner, *Business and Society*, 141.

[16]   There are at least two dimensions to this problem. On the one hand there is the question of whether corporations should operate in countries like South Africa, which institutionalize racism (or engage in equally objectionable practices). On the other hand, there is the question of whether corporations should transfer production to other countries at all, if the effect is to export employment from the United States to countries with large labor forces employable at cheaper wages (on this, see Richard J. Barnet and Ronald E. Muller, "U.S. Unemployment Is Clearly Affected by the Spread of Multinationals," *New York Times,* December 22, 1974). The former raises the question of whether corporations have social responsibilities to the citizens of other countries; the latter whether, even if they do, responsibilities to citizens of our own country override those in case of conflict.

[17]   K. William Kapp, *The Social Costs of Private Enterprise* (New York: Schocken Books, 1950), 13f.

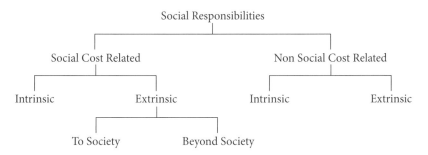

Now whether or not corporations have any obligation to do good, that is, have responsibilities in the area of non social cost related matters, it is clear that they have an obligation not to do harm. That is, they have at least a prima facie duty of nonmaleficence.[18] If there are any duties at all, we all have such a duty, corporation managers included. It is morally wrong for corporations to deceive the public into thinking that harmful drugs are beneficial, or that unsafe automobiles are safe, or knowingly to allow employees to work under conditions detrimental to health; all of these are wrong whether or not in violation of any laws. Moreover, if corporations have a duty of nonmaleficence, then it is plausible to maintain that they also have a duty of reparation when they have acted maleficently. The mere fact of having caused harm[19] creates a prima facie obligation to remedy that harm. This doesn't mean that every conceivable harm is of sufficient importance to require remedy, or that it will be possible to remedy all harms, or that all harms can even be calculated. Nor does it mean that every corporate action with social costs is wrong; if that were so, little that corporations do would be justified. Many social costs are offset by sufficient benefits as to be justified on balance.[20] What it does mean is that corporations have at least *some* social cost related responsibilities.

What specific social responsibilities a given corporation has this doesn't tell us, of course. To do that would require a case-by-case examination of alleged harms. The preceding doesn't in principle even presuppose that any corporation has in fact ever harmed anyone. All it says is that corporations have a moral obligation *not* to harm anyone, and that they owe reparations for such harm if it occurs. If that much is granted, then corporations have a social responsibility and the conservative position is refuted. The only questions remaining—and they are of the first importance, but from a practical moral standpoint, not that of the fundamental philosophical issue—concern which corporations have responsibilities, and which responsibilities should take precedence in cases of conflict. These deserve the most thorough analysis and discussion. But the debate over whether corporations have social responsibilities should be put to rest.[21]

---

[18]   In this and what follows I am following the analysis of W. D. Ross in *The Right and the Good* (Oxford: Clarendon Press, 1930).

[19]   And by "harm" I mean that which makes one worse off on balance.

[20]   Whether being offset by benefits is sufficient to justify all social costs, for example, in terms of the rights of persons who may not prefer the benefit over the cost, is a matter we cannot go into at present.

[21]   Originally published in *Ethical Theory and Business*, ed. Tom L. Beauchamp and Norman E. Bowie (Englewood Cliffs, NJ: Prentice-Hall, 1979), 151–60.

5

University Neutrality and ROTC

The role of American universities has changed in the recent past. Holmes argues that they face "an identity crisis." In his words, "No one is quite sure what they are anymore, much less what they ought to be." Caught between the European tradition of scholarship for its own sake and the American spirit of utility, can they combine scholarly studies with practical training? Ought they to be neutral morally and politically? And who should be neutral? Administrators? Faculty? Students? Or are we talking about an overall institutional neutrality? The role of American universities is obscured even more when we focus on their ties with Reserve Officer Training Corps (ROTC). No one will dispute that ROTC benefits the military and the US war machine. About 50 percent of each year's new crop of Army second lieutenants and about a third of all Army and Air Force and 12 percent of naval officers come from ROTC. Since the military is deeply embroiled in controversial political and moral issues, if the discussed views on the importance of neutrality are correct, then ROTC should not be present on American campuses. Holmes recommends instead establishing programs in military studies. Such programs would critically analyze all aspects of the military, including its historical, social, political, and moral dimensions. If in that way universities can contribute to a better understanding of the critical issues of the day, this may be among more important services that American universities can render to the society.

American universities face an identity crisis. No one is quite sure what they are anymore, much less what they ought to be. Looked at through different lenses, they are overgrown high schools, knowledge factories, corporations, employment agencies, farm clubs for professional football, or servants of the military-industrial complex. Sometimes, last if not least, they are also educational institutions. As such their primary purpose is not to make a profit, win games, improve the government, instill moral rectitude, or even teach. It is, rather, to encourage learning. Teaching is one way to do this, and for that reason teaching has an important role to play in the university. But learning can be fostered by research, discussion, independent study, and through countless other activities which do not, or need not, take place in the classroom. And these have a place in the university as well.

The problem of identity reflects the pluralistic character of American universities. Influenced in their fledgling years by both the European tradition of scholarship for its own sake and the American spirit of everything for the sake of utility, they sought to combine scholarly studies with practical training.[1] This was especially true of the land-grant colleges which sprang up largely in the rural areas, and whose purpose was to provide education for the working classes. The people they served, however, were accustomed to a life of toil and sweat; for them the "learning, poetry, and piety" promised to the community by President Eliot of Harvard at his inauguration was hardly enough. They had cattle to feed, crops to plant, machinery to repair; they wanted training geared to their way of life. Responding to this early demand for "relevance," the universities gave birth to a tradition of service to society, service which was at once more practical than skill in Greek or Latin and more immediate than the rewards of philosophy.

Long regarded as one of the strengths of the American university, this dual emphasis upon education and service today is at the root of its most critical problems. For it is an open question in a society wracked by controversial foreign and domestic problems whether a university can both serve outside interests and at the same time be neutral on the issues in which so many of those interests are implicated. It is even more of an open question whether the university can fulfill its primary educational purposes *unless* it is neutral.

Understanding university neutrality

There are two questions here. The primary one is whether universities *ought* to be neutral. There is a growing conviction among many students and faculty that the problems that confront us today are so serious that it is irresponsible, if not downright immoral, to fail to bring the full weight of the university's power and prestige down on the side of peace and social justice (and note that it is the neutrality of the university as an institution that we are discussing, not the propriety of individual members of the university community taking stands on issues, either as citizens or, say, in their capacity as students or faculty). This question, however, is ambiguous. It may be asked whether the university ought morally to be neutral, or whether it ought to be neutral from an educational standpoint or, if you like, from the educational point of view. In the latter case the relevant criteria would be whether or not neutrality is required for the promotion of the university's primary educational aims. The moral question is ultimately the decisive one, but we can limit ourselves to the educational question if we make the assumption that only morally defensible policies will be educationally sound in the long run. For then one can assume that in making a sound educational decision he will have covered (though not necessarily expressly considered) the relevant moral issues.[2]

The second question concerns what constitutes institutional neutrality. This needs clarification before the first question can be answered. The fervor with which neutrality

---

[1]   For a good historical study, see Frederick Rudolph, *The American College and University: A History* (New York: Vintage Books, 1962). See also Clark Kerr, *The Uses of the University* (New York: Harper & Row, 1966), Chapters 1 and 3, for a brief statement of this development and projection of where the universities are headed.

[2]   Such an assumption may not be self-evident, but it is sufficiently evident to stand until refuted, and is close to being a necessary article of faith for any philosophy of education.

has been both attacked and defended is often matched only by a lack of clarity about what it is.[3] During campus crises, administrators often spoke as if the universities were now neutral and that to accede to the demands of protestors would be to compromise that neutrality. They assumed both that the status quo was neutral and that neutrality is desirable. Protestors, on the other hand, charged that the problem was precisely that the universities are *not* neutral and are serving immoral causes. Their view was that neutrality is undesirable and should yield to the service of good causes.[4] With both sides thus starting from different conceptions of what constitutes neutrality, as well as from different premises about what the university should be and different perceptions of its current status, the stage was set for the typical confrontation.

Without intending any political connotations, I shall call the above views, respectively, the conservative and liberal views. Complicating the debate is a third position, which may be called the necessitarian view, which says that the university *cannot* by the nature of the case be neutral; that whatever it does, say, with regard to issues like ROTC, inevitably constitutes "political acts," and hence that all that is open to us is to get on with the business of deciding in which ways the university is going to be nonneutral.[5]

The problem in general, of course, is to define the university's proper role in society at large. More specifically, it is to determine the university's proper position with regard to social, political, and moral controversies. This undertaking must be a major part of the former enterprise. It requires distinguishing the question of whether the university should take a stand on such issues from the question of what the correct stand is on those issues. For sometimes whether to take a stand on a set of moral issues is itself

---

[3] A good recent attempt to clarify the notion with which I find much to agree is Robert L. Simon's "The Concept of a Politically Neutral University," in *Philosophy and Political Action*, ed. V. Held, K. Nielsen, and C. Parsons (New York: Oxford University Press, 1972), 217–33.

[4] The campus radicals perceived perhaps more clearly than anyone else that the status quo in American universities is not neutral. But instead of turning this to their advantage, they typically directed their fire against the concept of neutrality itself, claiming that it was a liberal camouflage of the real issues. Thus, they ended up defending the very principle they imputed to their opponents, i.e., that the university should serve political and ideological causes. This open espousal of what they alleged their opponents to be holding covertly only widened the gap between themselves and other students and faculty, which in turn enabled administrations to play one side off against the other and (with a little luck, the whole thing could backfire) to emerge the beneficiary. This same phenomenon, attesting to the shallowness of so much of what passes for radicalism, is a recurrent one. Accurately perceiving the abuse of notions like "reason," "tolerance," and "nonviolence" by liberals and their allies, militants rise to the bait and reject the genuine as well as the counterfeits of these, thereby guaranteeing the failure of their appeals for support far more certainly than their opponents could ever do.

[5] Henry David Aiken puts it that "a value-free academy, which is precisely what a university depoliticized in depth would try to be, is a contradiction in terms. At the least, the search for truth itself involves a commitment to the value of knowledge in every form, factual or normative. And an institution systematically committed to the search for and communication of truth in all its forms cannot in the nature of the case remain apolitical"; *Predicament of the University* (Bloomington, IN: Indiana University Press 1971), 97. In a similar vein, Robert Paul Wolff says: "As a prescription for institutional behavior, the doctrine of value neutrality suffers from the worst disability which can afflict a norm: what it prescribes is not wrong; it is impossible. A large university in contemporary America simply cannot adopt a value-neutral stance, either externally or internally, no matter how hard it tries"; *The Ideal of the University* (Boston: Beacon Press, 1969), 70. Whether the alleged impossibility here is of a logical sort, as implied by Aiken, or of a sort dictated by the circumstances in contemporary American society is not altogether clear.

a moral question and has to be assessed in the light of the consequences of action or inaction in the same way as the issues over which it initially arises. This makes the question of neutrality the prior question, inasmuch as whatever a university does with regard to these other controversies presupposes an answer to it.

Possible principles of university neutrality

Let us therefore begin by considering first how a plausible principle of university neutrality might be formulated. We may start by noting that neutrality can be assessed in light of both what a university says and what it does. Let us call these, respectively, official and de facto neutrality. The former is determined by the official pronouncements of the vested authorities of the university and can be expressed by a principle like the following:

1. A university ought not to take official stands on controversial social, political, and moral issues.

Most universities are neutral by this criterion. They only rarely commit themselves officially and explicitly in this manner. But as important as principle 1 is to an overall conception of neutrality, it is obviously too weak a principle if taken by itself, for it places no limits whatever on what a university does and what causes it supports as long as it carefully refrains from officially confirming what it is doing. It would, for example, allow a university to sponsor a program, say, to train Republican county chairmen (a program, let us suppose, financed, staffed, and controlled by the Republican party and—to make the analogy even more obvious—after graduation from which students were under contract to spend so many years in the service of Republicanism) and yet to claim neutrality on the grounds that it took no official stand on Republican policies. In the absence of similar services to other political parties, such a claim would be hardly credible. Taking an official stand suffices to violate neutrality, but refraining from taking such a stand in no way ensures neutrality.

This means that what is needed in addition to 1 is a principle to take account of a university's policies as well as its pronouncements, its implicit as well as its explicit commitments. It is tempting, in light of this, to think in terms of a principle like:

2. A university should do nothing which supports one side or the other on controversial social, political, and moral issues.

But this would be too strong a principle. It is one which a university could not help but violate in the normal course of performing its educational functions. If a university educates one student who joins the marines and another who joins the draft resistance, it contributes to the respective causes they serve. And there is no way to ensure that it will not contribute more to one cause than to another in the process. But educating students could not for that reason plausibly be called political act.

Principles like 1 and 2 have often been tacitly appealed to in disputes. When administrators represent the university as neutral when it sponsors recruiting by the military, the CIA, or Dow Chemical, or trains officers for the armed services, they frequently do so simply on the grounds that the university (meaning, in this context, themselves as its official spokesmen) has taken no official position on the policies of any of these agencies. When students, on the other hand, have charged the university with complicity in immoral acts, they have often done so on the grounds that it was in fact supporting the efforts and activities of these agencies. Even granting the correctness of the factual elements in respective claims, it is evident that the two were at cross-purposes right from the start, each opting for the conception of neutrality which supported their more general positions.

What is needed is a principle that is stronger than 1 but not as prohibitively strong as 2. The following, for example, would meet that condition:

3. A university ought not to adopt policies whose intention is to favor one side or the other on controversial social, political, and moral issues.

Like 1, 3 captures a necessary feature of any full-blown conception of neutrality. But also like 1, it is insufficient. The drunken driver may have had no intention of killing the pedestrian, but he is culpable nonetheless as long as he knows (or is accountable for knowing) the likely consequences of drunken driving; the point being that we are accountable in our actions for more than just what we intend, a fact which should be reflected in an account of neutrality. This suggests a principle which embraces 3 but goes beyond it:

4. A university ought not to adopt policies whose expectable consequences favor one side or the other on controversial social, political, and moral issues.

According to 4, a decision or policy would fail to be neutral if it in fact had foreseeable consequences of this sort, even if it were no part of the intention of the formulators of the policy that it does so.

But even this has a shortcoming. For it might be argued that the pursuit of a university's proper educational goals might sometimes have consequences of the sort described, and yet that in such cases we should be reluctant to characterize them as neutrality violating, particularly on the assumption noted earlier that sound educational policies will not in the long run contribute to unsound or immoral social or political causes. One might even argue that an official university stand on certain issues like free speech would be consistent with neutrality, the grounds being that free speech is an essential and integral part of the educational process without which the aims of education simply cannot be effectively pursued. To take account of this qualification to 4, let us propose:

5. A university ought not to adopt educationally nonessential policies whose expectable consequences favor one side or the other on controversial social, political, and moral issues.

This draws together the preceding considerations and yields a principle of de facto neutrality. Principles 1 through 5 represent varying degrees of neutrality. Principle 1 is the weakest, 2 the strongest, and the others fall between the two.

The preceding line of reasoning is not unattended with difficulties, however. Two objections in particular might be advanced against the qualification just introduced in 5 (as well as against the grounds for rejecting 2): first, that it arbitrarily rules out possible cases in which a university cannot help but violate neutrality, and hence begs the question against the necessitarian; and second, that because the survival of the nation is no less a necessary condition of the pursuit of educational goals than is, say, free speech, it makes virtually every major issue of foreign policy and national defense the proper business of the university, a state of affairs which if alleged to be consistent with neutrality reduces that notion to absurdity.[6]

On the first point, since much of the campus debate we have been trying to clarify has centered around whether the university *ought* to be neutral, we have indeed been guided partly by the desire to frame a plausible principle according to which a university *can* be neutral. But this need not be question begging against the necessitarian. His position, as we have stated it, implies that there is no meaningful sense in which a university can be neutral. And that view is clearly false with regard to official neutrality and probably false with regard to de facto neutrality. There are many issues on which a university can be neutral: it can refrain from supporting candidates for city council, mayor, the U.S. Senate, or the presidency, or from passing judgment on welfare reform, local dog-leash laws, coastal fishing rights, or abortion legislation. At most there are only certain respects in which a university cannot be neutral.[7] This means that even if the necessitarian view be conceded, a whole host of normative issues regarding whether or not the university should take certain stands will remain to be dealt with, and how they are dealt with will make an important difference to the overall character of the university. It is just that, contrary to the necessitarian position, it seems plausible to view these as involving neutrality.

But should even that much be conceded? Is it clear, that is, that there are *any* respects in which it is impossible that a university should be neutral? Without attempting to deal with this question at length, let me suggest only that arguments to this effect

[6] Not only that, but one could push the argument further and point out that since the existence of state and federally supported universities depends upon funding, they for that reason have a stake in state and national elections and should therefore be active in supporting political candidates for office. To pursue this line of reasoning is quickly to involve the university as an institution in almost every major political issue, foreign or domestic.

[7] Aiken (97–8) points this out when he says that "not every local political issue, of course, is a matter of immediate academic concern; nor am I contending that the university is obliged to take a stand on every matter debated in the state legislatures or the Congress. But this does not imply either that members of the university, in their capacity as scholars, or that the university itself as a collegial body, must remain aloof when, as in Nazi Germany, action and policies of the state undermine the very possibility of liberal learning or when, as in some of our own Southern states, prevailing social practices and prejudices radically limit the freedom of the academy in deciding policies of admission, appointment, or instruction." These remarks suggest not so much that the university cannot be neutral as that there are some circumstances in which it ought not to be neutral, which is the liberal rather than the necessitarian position. As will become clear later, I am in strong agreement with what Aiken says here, only I see it as having a different bearing upon the overall question of neutrality.

risk placing a greater burden on the concept of neutrality than it can bear. When any social consequences of education are taken to count against neutrality, or when a commitment to any values whatsoever—even if they are ones like learning, truth, or knowledge—is taken to be incompatible with neutrality, then surely we should have to agree that no university can or should be neutral. Neutrality has been ruled out by definition of the university and its purposes.[8] But is there any good reason to define neutrality in such a way? Not, I think, if we are to take our point of departure from the sorts of issues which have in fact most often given rise to the question of neutrality. For those issues have not arisen over the consequences of education and learning, but over the pursuit of educationally nonessential ends. And with regard to such issues, it is not at all apparent why a university cannot be neutral. A university does not *have* to sponsor recruiting by the marines, the CIA, or business-industrial firms; it does not *have* to do classified research for the Department of Defense; it does not *have* to train officers for the military. Nothing in the nature of the values of learning or the purposes of higher education requires it to do any of these things.[9] Even those who argue for these activities concede at least that the university's first business is not to be an employment agency, or a brain trust for the Department of Defense, or a training ground for military officers. Whether or not a university has any business doing these

---

[8] Aiken, in the first passage quote above, seems to take neutrality in this exceedingly broad sense to signify neutrality with respect to any values whatsoever. Wolff (73) sometimes sounds as though he takes it in a sense: "every university expresses a number of positive value commitments through the character of its faculty, of its library, even through the buildings it chooses to build. Astronomy departments ignore astrology, psychiatry departments ignore dianetics, philosophy departments ignore dialectical materialism. Universities build laboratories for experimental research, thereby committing themselves to the importance of the scientific enterprise; libraries devote scarce resources to the accumulation of rare and ancient manuscripts; whole faculties are organized to teach and study social welfare, veterinary science, law, or business. Each of these institutional decisions embodies an evaluation which can easily become the focus of a political dispute." It is difficult to believe that anyone has ever seriously proposed that a university can or should be free of any value commitments whatsoever. If this is what the necessitarian means by neutrality, then his conception is not covered by the foregoing principles; but by the same token, conceding his position does not entail an answer one way or the other to the normative question of neutrality as we have formulated it.

[9] Of course, if one characterizes both the doing and the not doing of such things as the performance of "political acts," then one can logically ensure that universities cannot be neutral. But one does so at the cost of depriving his claim of any real significance. For when neutrality is made logically impossible to achieve, we give rise to the need for a new term to do the same service as that within the category of so-called political acts, enabling us to distinguish between acts we can do or refrain from doing and those we cannot. Wolff seems inclined to take this line in *The Ideal of the University* (70ff.). While I do not find this plausible as an argument for the necessitarian position, it has the makings of a strong argument for the liberal position by calling attention to the fact that universities do have a certain amount of power (though less, I think, than is often suggested, and even less prestige) and implying that they should therefore apply it directly by taking stands on political issues. A full reply to this would require taking up in detail the question of what a university ought to be. I would suggest only that, if universities were the sorts of institutions they should be, they would not qua institutions have any particular political power to wield, and that it is only in proportion as they have forsaken their proper role that they currently possess such power. Rather, therefore, than accept the current trend and what it forebodes for the future (in which, in Clark Kerr's words, the university becomes a "prime instrument of national purpose"), I think it far better that effort be expended to transform the universities into genuine communities of learning, committed exclusively to the values which that implies.

things is another matter. What is incontrovertible is that it can avoid doing them and does not betray any commitment to the essential values of education if it does so.

But even if neutrality were understood in the above way so as to render the university practically or even logically incapable of attaining it, nothing whatsoever would follow with respect to the remainder of the necessitarian's argument. For that argument as often expressed says essentially that *because* universities cannot be neutral, they should take stands on a variety of other issues (being those of most concern to the persons advancing the argument). But if the premise of this argument means only that a university cannot by the nature of the case help but have a concern with education and its distinctive values and that education has social consequences, nothing follows regarding what the university should do with respect to noneducational matters. If it means more than this, and means that a university cannot help but address itself to noneducational issues,[10] then this claim in all probability is false and in any event has to be supported. And if it could be established, it still would not settle the question of what to do regarding the many respects in which a university can be neutral. So whether we characterize neutrality in such a way that universities cannot be neutral, and then ask independently what we should do about the many issues whose solution is not dictated by that observation, or characterize it as we have here in such a way that they can be neutral and then ask whether they should be, is ultimately of little consequence. Precisely the same normative questions remain to be answered either way. But as I have indicated, the latter focuses more clearly the issues which in fact have generated the problem, and for that reason seems a less misleading way of framing these questions.

The second objection to principle 5 is in many ways a more important one and deserves more attention than I can give it here. Let me simply indicate the general direction in which I think an appropriate reply to it can be framed. It involves distinguishing between conditions which are necessary to the very existence of a university and those which, additionally, are inextricably bound up in the educational process itself. To say that the pursuit of educational goals warrants taking a stand on all issues relating to the former conditions would indeed so attenuate the notion of neutrality as to deprive it of any real meaning. To say, however, that it warrants taking a stand on the latter issues (assuming for the moment that we are talking about official neutrality) would not similarly dilute it. For there clearly are certain values, particularly in the form of rights and freedoms pertaining to teaching, research, publication, and so forth, which are closer to the heart of the whole educational enterprise than others, even if some of the others are no less necessary in the last analysis to the existence of the university. The promotion and maintenance of these values is one of the specific functions of the university. There are many other issues of a political and foreign policy nature which have nothing to do with education, even though they may have a bearing upon the circumstances under which education takes place, or even upon whether it continues to take place in any particular context. Their resolution—calling as it does for concrete action of various sorts—is the proper business of society at large, as is the promotion and maintenance of many other values like peace, economic prosperity, and political freedom. All of these are proper subjects for research, study, and debate within the university, and the university at its

---

[10]   Other than those which are inextricably allied with the pursuit of educational aims.

best should exemplify certain of them; but it is not the university's job qua university actively to promote them in society or the world at large.[11]

While the preceding are not the only objections to this line of analysis, they are among the more important ones. But neither of them, if I am correct, is decisive, and I would therefore propose as a principle of institutional neutrality the combination of 1 and 5:

6. A university should neither take official stands nor adopt educationally nonessential policies supporting one side or the other on controversial social, political, or moral issues.

While there is room for refinement of such notions as what is educationally essential, or what constitutes a "controversial" issue,[12] there do not seem to be any insurmountable problems here, and I submit that 6 embodies the essence of any plausible conception of institutional neutrality.

Finally, it should be noted that 6 represents only what might be called a weak principle of neutrality. A strong principle could be formulated by substituting the word "any" for "controversial." Each of these might then be taken to reflect more basic views about the very nature of the university. These latter views might take the form of judgments like:

A. A university should adopt no educationally nonessential policies, programs, etc., whatsoever.
B. A university should adopt no educationally nonessential programs, policies, etc., which risk jeopardizing educational values.

These might be called principles of academic integrity. Principle A is the stronger of the two and would support the stronger principle of neutrality. Principle B yields the weaker principle 6 if conjoined with a premise to the effect that taking stands on controversial noneducational issues risks compromising educational values. I shall argue for such a premise in the next section. Principle A would rule out many institutionally sponsored extracurricular activities like intercollegiate athletics; B would allow them on condition that they in no way interfere with educational values. Some such conception of the university as is represented by principles A and B must, I suggest, underlie any defense of neutrality.

In the remainder of this discussion I shall be concerned only with 6, the weaker principle of neutrality, not because I think it is clearly preferable to the stronger one, but because it is sufficient for the argument I shall present. Accordingly, I shall tacitly assume only B, the weaker of the principles of academic integrity.

---

[11] I shall later maintain that there are circumstances in which a university is justified in taking social and political action but argue that these are circumstances in which a university has abandoned its primary mission.

[12] Controversiality, for example, is a relative notion, varying according to time and circumstance. Thus, although university-military ties during War World II were noncontroversial, they became exceedingly controversial during the war in Vietnam. It does not follow from this, of course, that they were ever a good idea, only that at one time they were not violative of neutrality as I have defined it while they were at another. While, as I shall maintain in the next section, neutrality is desirable, not everything which is consistent with neutrality is desirable.

In defense of university neutrality

Should neutrality so conceived be aimed at? I believe that it should and must, not because neutrality is itself an academic value like learning, truth, or academic freedom, but because it is necessary to maintaining the conditions under which these other values can flourish. For they can flourish only in an atmosphere of mutual confidence that they are prized to such a degree that no person or group will seek to transform the institution which sustains and nourishes them, and whose sole rationale is to do just that, into a vehicle for the promotion of other causes. Such confidence cannot exist if the time and energy of students, faculty, and administrators alike are consumed in an incessant struggle to prevail in the determination of the university's position with regard to the many nonacademic causes which may compete for its allegiance. Nor is there any way to create the mechanisms for supervising such a contest and adjudicating the differences it will bring to a head in a fair and equitable way and on a continuing basis without virtually transforming the university into a political institution. To try to have it both ways, as some universities have done, and to implicate the university deeply in controversial noneducational issues while at the same time withholding the full range of democratic rights and guarantees in the decision making that determines the nature of that involvement is to court disaster. Our country from its inception has expressly taught people to demand and if necessary to fight for just such rights in their political institutions.[13]

This means that if one takes neutrality seriously, he must be prepared to deny the relevance of some of his most fervently held convictions to the determination of institutional policy, and be prepared to see the character of the university shaped as nearly as possible by academic considerations alone. It also means that departures from the university's central educational goals in the interests of "public service" should be made if at all only when it is clear that they will not jeopardize neutrality.

All of this presupposes, of course, that the universities are worth preserving. There may be a point in the deterioration of a society, whether owing to domestic or to international causes, beyond which the objectives of an institution of higher learning are no longer attainable or even desirable. At that point the principle of neutrality

---

[13] I stress here considerations relating to the character and inner constitution of the university, because I think these are sufficient to establish the importance of neutrality. On the other side of the coin are all of the considerations relating to external pressures upon the university if it undertakes political action. As Walter P. Metzger points out regarding the landmark 1915 AAUP statement by Arthur O. Lovejoy, E. R. A. Seligman, and John Dewey, *et al.*, "The norm of institutional neutrality was not just an ethicist's abstraction: it was a denial of the proprietary claims of trustees, donors, and their spokesmen . . . it was an effort to reduce the sphere in which philistine administrators could take action"; *Dimensions of Academic Freedom* (Urbana, IL: University of Illinois Press, 1969), 14. Beyond the encroachments of "philistine administrators," of course, are those of the state. And these have more recently come to be recognized as a danger inherent in institutional nonneutrality. Even Wolff, who maintains that the notion of neutrality is a myth, recognizes this and seems to support the perpetuation of the myth, citing the "ever-present threat of pressure, censorship, and witch-hunting by conservative forces in society at large. . . . Let the university once declare that it is a political actor, and its faculty will be investigated, its charter revoked, and its tax-exempt status forthwith removed. . . . It is a bitter pill for the radicals to swallow, but the fact is that they benefit more than any other segment of the university community from the fiction of institutional neutrality" (75).

for which I am arguing is no longer binding.[14] For then, among other things, the assumption of the coincidence of the moral and educational points of view will no longer hold. I would argue that this is true in some Latin American countries and that it was true in Nazi Germany. It is for this reason that I am not persuaded by those arguments against neutrality which point to the case of Hitler's Germany and maintain that it is indefensible for universities to remain neutral in those contexts. One can only agree with the latter part of this claim, but not because nonneutrality is a sound and defensible position for an institution with an ongoing commitment to learning to take but, rather, because some situations are so bad, and some evils so great, that it is manifestly immoral for anyone to continue to occupy himself with teaching, study, and research, that is, to maintain that commitment at the expense of a wholehearted commitment to oppose that evil. To argue as though it were desirable to continue the so-called life of the mind in such situations, but just to do so in a way which at the same time leads the fight against the world's evils, seems to me wrongheaded. At times like that, universities should close down, or transform themselves into something other than educational institutions. What one cannot defensibly do, in my judgment, is to hold that universities should both continue to function as institutions of higher learning and at the same time serve political causes. In short, if there are to be institutions of higher learning, they should strive to be neutral; but sometimes the maintenance of such institutions is neither possible nor desirable.

ROTC Incompatible with university neutrality

While virtually all of the problems arising from the relationship between the military and the universities raise in one way or another the question of neutrality, ROTC brings the issue into sharper relief than do most of the others.

ROTC has its roots in the Morrill (or Land Grant) Act of 1862, according to which the purpose of the land-grant colleges is to teach agricultural and mechanical arts "without excluding other scientific and classical studies, and including military tactics." While it was unclear for many years precisely how this latter provision was to be interpreted, it has come to be expected that such schools will provide military training as part of their programs. Since the National Defense Act of 1916 establishing the Army Reserve Officer Training Corps (with Navy and Air Force programs appearing in 1926 and 1946, respectively), ROTC has been the vehicle by which this provision has been met. Its various programs, revised and expanded, and ranging far beyond the original grant schools, are currently administered under the ROTC Vitalization Act of 1964. Like other ties with the military— most of which developed during and after World War II—ROTC was largely taken for granted until the United States became deeply involved in Vietnam. After that time it came under heavy fire, and was forced out of many of the country's leading universities.

---

[14] This situation is characterized by Aiken when he describes the circumstances in which the "actions and policies of the state undermine the very possibility of liberal learning" (see n. 7 above). I agree with him that at such time the universities should take action. It is just that, while he clearly thinks the existence of such circumstances is sufficient to justify political action by the universities, he does not, if I understand him correctly, think that it is necessary.

Since universities do not as a rule officially endorse military policies, the question of neutrality with regard to ROTC hinges upon the issue of de facto neutrality, specifically upon whether ROTC is educationally essential and represents de facto institutional support of an agency deeply committed on controversial social, political, and moral issues.

The answer on both counts seems clear. To provide on-campus military training is not, and has probably never been claimed to be even by advocates of ROTC, a central part of the educational function of a university. The chief arguments for ROTC have been its benefit to the armed services, its contribution to national security, and its supposed moderating influence upon the military.[15] There is rarely any claim of benefit to the university or attempt to justify the training of officers for the military (as distinct from justifying credit for individual courses) on academic grounds. That ROTC benefits the military, moreover, no one disputes—about 50 percent of each year's new crop of Army second lieutenants and about a third of all Army and Air Force and 12 percent of naval officers come from ROTC. And that the military is deeply embroiled in controversial social, political, and moral issues is incontrovertible.

If so, then for a university to contract to supply the military with officers is to compromise its neutrality, not because it entails *saying* that the university approves of this or that policy of the military, or even because it necessarily signifies an intention on the part of decision makers to do so. Rather, it compromises neutrality because it *in fact* places the university in the service of a powerful outside agency which perhaps more than any other is at the center of the major moral, political, and ideological issues of the day. If, further, our reasoning about the importance of neutrality is correct, then ROTC should be discontinued.

Response to objections

Such a conception of the university may strike some as too high-minded. Universities train nurses, field football teams, and sponsor glee clubs, as well as host rock concerts,

---

[15] *The Report of the Special Committee on ROTC* to the Secretary of Defense, September 22, 1969, headed by George C. S. Benson, backs ROTC on the grounds that it is a "major procurement source of officers for the Army, Navy and Air Force," arguing further that in assessing the relationship for the military to the universities, "one overriding priority must be recognized, namely, the national security of the country." The committee maintains not only that it is proper for universities to host ROTC units, but that they have a responsibility to do so—presumably derivative from an alleged responsibility: to contribute to national security. This in turn is presumed to derive from the financial benefits which universities receive from the federal government: direct tax support in the case of public institutions and tax-exempt status in the case of private ones. The whole argument presupposes that the university as an institution has political obligations of a sort which preclude its being neutral on controversial moral and political issues. Interestingly, some of the staunchest advocates of university neutrality are among the first to insist that the university has an obligation to assist in national defense. Thus, a trustee of one university resigned in protest when his university's president signed a letter (joining thirty-six other college and university presidents) to President Nixon protesting the Cambodian invasion. He did so on the grounds that the university had no right "to become embroiled in public issues of political, military, or economic importance." At the same time he deplored the university senate's vote to discontinue ROTC, on the grounds that it showed that the university "does not wish to be closely associated with the defense of the United States." One cannot have it both ways. If the university has an obligation to assist in national defense, this precludes it from being neutral on the whole constellation of moral and political issues attaching thereto.

beer blasts, and political rallies—none of which is clearly any more central to the main purposes of a university than ROTC, and some of which have no conceivable justification on academic grounds. Should a university discontinue all of these as well, it might be asked, and if not, why ROTC?

The answer is twofold. First of all, remember that neutrality as it concerns us here is a property of the university as an institution, and governs only programs, policies, contracts, and so forth, representing an institutional commitment. This excludes from its scope the multitude of other events and activities like beer blasts and political rallies which merely occur within the university, usually on the initiative of individual students or student organizations, and are not in any real sense sponsored by the university as an institution. It is not only in keeping with, but indeed required by, the purposes of an open university that it allow as much freedom in these areas as is compatible with the preservation of academic values.

Second, there is a clear distinction between ROTC and even such institutionally sponsored programs and activities as nursing, football, and glee clubs. For in none of these other cases is the university party to a contractual arrangement whereby a student even before entering college makes a ten-year commitment to an outside agency;[16] becomes subject to immediate call to active duty if adjudged to have "willfully evaded" the terms of his contract; becomes subject to immediate separation from the program, with termination of financial support, any time it is deemed in the interest of the agency in question; and is prevented from marrying or (in NROTC) from majoring in some thirty-three areas while in college. And in none of these other cases is the curriculum controlled (by law) in whole or in part by a noneducational outside agency which staffs a university department with its own paid representatives whose primary allegiance is to it (the university being only able to accept or reject nominees it puts forward) and in which federal law requires that the university appoint the agency's chief representative as chairman of a department at the rank of full professor.[17] If and when nursing, football, and glee clubs mark such a violation of the spirit of an open and autonomous community, or become as deeply committed on one side of the major issues of the day as the military, then by all means let us ask seriously whether they should continue to enjoy university sanction. But at present there is no significant analogy between them and ROTC other than that they all have their primary justification at least partly on nonacademic grounds.

A more difficult objection is that termination of ROTC would represent a de facto taking of sides with antiwar forces. This is the sort of objection advanced by those

---

[16] Speaking here, and in what follows, of the NROTC Regular Student Program (see Contract for Regular Students [NROTC], NAVPERS 1110/24 [6–67] [Washington, D.C.: Bureau of Naval Personnel]). There are variations in the programs from one service to the next. The NROTC student becomes a member of the armed service during his training and is committed to a minimum active-duty service period of four years following commissioning, plus two years of reserve duty. He may voluntarily disenroll during his first year, and thereafter only at the risk of being called to active duty.

[17] The ROTC Vitalization Act of 1964 specifies that no unit may be established unless "the senior commissioned officer of the armed forces concerned who is assigned to the program . . . is given the academic rank of professor," and unless the institution establishes "as part of its curriculum, a four-year course of military instruction, or a two-year course of advanced training . . . or both, *which the Secretary of the military department concerned prescribes and conducts*" (italics added).

who hold the necessitarian view. Certainly a university *could* drop ROTC as a means of antiwar protest. But equally clearly, it need not do so and can take obvious steps to guard against being interpreted as doing so (such as by announcing that it is acting in the interests of neutrality). It is true that once an institution adopts a program which compromises neutrality, then to discontinue the program will gladden the hearts of those who oppose it. It is this which gives superficial plausibility to defenses of the status quo by appeal to neutrality and to the argument that a university cannot be neutral. But one must distinguish between dropping ROTC in order to take an antiwar stand and doing so in the interests of neutrality, since one and the same action could be taken on either ground. In the former case it would violate neutrality, in the latter not. When the foreseeable actual or symbolic benefit to one side in a controversy derives from an action necessary to undo an arrangement which compromises neutrality, such benefit cannot plausibly be said to be violative of neutrality. Otherwise, to side with those who favor neutrality would itself be to violate neutrality, which would mean that a principle of neutrality could never be implemented so long as there were some who favored it. And this would render the principle useless. Thus, if my analysis is correct, the objection that to discontinue ROTC would necessarily be to ally the university with antiwar forces cannot be sustained.

None of this is to deny that modern universities inevitably have complex ties with society. Nor is it to deny that it would be impossible and perhaps even destructive of the university to try to break all of these ties even if it were desirable to do so. These are the unchallengeable premises in the liberal position. But insofar as a principle of neutrality prescribes what a university *ought* to do, it applies only to what it *can* do. And while a university neither can nor should dissociate itself completely from society at large, there are some things it can readily do (like terminating certain contracts) and others toward which it can work in the long run (like altering investment policies when this is dictated in the interests of neutrality).[18] There are as well, as we have seen, many things violative of neutrality which it can refrain from doing.

Nor is the preceding to disregard the academic freedom of students enrolled in ROTC—a matter which rightfully concerns many faculty. Since no academic consideration confers upon a person the right to institutionally sponsored military training as part of his college program, there is no academic obligation on the part of a university to provide such training, and no violation of academic freedom if it does not do so. It would nonetheless be unfair to students currently enrolled in ROTC to pull the

[18] A university's investment policies pose more complex problems than does ROTC. Harvard has been notable in addressing itself to this aspect of the problem through a Committee on University Relations with Corporate Enterprise. The committee supported university neutrality but acknowledged certain issues—including "respect for freedom of expression, regard . . . for individual political rights and constitutional processes, and hostility (whether in the University's role as center of learning, contractor, employer, or investor) to anything smacking of racism"—on which there presumably should be no room for question about where the university stands. Harvard has adopted the view that its investment policy should strive for maximum return, while nonetheless recognizing a "right and duty to achieve purposes other than educational purposes" through its investment practices. This latter qualification might be regarded as coming within the scope of our principle of neutrality by virtue of the further recognition that it arises "solely out of our obligations to take the long view of our education mission and to act as a good citizen in the performance of it" (as reported in *Harvard Today*, Spring 1971).

rug from under them partway through their program, and for that reason universities should either phase the programs out over a period of years or provide comparable financial assistance to such students for the remainder of their college education.

Perhaps the biggest obstacle to the removal of ROTC from the campuses, however, is faculty themselves, who too often sidestep the bedrock issue of neutrality and confine themselves instead to more "manageable" questions of academic credit, hours of drill, and so forth. This is true of defenders and critics of ROTC alike. They do not face squarely the fact that if one's criterion is stringency of standards, ROTC courses often are—and can easily be made to be—academically as respectable as anything else for which credit is given. Any "subject matter" from chemistry to concentration camp management can be taught well or poorly. That is not the issue. The issue is whether certain kinds of programs, with whatever degree of excellence they are taught, have any business in the university in the first place.

When faculty do address the broader issues, they often argue not so much from the benefit to the armed forces as from ROTC's supposed "moderating influence" upon the military: ensuring civilian control and a continuous infusion of civilian values into the military establishment.[19]

This is a seductive argument. Critics of the military rally to it as readily as supporters. It calls up images of a vigilant citizenry over a potentially dangerous military establishment (a necessary evil as long as there are threats to freedom in the world) and of the university as custodian of that citizenry's highest ideals, guaranteeing, as it were, that young men will emerge humane and responsible warriors, responsive to civilian leadership, if only they pass first through its portals.

Insofar, first of all, as the motive behind the argument is fear of a professional military elite insulated in background and education from the rest of society, ROTC probably does little to mitigate such a danger. The dangers of professionalism come not so much from enlisted men (as opponents of a volunteer army would have us believe) or junior officers as from the top-echelon officers' corps. And at that level, we already have a professional army with or without ROTC. It is worth remembering, in any event, that in Nazi Germany the strongest military opposition to Hitler came not from the younger officers and enlisted men but from the professional military elite, and yet it was the former who more nearly embodied the prevailing sociopolitical values of the civilian population.[20] The point is that the appeal to civilian values is next to meaningless unless those values are specified. If one means only certain values widely held by the civilian population, they may or may not be worth preserving. If one means values which are both widely held and properly so, then one must show, and not merely assume, that programs like ROTC will foster rather than undermine them.

[19] This argument was used in support of the original Morrill Act as well as more recently by the Report of the Special Committee on ROTC to the Secretary of Defense, which states ominously that "if ROTC were to be removed from the nation's campuses there would be grave danger of isolating the services from the intellectual centers of the public which they serve and defend!" Secretary of Defense Laird played upon this same theme before Congress when he professed to be mystified "by those who on the one hand oppose the so-called 'militarization' of our society and on the other hand seem determined to dry up the important source of civilian trained officers of our armed forces" (*New York Times*, May 31, 1970).

[20] See Telford Taylor, *Sword and Swastika* (Chicago: Quadrangle Books, 1969), 244.

ROTC, in any event, has had little impact of the alleged responsible and humanizing sort, at least as measured by the actions of the United States in Indochina. ROTC students have scarcely been identified with antiwar activity, much less in the forefront of it, which suggests either that ROTC does not attract young men much susceptible to the kind of influence in question or that it fails to instill in them the proper values—at least in sufficient strength to hold sway against military values like obedience—or both. Either way, the salutary influence of ROTC upon the military by one of the most obvious of criteria has been negligible.

This is hardly surprising. What is surprising is that it should seriously be thought that if you screen out a group of teenage youths through the lure of an expense-paid college education, exact from them a military commitment at an age when they are still maturing, and place them throughout the duration of their higher education—when, ideally, at least, they should have the greatest freedom to grow intellectually and morally, and to do so with a minimum of pressure to conform and to obey external authorities—in a program of military training under the scrutiny of a commanding officer whose job is to screen them still further if necessary, the whole process will in the long run civilianize the military rather than militarize the citizenry. Carried to its conclusion, such reasoning would argue for giving the military a foothold in all of the civilian institutions of the country—perhaps, to be only slightly unfair, a quota of congressional seats and representation on the Supreme Court—the better thereby to expose it to the whole range of civilian values. It takes little imagination to picture the direction in which the influence would flow. The military already sit on top civilian commissions of government and increasingly move into influential roles in business and industry following retirement; and historians and analysts have repeatedly noted their growing influence upon foreign policy since World War II. Should this trend continue, we shall one day be describing what for all intents and purposes is a garrison society and calling it a civilianized military. And while it is true that a society geared at all levels to the service of the military has little to fear from an internal military takeover, that is only because it has already handed over virtually everything worth taking.

If one were seriously interested in exerting deliberate pressure upon the military through the universities—and if this were an appropriate use of the universities, which I contend it is not—this could better be accomplished by keeping the universities autonomous and expecting the military to transform itself in such a way as to attract college graduates in competition with other professions. As it is, it is no more the university's job to temper the military virtues than it is to foster them.

Conclusion

The upshot is that neither the liberal student view nor the conservative faculty-administration view is adequate. Faculty and administrators have often had the better grasp of the principles[21] involved in their recognition that the university

---

[21]   Educational, not moral. They have often been remarkably insensitive to the latter.

should strive to be neutral. Where they have gone wrong is in supposing that the current status quo is neutral. Students, on the other hand, have often had the more perceptive analysis of the actual facts and have seen that the universities long ago forsook neutrality, in fact if not by design and intention. Where they have gone wrong is in believing that the remedy lies in merely getting the university to serve other causes than it has served in the past. Recognition of what is sound in both of these positions leads to a more complex analysis than either one of them represents. And—as in the case of ROTC—it leads to conclusions which support many of the substantive changes students have urged over the years, but does so on precisely the grounds on which faculty and administrators have resisted those changes.

For all of this, there is considerable truth in B. H. Hart's claim that "if you wish for peace, understand war," and the one place above all others where such understanding should be attainable is the university. But its pursuit should be under the guidance not of those who are charged with the responsibility to wage war, but of scholars whose independence and objectivity is the same as that expected in any other academic discipline. For this reason, universities might seriously consider establishing programs of military studies. But they should be programs which deal with *all* aspects of the military, including the social, political, and moral dimensions. And they should be programs which are university initiated and controlled, staffed by scholars recruited in normal ways, and governed at all levels by properly established academic criteria. All of this is within the province of an academic institution's proper concerns. And insofar as public service is measured first and foremost by a university's contribution to a better understanding of the critical issues of the day, it may be among the more important services a university can render to society.[22]

---

[22] Originally published in *Ethics*, Vol. 83, No. 3, April 1973, 177–95.

6

The Philosophy of Political Realism in International Affairs

In this essay Holmes masterfully dissects two competing currents in twentieth-century American political thought. The first is that of Wilsonian idealism, which would keep the country focused on its domestic issues and leave the search for solutions to various international problems to those who are directly involved in them. The second is that of so-called Political Realism, which is based on interventionism and willingness to wage wars. Holmes' analytical knife is mostly directed toward various justifications for Political Realism: from Niebuhr's view of corrupt human nature, to the submission of morality to politics. Political realists seem incapable of resisting the temptation to try to solve all political problems—domestic as well as international—by military means, by threats and punishments. Holmes outlines how the unchallenged dominance of the philosophy of Political Realism has turned the country into a "virtual garrison state, geared to intervention abroad and chained to a permanent war economy at home." It has led the country to catastrophic wars, like the one in Vietnam, and also to massive violations of human rights at home. He urges a return toward a version of the Wilsonian idealism, but of the kind that would be squarely based on nonviolence and committed to equally respect all citizens of the world.

Many who concede that violence always needs justifying where questions of morality are pertinent contend that in international affairs, particularly in matters of warfare, morality either has no relevance at all or has at best limited relevance. Hence, they say, appeals to morality in foreign affairs are best foregone in the interests of clear thinking and effective action.

This view has been called Political Realism, and is sometimes said to have been the dominant outlook in American foreign policy since World War II.[1] Whether the latter is true is difficult to judge with confidence, of course, since the haze of secrecy surrounding high-level decision making makes such judgments almost unavoidably partly conjectural. But much of post–World War II foreign policy conforms closely to the prescriptions of the realists, and Political Realism has unquestionably been a leading—and perhaps even the dominant—theoretical approach to foreign policy thinking in America since World War I, with adherents among leading theologians, historians,

---

[1] Robert L. Rothstein, "On the Costs of Political Realism," *American Political Science Quarterly*, Vol. 87, No. 3, September 1972, 347–62.

diplomats, and political scientists, including Reinhold Niebuhr, George Kennan, Robert E. Osgood, Hans Morgenthau, and Arthur M. Schlesinger, Jr.[2]

Despite its importance, however, and the fact that it abounds with philosophical assumptions, Political Realism has rarely been subjected to close philosophical examination.

I wish to initiate such an examination here. I do not presume, in such limited space, to be able to do justice to all of the theories which have some claim to be called forms of Political Realism, or even to all of the particulars of those theories I shall discuss. The differences among realists on many matters of political, military, and historical judgment are too great for that. My aim, rather, will be, first, to clarify what Political Realism is and what some of the grounds are upon which it has been, or might be, held; and second, against this background, to place in general perspective two of the main currents of recent political realist thought in America. In the latter undertaking I shall concentrate upon analyses of American foreign policy between the two world wars, and deal only incidentally with the views of "neorealists" who attempt to update Realism for the nuclear age, and not at all with the forms which the doctrine has taken in European thought. Finally, I will, in the process, indicate the points at which I think that Political Realism has been in error. For despite the differences among the theories it embraces, it seems to me that Political Realism not only embodies some serious confusions but that it has provided a rationale (whether or not rational, a factual question I shall not attempt to answer) for the policies which eventuated in the Vietnam-Indochina War.

Let me begin the first task, of clarifying what Political Realism is.

The nature of Political Realism

Often as not, "Political Realism" is used simply as a commendatory label, to stand for a sound, effective, clear-headed and rational approach to foreign policy;[3] a sense in which no one in his right mind would admit to being anything but a realist. "Idealism" is then reserved for possibly well-intentioned but naive, impractical, and faint-hearted approaches to word problems; a sense in which no one in his right mind would admit

---

[2]   While not usually identified with Political Realism, Schlesinger defends what is in effect a political realist position in his "National Interests and Moral Absolutes," in Ernest W. Lefever, ed., *Ethics and World Politics: Four Perspectives* (Baltimore: Johns Hopkins University Press, 1972), 21–42.

[3]   Speaking here of its use by advocates. Thus Robert E. Osgood, in his *Ideals and Self-Interest in America's Foreign Relations* (Chicago: University of Chicago Press, 1953), says (10) that "realism—with a small 'r'—is used in this book to refer to an accurate assessment of the ends and motives that determine the conduct of nations; it implies a disposition to perceive and act upon the real conditions under which a nation may achieve its ends in international society." See also J. W. Burton, *International Relations: A General Theory* (Cambridge: Cambridge University Press, 1965), 245. Critics, on the other hand, characterize it in equally uncomplimentary terms. Marxists, for example, represent it as functioning "to conceal by more subtle means than hitherto had been the case the threat to peace constituted by imperialism," and as "an apology for the use of violence as a means of halting socio-historical progress." See the study by Soviet philosophers *et al.*, *Problems of War and Peace: A Critical Analysis of Bourgeois Theories*, trans. Bryan Beau (Moscow: Progress, 1972), 191, 198.

to being an idealist. With one side having no voluntary defenders (at least as its position is defined by the other side), the issue between Idealism and Realism then becomes a pseudo-issue, useful perhaps in polemical disputes, but doing little to illuminate the problem of the place of morality in international affairs.

While it is tempting at times to scrap the notions of Idealism and Realism altogether as being hopelessly muddled, their use is so deeply embedded in foreign policy that it seems best to retain them, but to try to give them some useful meaning. This I shall try to do. Such a meaning, one which accords with much of the actual discussion of realism, and which highlights substantive issues of importance, can be arrived at by distinguishing four theses. Three of these concern national self-interest, the fourth, morality:

1. That "nations *in fact* always act from self-interest," may be taken as a purely factual claim, implying nothing about the possibility of altering the conduct of nations or about how nations ought to govern their affairs. It should thus be distinguished from
2. "Nations *necessarily* always act from self-interest," which can be taken in either a strong sense, in which the necessity is alleged to be of a conceptual or logical sort, determined, say, by the very meanings of such concepts as that of a nation or national conduct; or in a weak sense in which it is held that, perhaps because of the nature of man or the state of the world, it is virtually inevitable—though not logically necessitated—that nations pursue their own self-interest. Thesis (1), of course, does not imply (though it is implied by) (2) in either the latter's weak or its strong sense.

Thesis (1) I shall take to define *Descriptive Realism*, thesis (2) to define *Necessitarian Realism*. Both should be distinguished from what we may call *Normative Realism*, expressed by the claim that,

3. "Nations *ought* always to act from self-interest." On the assumption that there is some point to prescribing what one ought to do only if he is not already doing it, the normative realist will deny what the descriptive and necessitarian realists assert, and the necessitarian—and perhaps the descriptivist as well—will at least deny that there is any point to what the normative realist asserts. It makes sense, that is, to urge that nations act self-interestedly only if they do not already in fact do so, necessarily or not.

Whatever else is entailed by the various forms of Political Realism[4]—and there are many differences among them on such questions as the nature of power, the role of law in international affairs, and the nature of diplomacy—they are in agreement in denying the further thesis:

4. Nations *ought* always to govern their conduct by moral consideration.

---

[4] It should be stressed that I am not taking Descriptive, Necessitarian, and Normative Realism by themselves to be forms of *Political* Realism; though as I am characterizing the latter it will be either descriptive, necessitarian, or normative in the senses indicated. I am also taking self-interest broadly enough to include within it conceptions of national honor, self-realization, national aggrandizement, and the like, any of which may constitute the governing point of view in the determination of a nation's policies.

Indeed, I shall define Political Realism as the assertion of (1), (2), or (3) *and* the denial of (4). What we may call Political Idealism can then be defined, as the assertion of Political Idealism in this sense will obviously contrast with Normative Realism and, on the assumption that "ought" implies "can," with Necessitarian Realism; but it will be compatible with Descriptive Realism.

The denial of (4) may have varying strengths, however, and political realists theoretically fall into two camps according to which they intend. According to what I shall call *Positivistic Realism*, moral concepts simply do not apply to international affairs at all—any more than they do, say, to the phenomena of nature or the operation of machines.[5] On this view morality neither has nor can have any bearing upon the conduct of nations. Not that international violence is therefore morally justified; it is, rather, that it is neither justified nor unjustified; its justification, if it is to have one, must be found on nonmoral grounds, such as those of national interest.[6]

---

[5] Value concepts like good and bad do, of course, apply to the phenomena of nature; but notions like right, wrong, permissible, prohibited, blameworthy, and the like do not, other perhaps than in attenuated or metaphorical senses. Interestingly, according to what Anatol Rapoport calls "cataclysmic" philosophies of war, wars are indeed like fires, natural disasters, or epidemics; catastrophes which afflict mankind but for which no one is really blameworthy. See his excellent introduction to *Clausewitz on War* (New York: Penguin Books, 1968). Such a conception of war may be part of a broader historicist approach to history as a whole. There is a strain of this approach in the writings of realists like Niebuhr and Kennan. The latter, for example, says regarding World War I as a determinant of World War II, that "all the lines of inquiry, it seem to me, lead back to it [World War I]. World War II really seemed so extensively predetermined; it developed and rolled its course with the relentless logic of the last act of a classical tragedy." See Kennan, *American Diplomacy, 1900–1950* (New York: Mentor Books, 1951), 51. And the former attaches a near-cosmic significance to war as a "final revelation of the very character of human history," in "An Open Letter," in D. B. Robertson, ed., *Love and Justice: Selections from the Shorter Writings of Reinhard Niebuhr* (New York: World Publishing Company, 1967), 268.

[6] There are a number of grounds upon which Positivistic Realism might be held. The most extreme would be that which says that all moral discourse, hence moral discourse about international affairs, is simply meaningless. Less extreme views may distinguish between relations among individuals and relations among nations in such a way as to preserve morality in the one case but preclude it in the other. If, for example, it is held that morality comes into existence only through the institution of a state authority with power to make rules and enforce sanctions—as one finds in Machiavelli and Hobbes—then the absence of such a power over nations would entail that moral relations do not and cannot exist among nations. A similar view, but one which differs in that it appeals to social organization, rather than political power, is expressed, by John Dewey: "States are non-moral in their activities just because of the absence of an inclusive society which refines and establishes rights. . . . The actual fact is that until nations are bound together by the law of a social order, there cannot be any truly moral obligations existing among them"; in Joseph Ratner, ed., *Intelligence in the Modern World: John Dewey's Philosophy* (New York: The Modern Library, 1939), 508f. Still another path is to deny that the problem is simply one of the absence of certain conditions which could, but do not at present in fact obtain on the international scene (as is implied by the preceding lines), and to maintain instead that nations by their very nature are not the sorts of entities which can enter into moral relations under *any* circumstances. On this view, there would be no point to trying to institute morality among nations by means of international organizations which attempt to duplicate on the international scene the legalistic structures which obtain within societies. Moral judgments ostensibly about the conduct of nations would either be translatable into judgments about the conduct of individual persons—say, governmental leaders—or they would be devoid of literal meaning. Nonpositivistic realists like Niebuhr also regard as naive what they call the legalistic-moralistic attempt to institute the conditions of morality by means of international organizations. But rather than conclude, as the positivist does, that morality cannot apply to international affairs, they persist in making moral judgments about the conduct of nations to the effect that that conduct is irredeemably immoral.

According to *Nonpositivistic Realism*, on the other hand, which may take either descriptive or normative forms, moral considerations are applicable to the conduct of nations, but they either do not, or ought not to, have a decisive bearing upon the assessment of such conduct. This view itself, however, may assume one or the other of two forms. According to the stronger form (henceforth "hard Realism"), morality has (or should be given) no weight whatsoever in foreign affairs; it is a mode of assessment intelligibly applied to such affairs but best foregone as naive or downright dangerous. On the weaker version (henceforth "soft Realism")—which is the form taken by the theories we shall be discussing—morality has (or can be given) a place in international affairs, but only a secondary one, as a kind of embroidery to the claims of power politics;[7] finding its true value, in the words of the distinguished diplomat George Kennan—words perhaps more revelatory of the deeper springs of Political Realism than may have been intended—in the "unobtrusive, almost feminine function of the gentle civilizer of national self-interest."[8]

This denial of (4), however, places a burden upon the realist. For just as no one wants to be unrealistic, no one—or scarcely anyone—wants to be, or at any rate to admit to being, immoral, and the denial of (4) is prima facie immoral. This means that realists must make their case against (4) in such a way as to defeat that presumption. The focus of the following discussion will be a consideration of whether they have succeeded in doing this. Before turning to that, however, let me comment briefly upon two of the more obvious ways in which they might try to do this.

One way, of course, would be to take the necessitarian line and to argue that nations *cannot* act other than from self-interest, since if that could be established, one could scarcely urge that nations ought to act otherwise.[9] Such an argument might develop in various ways, such as by trying to produce a plausible conceptual analysis of the notion of a nation according to which it would be logically impossible for nations to act other than from self-interest; or by advancing theological or metaphysical claims, in the manner of Niebuhr, about the nature of man or the human condition, according to

---

[7] More specifically, of the two negations of (4), namely, (5) It is not the case that nations ought to govern their conduct by moral considerations and (6) Nations ought *not* to govern their conduct by moral considerations, the positivistic realist is asserting (5) and the non-positivist, at least of the normative variety, is asserting (6). It should be noted that (6) may be asserted on either moral or non-moral grounds. In the former case, it would amount to saying that, for moral reasons, moral considerations should be given no role, or at best a secondary role, in international affairs, and hence would not, strictly, be a form of Political Realism (since, to be intelligible, it would have to be taken, not to be denying (4) *simpliciter*, but only to be denying that "moral" considerations other than those pertaining to national interest should govern national conduct). Such a position, though at first blush paradoxical, is a consistent one, and one finds it suggested at least some of the time in Osgood's *Ideals and Self-Interest in America's Foreign Relations*.

[8] Kennan, *American Diplomacy, 1900–1950*, 80. The association of morality with feminine weakness and hard-headed "realism" with masculine virility runs through much of the writing on international relations; as though there were agreement with the nineteenth-century German historian, Heinrich von Treitschke that, "The features of history are virile, unsuited to sentimental or feminine natures"; *Politics*, ed., Hans Kohn (New York: Harcourt, Brace and World, 1963), 13. For a good study of this phenomenon, particularly in contemporary literature, see Lucy Komisar's "Violence and the Masculine Mystique," *Washington Monthly*, Vol. 2, No. 5, July 1970.

[9] Schlesinger shows some inclination in this direction when he says that "governments in their nature must make decisions on different principles from those of personal morality," where the implication is that, save for "questions of last resort, national interest should guide foreign policy"; National Interests and Moral Absolutes," in Ernest W. Lefever, ed., *Ethics and World Politics*, 26.

which it would be virtually (though not logically) impossible for them to act otherwise. A second tact, different altogether from the necessitarian line, would be to try to show that acting from moral considerations has, or tends to have, worse consequences than does acting from self-interest (or some other norm), a line taken by Kennan and Schlesinger. The latter, in particular, would require the substantiation of a range of historical, philosophical, and valuational judgments.

These two strands, the first primarily theoretical, the second historico-valuational, are often interwoven, but it is important to distinguish them and I shall do so in what follows. I shall discuss primarily the historico-valuational view and comment upon only one version of what I am calling "the theoretical approach," namely, the nonlogical necessitarian position which appeals to a theological conception of the nature of man.

Let us begin with the former, which we may call historical Realism.

Historical realism

This approach focuses upon America's foreign policy during the first half of the twentieth century and alleges that that policy bore near-disastrous fruits in the intervening years between World War I and World War II.[10]

The problem on this view has its roots in America's history of isolationism. It reached a critical point with the country's flirtation with imperialism in its seizure of the Philippines during the Spanish-American War. For the country then discovered a distaste for this departure from its traditional stance and as a result turned its "back on the beckoning role of world power." Whereas the older European nations were perceived as war-prone, beset with corruption, and committed to an immoral balance of power system of international politics, America thought of itself as principled and righteous. Equally as important, it thought of itself as secure. The young Lincoln had proclaimed that "all the citizens of Europe, Asia, and Africa combined . . . could not by force take a drink from the Ohio or make a track on the Blue Ridge in a trial of a thousand years."[11] If this was a piece of youthful hyperbole, it nonetheless reflected a deeply rooted sense of geographical security. Seeing no reason, from such a vantage point, why it should become entangled in the petty quarrels of others, America elected to stand alone in majestic isolation: proud, strong, and unconquerable.

If Lincoln epitomized the complacency in this outlook, it was Woodrow Wilson who brought the idealistic strain to its highest pitch. It was his conviction that it had fallen to America to play a unique moral role in community of nations. That role was one of conciliator and peacemaker, a role, he thought, which only a nation which stood apart from the travails of conflict could perform. It was this conviction, and the sense of moral superiority it reflected, which provided the stuff of America's resolve to

---

[10]   Osgood gives the most sustained analysis of this line of argument, and I shall rely heavily upon his account in what follows. I shall, however, attempt to capture the spirit of this general approach rather than to represent in full the views of any one writer.

[11]   Quoted, from "Abraham Lincoln on the Challenge of Violence," in *American Violence,* ed. Richard Maxwell Brown (Englewood Cliffs, NJ: Prentice-Hall, 1970), 8.

stay out of war. That resolve was eventually washed away, of course, by the turbulent waters of World War I. But the foundation upon which it was based remained intact, and when the country did go to war it did so for reasons every bit as elevated, and in keeping with this conception of America's high calling in the world, as those which previously had dictated neutrality. It went to war—as we are now so often cynically reminded—to save Democracy and end all wars.

This Wilsonian idealism, the realists contend, distorted our perspective on our proper role in the world and misled us as to where our true interests lay. It not only obscured the fact that those interests should be at the heart of foreign policy, but also delayed America's awakening to the fact that the protection and advancement of those interests may require taking up the sword even when our own security is not directly threatened.[12] This signified a willingness to become involved in overseas wars. Wilson's mistake on this view was not to have involved us in a foreign war but, in Osgood's words, to have failed to "prepare the people to see their entrance into a foreign war as an act consistent with imperative principles of national self-interest, as well as with national ideals and sentiments."[13] In other words, we fought the right war under Wilson but for the wrong reasons.

Wilsonianism also allegedly affected adversely both the prosecution of the war and the postwar evolution of American foreign policy.

Kennan, for example, argues that the war threatened the European balance of power upon which our own security as well as that of the European nations depended,[14] and for that reason needed to be ended quickly, without thought of total victory. But it was precisely, he says, because considerations of power balance "argued against total

[12] America had, of course, long been interventionist within its own hemisphere. Realists tend to ignore the extent to which Wilson was "realistic" in much of his foreign policy, as in the invasion of Haiti and the Dominican Republic.

[13] Osgood, *Ideals and Self-Interest in America's Foreign Relations*, 262. Osgood also says that Americans were not wrong in their idealism, but rather that they "failed from the first to guide and restrain their aspirations and sentiments with a realistic view of national conduct and a prudent recognition for the practical consequences of specific policies," which suggests that from a theoretical standpoint it was peripheral matters that were at fault and not idealism itself. This interpretation, however, conflicts with the main emphasis of his argument, which is that "as long as men owe their supreme loyalty to nation-states, nations ought to act upon idealistic ends only in so far as they are compatible with the most fundamental ends of national self-interest," (21) and it is the latter which I shall stress. Notice, in any event, that the sentiments of the American people have pretty consistently been opposed to war. It is usually only after their leadership has involved them in war that they have—if then—come to support it wholeheartedly. Realists give insufficient attention to the fact that the attitude with which they would have us go to war—namely, a cool, dispassionate willingness to kill for limited objectives—is one which Americans have refused to adopt. Even the military have sometimes been reluctant to accept it, often, like Clausewitz, finding it incomprehensible why anyone should wage war without doing so to win. If one is concerned about the "realities" of international affairs, this suggests that the hope of gaining widespread acceptance of a political realist outlook in the country may be unrealistic.

[14] Wilson did, of course, disagree with this assessment. As he said before the Senate on January 22, 1917: "If [the present war] be only a struggle for a new balance of power, who will guarantee, who can guarantee the stable equilibrium of the new arrangement? Only a tranquil Europe can be a stable Europe. There must be, not a balance of power, but a community of power; not organized rivalries, but an organized common peace." Here he put his finger upon what has been and is the key problem with balance of power theories, namely that they presuppose what almost never exists on the international scene, at least for any extended time: a stable system of relations among nations. This conclusion has been persuasively argued by Partha Chatterjee, "The Classical Balance of Power Theory," *Journal of Peace Research*, Vol. 1, 1972, 51–61.

victory" that people "rejected them so emphatically and sought more sweeping and grandiose objectives, for the accomplishment of which total victory could plausibly be represented as absolutely essential."

It was thus that "a line of thought grew up, under Wilson's leadership, which provided both rationale and objective for our part in fighting the War to a bitter end."[15] When the cause is great and the enemy is perceived as the incarnation of evil, there is no stopping short of his total destruction, or at least unconditional surrender. To settle for less is to compromise with evil.

It was such thinking as this which allegedly bred the righteous intransigence which prolonged World War I to the point where the essential balance of power in Europe was destroyed and the seeds of World War II sown.

Further contributing to these longer-range consequences was the postwar disillusionment with the war and America's role in it. The lofty ideals in whose name the war was fought were incapable of fulfillment, and the resultant disappointment—nourished as it was by revisionist historical analyses reallocating responsibility for the war—led to an even greater withdrawal of America from world affairs. "Since war could only be justified by exalted goals," as Osgood puts it, "and since this war had failed to achieve exalted goals, it seemed to follow that all war is useless."[16] America's consequent reluctance to become involved in another war, the realists felt, emboldened Nazism and Japanese militarism at a time when greater firmness might have forestalled World War II.

Thus, whether American foreign policy during the crucial decades of the twentieth century quite verged on the commission of national suicide, as Osgood maintains,[17] or whether the policies of Christian isolationists were tantamount to "connivance" with tyranny, as Niebuhr contends,[18] both were, in the view of the realists, at best seriously wrongheaded, and the moralism from which they were believed to have sprung itself came to be looked upon as a cause of war.

Reinhold Niebuhr's realism

Supervening upon, and helping to explain accounts like the preceding, is the more conspicuously theory-laden approach of Reinhold Niebuhr, whom Kennan, acknowledging the former's influence, has called "the father of us all."[19]

[15] Kennan, *American Diplomacy, 1900–1950*, 60. Kennan does, however, clear Wilson of responsibility for actually holding this view prior to early 1917. Ibid., n. 6. Indeed Wilson himself, in that same Senate speech of 1917 (see n. 14 above) said prophetically that "*Victory would mean peace forced upon the loser, a victor's term imposed upon the vanquished. It would be accepted in humiliation, under duress, at an intolerable sacrifice, and would leave a sting, a resentment, a bitter memory upon which terms of peace would rest, not permanently, but only as upon quicksand.*"
[16] Osgood, *Limited War: The Challenge to American Strategy* (Chicago: University of Chicago Press, 1957), 99.
[17] Osgood, *Ideals and Self-Interest in America's Foreign Relations*, 430.
[18] Niebuhr, "To Prevent the Triumph of an Intolerable Tyranny," in D. B. Robertson, ed., *Love and Justice: Selections from the Shorter Writings of Reinhold Niebuhr*, 278.
[19] Quoted in Kenneth W. Thompson, *Political Realism and the Crisis of World Politics* (New York: John Wiley & Sons, 1968), 23. Not that the preceding was subscribed to in all of its particular by Niebuhr,

Niebuhr's analysis keys upon the very nature of collectivities and the theological and metaphysical foundations of the processes of history at work in their development and interaction. While not as clear at all points as it might be, his position is best characterized as a qualified non-logical necessitarianism. Its central contention is that group relations inevitably express a collective egoism and hence "can never be as ethical as these which characterize individual relations."[20] This is an inherent feature of the very nature of collectivities, one which severely limits the moral possibilities in their conduct. It is this fact which gives social and international relations their distinctive character by rendering nations incapable of responding to moral considerations, or of responding in more than a limited way.[21] Statesmen, as well as social reformers who must contend with the same phenomenon in their dealings with society and intra-societal groups, must reconcile themselves to this circumstance.

But this collective egoism itself calls for explanation, and the explanation for Niebuhr is to be found in the theologico-metaphysical orientation of neo-orthodox Christianity; specifically in the "stubbornness of sin in all men," an allegedly unalterable fact of the human condition whose ramifications are magnified at the international level. Failure to perceive this is the chief error, on his view, of those "modern moralists"[22] who assume that "with a little more time, a little more adequate moral and social pedagogy

or that other realists subscribe to all of Niebuhr's account; it is rather that the Niebuhrian analysis sustains the essentials of the analyses of other soft realists and yields a similar conclusion about the role of morality in international relations.

20   Niebuhr, *Moral Man and Immoral Society* (New York: Charles Scribner's Sons, 1932), 83. Although Niebuhr sometimes seems to embrace a nearly iron-clad necessitarianism about the role of self-interest in group relations, he more often says, as above, that group relations cannot not be *as* ethical as interpersonal relations. It is this which qualifies his necessitarianism by suggesting the possibility (in principle) of a least a partial transcendence of collective self-interest. This means that Niebuhr is basically a nonpositivist and a soft realist, in that he does not rule out altogether a role for morality in international relations. One suspects that he regards morality in international affairs in much the same light as he does Christian love in interpersonal affairs as an "impossible ideal" to be striven for but realistically understood to be unattainable. See his *An Interpretation of Christian Ethics* (New York: Meridian Books, 1956).

21   It is the possibility that nations can to a limited extent act morally which qualifies Niebuhr's necessitarianism. Although it sometimes sounds as though he believes that nations cannot transcend self-interest at all, he more often speaks as though their ability to do so is only more restricted, than that of individual persons. It should be noted, however, that this claim conflicts with much of the analysis realists give of World War I (and in some cases World War II and Vietnam as well). For in that analysis it is often contended that the United States *was* acting on moral considerations in those cases; but naively so and to its own detriment. One cannot have it both ways, of course. If nations cannot rise above self-interest and respond to moral considerations, then whatever the proper analysis of America's foreign policy through the first half of the 20th century, the problem with that policy cannot be that it was guided by morality. It cannot even be, as Niebuhr maintains, that the country was acting hypocritically—which implies that it could have acted morally but instead merely sought the appearance of doing so.

22   Like Dewey whom he is fond of chiding. Dewey did, however, recognize a darker side to human nature, saying that "The old Adam, the unregenerate element in human nature, persists. It shows itself wherever the method obtains of attaining results by use of force instead of by method of communication and enlightenment"; *The Public and Its Problems* (Denver: Alan Swallow, 1927), 154. And Dewey, too, deplored naive optimism in social and international affairs, but he traced it to "our traditional evangelical trust . . . in morals apart from intelligence." See Joseph Ratner, ed., *Intelligence in the Modern World: John Dewey's Philosophy*, 497. For more recent challenge to optimism in social matters, see Stuart Hampshire, *Morality and Pessimism* (Cambridge: Cambridge University Press, 1927).

and a generally higher development of human intelligence, our social problems will approach solution"; a view, he contends, which goes back to our culture's "romantic overestimate of human virtue and moral capacity." [23]

In this way the problem is tied first to self-interest, then to sin, and finally to the whole traditional Christian outlook upon the world. When men have lost the fear of God and the conviction that we are all sinners survives mainly in tepid Sunday morning generalities, new life is injected into that outlook by shifting its focus from individuals to collectivities. "Thus," Niebuhr says, "the international situation is a perfect picture of human finitude and a tragic revelation of the consequences of sinful dishonesty which accompany every effort to transcend it."[24] The upshot is a profound pessimism, not only about human goodness but also about the power of human resources, even when governed by the best of intentions, to redress the world's evils.

This refrain is a common one, and one finds wholesale indictments of human nature repeatedly advanced as explanations of the world's problems. It was in this spirit that Kennan took to task the antiwar youth of the 1960s for failing to see that "the decisive seat of evil in this world is not in social and political institutions, and not even, as a rule, in the will or iniquities of statesmen, but simply in the weakness and imperfection of the human soul itself, and by that I mean literally every soul."[25] And it is in this spirit that secularized versions of this approach explain war and violence by appeal to innate aggression, will to power, or a territorial instinct[26]—notions which have more respectable ring than sin and corruption to those who aspire to a political or naturalistic science of such matters, but which make it no less difficult to avoid an equally gloomy assessment of social and international affairs.

It is difficult even to know what to make of such sweeping claims as that the whole of human nature is corrupt, "literally every soul" flawed. We understand easily enough what it is for this or that individual to be evil. But in that sense it is patently false that everyone is evil; indeed, it is precisely because our expectations regarding the conduct of the occasional person *contrast* so sharply with those we have regarding the conduct of others that such an assessment is intelligible; remove those differentiating conditions and the clear cases at the heart of our understanding of good and evil disappear. And if one tried to preserve the clear cases, but at the same time to include everyone in the indictment, the effect is to so dilute the general claim as to make it acceptable to anyone who holds the opposite; who holds, that is, that human nature is basically good, or that such issues simply cannot be substantiated one way or the other. For then the evidence for the general claim is reduced to little more than such considerations as that we all sometimes make mistakes, sometimes yield to temptation, sometimes do wrong, and sometimes are basely motivated; incontrovertible facts which no one ever thought of denying and only those determined to think the worst of human nature could suppose

[23]   Niebuhr, Introduction to *Moral Man and Immoral Society*, xiii. See also his *The Nature and Destiny of Man* (New York: Charles Scribner's Sons, 1949), 94f and 100.

[24]   Niebuhr, *An Interpretation of Christian Ethics*, 119.

[25]   Kennan, *Democracy and the Student Left* (New York: Bantam Books, 1968), 8f.

[26]   See, for example, Konrad Lorenz, *Human Aggression* (New York: Harcourt, Brace & World, 1963); Hans Morgentahu, *Politics among Nations* (New York: Alfred K. Knopf, 1949), Chapter 8; and Robert Ardrey, *African Genesis: A Personal Investigation into the Animal Origins and Nature of Man* (New York: Delta, 1961), esp. Chapter 6.

indicated corruption. Hannah Arendt has said of guilt, in another connection, that when everyone is guilty no one is guilty. Much the same is true of sin and corruption; spread them thinly enough and they evaporate.

Were Realism to go no further than this it would take its place among the tired rationalizations of the status quo in social and political affairs. For if man is so thoroughly evil that he cannot consistently do good, and if societies and collectivities are by their nature inherently immoral, then there is, indeed, little point to trying to change things in essential respects. One might as well, in that case, resign himself to the way things are and indulge in pious lamentations about the tragedy of it all. By the status quo, however, I do not mean those relatively inconsequential points of detail in a given social state of affairs which are the focus of debates between liberals and conservatives; the status quo in that sense is in almost constant flux and varies with the fortunes of those in power. For I do not mean the particular configurations of alliances on the international scene at any given point in history, since Realism is no more committed to the status quo in that sense than is any other theory. I mean rather the more deeply engrained attitudes toward man, society, and institutions which persist throughout such changes and are usually shared by all sides to the typical political debates; attitudes which accept the use of coercion, force, and violence as the established means of getting along in the world, and regard the suffering and injustice they entail as an acceptable cost. One can scarcely do less than accept these attitudes if his estimate of man is low enough. For this outlook standardizes the response to problems and, by virtually defining the range of thinkable options, devitalizes any impulse to new and creative thinking. In so doing it so diminishes the quality of human life and the prospects of a better future that acquiescence to it should come, if at all, only under the weight of the most compelling of intellectual reasons. Such reasons the articles of faith of Christianity—or any other religion, for that matter—are not.[27] Nor, without vastly more substantiation, are those pseudo-scientific accounts of human nature which reiterate tiresomely—with the profundity of cocktail-party wisdom—that before you can change the world you must change man.

Hypostatic Realism

But although Realism does sometimes go no further than this, there is another, potentially more challenging strain to be found within it. Interestingly, it is also found in Niebuhr, though it is relatively undeveloped there and conflicts with the line of reasoning we have just been considering.

The latter reasoning holds that the evil of collectivities is incompatible with the supposition that individual men are good. "No school asks," Niebuhr wrote in *The Children of Light and the Children of Darkness*, "how it is that an essentially good man

---

[27]   Unless we assume in advance the theologico-metaphysical outlook of Christianity, in which case the alleged evil is not an antecedent datum to be explained but a conclusion which follows from the acceptance of that outlook.

could have produced corrupting and tyrannical political organizations or exploiting economic organizations, or fanatical and superstitious religious organizations."[28] The intended point is, of course, that there is no answer to this question. But he himself had already given an answer in *Moral Man and Immoral Society*. He wrote there, in one of his most insightful passages, that,

> There is an ethical paradox in patriotism which defies every but the most astute and sophisticated analysis. The paradox is that patriotism transmutes individual unselfishness into national egoism. Loyalty to the nation is a high form of altruism when compared with lesser loyalties and more parochial interests. It therefore becomes the vehicle of all the altruistic impulses and expresses itself, on occasion, with such fervor that the critical attitudes of the individual toward the nation and its enterprises is almost completely destroyed. *The unqualified character of devotion is the very basis of the nation's power and of the freedom to use the power without moral restraint. Thus the unselfishness of individuals makes for the selfishness of nations.*[29]

Here it is the basically good, unselfish, self-sacrificing qualities of individual persons—not their egoism or sinfulness—which is held to be the source of the immorality of groups.[30] And it is this which creates the conflict with the other line in Niebuhr's thought. For if man exhibits intrinsically commendable traits to the degree required by this theory, one can no longer credibly maintain—in anything like the sense found in Niebuhr and traditional Christianity—a doctrine of the inherent corruption of each and every individual soul.

The particulars of this "transmutation" of altruism into collective egoism are not detailed for us by Niebuhr.[31] But at least the rudiments of a theory of how it comes about have been given by others. Osgood, among realists, gives one of the more plausible accounts. He writes that,

> A citizen's dependence upon his nation assumes a distinct intimacy because he confers upon the object of his allegiance the attributes of a person so closely identified with his own personality that he virtually acquires a second self, in whose behalf he can feel friendly, hostile, generous, selfish, confident, afraid, proud, or

---

28   Niebuhr, *The Children of Light and the Children of Darkness* (New York: Charles Scribner's Sons, 1944), 17.
29   *Moral Man and Immoral Society*, 91; italics added. See also *An Interpretation of Christian Ethics*, 107.
30   Carried to one of its conclusions, this line of reasoning argues for the perpetuation of war precisely in order to foster these traits. See, for example, Benito Mussolini, "The Doctrine of Fascism," in J. Somerville and R. E. Santori, ed., *Social and Political Philosophy* (Garden City, NJ: Doubleday, 1963), 424–41. Niebuhr is at times attracted by other beneficial effects of war. He wrote during World War II, for Robertson, ed., *Love and Justice: Selections from the Shorter Writings of Reinhold Niebuhr*, that "only the chastisement of a fairly long war can prompt a really thoroughgoing repentance and conversion from those sins of the democratic world which helped to produce the Nazi revolt against our civilization. We were much too soft and fat, much too heedless and indifferent to the ultimate issues of life to be changed by the only casual chastisements of brief belligerency" (81). He also saw increased international cooperation and a reduction of the "inequalities of our economic system" as by-products of the war.
31   He does, however, offer an historical account of how the "deification" of the nation is outgrowth of romanticism. See Niebuhr, *The Nature and Destiny of Man*, 83.

humiliated almost as poignantly as he would feel these emotions for himself in his relations with other individuals.[32]

Much of this rings true psychologically, and there is supporting testimony for the essentials of this account from other sources, including Koestler, Lorenz, Frank, Dewey, and Tolstoy. Indeed, this account is in keeping with the insight—far profounder, in my judgment, than appeals to original sin or corrupt human nature—that the source of the world's greatest evils lies less in the works of evil men than in the works of basically good people whose efforts go awry through ignorance, misunderstanding, misplaced loyalties, and too much rather than too little willingness to sacrifice themselves, both for the sake of others and at the behest of others, particularly those who govern them. As Plato said, "evil is a worse enemy to the good than to the indifferent."

But if this account is correct in its essentials, as I believe it is, it means that the alleged inevitability of egoism in international affairs, and the structural commitment to violence which it entails, rests upon an illusion, a collective self-deception about the nature of the nation or state. For neither the nation nor the state are, *in fact*, super-personalities or even remotely like them. They do not have feelings, thoughts, aims, or interests independently of those projected into them by individual persons. Nor, as imaginatively personified super-beings, are they fitting objects of devotion, much less of the sacrifice of a single human life. Only individual persons feel and suffer, live and die, and only their survival or extinction and the quality of their lives can be of ultimate moral concern.[33] To think otherwise is to generate myth from metaphor. It is to mistake that convenience of language by which we speak of nations as deciding, choosing, acting, as though they were rational super-beings, for a literal reflection of reality; "as sheer a case of animism," Dewey once wrote of this outlook, "as is found in the records of any savage tribe."[34] It is worst of all to populate the world of international politics with functional equivalents of the Homeric gods and to seed that world with all the deceit, cruelty, and violence to which theirs was prey.

I shall call realist theories which hold that the state or nation is super-personality, or should be regarded as though it were one, forms of hypostatic Realism.[35] What is disturbing about such theories is not the importance they attach to the phenomenon to which Niebuhr and Osgood call attention, but rather their recommendation concerning what we should do about it. For they do not urge that we disabuse ourselves of such illusions and put an end to the trail of tragedy they have left through modern history.

---

[32] Osgood, *Ideals and Self-Interest in America's Foreign Relations*, 11. Another line is suggested by Walt W. Rostow, who says that "The same religious and philosophical beliefs which decree that we respect that uniqueness of each individual, make it natural that we respect the uniqueness of each national society"; "Countering Guerrilla Attack," in Richard A. Falk, ed., *The Vietnam War and International Law* (Princeton, NJ: Princeton University Press, 1968), 129.

[33] I do not mean here that well-being of non-humans, like animals, is not of legitimate moral concern, perhaps equally so with that of humans; but rather the well-being of "collective persons" like the nation or the states is in itself of no moral concern, because the latter entities are mere fictions. Such claims, rights, privileges, and so forth as they seem to have from a moral standpoint are either translatable into those of individual persons or they are non-existent.

[34] Ratner, ed., *Intelligence in the Modern World: John Dewey's Philosophy*, 471.

[35] Such Realism has a kinship with metaphysical idealism, which conceives of mind or consciousness as embodied in a nation, an age, or the universe at large.

They urge, in effect, that we reconcile ourselves to their predominance of the collective egoism which they generate and the inevitability of war which that entails; that we regard statesmen as duty-bound to promote the interests of what realists themselves concede is a fiction; that we leave forever in the hands of a few—men of like minds unto themselves, who have access always to undisclosed "facts" to license them—the life and death decisions affecting whole populations; and that we dismiss as romantically idealistic the hope that we can never change all this and put an end to war. All in the name of Realism.

The concession to ignorance and deception in this outlook is so great, in my judgment, as to deprive it of any serious claim upon our conviction. If realists believe that the state is indeed a super-personality, we should see their arguments for such a dubious metaphysics. If they do not, but believe that others should be encouraged in that illusion, we should see their arguments for such a dubious normative conclusion.[36] As it is, one cannot but feel that as great a danger to mankind as the collective egoism they descry is the collective self-deception they foster.

Principles and consequences

It should be stressed that historical Realism, as interwoven with the theologico-metaphysical view (including hypostatic Realism) as it often is, does not require that account and stands or falls by itself. And it is far the more compelling of the versions we are considering, and for that reason warrants closer examination.

Its central contention, we recall, is that the dominance of moral ideals on international relations has had (or does or would have) bad consequences, and this contention is assessable independently of the foundation which the Niebuhrian approach provides for it. For it is basically an evaluative contention. It raises principally two questions: first, whether the realist's representation of the Wilsonianism can properly be charged with responsibility for the consequences alleged by the realists. There is, of course, the further question of whether the consequences in question were (are, or would be) as bad as the realists content, but I shall not deal with that here.

Although I believe that the realist's interpretation of Wilsonianism is a challengeable one, I shall leave that matter to the historians and confine myself primarily to the second question. For I do want to challenge the standard indictment of Wilsonianism.

---

[36] Perhaps the best argument in this vein—and one which must be taken seriously, though there is no space to deal with it here—is that given by Osgood, who maintains that the identification of the individual with the state is so strong that his very happiness is tied up with the latter's fortunes (*Ideals and Self-Interest in America's Foreign Relations*, 12). This gives Hypostatic Realism ultimately a utilitarian rationale. In this respect it contrasts with the rationale given by German writers like Treitschke, whose justification proceeds upwards, so to speak, assigning a genuine metaphysical being to the State. Osgood's proceeds downwards, to the happiness of individual persons. *If* any such justification can be made convincing, it must follow generally the latter rather than the former course. Such an approach suggests the paradoxical position alluded to earlier (n. 7 above), in which a moral argument is given for ruling morality out of international affairs and basing the conduct of those affairs upon national self-interest.

That indictment, we recall, charges that Wilsonianism consisted of self-righteous moralism and did not prepare the American people adequately for entry into war; that once into war it was uncompromising in its determination to settle for nothing less than total victory; and that after the war it left the country adrift on the seas of isolationism at a time when it should have been steering boldly the course of national self-interest.

It is arguable that Wilson's error was not to have failed to steep the American people in the attitude of national self-interest before leading them into war, but rather to have departed from the principles which prescribed to stay out of war in the first place. For if the events during and after World War I which the realist perceives as consequences of Wilsonianism were indeed near-disastrous, it was certainly no less a condition of their occurrence that the United States entered the war than that it did so from a particular set of motives. Had Wilsonian idealism and its conviction about the importance of neutrality prevailed, *those* "consequences" would not have taken place. Whether equally bad ones would have taken place instead is a matter of conjecture; but it cannot simply be assumed that they would have. It may well be that far better than either the course which history in fact took, or the one which it would have taken had we entered the war sooner and from the motive of self-interest, is that which it would have taken had we stayed out of the war altogether, as Wilson originally intended, and as the overwhelming majority of the American people desired. The comparative assessment of these counter-factual sequences of events would be difficult, of course, and beyond a certain point largely speculative; but the realists cannot be conceded their assessments in the absence of such an undertaking, and in the absence of some plausible reason to suppose that it would support the particular historical and evaluative judgments essential to their analyses.

In short, it may well be that the failure lay not with Wilsonianism but with Wilson the man; and not with the principles but with the policies.[37] And it may have consisted less in the fact that he held the moral perspective that he did, and tried to keep the country out of war, than in the fact that, rather than adhere to his own original convictions, he eventually yielded to the course which his critics advocated.

This distinction between Wilson the man and Wilsonianism as a moral perspective on international affairs highlights the further point that, even if we grant the realist his assessment of the preceding alternatives, and his contention that it was Wilson's attitudes and not the waging of the war itself which led to World War II, the further conclusion does not follow that morality should be discounted in foreign affairs. To suppose that it does is to misconstrue the nature of morality. For there is nothing to make the attitudes of intransigence and self-righteousness which the realist attributes to Wilson any more

---

[37] Wilson's critics urged entry into the war often from precisely the moralistic point of view which the realists decry, claiming that it was "supreme battle between right and wrong." See Arthur S. Link, *Wilson: The Struggle for Neutrality 1914–1915* (Princeton, NJ: Princeton University Press, 1960), 13. And Wilson by 1915 shifted his emphasis from the broad moral one of humanitarian considerations to the narrower one of American rights on the seas. It is hard to see why this shift does not accord with the point of view urged by the realists.

closely tied to morality than to any other normative perspective.[38] Men can be, and are, as inflexible, dogmatic, and arrogant about national interest as about morality; or about interventionism as about isolationism; just as they can be as clear-headed, objective, and unemotional about the one as about the other.[39] Neither these virtues nor these defects are the special province of the moralist. To claim for Political Realism all and only of what is commendable among the attitudes which may attend, the holding of a normative point of view, and to lump together under the heading of Idealism all that is uncommendable, is to stack the cards against the idealist in advance.

There is, finally, a still more serious confusion here. It is the supposition that morality is a matter of principle to the exclusion of consequences, a blind pursuit of righteousness to the disregard of facts.[40] It seems to be such a conception that Osgood has in mind when he indicates that a fitting motto for America's attitude toward its involvement in World War I would have been the dictum: "Fear not the consequences when you know you are right."[41] But whether or not this accurately represents the Wilsonian position at that time, it does not accurately reflect anything about the nature of morality or the moral point of view. For while it is true that one *can* subscribe to principles in such a rigid and uncompromising way as this suggests, one need not do so, and if he does do so the principles can as easily be non-moral ones as moral. One can follow any principle to the exclusion of consequences (with the exception, to be noted below, of consequentialist principles themselves), and people do so with respect to moral principles probably no more than with respect to any other principles.

Even the contrast between principles and consequences is misleading from the outset. Those, like utilitarians, who stress consequences in ethics do not do so in *lieu* of subscribing to principle, but rather in accordance with a principle, namely, that one should maximize value in the consequences of his actions. What distinguishes them from the deontologist is not that the latter subscribes to a principle and they do not, but that they subscribe to a principle which prescribes

---

[38] One suspects that the realists have confused moralism, in the pejorative sense, with morality, and having thought that they perceived the one, rejected the other. Ernest W. Lefever, by taking account of this distinction, is a notable exception in his "Morality versus Moralism in Foreign Policy," in Ernest W. Lefever, ed., *Ethics and World Politics*, 1–20. See also K. W. Thompson, *Political Realism and the Crisis of World Politics*, 140.

[39] It was, interestingly, precisely the calm, even-handed, accommodating spirit of neutrality in the years 1914–15 which Wilson's critics so deplored in him. The Wilson of 1915, coolly going about his usual golf game after the sinking of the Lusitania to avoid even the appearance of being swept away on the tide of high emotion, contrasts with the near hysterical cries for action by some of his critics.

[40] Also in this spirit Henry A. Kissinger says that "moral claims involve a quest for absolutes, a denial of nuance, a rejection of history"; *A World Restored* (London: Weidenfeld & Nicolson, 1957), 316.

[41] Osgood, *Ideals and Self-Interest in America's Foreign Relations*, 261. This dictum is ambiguous, of course. It may mean, as Osgood seems to take it, that what is right can be ascertained independently of consequences. But it may also mean that once a determination of rightness has been made—where this may involve giving due regard to consequences—one should then have the courage to proceed, whatever the actual outcome. In any event, notice what the realist Niebuhr said: "Nazi tyranny had to be defeated. There are certain crises of evil in history in which we are forced to move against a threatening evil without too much regard for the ultimate consequences"; "The Possibility of a Durable Peace," D. B. Robertson, ed., *Love and Justice: Selections from the Shorter Writings of Reinhold Niebuhr*, 196.

the performance of *one type* of act exclusively (namely, those which are conducive to goodness) and he does not. When the deontologist does subscribe to rules or principles—and he need not do so, though many do, and rule-following is often associated with deontologism—he typically holds that there are many different properties of acts which bring them within the scope of moral rules, among them being the extrinsic property of being conducive to goodness, but also among them being purely intrinsic properties like that of being an instance of promise-keeping; properties whose verification requires no reference to consequences. In short, the deontologist is a pluralist with respect to the kinds of morally relevant property whereas the utilitarian is a monist. But both may equally subscribe to principle (in fact, it may well be that deontological theories are the only ones which can *dispense* with principles, since it is difficult to see how a consequentialist theory could even be stated other than in terms of a principle).

What those who contrast principle with consequences seem actually to have in mind is the distinction between the commitment to one *kind* of principle, that which involves no appeal to consequences, and the commitment to another kind, namely, that which makes express reference to consequences. While this is a legitimate and important distinction (though not the one which coincides with the distinction between teleologists and deontologists), it is misleadingly represented as a distinction between "principles" and "consequences." And there is no more reason to associate advocates of morality in international relations with one of these conceptions than with the other.

These considerations would scarcely warrant mention were they not so commonly ignored. What they indicate is that one cannot extract the conclusions of either hard or soft Realism from the imputation to morality of an exclusive concern with principle to the exclusion of consequences, or by equating morality with moralism and discrediting the latter. One suspects that the historical realists have simply disagreed so strongly with the particular normative judgments of Wilsonianism—judgments which Kennan apparently thinks represented the "nonsensical timidities of technical neutrality"[42]—that rather than merely reject the judgments themselves they have rejected the whole perspective from which they issued; thrown out the moral baby with the moralistic bathwater. Their mistake has not been chiefly an historical one—though as I have indicated their accounts are challengeable on that score—but a philosophical one, a failure to appreciate what the whole concept of morality is all about.

This does not mean that it is not *possible* that to adopt a moral point of view in the conduct of foreign policy would have bad, or even disastrous, consequences. What it does mean, if I am correct, is that this has not been shown to be the case, and that this conclusion derives little support from that particular frame of history to which realists have so often appealed. This in turn means that neither of the approaches we have been examining succeeds in making the case against thesis (4), that nations should govern their conduct by moral considerations.

---

[42] Kennan, *American Diplomacy, 1900–1950*, 63.

Realism and U.S. foreign policy

What bearing, finally, does this assessment have upon more recent developments in American foreign policy?

To answer this in full would require a detailed examination of the works of the neo-realists, as well as an appraisal of America's foreign affairs since World War II, and there is no space for that here. But I do want to suggest that if one looks at some of the specific prescriptions of political realists, it is clear that the drift of U.S. foreign policy in the post World War II era has been decidedly in the direction indicated by them, and in the instance of Vietnam seems to have been tailor-made to their specifications. If this is correct, it means that recent history provides some compelling evidence of the fruits of following such a philosophy.

Consider, in this connection, the following statement by Osgood, in which he describes approvingly the course on which the country embarked soon after World War II:

> The astounding growth of America's willingness to take an active part in world politics, the amazing speed with which Americans have junked old concepts of neutrality and readily entangled their affairs in political and military arrangements with other nations, deliberately adopting extensive world-wide commitments unthinkable a short while ago; these developments reflect a widespread recognition of the exigencies of survival. They may also signify the emergence of a more stable and effective foreign policy.[43]

This, he maintained, represented a maturing of the American people, in "which they gradually adapted their conduct of foreign relations to the realities of international society."[44] It was stressed that in order to achieve the aims of that more effective policy, liberal idealists and international reformers would

> be forced to put the exigencies of power politics ahead of their moral sensibilities. Similarly, if they want to pursue their ideals effectively, they must base American aid to foreign peoples primarily upon the power advantage of the United States and only secondarily upon humanitarian considerations. They must, at times, support reactionary and anti-democratic regimes with arms and money. They must even put themselves in the position of resisting with force the misguided proponents of a social revolution, which arises, in large part, from basic human aspirations which the American mission itself claims to fulfill.[45]

---

[43] Osgood, *Ideals and Self-Interest in America's Foreign Relations*, 432.

[44] Ibid., 431.

[45] Ibid., 438. Notice that Osgood speaks here of what America must do in order to pursue its ideals effectively, as though perhaps ideals were to supersede self-interest. This indicates ambivalence in his thought—characteristic of many soft realists—between the desire to affirm the paramountcy of national interest and a reluctance to part altogether with morality. The result is sometimes one of trying to have it both ways, but it is more often one of subordinating morality to national interest. Thus while Osgood contends that, "the calculation of national advantage without regard for the interrelation of ideals and self-interest is not only immoral as a national end but unrealistic as a means to an end" (442), he also says that "If the United States is to have a stable and effective foreign policy, neither egoism nor altruism must interfere with the rational, objective assessment of the real long-run conditions of American self-interest" (441).

It is hard to see that much was lacking in the implementation of these guidelines in the Cold War era. The United States supported reactionary governments in Spain, Portugal, and Latin America; based aid upon considerations of advantage to itself in Greece and South Africa; and fought against "misguided" revolutionaries in Vietnam and the Dominican Republic. And in both Korea and Vietnam it fought the limited wars which realists would have our wars be, wars in which unconditional surrender was never an objective, and in which—despite excesses, particularly in Vietnam—major constraints in design and execution were continually in operation. And Vietnam, at any rate, was a war directed for the most part by dispassionate efficiency experts making calculated use of the best of modern technology and military science; precisely the opposite of the moralistic crusade which some realists tried to paint it as being once its failure was manifest.[46] And it was a war rationalized by an entangling alliance (SEATO), waged about as far from our borders as one can get, and justified by appeal to national self-interest.[47] Had that intervention been successful, say in 1955 or 1963 or 1968, one suspects that political realists would today be applauding it (as some do in any event) as bold, forthright and hard-headedly pragmatic—and chalking it up to a policy of Realism.

That much of the post–World War II direction of America's foreign affairs seems to conform to the realist philosophy does not mean, of course, that political realists themselves are irrational war-mongering jingoists who would have us fighting continuously all over the globe. To the contrary, they are forward-looking, often liberal men of intelligence whose analyses are as thoughtful and restrained as they would have our statesmen be. And if Schlesinger overstates things when he says that it was realists who were most skeptical about Vietnam from the beginning, it is certainly true that some of them, like Osgood, thought Vietnam intervention ill-advised as far back as 1957,[48] others, like Morgenthau, were long-standing and prominent critics of the War, and still others, like Schlesinger himself, came to be seriously disenchanted

---

[46] See, for example, Schlesinger's statement: "Since it is painful to charge our national leaders with stupidity, one must suppose that this foolish analysis of the relation of Indo-China to the American national interest was only a secondary motive for our involvement in Indo-China. The primary motive, it seems probable in retrospect, had little to do with national interest at all. It was rather a precise consequence of the belief that moral principles should govern decisions of foreign policy. It was the insistence on seeing the civil war in Vietnam as above all a moral issue that led us to construe political questions in ethical terms, local questions in global terms, and relative questions in absolute terms"; "National Interests and Moral Absolutes," Ernest W. Lefever, ed., *Ethics and World Politics*, 37. See also his *The Crisis of Confidence* (New York: Houghton Mifflin, 1969). This way of viewing matters has come to constitute almost a formula for instant—and superficial—analyses of American foreign policy over the years. Major failures are automatically explained as owing to "not enough realism," to the holding sway of visionary idealism, to the unrealistic attempt to implement moral judgments in foreign policy. And thus the cry is raised anew—as after World War I, and after World War II, and again after Vietnam—for a return to a hard-headed understanding of the realities of international affairs; in short, for a return to Realism.

[47] At least much of the time; almost every remotely marketable "justification" was given a try at one time or another.

[48] See Osgood, *Limited War: A Challenge to American Strategy*, 214–26.

with it.[49] But the fact remains that their philosophy would have us be quicker on the trigger than we have been throughout most of the twentieth century (and that the majority of the public would have had us be, as judged by public opinion polls of attitudes toward entry into our major wars), and that it would have us be radically more interventionist than we have historically been. Most of all, however, in assigning a position of paramountcy to national interest the realist commits himself to the rationalization of *any* magnitude of evil which circumstances render necessary to maintain or further that interest; either that or he takes it on faith that America's national interest can never require depredations against others, a faith as naive as anything he attributes to the idealist. What his philosophy cannot allow (or allow to be decisive) is that a war like Vietnam could be successful beyond the wildest dreams of its originators and executors, and yet, morally, be totally and unqualifiedly wrong.

That Vietnam was an unprecedented tragedy militarilly, politically, and morally some will dispute. That it was never in the national interest to have intervened there in the first place some will dispute. But that it was a product of the *kind* of foreign policy advocated by the realists I submit it indisputable. This suggests that as decisive a verdict as we are every likely to have in such matters is to be had of Political Realism by an assessment of Vietnam in the American experience. But that assessment is another story.[50]

[49] See Schlesinger, *The Crisis of Confidence*, ch. IV. Kennan wrote in 1954 of our involvement in Indochina that "Our government is obviously making a concentrated and determined effort to come to grips with the problem. We can only wish them well and give them our confidence and support"; *Realities of American Foreign Policy* (Princeton, NJ: Princeton University Press, 1954), 95f. In 1967, acknowledging that "the Vietnam involvement . . . marches under the same semantic banner"—namely, that of "containment"—which had become closely associated with him in the early 1950's (though see his comments on the allegation that he authored a "containment policy" in his *Memoirs 1925–1950* [Boston: Little, Brown and Co., 1967], ch. 15, he said that it should be apparent to anyone who reflects upon the "official rationale and methodology" of Vietnam policy that it does not accord with the concept which he advocates). From an abbreviated version of an address delivered at Harvard in Spring, 1967, under the auspices of the Charles Warren Center for Studies in American History, published as "The Quest for Concept," *Harvard Today*, Autumn, 1967. Nonetheless, in keeping with his realist predisposition against judging morally, about the most he can bring himself to say about the "totality of our action in Vietnam" is that it "might well classify as a massive imprudence but scarcely as a deliberate crime"; *Democracy and the Student Left*, 139. In any event, as Rothstein observes, it is often "difficult to relate an individual Realist's position on policy to his philosophical convictions"; "On the Costs of Realism," *American Political Science Quarterly*, September 1972, 352.

[50] This essay has not been previously published. (Some of its material was used in Holmes' book, *On War and Morality*, Chapter 2, 50–82.)

7

The Challenge of Nonviolence
in the New World Order

Historical developments occasionally create an opportunity for a radical redirection in world politics; they present a chance for a new world order. In the twentieth century, such opportunities existed three times: after the first and the second world wars, and at the very end of the Cold War. Holmes writes this essay after the collapse of the Soviet Union. All of a sudden, the United States finds itself at the crossroads—to continue building up as a superpower and create a world empire, or to emerge as a leader of a new world order based on genuine collaboration among nations and universal respect for the international law. One path meant continuing with a gigantic war economy and establishing an undisputed military presence all over the world. The second called for a radical departure from traditional military missions and, Holmes argues, the development of nonviolence. The second path was suggested by Lithuania's peaceful separation from the Soviet Union, which led to further secessions of the former Republics and, ultimately, to a peaceful disintegration of the Soviet military power (created by violence and maintained by violence). Unfortunately, Holmes laments, the dilemma was resolved before it could be properly publicly discussed. A creation of a new world order based on nonviolence and genuine collaboration among nations was never given a chance. The temptation to build an empire proved too strong, with all the tragic consequences to which such a choice will lead for decades to come.

History may well record the social and political changes of the twentieth century's closing years as unrivaled in swiftness, scope, and consequence. Time has, to be sure, always rearranged the landscape of human affairs in its course. But wars and revolutions notwithstanding, this has often occurred gradually, one era's promontories of power metamorphosing almost imperceptibly into the next era's valleys of decline. Abrupter changes, even when they were to be of momentous eventual consequence, were localized in immediate effect because of limitations in travel and communication.

That has now changed. With benefit of near-instantaneous communications, today's major events reverberate quickly throughout the world, their effects augmented by the increased capacity for global action and reaction. Most dramatic of such recent events has been the transformation of Eastern Europe and the Soviet Union. In little more than a moment by historical standards, a great nation, whose rivalry with another great nation shaped the international scene for nearly fifty years, has ceased to exist, and along with it an empire forged in the name of a global ideology. This has left America as the world's sole superpower, with the problem of what to do with its vast military power. Its response to that challenge will, more than the actions of any other nation, largely determine the direction of humankind's course and the nature of the emerging new world order, at least for the foreseeable future. As put disarmingly by General Colin L. Powell, Chairman of the Joint Chiefs of Staff, "We no longer have the luxury of having a threat to plan for. What we plan for is that we're a superpower."[1]

What planning to be a superpower means needs translating, of course, and there is growing debate between those, on the one hand, who want the U.S. to rein in its military power to focus upon domestic needs and those, on the other hand, who relish the prospect of the virtually unimpeded exercise of that power abroad. Neo-isolationism and neo-imperialism, as these positions may be called respectively, represent extremes on a spectrum that admits of many gradations.

Neo-isolationism and neo-imperialism are normative positions, prescribing how the U.S. ought to proceed in the years ahead. It is with the normative dimension of the world situation that I am primarily concerned. Description and explanation are useful only if brought to bear on the guidance of conduct. However much some may deny it, virtually all analysts of the international scene implicitly or explicitly advance normative claims. And all of them, without exception, rely upon normative assumptions, if only because it is impossible to do otherwise.

But normative judgments require understanding the world. And different observers looking at the same facts following the collapse of the Soviet Union perceive different things. Some see a unipolar world with the U.S. as the dominant power. Others see a multicentric concert of powers, consisting of the U.S., Europe, Russia, Japan, and China.[2] Still other see an essentially intact but evolving state–centric system in which national sovereignty still has preeminence.[3] And still others question whether there is a new world order to be seen at all.[4]

Two conceptions of a new world order

Let me begin by saying what the new world order is not. It is not the order of the Bush administration's Gulf War rhetoric, according to which strong U.N. action in the Gulf crisis has ushered in an era of peace and order through collective security. The U.N. actions from August 8, 1990 on were largely orchestrated by Washington, which sought a military solution to the crisis virtually from the outset. More importantly, Washington made clear—most emphatically from its August 12th announcement of a unilateral blockade of Iraqi and Kuwaiti shipping—that it did not need Security Council authorization (or congressional either, for that matter) for its actions. Only in the face of growing criticism within the U.N. did it undertake an intensive diplomatic campaign to get that authorization, which it succeeded in doing on August 25th. Far

---

[1] *Washington Post National Weekly Edition,* May 27–June 2, 1991.
[2] See Richard Rosecrance, "A New Concert of Powers," *Foreign Affairs* 71 (Spring 1992), 64–82.
[3] See Joseph S. Nye, Jr, "What New World Order?" *Foreign Affairs* 71 (Spring 1992), 83–96.
[4] See, for example, Ted Carpenter, "The New World Disorder," *Foreign Policy* 84 (Fall 1991), 24–39.

from representing the realization of the heralded role for which the U.N. was created, these events transformed the Security Council almost overnight from a position of ineffectuality brought about by years of superpower neglect and obstruction to one of near-subservience to the remaining superpower.

So if by a new world order is meant one fashioned deliberately by the Bush administration and heralding a new era of international peace and order, there is no such thing—scarcely, any longer, even in the rhetoric of the U.S. government. But if by a new world order one means simply a radically changed world, with realigned powers and new challenges, then a new world order there will inevitably be. For when the transitional period we are now in stabilizes, there will have taken shape a world that, at least in traditional geopolitical terms, cannot help but be radically different from the one that has existed since the end of the Second World War.

A major candidate for such an order is set forth in the Pentagon Defense Planning Guidance for the 1994–1999 fiscal years.[5] The role initially envisioned there for the U.S. was that of preventing other nations from ascending to superpower status and maintaining a world order congenial to U.S. interests. Although that goal appears to have been dropped from a later draft, more moderate in tone, the document clearly sees the U.S. as the world's paramount military power and conducting itself accordingly.[6] Conflict in third world countries has been thought for some time to be the likeliest military challenge to the U.S. With Grenada, Panama, and the Gulf War as models, the expectation is that the U.S. military will visit swift, massive, and decisive force upon those countries, or elements therein, who seriously threaten that status or the order on which it depends. To the extent that this represents the de facto position of the U.S. government, which remains to be seen, it brings policy planners down squarely on the side of neo-imperialists.

Thus two conceptions of a new world order need to be reckoned with. The first, which many believe to have been born of the Gulf crisis, and which I shall call WO1, envisions collective security and international law as the paramount features of the international world. It represents a refurbishing of the conception George Kennan saw the U.S. aspiring to in much of the first half of the twentieth century.[7] The second, which I shall call WO2, may maintain the appearance of including some of structures (such as the International Court of Justice and the U.N.). But it envisions the U.S. as remaining the sole global superpower, whose will and determination guarantee stability designed to enable its interests to flourish. It represents the world dreamed of by political realists, in which power and national interest, rather than legalistic/moralistic norms, prevail; a world transfigured by the collapse of the Soviet Union to feature a resplendently victorious United States.[8] WO1 is internationalist in character, but allows wide latitude in how extensive nations' international commitments will be. It is compatible with all but the more extreme forms of neo-isolationism. But it is

---

[5] A report on a draft of the document was published in *New York Times*, March 8, 1992.

[6] See the *New York Times,* May 24, 1992.

[7] He also saw this conception as lamentably lacking in realism. See George F. Kennan, *American Diplomacy, 1900–1950* (New York: New American Library, 1951), 82.

[8] I have stated both in pure forms, ignoring the complexities and permutations of each and the extent to which there might be a mix of the two.

incompatible with neo-imperialism, which, though it is internationalist in character, is individualist rather than collectivist in its conception of the form such internationalism should take. WO2, on the other hand, represents an imperial order, consistent only with, indeed embodying the objective of, the neo-imperialist philosophy.

Will either world order prevail?

Whether either WO1 or WO2 will in fact be realized in anything like full-blown form remains to be seen. But three factors will almost certainly play a major role in determining the answer to that question.

The first is that even before the close of the century, the defeated nations of the world's greatest war loom once again as major powers. Japan is not yet a military power, but despite a constitutional ban on remilitarization there is a growing aspiration among many on Japan's right to restore Japanese military might—an aspiration encouraged by the U.S. throughout much of the Cold War, as it sought to counteract Soviet influence in Asia. The historic vote of the Japanese parliament to allow deployment of Japanese troops abroad, even as only part of a U.N. peacekeeping force, is an ominous step in that direction. Germany is a military power, however, though with fragile constraints against the use of that force outside of NATO, and is now looking for a new mission for its military in the post-Cold War era.[9] Some are calling for "selective" nuclear proliferation to allow Germany to become a nuclear power as well.[10] Meanwhile, neo-Nazism—a resurgence of the very plague that led the world into WWII is alive and flourishing in Germany, various Eastern European countries, and the U.S., and proto-Nazi nationalism asserts itself in Russia and what remains of Yugoslavia.

The second factor is that, as the West glows with satisfaction over the collapse of communism in the Soviet Union, a powerful, revolutionary Marxist movement, the Shining Path, with the potential of creating another Vietnam, gains strength in Peru; and another, the Khmer Rouge, even more ominous because of its past record, becomes a growing threat in Cambodia. Their rhetoric aside, the ruthless, oppressive, centralized bureaucracies of the Soviet Empire bore about as much resemblance to the Marxist vision as Western nations do to Christ's vision in the Sermon on the Mount. It would be naive to suppose that the collapse of that empire signals the end of Marxism's appeal to the world's disadvantaged, particularly to those in the third world who feel the continuing effects of colonialism's legacy.

The third, and perhaps least appreciated, factor is the extent to which Marxist predictions for capitalism show signs of being confirmed by developments in the U.S.: increasing numbers (now more than 30 million) living in poverty, a shrinking middle

---

9   The German military sent mine sweepers to the Gulf waters following the Gulf War, and has contributed helicopters to U.N. observer units in Iraq. In addition to aiding the Kurds in northern Iraq, it helps operate a U.N. hospital in Cambodia. On these issues, Francine S. Kiefer, "Germany Tiptoes toward Greater Use of Military," *Christian Science Monitor,* July 16, 1992.

10 See, for example, John J. Mearsheimer, "Back to the Future: Instability in Europe After the Cold War," *International Security* 15 (Summer 1990).

class, increasing concentration of wealth in the hands of a few, and—conforming to projection for the final, imperialistic stage of capitalism—a flight of American companies to the third world in search of cheap labor. There is not, to be sure, anything like a proletarian class consciousness; nor a self-appointed revolutionary vanguard to lead the oppressed masses to freedom. Nor is it at all clear that American capitalism may not yet prove resilient enough to hold together indefinitely. But tensions of the sort Marxists call contradictions are intensifying in the capitalist system at a rate that should be of concern to defenders of free enterprise. In the long run, they may represent a more insidious threat to America's social well-being than ever did the Soviet military.

The armed forces' current role

What is the role of the armed forces in this period? The world over, it is business as usual: the business, in part, of defending national boundaries, but often that of aggressing against other peoples, or of oppressing the very people they are ostensibly defending, the citizenry of their own country. The particular mix of these functions varies from region to region and time to time. Where there are few external threats, as in Latin America, control of a country's citizenry often predominates. Where there are external threats, real or imagined, national defense tends to predominate. Even nations that do not use their militaries directly to oppress other peoples often back antidemocratic regimes whose military do this.

This has long been true in Latin America, but it is now particularly true in the Middle East, none of whose beneficiaries of massive U.S. and Soviet arms sales— with the notable exception of Israel (and Israel only for a portion of the population it controls) is a democracy. U.S. policies there, once designed to counteract Soviet influence, now serve more to preserve its position as the dominant power of the region than to encourage democratization. Indeed, the movement toward democracy, particularly in countries like Algeria and Jordan, and the attempt to maintain the status quo in countries like Egypt, increasingly risks bringing to power fundamentalist Islamic movements with a decidedly anti-Western orientation.

Here we see the inherent incompatibility between WO1 and WO2.[11] WO1 would primarily ensure peace through collective security. It may be interventionist, on the grounds that national sovereignty immunizes governments against anything other than moral reproach for their treatment of their own citizens. But it may also be expressly interventionist, an understanding of it that is gaining acceptance today. Intervention may be thought to be warranted (and perhaps even mandated) when necessary to protect human rights.[12] According to WO2, on the other hand, the preservation of an order congenial to perceived U.S. (and perhaps Western) interests is the dominant

[11]   Despite the fact that some, like Joseph Nye, Jr, seem to think that effecting a blend of the two will best serve U.S. interests. See his "What New World Order?"
[12]   For a good recent statement of the case for human rights based interventionism on internationalist grounds, see Fernando R. Teson, *Humanitarian Intervention: An Inquiry into Law and Morality* (Dobbs, NY: Transnational, 1988).

concern. When democratization is thought to threaten those interests—as it did in Chile under the Allende regime, does in parts of the Middle East today, and may come to in Peru—it is democratization which suffers. Kuwait, Saudi Arabia, Egypt, and the Israeli occupied territories are all cases in point.[13]

America's departure from traditional military missions

In the U.S. there is increasing use of the military to deal with nonmilitary problems, a change from its traditional role.[14] The sending of 27,000 troops into Panama to apprehend a head of state wanted on U.S. drug charges is only a particularly dramatic example.[15] The militarization of the so-called "war on drugs" in general symbolizes this change. It shows how tensions can be created even within this approach itself. For not only has the U.S. begun to depend increasingly upon the military to deal with the drug problem, it has encouraged others to do so as well. In Peru, U.S.–encouraged efforts to militarize the drug problem led to the alliance of many in the military with coca producers.[16] The beneficiary of millions of dollars in U.S. support and inkind assistance in training, Peru's military has backed the suspension of democratic processes there, a development that did not go unnoticed in Bolivia, where there are concerns about a possible military coup.

In these cases, the military (in the first instance, that of the U.S. itself, in the second, that of other countries and trained by the U.S. military) are employed to use or threaten force directly in pursuit of the desired objectives.

But other roles are envisioned for the military—or for the war system in general. As General Carl E. Vuono wrote, when serving as the Army chief of staff:

> The United State provides military training, in one form or another, to 75 percent of the world's armed forces. This training is crucial to the successful assimilation of new weapons and tactics by friendly forces. More important, U.S. military training is a unique medium for encouraging the adoption of the values of professionalism, respect for human rights and support for democratic institutions. . . . Conventional forces, particularly the U.S. Army, actively support nation-building in countries throughout the world, assisting in the development of infrastructure that in turn helps alleviate some of the root causes of instability and violence.[17]

---

[13] This readiness to see democratic aspirations stifled may coexist, of course, with a willingness to shake a finger at human rights violations and the undermining of democracy, as it does in Haiti and Peru. But that coexistence, not the intention, will likely serve mainly to preserve the appearance of WO1 all the while the forces of WO2 are at work.

[14] Though not altogether without precedent, as the Army Corps of Engineers has long been involved in civilian projects and the Civilian Conservation Corps was run by the military.

[15] This was not the sole purpose, which included protecting American lives and safeguarding the canal.

[16] As it has also in Colombia, as Colombian lawyer and human rights advocate Jorge Gomez Lizarazo writes in an op ed piece: "U.S. aid, justified in the name of the drug war, is furthering the corruption of the Colombian security forces and strengthening the alliance of blood between right-wing politicians, military officers and ruthless narcotics traffickers"; *New York Times,* January 28, 1992.

[17] Carl E. Vuono, "Desert Storm and the Future of Conventional Forces," *Foreign Affairs* 70 (Spring 1991), 55.

One might add to this the 1991 relief operations on behalf of the Kurds in northern Iraq and Turkey, on behalf of flood victims in Bangladesh, and on behalf on Haitian refugees following the overthrow of the government, as well as efforts to save an Italian village from the lava flow of Mount Etna.[18] The Army provided disaster relief following the California earthquake and Hurricane Hugo, fought forest fires in the West and supported antidrug campaigns on the border with Mexico. Both Army and Marine units were called in during the Los Angeles riots in 1992. What amounts to an institutionalization of such uses is contained in a Civil-Military Cooperative Action Program, proposed by Sam Nunn, chairman of the Senate Armed Services Committee, committing the military, at least during peace time, to a wide range of domestic activities, from rebuilding schools and bridges to providing a military-based youth training corps.[19] When one notes further the deep-rootedness of ROTC in American colleges and universities; the appointment of retired military personnel to the boards of directors of corporations; and, more recently, their hiring in increasing numbers for teaching positions in public schools, it is clear that, despite a reduction in military spending, there is an increase in the projected use of the military in the country's dealings abroad, and a growing role for it, and those trained in its values, in traditionally nonmilitary domestic institutions.

We are witnessing in the U.S. an almost imperceptible assimilation of military values to the approach to social, political, and moral problems, both domestically and internationally. This is happening at a time of decay in the country's social fabric. The educational system is deteriorating, poverty is increasing and punishment rather than social reform is looked to more and more as a solution to domestic problems. This is not "declinism" in a pejorative sense;[20] it is a realistic appraisal of tendencies inherent in the current course of events.

This social and economic decline is occurring at a time when the U.S. enjoys unrivaled global military power. But, if I am correct, that power, while it almost certainly will remain superior to any other for a long time to come, will likely be challenged eventually by Japan and Germany, as well as China. Add to this the growing signs that America's international prestige is declining as well, and the mix is volatile.[21] The temptation will be to try to compensate for our deteriorating social and economic situation by the exercise of military power to try to solve international problems in the way we increasingly try to solve domestic problems, by threats and punishment. What lies at the end of this road is not the world order dreamed by neo-imperialists, but a world of increasing instability as the surviving superpower lashes out militarily at real or imagined threats in the attempt to stave off a more drawn-out version of the decline of its erstwhile adversary.

---

[18] See Eric Schmitt, "U.S. Forces Find Work as Angels of Mercy," *New York Times,* January 12, 1992; Scott Shuger, "Pacify the Military," *New York Times,* March 14, 1992; and Alan Cowell, "It's Plug Up Mt. Etna or Go the Way of Pompeii," *New York Times International,* April 25, 1992.

[19] Eric Schmitt, "Civilian Mission is Proposed for Post-Cold War Military." See also Scott Shuger, "Pacify the Military."

[20] As characterized by Samuel P. Huntington, in "No Exit: The Errors of Endism," *National Interest* (Fall 1989), 3–11.

[21] As John Lukacs writes, "The power of a nation, like that of a person, is inseparable from the unquantifiable asset of its prestige"; "The Stirrings of History: A New World Rises from the Ruins of Empire," *Harper's Magazine,* August 1990.

I emphasize that I am speaking only of tendencies here, for none of this is foregone. It will be the choices made through this transitional period that determine whether or not it comes to pass.

These choices, I suggest, need to reflect a redirection of our course as a nation, starting with a reconceptualization of the very idea of security. For just as social problems cannot in the long run be solved by SWAT teams and prisons, so security cannot in the long run be preserved solely or even primarily by military means. Even if we could keep our borders inviolate indefinitely, and could project sufficient power globally to be able to prevail in conflicts anywhere in the world, to do so would jeopardize the very values we would preserve. It would require becoming a virtual garrison state, geared forever to intervention abroad and chained to a permanent war economy at home.[22] This most likely would not happen by design, but gradually, almost imperceptibly, through prolonged breathing of the air of militarism, deceptively scented by the language of democratic values. A hint of this is found in the assertion that U.S. military training is a "unique medium" for encouraging respect for human rights and democratic institutions. Stripped of its glamour, and in plain language, military training aims in the first instance to produce specialists in the infliction of death and destruction—men and women who will perform efficiently, effectively, and on command. It is not a grand job-training program, or a prolonged summer camp, or a college preparatory school, as a surprising number of young people—influenced by aggressive advertising and recruiting—seem to view it. Those who undergo such training prepare either to engage in such killing and destruction themselves or to support (or in some cases, command) those who do. In so doing they must overcome, or help others to overcome, the natural inhibitions toward killing and causing harm—particularly on a large scale and to those they do not know and by whom they have never been personally wronged. The rest of what they do is incidental, whatever other functions it may serve. Seriously to encourage respect for human rights and democracy would be to support institutions designed to promote those values; to explore the historical, ethical, and political dimensions of the issues they raise in a spirit of open, critical inquiry. To expect respect for such values somehow to materialize as a byproduct of the operations of a vast, bureaucratic institution that by the very nature of its mission is undemocratic and authoritarian, and that stands only a command away from being used in ways antithetical to those values, is wishful thinking.

Security and how to get it

Security exists only when the conditions of a good life are present and sustainable. Physical survival is one of those conditions, but only one. An obsessive preoccupation with it, as one sees in so many nations, not only cannot guarantee the realization of the other conditions, it can actually obstruct their attainment; as it does in nations that

---

[22] I borrow this term from Seymour Melman, *The Permanent War Economy* (New York: Simon and Schuster, 1974).

squander their resources in an endless pursuit of physical security through armaments to the detriment, and sometimes impoverishment, of their own people, and often of those around them as well. Absolute security is an illusion, no more attainable by people collectively than by individuals. Acceptance of that fact is as essential for the well-being of a society as for the mental health of an individual.

The promotion and maintenance of the conditions of a good life, among them, notably, social justice, trust and respect for persons, requires cooperation, not only among members of one's own society, but among those persons and the members of other societies as well. This, in turn, requires a regard for the well-being of other peoples as well as one's own. In the end, the well-being of all peoples is interconnected; not in precisely the same way, or to the same degree, but in such a manner that no peoples' lasting security can be achieved at the expense of others. The exploitation, domination, or oppression of others eventually victimizes the victimizer as well, if only through the moral corruption it works in the oppressor's national character.

We think of military power as the best guarantor of security. But the collapse of the Soviet empire reveals the fragility of power understood principally as the capacity to inflict violence. A militarized state that could have been overcome, if at all, only at a horrendous cost if confronted head-on by military might, disintegrated once the true source of its power—the willingness of its people to continue acquiescing in the rule of a government in which they had long lost confidence—was removed. That happened once people lost their fear, as they did, not only in the Soviet Union, but also in the essentially nonviolent revolutions of Eastern Europe: from the ten-year struggle of Solidarity in Poland (whose members point with pride to the fact that they did not so much as break a single window during that time) to the six-week inspired uprising in Czechoslovakia. What they achieved almost certainly could not have been achieved through violence.

Lithuania is a case in point. The first of the Soviet Republics to declare its independence on March 11, 1990, Lithuania, under defense minister Audrius Butkevicius, mobilized a system of nonviolent defense against the Soviet military. Volunteers from throughout the country converged on Vilnius, setting up shacks in the newly christened Independence Square, site of the parliament building, and establishing communications networks. Lithuanians responded by the thousands when called out to confront Soviet troops nonviolently when they moved against key governmental and communications centers.[23] To be sure, the Soviets could have taken the parliament building—the seat of the new government, and symbolic of Lithuanian defiance of Moscow—in a few hours had they chosen to; and had not the Soviet government collapsed when it did, the Lithuanian struggle for independence would have been a protracted one of less certain outcome. But these considerations only highlight the fact that any successful nonviolent action, like any successful military action, presupposes conditions in whose absence the action might not have succeeded.

---

[23] The most dramatic event was the move by Soviet tanks against the Vilnius television tower, only to find thousands of Lithuanians converging on the tower, which they surrounded in nonviolent defense. The Soviets killed thirteen people in the course of occupying the tower, but this left them in a position of moral vulnerability, as they sat, surrounded by fence and barbed wire, peered at by Lithuanians gathering to lay wreaths honoring the dead.

Nonviolence did not succeed in Tiananmen Square. It did in Lithuania and throughout much of Eastern Europe. What is particularly significant about Lithuania, however, is the fact that nonviolence was deliberately incorporated into the government's defense strategy; indeed, it became its paramount—though never its sole—dimension. At no time, has a country expressly committed itself wholly to nonviolence. And only a very few (today, notably, Scandinavian countries) make nonviolence a component of their defense strategy. Nevertheless, it is in this direction, I want to suggest, that creative thinking must go in the quest for an alternative conception of security.

Pragmatic and principled nonviolence

Nonviolence can be thought of exclusively in practical terms, as simply another instrument of power for the attainment of social and political ends, or as a moral or spiritual philosophy—even a way of life—which may, though need not, be held to have broad social and political uses. The first conception may be called pragmatic, the second principled. Pragmatically, nonviolence is a form of power, differing from violent and violence—threatening forms but capable of serving the same kinds of ends, whether just or unjust. Disavowing as it does an essential moral or religious orientation, pragmatic nonviolence is open to anyone to accept. It does not require superhuman, or even extraordinary, capacities—say, in the manner of a Gandhi or a Martin Luther King, Jr. The use of nonviolence particularly relevant to the issues under consideration here—that is, nonviolent national defense (or Civilian-Based Defense, as it is sometimes called)—requires only training and discipline on the part of ordinary citizens.

Principled nonviolence, on the other hand, though often viewed as a practical alternative to violence, and as requiring training and discipline, is taken to have a moral and/or spiritual foundation, usually requiring something of a transformation of its adherents. Nonviolence, on this view, is not simply a tactic or tool, to be dispensed with if it does not work. It has a different rationale. Living nonviolently, or being a nonviolent person, may be the principal objective. And it is one that may be attainable even in the face of failure to achieve more usual social or political objectives.

So there is a twofold difference between principled and pragmatic nonviolence: first, in the conception of what constitutes the justification of nonviolence, specifically whether it is moral (or spiritual) or purely practical, and second, in what a commitment to nonviolence is thought to entail—whether it requires leading a consistently nonviolent life or merely acquiring the necessary training and discipline to engage in nonviolent action where appropriate.

But whether principled or pragmatic, nonviolence does not threaten the lives or well-being of those against whom it is used; hence it minimizes the risk of at least such violence as is borne of fear for personal safety. And it is usable by virtually a whole population. Unlike military defense, which singles out one group (normally young men, though in this country increasingly young women as well) to bear the full burden of that defense, nonviolent national defense distributes responsibility throughout society. Not only can this give ordinary persons a stake in the defense of what they value, it can help alter the situation in which older men send boys and young men to fight without risk to selves—a situation that does little to discourage military adventurism by heads of state.

There is not space here to detail the many techniques of nonviolent struggle—more that 180 of them have been catalogued by Gene Sharp.[24] But their aim, when used to counteract aggression, particularly an attempted takeover of one country by another, is the same as one of the stated objectives of military action: to deny to an adversary the ability to achieve his objectives. Rather than seeking to do this through force, however, nonviolence seeks to do it chiefly by withholding the cooperation necessary for the attainment of those objectives. In so doing it operates with a broader than usual understanding of power.[25] For political power involves more than merely the capacity to apply physical force. It requires the acquiescence of those over whom such power is held, and a willingness on their part to cooperate with the enterprises of those who govern them. Once that willingness ceases and cooperation is withdrawn, that power evaporates. There remains, of course, the capacity to inflict violence, to kill and destroy. But that alone rarely suffices to achieve one's objectives. And even that power presupposes a continuing willingness on the part of the military to carry out orders, and, at least in the long run, on the part of the citizenry of the offending country to support its government's aggression. All of these represent points of potential vulnerability that can be exploited by nonviolence, which seeks both to confront an aggressor's actions and to undermine his legitimacy.[26]

Choosing between violence and nonviolence

Does nonviolence work? As with military action, sometimes it does and sometimes it does not. There is no more assurance (at least when nonviolence is pragmatically conceived), than with violence, that any particular nonviolent campaign will succeed.

---

[24] According to eyewitness accounts, Sharp's list of nonviolent techniques was publicly posted near the Russian White House early in the August 1991 coup attempt.

[25] As Gene Sharp says, "Civilian-based defense rests on the theory that political power, whether of domestic or foreign origin, is derived from sources *within* each society. By denying or severing these sources of power, populations can control rulers and defeat foreign aggressors"; *Civilian-Based Defense: A Post-Military Weapons System* (Princeton, NJ: Princeton University Press, 1990), 7.

[26] As may the use of so-called "indirect force" as understood by Sun Tzu as well. As Max G. Manwaring observes, in characterizing such force as an adjunct to military force: "Indirect force is applied or conducted through the use of moral power. If carefully done, the use of moral influence can undermine the legitimacy and the position of another actor by breaking the bonds which unite a people, its political leadership, and its protective military/police organization. When legitimacy is seriously questioned, will is destroyed and the opponent is weakened to the point where only a minimum of direct military force is necessary to assure the desired change. Moreover, by transforming the emphasis of war from the level of military violence to the level of a struggle for legitimacy, an actor can strive for total objectives (e.g., the overthrow of a government) instead of simply attempting to obtain leverage and influence for 'better terms' in the classical dimension." "Limited War and Conflict Control," in Stephen J. Cimbala and Keith A. Dunn, ed., *Conflict Termination and Military Strategy: Coercion, Persuasion, and War* (Boulder, CO: Westview Press, 1987), 60.

That depends upon circumstances, including the training, discipline and morale of the practitioners of nonviolence, as well as upon that of their adversaries. But nonviolence has worked at specific times in the past—against the British in India, the French and Belgians in 1923, the Nazis in Norway and Denmark during World War II, and of course, in the civil rights movement in the U.S. in the 1960s. And (though neither of these represents a clear commitment to nonviolence) it has played a significant role in the Palestinian Intifada, most notably in the civil disobedience against Israeli authorities in the tax resistance of the West Bank town of Beit Sahour, and is playing a role in the struggle of the Albanian majority against Serbian domination in the Yugoslavian province of Kosovo. Nonviolence does not promise simple solutions. It cannot guarantee there will be no bloodshed. It cannot, and does not seek to, end conflict. It holds open, rather, the promise of dealing creatively with conflict, resolving it where possible, managing it where not. It seeks to channel conflict constructively where its elimination would be undesirable. It holds open the promise, on the large scale, of providing an empowering, effective and less costly means of national defense.

But the question is not really whether nonviolence works. It is whether it works as well as, or better than, violence. For the choice is between those two approaches, and the shortcomings of either are relatively unimportant if, by comparison, those of its alternative are even greater. If nonviolence is relatively untried, violence is not, however, and its record is less impressive than is often supposed.[27] Every war that has a winner also has a loser, so that in every case in which violence succeeds on the victorious side, it fails on the losing side—an exact balancing of the scales.[28] Even the military success of Operation Desert Storm is offset by the failure of violence in the initial Iraqi aggression against Kuwait. Interestingly, the threat of force, which was represented as the surest way to peace during the military buildup of the fall of 1990, failed to dislodge Iraq from Kuwait; a fact that represented a failure of policy based on that threat when the 15 January 1991 deadline for Iraqi withdrawal passed. Even the military rout of Iraq, as effective as it was in getting Iraq out of Kuwait, did not achieve the clearly intended, though unstated, objective of bringing down Hussein. And it failed to achieve what came after the war to be represented as one of the war's principal aims, to destroy Iraq's nuclear capability. Iraqi compliance with U.N. resolutions in this regard, such as it has been, may well have owed more, in the end, to the effects of the embargo—the nonviolent sanction that was given less than a week to work before military measures were undertaken in August of 1990— than to the threat of force. And if one views the matter from the other side, Iraq has arguably been more effective in resisting U.N. pressures since the end of the war by what has, in effect, been a program of passive resistance (delay, indirection, noncooperation, tactical capitulations) than ever it was in its use of military force.

Both WO1 and WO2, and their many variants, as different as they appear on the surface, perpetuate the reliance upon force to get along in the world. In that sense there

---

[27] John Mueller, in a critical assessment of the efficacy of the nuclear threat, argues in fact that, "It seems likely that the vast majority of wars that never take place are caused by factors which have little to do with military considerations." See his "The Essential Irrelevance of Nuclear Weapons," *International Security* 13 (Fall 1988), 18.

[28] For a discussion of this issue, see the General Introduction to my *Nonviolence in Theory and Practice* (Belmont, CA: Wadsworth, 1990).

is nothing new about them. The most they can hope to achieve is a peace built upon violence and fear.

Building institutions for nonviolent conflict resolution

There is an unprecedented opportunity for the U.S., now that it is finally free of the Soviet threat, actively to promote the creation of institutions and mechanisms for nonviolent conflict resolution throughout the world.[29] This would hold some promise of creating a new world order in substance as well as name. Instead, it is pouring yet more arms into the hands of those who represent the status quo, as the militarization of the Middle East and Latin America, in particular, continues and that of South Asia gets underway in earnest.[30] This not only will not, but cannot, I suggest, bring about a new world order worthy of the name. The essential character of any world order is determined by the principal means relied upon to maintain it. And the means now envisioned in WO1 and WO2 are those of every failed order of the past—the use and threat of violence.

As long as the emphasis is primarily upon ends—even noble ends like freedom, democracy, and respect for persons—the way remains open for continuing reliance upon means that eventually subvert efforts to realize those ends. We need to shift our emphasis away from ends to means; to commit ourselves to nonviolent means that respect all persons equally, whether they happen to be Americans or not; and to limit ourselves in the pursuit of ends to those that are consistent with such means. This represents a reversal of the usual understanding of means and ends. Rather than adopting ends and then devising means to their attainment (which, on the international scene, invariably involves ultimately relying upon the instruments of violence), it counsels adopting means, specifically nonviolent means, and then pursuing only such ends as accord with them. Rather than the ends justifying the means, it is the means—at least to a significant degree—that justify the ends. This gives recognition to the fact, stressed by Gandhi, King, and others, that, at least insofar as we are viewing them from a moral perspective, means and ends cannot be separated from one another.

Commitment to promote a nonviolent world order would in this country, as well as in many others, require conversion to a peace-oriented rather than a war-oriented economy. Worldwide it would over time almost certainly entail a transformation of the

---

29   One of the few public calls for this is found in Helena Cobban, of Search for Common Ground in Washington, who writes: "We should actively promote, worldwide, the work of those American individuals and institutions that over past decades have pioneered nonviolent ways to resolve intergroup conflicts. . . . These institutions have put the U.S. at the cutting-edge of the discipline of conflict resolution. This kind of 'software,' rather than further sales of military hardware, is what we ought to be offering a world facing new insecurities at every turn"; *Christian Science Monitor,* March 19, 1992.

30   With the U.S. having sold more $14.8 billion in arms to Saudi Arabia, $2.17 to Egypt, $737 million to the UAR, and $3.2 billion to South Asia during the year following the Gulf War. James Adams, *Washington Post National Weekly Edition,* March 23–9, 1992. During 1990, the U.S. became the world's biggest arms supplier overall, accounting for 40 percent of the market. Ira Shorr, "Making History in a Post Cold War World," *Global Security News,* Winter 1991–2.

nation-state system. For the modem nation-state gives social and political embodiment in today's world to centuries of humankind's habituation, through custom and convention, to relying upon the sword to achieve its ends.

Events in the former Soviet Union and parts of Eastern Europe are instructive in this regard. Many peoples there are trying to replicate on a smaller scale the same coercive state system they previously found oppressive as minorities within larger states; and doing so often with little regard for other ethnic groups that suddenly find themselves minorities in these newly established states (or, where they were minorities to begin with, finding themselves minorities under governments controlled by what had been another minority alongside them before independence). Ironically, they are in many cases insisting upon, and in the worst cases fighting over, boundaries established by the very regimes they now repudiate. In the overall process in which they are engaged, they are inadvertently laying bare the full nature of the institutionalization of violence represented by the state. It is as though, in these events, the world is witnessing in concentrated form, and at accelerated speed, the way in which most nations have been formed over the centuries: through forcible domination of some people by others.

But for the bloodshed to which it is leading, the dissolution of the Soviet Union would be a blessing to the world—as (all other things being equal) would be that of the world's other major military powers as well. The power to destroy countless persons at will, and perhaps even civilization itself, cannot safely be centralized in a handful of men or women, however chosen, and however seemingly trustworthy. Nation-states are not part of the nature of things. They certainly are not sacrosanct. If they perpetuate ways of thinking that foster division and enmity among peoples, ways should be sought to transcend them. Such ways are beginning to evolve now in any event, with the development of a global economy and increased travel and communications. The challenge is to give the process conscious, thoughtful direction.

There is the moral dimension to this, of course, in that if there should be a way for peoples and societies to get along in the world without depending upon military force, it behooves us to find it. It would represent an accomplishment for humankind surpassing any of science and technology. But moral considerations aside, national interest (or a public interest that might take its place with the transformation of the nation-state system) would call for finding it. We are on a course now in which the very fabric of society shows signs of coming unraveled through saturation with violence—not only as found in the streets, and increasingly in the schools, but as depicted in television, film, newspapers, popular music and culture. For this cannot help but take a toll on our greatest resource, our children. Not that conversion to nonviolent national defense would magically solve all domestic problems, including that of violence. But it would institutionalize a different set of values for dealing with international problems, setting the stage for the possibly even more difficult problem of cultivating methods of nonviolent conflict resolution for domestic problems as well. We cannot be a Rambo on the world scene, then turn around and tell young people to be nonviolent.[31] They will be what we as a people and a country are.

---

[31] As one sixteen-year-old girl reportedly said with exasperation to then presidential hopeful, Governor Bill Clinton, at a New York high school, "I mean, we went to war over oil, and we're telling our kids not to shoot each other?" *New York Times,* March 1992.

If the transition to a nonviolent world order should be possible (and it may not be), it is possible that ignorance and narrowness of vision are so deeply rooted that it cannot be done; I do not believe this, but it is possible—if, I say, such a transition should be possible, then at the very least discussions of strategy must begin to take seriously the possible role of nonviolence, initially, at least, as a component of current military thinking. Indeed, some conceptions of strategy already suggest as much (not by design, so far as I know, but in effect). As in one recent statement: "Today, strategy is not confined simply to devising ways to win battles; it is a daily preoccupation of most modern governments—certainly most industrial states—and its scope has broadened to include all of the elements of national power, not just the military."[32] Taking this at face value, the potential of nonviolence, and its possible effectiveness in national or social defense, must be reckoned among the elements of national power,[33] and hence taken into account in strategy, even from a position of *realpolitik*. For the effectiveness of nonviolence—leaving moral considerations aside—is an empirical issue. It can be assessed only by the same rigorous scrutiny and testing commonly brought to bear upon alternative military strategies; it cannot be assessed a priori.

If the vast material and human resources we now expend in the quest for security through military means are not affording us that security, and if that effort is costing us more and more in our ability to deal constructively with challenges to the values we profess to cherish, realism in any meaningful sense argues for taking up the challenge of nonviolence.[34]

---

[32] Keith A. Dunn and William O. Staudenmaier, "US Military Strategy in the Nuclear Era," in *Alternative Military Strategies for the Future*, ed. Dunn and Staudenmaier (Boulder, CO: Westview Press, 1985), 213.

[33] In a glimmering of recognition of this shortly before the collapse of the Soviet Union, John Lewis Gaddis wrote: "What seems most likely is not that some new rival will emerge, capable of challenging the superpowers militarily, but rather that the standards by which we measure power will begin to evolve, with forms other than military—economic, technological, cultural, even religious— becoming more important"; "How the Cold War Might End," *Atlantic Monthly* (November 1987).

[34] Previously published in James Burke, ed., *The Adaptive Military: Armed Forces in a Turbulent World* (New Brunswick, NJ: Transaction, 1998), 201–20.

8

St. Augustine and the Just War Theory

St. Augustine occupies a strange position in the history of Western thought. He is a developer of the Christian tradition, which focuses on love of God and love of one's neighbor. Following this tradition, he is a "personal pacifist"— unwilling to engage in war himself but refraining from asserting that others should do so as well. Moreover, he is also widely considered to be one of the original defenders of the Just War Theory. Holmes' exemplary essay covers the whole spectrum of Augustine's views: from the ambiguity of his decree, "Love, and do what you will," to his puzzling acceptance of human practices dealing with war, death, and destruction. Holmes agrees that the problem of war is of the first importance to Augustine's thought yet maintains that he is given too much credit for the launching of the Just War Theory. What Holmes finds instead in numerous of Augustine's writings dealing with war is a too easy acceptance of war—enabling the rulers to go to war whenever they deem it "necessary." With this view justifying an almost unlimited power on the part of rulers and calling for submissive obedience on the part of their subjects, Holmes sees Augustine as setting the stage for Hobbes and the twentieth-century political realists far more than establishing a ground for the Just War Theory.

The just war theory represents a continuing and virtually unparalled effort to bring moral considerations to bear upon one of the most pervasive, complex, and destructive of human practices, one that has played a historic role in shaping modern societies and their institutions.[1] The resurgence of interest in the theory during the last half of the twentieth century has brought a better understanding of the traditions from which it has evolved, as well as a better appreciation of its religious and secular dimensions and the parallels among Christianity, Judaism, and Islam.[2]

---

[1] Indeed, Paul Remsey, in *War and the Christian Conscience: How Shall Modern War Be Conducted Justly?* (Durham, NC: Duke University Press, 1996), xxiii, characterizes the just war theory as the "longest-continuing study of *moral decision making* known in the Western World." The nature and justification of political authority represents a longer tradition, although for the most part it deals with the justifiability of social and political systems rather than with specific, deliberately undertaken actions of a sort common to nearly all social arrangements. Historians of ethics focus primarily upon the history of ethical theory. But some of the most important contributions to philosophical ethics, from Plato through the classical utilitarians, have been in applied ethics, and it is to applied ethics that the just war theory belongs.

[2] See particularly John Kelsay and James Turner Johnson, ed. *Just War and Jihad: Historical and Theoretical Perspectives on War and Peace in Western and Islamic Traditions* (New York: Greenwood Press, 1991), 2.

The prevailing view is that, at least within Christianity, the father of just war thinking is St. Augustine,[3] a view supported by the medievalists' heavy reliance upon him[4] and the deference to him by both early jurisprudentialists and just war revivalists in the twentieth century. The extent of his influence is documentable. If that is all that is meant by his being called father of the just war theory (or of the just war tradition, as some prefer to put it), the claim is certainly correct. But if one means more than that, the claim needs closer scrutiny. For although Augustine clearly seeks to justify war, what is less clear is what he offers in the way of original thinking about war, and whether his views hold together in a coherent and consistent fashion—both on their own and within the broader context of his overall thought, which is vast in scope and rich in social, psychological, and philosophical insights.

What makes this issue difficult to assess is that Augustine's discussions of war are brief, scattered, and unsystematic.[5] In fact many who deal with topics in his writings to which war would seem to be relevant either do not discuss his views on war at all or do so only in passing. At the same time metaphors of war recur in his writing. Perhaps most notably, Augustine, like Plato, uses the language of war to characterize what he sees as an ongoing psychological conflict within each person,[6] which suggests that whatever its role in shaping his beliefs about the actual practice of armed conflict, the idea of war has deep roots in his thinking. But whereas Plato and Aristotle understand war in the context of an impersonal teleological natural order,[7] Augustine understands it in terms of a divine order and—as do writers in Judaism, Christianity,

---

[3] For example, Roland Bainton writes that Augustine's view "continues to this day in all its essentials to be the ethics of the Roman Catholic Church and of the major Protestant bodies"; *Christian Attitudes toward War and Peace* (New York: Abingdon Press, 1960), 99. For challenges to this interpretation see particularly David Lenihan, "The Just War Theory in the Work of Saint Augustine," *Augustinian Studies* 19 (1988), 37–70; George J. Lavere, "The Political Realism of Saint Augustine," *Augustinian Studies* 11 (1980), 135–45; and Reinhold Niebuhr, "Augustine's Political Realism," in *Christian Realism and Political Problems* (New York: Charles Scribner's Sons, 1963), 119–46. For a balanced analysis of the issue see William R. Stevenson, Jr, *Christian Love and Just War: Moral Paradox and Political Life in St. Augustine and His Modern Interpreters* (Macon, GA: Mercer University Press, 1987).

[4] On Augustine and the medievalists see Frederick H. Russell, *War in the Middle Ages* (Cambridge: Cambridge University Press, 1975).

[5] The principal passages in which Augustine discusses war have been usefully compiled by David Lenihan in "Just War Theory in the Work of Saint Augustine": 1. *De libero arbitrio* 1.5; 2. *Contra Faustum* 22; 3. *Epistulae* 138, to Marcellinus; 4. *Epistulae* 189, to Boniface; 5. *Epistulae* 222, to Darius; 6. *Quaesteiones in Heptateuchum* 6.10; 7. *De sermone Domini in monte* 30; 8. *City of God.*

[6] As Plato has Clinias say, "Why, here . . . is the field in which a man may win the primal and subtlest victory, victory over *self*, and where defeat, defeat by *self*, is most discreditable as well as most ruinous. There lies the proof that everyone of us is in a state of internal warfare with himself"; *Laws* 626; trans. A. E. Taylor, in *Plato*, ed. Edith Hamilton and Huntington Cairns (Princeton, NJ: Princeton University Press, 1971). Compare Augustine: "What war, then, can be imagined more serious and more bitter than a struggle in which the will is so at odds with the feelings and the feelings with the will, that their hostility cannot be ended by the victory of either?"; *City of God*, 19.28; trans. Henry Bettenson (New York: Viking, 1986). See also *City of God*, 19.4.13; 21.15.16; *Contra Faustum* 22.22; *Confessions* 10.

[7] Plato understood war in the broader context of the nature of the state, viewing it as an art of acquisition to facilitate expansion when expensive tastes created wants that outstripped needs. In this way he thought it sprang from the same causes as all of the evils of the state (*Republic* 2). Aristotle added that some people were meant to be dominated by others, and when refused to submit it was "naturally just" that war be made against them (*Politics* 1.8). There was believed to be a teleological order to nature and a natural justice to war when it conformed to this order.

and Islam alike—accordingly seeks war's legitimation in the relationship between God and humankind. The problem for Christianity is that Christ seems to proscribe war and violence in the commandment to love, particularly as that applies to enemies. To overcome this presumption against war is the central challenge to Augustine.[8]

It is a challenge I believe he fails to meet. Despite a complex and sophisticated attempt,[9] Augustine in fact departs radically from the pacifism of the early church,[10] wedding Christianity to a militarism that to this day is a hallmark of societies that profess it. Indeed, the most striking feature of his position is its acceptance of war, just or unjust, as an inevitable part of the human condition. Insofar as the just war theory is thought to provide moral criteria by which to judge whether to go to war (*jus ad bellum*), and how to conduct war once in it (*jus in bello*), there is, I maintain, little of such guidance in Augustine, hence little ground on that score for representing him as the father of the just war theory. Indeed, the practical import of his views puts him closer to the tradition of Hobbes and recent political realists than to either the pacifists of the early church or subsequent just war theorists.

A contrary view merits consideration at the outset, if only because it enables us to highlight one of the central problems in understanding Augustine on the issue of war. Although the prevailing view is that Augustine is progenitor of the just war theory, he has also been read as a personal pacifist, whose views are peaceful in essence, on a continuum with pacifists of the early church.[11] Augustine's thought, on this view, is distorted by later writers who obscure its essentially pacifistic character and give it an increasingly militaristic coloration.

That Augustine was almost certainly a personal pacifist may be granted. He denies that private individuals may kill even in self-defense. Short of assuming the duties of an official of the state or an agent thereof (as he understands soldiers to be), one not only need not but may not, on Augustine's view, engage in killing. It should not be surprising that as a bishop of the church, and not an official of the state, Augustine would have been unwilling personally to participate in war. In later medieval writers the prohibition of clergy from participating in war came, in any event, to be thought consistent with the Christian sanction of war. One can personally renounce war and yet believe in its justifiability as waged by others. Moreover, it is arguably true that Augustine stands on a continuum in many respects with earlier Christian writers—certainly if one counts

---

[8] On the moral presumption against war in recent Catholic thought, see *The Challenge of Peace: God's Promise and Our Response*, A Pastoral Letter on War and Peace, May 3, 1983 (Washington, D.C., American Catholic Conference, 1983).

[9] This attempt is motivated in part by the desire to respond to Christianity's critics who charged that its teaching had weakened the Roman state and thus made it vulnerable to attacks like that of the Visigoths in 410.

[10] At least partially in support of this his biographer, Peter Brown, writes: "In an atmosphere of public disaster, men want to know what to do. At least Augustine could tell them. The traditional pagans had accused the Christians of withdrawing from public affairs and of being potential pacifists. Augustine's life as a bishop had been a continual refutation of this charge. He knew it was to wield power with the support of the Imperial administration. Far from abandoning civil society, he had maintained what he believed to be its true basis, the Catholic religion; and in his dealings with heresy, lawlessness and immortality, he had shown not a trace of pacifism"; *Augustine of Hippo* (New York: Dorset Press, 1967), 291.

[11] See Lenihan, "Just War Theory in the Work of Augustine."

St. Ambrose among those writers, since he expressly supports war and killing. Even discounting Ambrose, and emphasizing those typically identified with the pacifistic sentiments of the early church—like Origen, Tertullian, Lactantius—there are many similarities. Augustine talks continually about peace and love and laments the horrors of war. That is not in question. What is in question is whether, despite this, his thought places Christianity on a different path from what it was in the view of most Christian writers prior to Ambrose and prior to its de facto militarization by Constantine.

The claim I believe needs close scrutiny is that Augustine's interiority, as it is often called—his emphasis upon subjective inner states—renders consistent his probable personal pacifism and denunciation of war's horrors with his justification of war. For Augustine unquestionably turns Christianity inward. He says that Christ's injunctions in the Sermon on the Mount do not apply to outward action but rather to inner attitude; the "sacred seat of virtue," he says, is the heart.[12] And this, if it can be rendered both intelligible and plausible, does indeed seem to open the door to one's being a pacifist in his heart and yet supporting the killing of warfare. And that in turn would be a step in the direction of enabling Augustine, at one level, to remain committed to the pacifistic testimony of the New Testament and at the same time, at another level, to reorient Christianity to the path of militarism.

The motive of love

Augustine's interiority stands out in his statement that "not what the man does is the thing to be considered; but with what mind and will he does it." Contrasting God's giving up of his Son and Jesus' giving up of himself with Judas' giving up of Jesus in betrayal, Augustine says, "The diverse intention therefore makes the things done diverse." With regard to the acts of Jesus and Judas, "though the things be one [presumably a giving], yet if we measure it by the diverse intentions, we find the one a thing to be loved, the other to be condemned; the one we find a thing to be glorified, the other to be detested. Such is the force of charity. See that it alone discriminates; it alone distinguishes the doings of men."[13]

Here the thing done is presumed in some sense to be the same, but intentions determine whether it is praiseworthy or blameworthy. Then Augustine speaks of cases where the things done in two cases are different: a father beating a boy, a boy-snatcher caressing one. The first case represents "a man by charity made fierce," the other, a man "by iniquity winningly made gentle." Here not only do the outward acts differ, they

---

[12] "If it is supposed that God could not enjoin warfare, because in after times it was said by the Lord Jesus Christ, 'I say unto you, That ye resist not evil: but if any one strike thee on the right cheek, turn to him the left also', the answer is that what is here required is not a bodily action, but an inward disposition. The sacred seat of virtue is the heart"; *Contra Faustum* 22.76, in Saint Augustine, *Writings in Connection with the Manichaean Controversy*, in Philip Schaff, ed., *Select Library of the Nicene and Post-Nicene Fathers*, vol. 4.

[13] St. Augustine, *Homilies on the First Epistle of John* 7.7, trans. H. Browne, in *Select Library of the Nicene and Post-Nicene Fathers*, vol. 7.

differ deceptively. The beating is an act of love, the caressing an act of evil. It is the "mind" or "will" with which they are done that makes the difference.[14]

In this latter case, however, it is not merely that the intentions differ. It is that the motives differ as well—love in the one case, concupiscence in the other. Neither Augustine nor Aquinas after him carefully distinguishes motives and intentions. But the distinction is of the fist importance for understanding his position.

At stake is the grounds for sometimes judging similar acts differently and different acts similarly ⸻ 's that he believes requires looking beyon   as he says:

> For   happen that, at the same moment,
> one   n may not, because of a difference
> not   s it, so in the case of one and the
> same   ty formerly is not duty now, not
> beca   lf, but because the time at which
> he dc

Augustin   y of moral judgments,[16] intending us to und   ⸻ ..ay be prideful or loving, hence may have different moral characters. "In the works," he says, "we see no difference."[17] Ever ready to expose hypocritical do-gooding, Augustine emphasizes that as measured by outward acts there need be no difference between pride and charity.

Although Augustine speaks in this passage as though a difference of time *simpliciter* were a morally relevant difference, a more charitable understanding of him is as holding that motives and intentions, representing as they do "mind and will" as distinguished from outward act, are morally relevant aspects of situations. They differ from outward acts, yet are transformative of the moral character of such acts. The implication is that without some difference in motives or intentions, or both, acts cannot differ morally.

Augustine emphasizes diverse intentions in the case of giving. But a specification of intentions does not suffice to reveal the "inward disposition" of the heart. One can intend good but do so from pride. One who fights the flames in a burning building may intend to save the child but do so from a desire for praise. A right intention, to be sure, is necessary for a rightly done act (Augustine sees a bad intention as sufficient to condemn Judas). But it is not sufficient. Indeed all of the acts of charity—from feeding the hungry to clothing the poor—can be done from pride. When they arc, the intentions (to see the hungry fed and the poor clothed) will be the same as if they

---

[14] Ibid.

[15] Letter 138.4, trans. J. G. Cunningham, in *Select Library of the Nicene and Post-Nicene Fathers*, vol. 1.

[16] That is, he seems to be denying universalizability if that thesis is understood to require that similar acts be judged similarly. It is doubtful that he is denying the thesis, however, if one interprets it more broadly as requiring that relevantly similar *cases* or *situations* be judged similarly. For he does think that there are relevant dissimilarities in the cases he would have us judge differently. And he is almost certainly not denying the thesis if it is taken to mean that acts or cases must be judged similarly unless there are relevant similarities between them.

[17] *Homilies on the First Epistle of John* 8.9.

were done from charity. Not acts of charity but only the motive of charity can properly be the root of our conduct. "It alone," says Augustine, "distinguishes the doings of men."[18]

Thus while it is arguably true that evil intentions can spring only from evil motives, good intentions can spring from either good or evil motives. This makes possible the seduction of "good deeds" against which Augustine cautions. With prideful motives concealed, we seek praise through outwardly good acts. Such acts can abound. We can easily identify them. Truly good works we cannot—at least reliably—because they are done from love, and that motive is hidden from us.

If this is correct, it means that Augustine's interiority is rooted in motivation, not (merely or basically) in intention. Both motives and intentions can determine the moral character of acts (though intentions cannot do so invariably, since a well-intentioned act can yet be basely motivated). But motives are basic, because they determine the character of intentions as well as of acts.[19]

There remains, however, the question of the precise role of motivation in determining correct conduct. This is crucial to understanding the justification of war and brings us to one of the most difficult areas of Augustine's philosophy. There arises here a problem that continues to plague love-centered ethics. It is found in one of Augustine's homilies on the Epistle of St. John:

> See what we are insisting upon; that the deeds of men are only discerned by the root of charity. For many things may be done that have a good appearance, and yet proceed not from the root of charity. For thorns also have flowers: some actions truly seem rough, seem savage; howbeit they are done for discipline at the bidding of charity. Once for all, then, a short precept is given thee: *Love, and do what thou wilt*: whether thou hold thy peace, through love hold thy peace; whether thou cry out, through love cry out; whether thou correct, through love correct; whether thou spare, through love do thou spare: let the root of love be within, of this root can nothing spring but what is good.[20]

At the heart of this passage is the directive, Love, and do what you will. But the directive is ambiguous. It could mean, as it most readily suggests:

1. Love, then do whatever love moves you to do.

This would give full weight to love as a motive. If love is commanded, and to be motivated by love is to be governed by that motive (as opposed, say, to merely being inclined in the direction it points), then everything one wills when one loves would

---

[18] Ibid., 7.7.
[19] Barry Gan has suggested to me that if good intentions were understood as those that aim at creating or maintaining a virtuous character, and if it were assumed that a virtuous character entailed good motive, then, while it would still be true that the moral character of motives determines that of intentions (or, at least, that good motives determine good intentions), this would not allow that good intentions may be produced by evil motives. It would then be difficult to explain how the road to hell can be paved with good intentions, as Augustine pretty clearly thinks it may be.
[20] *Homilies on the First Epistle of John* 7.8; emphasis added.

issue into right outward conduct.[21] And if (*per impossible* for humans) love fully and completely motivated us, then all of our conduct (at least all of it that is voluntary) would be right. Where for Plato to know the good is invariably to do it, for Augustine, on this interpretation, to love perfectly would be invariably to act lovingly.

But a second interpretation is suggested by that part of the passage that says, "whether thou hold thy peace, through love hold thy peace; whether thou cry out, through love cry out; whether thou correct, through love correct; whether thou spare, through love do thou spare." Here it looks as though the directive may actually mean:

2. Do what you will, but whatever you do, do it from love.

This suggests something different. It suggests that what you do in the way of outward conduct may, in the end, be unimportant; what is important is that whatever you do, you choose to do it from love. Whereas (1) implies that love moves us to perform certain outward acts, presumably because there is something about those acts (for example, their goodness) that makes them the appropriate objects of love, (2) implies that outward acts are indifferent in themselves and that it is only when they enter into the appropriate relationship with love—being selected (or rejected), as it were, by loving persons—that they acquire their particular moral significance.[22] According to both (1) and (2) any act is right if done from love. But according to (1) that is because love reliably guides us to perform only those acts that are antecedently and independently right. According to (2) it is because any acts chosen by love thereby become right.[23]

Augustine at times inclines toward the consequentialist view suggested by (1)—that love moves us as it does because that is the direction in which the good lies (and ultimately, of course, because that is what God has ordained). At other times he inclines toward the nonconsequentialist view suggested by (2)—that whatever love produces in

---

[21] If, on the other hand, it is supposed that one can love but not always be governed by love—if, that is, love, when present, does not invariably provide a motive or at any rate a governing motive for conduct—then doing "whatever thou wilt" would authorize doing only those things actually impelled by love. This would leave open whether acts not motivated by love should be foregone or judged by some other criteria.

[22] This would accord with what Augustine says in the well-known passage regarding the seat of virtue being in the heart, as well as with the Stoic doctrine that, in the classification of all things as good, bad, or indifferent, everything other than virtue (an intrinsic good) and vice (an intrinsic bad) is indifferent, including human actions. This appears to be the understanding of William R Stevenson, Jr, when he says of Augustine's view that, "So long as one truly loves, *what* one does, does not really matter; any action based in and arising out of true love is by definition 'right.'" *Christian Love and Just War*, 107.

[23] The difference between (1) and (2) is analogous to that involved in divine-command ethics. Whereas one can ask whether God commands what he does because it is right, or whether it is right because God commands it, here one can ask whether love motivates us to do what is right because it is right, or whether what is right is so because love motivates us to do it. There are further possible complexities that we cannot explore fully here. It may be that love selects certain acts not because they are right but because they are good and that they are then rendered right because of the good they promise to actualize. This would make Augustine basically a divine-command deontologist, holding that we ought always and invariably to do as God commands, but at the same time a pragmatic teleologist, holding that when we do as God commands (that is, act lovingly in all that we do) we as a matter of fact do what is best, given God's ordering of things.

the way of conduct is thereby constituted good and hence right.[24] The consequentialist rendering is suggested by Augustine's saying that "there is a certain friendliness of well wishing, by which we desire at some time or other to do good to those whom we love"[25] and that, when we are not situated so as to be able to do good, benevolence—the "well-wishing"—must suffice. Loving, it seems here, means doing good (acting beneficently) when we can and wishing good (being benevolently disposed) when we cannot. By extension we may presume that acting beneficently when possible (and benevolently otherwise) is to do what is right. In this spirit Augustine contends that love of enemies has an end that is an obvious good: the transforming of them so that they are no longer enemies.[26] The problem with this rendering is that it seems to reduce love to benevolence, which, though a motive, is only a motive to do good. And this would leave unexplained why God commands love rather than benevolence.[27] Yet Augustine seems to regard love and benevolence as two different things. He says, for example, that when one cannot act beneficently "the benevolence, the wishing well, of itself sufficeth him that loves."[28] If they are not two different things, love becomes vacuous, its content emptied into the notion of benevolence.

The nonconsequentialist interpretation, on the other hand, is suggested by the final thought of the above passage in which Augustine says, "let the root of love be within, of this root can nothing spring but what is good." This suggests that love cannot fail to produce good.[29] If this means only that love reliably directs us to the good, and invariably moves us to it (or promotes it), then it is consistent with interpretation (1). But if it means that love cannot in a logical or conceptual sense fail to produce good, then it supports (2). It is not that the good is out there and love simply directs us to it; it is that something's being good (and perhaps right) simply is its issuing from love. It is as though when one loves one necessarily (given how God has ordered the world) brings about good. Thus identical acts may have different moral characters depending upon whether they are done from love. Acts done from pride sometimes produce good and sometimes not. But acts done from love necessarily produce good.[30]

[24] Strictly speaking, both (1) and (2) would appear to be nonconsequentialist if they are taken without elaboration and also taken to be basic principles. It is when one understands (1) (as I am) to presuppose that love impels us to do good that it becomes consequentialist and axiological, for then it requires of us that we calculate the value of the consequences of our acts in the determination of what is right.

[25] *Homilies on the First Epistle of John*, 8.5.

[26] Ibid., 8. 10. It is possible that there is something else about the character of certain acts besides their goodness or rightness that leads love to move us to do them, but it is difficult to see what that would be for Augustine.

[27] For related topics see William K. Frankena, "Love and Principle in Christian Ethics," in Alvin Plantinga, ed., *Faith and Philosophy: Studies in Religion and Ethics* (Grand Rapids, MI: Eerdmans, 1964), 203–25.

[28] *Homilies on the First Epistle of John* 8.5.

[29] And if one is troubled by the possibility that some of what one does from love may seem harmful to others (and here we should be mindful that, as Augustine conceives of love, it can lead to war and killing, Augustine counsels: "Therefore hold fast love, and set your minds at rest. Why fearest thou lest thou do evil to some men? Who does evil to the man he loves? Love thou: it is impossible to do this without doing good"; *Homilies on the First Epistle of John* 10.7.

[30] To render all of this coherent, one would have to say that it is sufficient to make an act (and presumably its consequences) good that it be performed from love, but it is not necessary, since good can be done from pride as well. It may, on the other hand, be both necessary and sufficient

Augustine and personal pacifism

Let us now return to Augustine's alleged personal pacifism and the question of whether he stands more in the tradition of the church's earlier pacifism than in that of subsequent just war theorists.

A "personal pacifist" is one who is unwilling to participate in war himself but who refrains from judging that others should do so as well. Such a person might believe that wars must sometimes be fought but simply not want to be personally involved; in that case the maintenance of clean hands is paramount. On the other hand such a person might believe that war is wrong but, perhaps owing to humility, or moral tolerance, or both, simply be unwilling to legislate morally for others, leaving it to them to make up their own minds about what to believe and how to act.

If Augustine were a personal pacifist of the second sort, it would indeed put him closer to early Christian pacifists than to later just war theorists. But then we could make little sense of his determination to justify war—which after all represents an attempt to justify it for all Christians, and by implication at least, for non-Christians as well. So to render his position consistent we must view him, it seems, as a personal pacifist of the first sort: as one who believes that wars are sometimes justified but who would be unwilling, even then, personally to participate in them.

If one reads him as a personal pacifist of this first sort, there is no difficulty in reconciling his position with the justification of war, hence no ground, on this basis, for challenging the standard view of him as progenitor of the just war tradition. If that is the case, then the interpretation that would put Augustine more in the tradition of the early Christian pacifists than in that of later Christian just war theorists derives little support from Augustine's personal pacifism. Even if Augustine maintained that not only he but others as well should be pacifists, the situation would not change. His interiority would render even universal pacifism consistent with the waging of war and with doing so justifiably.[31] If the command to love is God's principal directive, and if it requires a right inner disposition rather than specific outward conduct, then there is no inconsistency between advocating pacifism and justifying war. This is true on either interpretation of the precept to love and do as you will. If that precept is understood, as in (2), to require an inner transformation that is compatible with any outward conduct (normally described)—and I tend to believe this is Augustine's view—then, rather than outward conduct being changed by love, that conduct is simply given a moral coloration when motivated by love. It is what love is thought to require that is changed, refashioned to fit the exigencies of the temporal world. Turning the other cheek, loving one's enemies, and not returning evil for evil then become fully consistent with striking back, killing one's enemies, and returning suffering, death, and destruction for evil.

---

for an act's being right that it be done from love. In that case acts and consequences would not be fully value-neutral independently of their being produced by love; but their character as right or wrong would be. This, however, takes us well beyond anything that can reliably be attributed to Augustine's actual thought.

[31]   That is, it would render it consistent in his own mind. Whether in fact one can render wholly consistent this combination of positions is less clear.

But even if one adopts the consequentialist rendering of the love commandment, as represented by interpretation (1), there is still no inconsistency between pacifism and the justification of war. For when one looks at what Augustine considers loving conduct (as opposed to merely motivation) one finds it repeatedly associated with notions like "severity," "discipline," "correction," and "chastisement." Love is not preserved by gentleness.[32] It can inflict terrible suffering, and often does.[33] Whereas on interpretation (2) love so transforms the moral character of conduct that otherwise indifferent acts become permitted, on interpretation (1) the pain, suffering, and death almost universally taken to be evil become good when inflicted by love.[34]

Even though interpreting Augustine as a personal pacifist of this sort lends little support to the view that he belongs in the tradition of early Christian pacifists, nothing in the preceding compels placing him in the later just war tradition either. The appeal to his interiority does not settle the question one way or the other whether he belongs more to one tradition than to the other. If we accept the sharp inner-outer dualism of his interiority, there is no inconsistency in representing him as both pacifistic and militaristic in different respects, and it becomes a matter of emphasis which side of him one takes to be most important. Where that emphasis properly belongs then becomes a matter of judgment based upon a consideration of the specifics of his views on war. Moreover, as I shall suggest, nothing in the preceding precludes the possibility that Augustine has carved out a position that distinguishes him from both the pacifists of the early church and the just war theories of the later church. So let us turn now to the specifics of his views on war.

Just wars not commanded by God

With regard to the two recognized dimensions of just war theory, *jus ad bellum* and *jus in bello*, Augustine says little about the second, beyond sanctioning ambushes,

---

[32]   *Homilies on the First Epistle of John* 7.10.
[33]   Despite the death and destruction love can inflict upon enemies, it may be that Augustine thought that love of enemies is a purer form of love even than love of the poor and needy. This is speculative, it should be cautioned. He does imply that there is an ordering of the purity or perfection of love when he points out that loving the poor and needy is fraught with pitfalls because of the risk of pride creeping into one's motivation. "With a truer touch of love," he says, on the other hand, "thou lovest the happy man, to whom there is no good office thou canst do; purer that love be, and far more unalloyed" (ibid., 8.5). When shortly later he discusses love of one's enemies, he says: "Thou lovest not in him what he is, but what thou wishest him to be. Consequently, when thou lovest an enemy, thou lovest a brother. Wherefore, perfect love is the loving an enemy: which perfect love is in brotherly love" (ibid., 10). He may mean here only that perfect love entails loving one's enemy. But the fact that he apparently recognizes an ordering of degrees of purity of love suggests that he may mean that, just as loving a happy person will likely be freer of pride than loving those for whom we can provide outward manifestations of charity, so love of an enemy is purer still, since it requires overcoming and going against the very interests of the temporal self pride cherishes.
[34]   A problem for this interpretation is that if the infliction of death and destruction is reckoned good for purposes of understanding the conduct of warriors and civil magistrates, it is hard to see (consistent with this interpretation) how such actions can fail to be good when performed by evil persons. For it is the evaluation of the outward conduct (and its effects) that is here involved, not the motivation. If one says that it matters whose conduct it is, so that what is done from loving motives is good and what is done from motives evil, then interpretation (1) collapses into (2). For then, once again, it is only in *relation* to good or bad motives that conduct is good or bad.

prohibiting vengeful cruelty (see below), and acknowledging the need for truthfulness in dealing with an enemy. He says more about *jus ad bellum* but even there without much elaboration.

The exception to this is with regard to wars commanded by God. Like Ambrose, Augustine looks for much of his justification of war to the Old Testament and God's directives to the Israelites to conquer, and in some cases annihilate, various peoples. What is commanded by God, for Augustine, is absolutely obligatory.[35] Thus there is a sharp dichotomy in his justification of war between his treatment of wars approved by God which are unquestionably just, and those not so approved, which may or may not be just.[36] To be justified in waging a war not approved by God, one must have legitimate authority and a just cause. Sometimes it is thought that he requires a right intention as well. I shall maintain that this is true, but only in a trivial sense; it is not until Aquinas that right intention is fully enshrined in Christian thinking about just war.

Just cause is provided by a state's having suffered a wrong at the hands of another state, either by direct action of the other or by actions of its citizens for which it refuses to make restitution.[37] The war such a just cause warrants is punitive in nature, to avenge that wrong. It may be a war of self-defense, but it need not be. A just cause may entitle a state under a ruler with legitimate authority to initiate a war. This sets Augustine against those contemporary theorists who see self-defense as the *only* justification for war. It also sets him against the twentieth-century paradigm for a justified war, which is one fought in self-defense against an aggressor.

Legitimate authority is framed by Augustine's Christian world view. In his hierarchical ordering of things husbands dominate their families, monarchs their subjects, and God all persons, who ought to be submissive and obedient to his will.[38] As war takes place between states, only persons with the appropriate authority within states may initiate war, and only their agents may fight. When those agents do, they do so with impunity.[39] As William R. Stevenson, Jr, effectively summarizes this aspect of Augustine's thinking:

> For the subjects of rulers, the fact of the *providentia voluntaria* means that they should obey, essentially without question. Whatever the content of a particular regime, it serves a purpose ultimately good and consequently should not be hindered through disobedience. God bestows power on representatives of all degrees of human perversion; nonetheless, Augustine asked rhetorically, "although the causes be hidden, are they unjust?" Consequently, subjects ought to be both passive and obedient in the face of superior human power. For them, too, power equals authority. If the subjects are soldiers, they are obliged to carry out the orders

[35] See *City of God* 1.21.
[36] I shall speak of "approved" here, because Augustine speaks of acts of killing—presumably intending acts of war as well—that are permitted although not specifically commanded by God, and I shall consider those to be covered by "approved." See, for example, his treatment of Moses' killing of the Egyptian as recounted in Exodus 1.2; cf. *Reply to Faustus the Manichean* 22.70.
[37] *Quaestiones in Heptateuchum* 6.10, in John Eppstein, *The Catholic Tradition of the Law of Nations* (London: Burns, Oates and Washburn, 1935), 74.
[38] Interestingly, the traits that are at the heart of Augustine's conception of the relationship of humans to God are the feminine traits of submissiveness and obedience.
[39] *City of God* 1.21.

of their commanders even if those orders require fighting and killing. If they kill under military orders they are not guilty of murder; on the contrary, if they do not kill when ordered, they are guilty of treason. Soldiers ought therefore to obey even the possibly unrighteous commands of infidels, such as Julian the Apostate. Even in such a case, "the soldier is innocent, because his position makes obedience a duty." Within the framework of historical providence, then, the matter of authority is a simple one: the ruler, whoever he might be and whatever he might do, rules with God's sanction. He can do nothing without God's foreknowledge of the deed and, if the deed issues from a perverted will, without God's ultimate compensatory historical intervention. Rulers thus war at their discretion, and subjects fight in obedience to their rulers.[40]

The one part of this that is misleading is that which says that rulers war "at their discretion." As descriptive of the behavior of rulers this may well be true. But as normative of what rulers may justifiably do, it is not quite accurate. For rulers are constrained morally by the requirement of a just cause. What is left to their discretion is the determination of what constitutes such a cause. As Augustine sees the matter, "it is the wrongdoing of the opposing party which compels the wise man to wage just wars."[41]

What of right intention? It is true, in a sense, that Augustine expects there to be a right intention in warfare, in that he believes that everyone who wages war—justly or unjustly—does so for the sake of peace.[42] It is just that different rulers have different conceptions of what peace is. The question is whether any particular "right intention" deserves to be realized. And that goes back to whether that intention is in the service of a just cause. It will be useful to speak here of a formally right intention, by which I mean one that aims at the perceived good of a particular peace. Augustine recognizes a right intention of this sort. But since it characterizes the unjust and the just alike, and hence can always be presumed to be present,[43] it cannot be normative of what constitutes a just resort to war.

This provides a preliminary account of the specific conditions Augustine lays down for *jus ad bellum*. But its full import can be understood only by seeing how it fits with our account of Augustine's interiority. For here the radical dualism of Augustine's metaphysics affects his ethics and social and political philosophy as well. Moreover, we have seen earlier that a right intention can issue from either a good or a bad motive and that it is the motive that ultimately determines the character of what one does; "it alone," Augustine says, "distinguishes the doings of man."[44] The possibility of a formally right intention, therefore, cannot suffice to provide a viable condition in the criteria to distinguish just from unjust wars.

[40] Stevenson, *Christian Love and Just War*, 69.
[41] *City of God*, 19.7, trans. Marcus Dods, in *Select Library of the Nicene and Post-Nicene Fathers*, Vol. 2.
[42] *City of God* 19.12.
[43] The American Catholic bishops, on the other hand, tie right intention to just cause, saying, "Right intention is related to just cause—war can be legitimately intended only for the reasons set forth above [protecting innocents, preserving conditions of decent human existence, and securing basic human rights] as a just cause"; *Challenge of Peace*, 30.
[44] *Homilies on the First Epistle of John* 7.7.

Because rectitude is tied to virtue, and virtue to love, we can know whether someone acts rightly only by knowing that person's motivation. And that, according to Augustine, is hidden from us—often even in the case of our own actions. We presumably know when we are deliberately acting pridefully. But when we think we are acting lovingly, we may unwittingly be motivated by pride. In any event, as we have seen, it is difficult to know what love requires in any given case.[45] It is God, after all, who has commanded us to love. And Augustine says repeatedly that God's ways are inscrutable. So whether we read Augustine in consequentialist terms or in nonconsequentialist terms, it is evident there is no sure way to determine in specific cases what constitutes right conduct, certainly not with regard to justice in war. Even if we were able to determine accurately the consequences of our actions and their value, hence to know what beneficence calls for, we would remain unable to know whether our underlying motivation is correct.[46] And if we cannot know when we are motivated by love, we cannot know when we are acting rightly. Add to these cognitive deficiencies our motivational inadequacy even to love fully without divine grace, and the obstacles to acting rightly are formidable. They may not be insurmountable, but the obstacles to our ever knowing they have been surmounted seem insurmountable.

This means we must recognize a distinction between true virtue and temporal virtue and, in the case of war, between true justice and temporal justice. True justice is that which is actually just according to what God ordains both in broad historical terms and in particular circumstances; temporal justice is that which humans warrantably *judge* to be just according to standards accessible to them and in view of their cognitive and motivational limitations. Reliance upon temporal justice is necessitated by our inability both to know what true justice requires and to know, either in general or in any given case, whether our conduct accords with it.

The conditions of a truly just war can now be filled out in keeping with our earlier discussion. In addition to legitimate authority and just cause we may now include right intention, appropriately qualified. I have said that since rulers who go to war do so with the intention of achieving the perceived good of a peace of their choosing, both sides in a war can be presumed to have a right intention. But in addition to a formally right intention in this sense we can distinguish (though Augustine does not) a materially right intention—one that aims not only to bring about a perceived good but also to achieve a rightly chosen, just peace. Peace, for Augustine, entails order, and a given temporal order can be just or unjust (at least, can vary in degrees of injustice, since, strictly, no temporal order can be completely just). One ought only to aim for just peace.

---

[45] This applies, strictly, only to (1), since according to (2) love does not specifically direct our outward conduct.

[46] It might be argued, in defense of Augustine, that the consequentialist interpretation does not require that we be able to determine consequences. It requires only that love (so to speak) do that in moving us always to perform acts that are best, whether or not we can see them to be best. This I think is plausible. But it still leaves the problem of knowing precisely when we are motivated by love. Knowing that will be practically equivalent to knowing what acts will have best consequences. To the extent such knowledge is hiding from us, so, it seems, must be the knowledge of what would be best in conduct.

But if what we have said earlier is correct, even the best of intentions, if measured only by the states of affairs it is their purpose to bring about, are not enough. For good deeds can be done from pride. It is only when intentions issue from love that they are materially right. But even that is not quite enough. We have been assuming that by "love" is intended the love commanded by God. But sometimes Augustine speaks as though love in another sense is at the root of sinful conduct—the love of things that can be taken from us against our will.[47] As with formally right intentions such temporal love (as we may call it) can always be presumed to be present when states go to war, hence cannot be normative of what constitutes true justice in war. Only love as prescribed by Christ—that is, *agape*—can provide a proper love. This "right love," as Stevenson calls it, must be the soil from which intentions spring if they are to be materially right. What forces us to rely upon the conditions of temporal justice is not that these conditions can never be met. It is that we can never know that they have been met. When the conditions of temporal justice are met, we then have a warrant for acting, if only because that is the best we can do. Such conduct is then actionably just.

The completed picture of the Augustinian view with regard to the justification of war is thus a complex one, varying both to the relationship of the war in question to God's express will (all wars ultimately accord with God's will in the sense that he allows them to take place and turns them even when they are unjust to his purposes) and according to the dichotomy between true justice and temporal justice. These interrelations can be represented as follows:

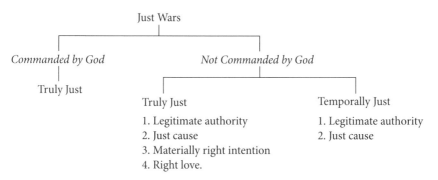

Because God indisputably commands wars in the Old Testament, there can be nothing intrinsically wrong with war. For early Christians this created the dilemma of how to reconcile the Old Testament's sanction of some wars with the New Testament's implied rejection of war—a dilemma they resolved by supporting the New Testament over the Old. Augustine resolves it by reinterpreting the New Testament to accord with the Old. The result is a sharp division in his thinking between true justice and temporal justice.[48]

---

[47]   *De libri arbitrio* 1.
[48]   This dualism is probably prompted partly by Augustine's desire to reconcile the New Testament with the Old, but it is almost certainly facilitated by his Platonistic inclinations. For an account that alleges an expanded list of conditions for Augustine, see Franziscus Stromann, *The Church and War: A Catholic Study* (New York: P. J. Kennedy and Sons, 1928), ch. 3.

While we can, on Augustine's view, know when God commands us to go to war and can in the absence of such commands make determinations of temporal justice with sufficient confidence to act upon them, true justice in such circumstances cannot be known, hence cannot provide an effective guide to conduct.

True justice and temporal justice

Despite the otherworldliness of his theological outlook, and the sharp dualism entailed by his interiority, Augustine seeks to understand and provide guidance for this world, not least of all in its social and political dimensions. Much of his work as bishop was devoted to providing such guidance, as were many of his letters, including those to men troubled by war and killing. How to provide such guidance in the face of the unknowability of true justice creates a continuing, unresolved tension in his thought.

There are, however, grounds in Augustine's thought for partially bridging the gap between true justice and temporal justice. The direction in which they point is not one that Augustine pursues, perhaps because it would almost certainly have led him back to the early church's renunciation of war. But it makes of the commandment to love something more than the "impossible ideal" that it later becomes for Niebuhr, the twentieth-century's leading Augustinian in social and political thought.[49]

The first ground is broadly epistemological and is tied to Augustine's understanding of the state and its authority. The fundamental pragmatic imperative for Augustine is to obey the state. Even an oppressive state at least serves as the agent of God's chastisement for our sins and, moreover, provides order, which is essential to peace. In its restraint of sinful conduct the state provides an opportunity for such transitory moments of happiness (or, perhaps more accurately for Augustine, relief from misery) mortal life provides. This need for obedience extends to participation in war. Even when the cause is unjust,[50] one must fight when commanded to do so by the appropriate authority. One does so, in that case, with legal immunity from the standpoint of temporal justice. Moreover this gives soldiers on both sides in a war—the just and the unjust alike—a kind of moral immunity as well. Each has an equal right to kill, establishing a moral equality among soldiers.[51]

In his early writings Augustine is troubled by this. He expresses uncertainty whether, by the eternal law, even those who kill with full legal sanction are free of sin.[52] But, as though resigned to the unfathomability of the answer to that question, he proceeds later to view the duty of obedience as very nearly absolute,[53] even when one is confronted with (temporally) unjust commands. Moral license, therefore, extends

---

[49] See, for example, Reinhold Niebuhr, *An Interpretation of Christian Ethics* (New York: Meridian Books, 1956).

[50] And, presumably—though Augustine is not clear about this—when the cause is known to be unjust as well, at least from the standpoint of temporal injustice.

[51] As Michael Walzer puts it in defending what he calls the moral equality of soldiers; *Just and Unjust Wars* (New York: Basic Books, 1977), ch. 3.

[52] *De Libero Arbitrio* 1.15.12, trans. Caroll Mason Sparrow (Charlottesville, VA: Dietz Press, 1947).

[53] Excepting only commands that one do things disrespectful of God.

to soldiers on all sides in war, providing only they are acting as agents of a legitimate authority.

Are those who must fight if commanded to do so by a legitimate authority free of guilt no matter with what inward disposition they do so? More specifically, if right love and intention are requirements of true justice, will not their absence mean that, whatever the standards of temporal justice, those who fight do so wrongly by the standards of true justice? It is hard to see how Augustine can consistently answer this other than by an affirmative. It is just that he would contend that the unknowability of the presence of right love and intention makes temporal standards nonetheless actionable for practical purposes.

The problem with this contention is that we can know, so it seems, and so Augustine gives reason to believe, when we are willfully and self-consciously acting from motives other than love—motives like selfishness, greed, malice, and the like. Augustine reveals no skepticism on this score. It is not as though when we deliberately give rein to selfish, greedy, or lustful impulses we may be mistaken and actually be acting from love. Although when we strive to act from love we can never be certain we are in fact doing so, when we self-consciously act from these other motives we can be certain we are not acting from love. In those cases, then, we can know that our conduct does not accord with true rightness. And in the case of war we can know that temporal justice when accompanied by illicit motives does not accord with true justice. On the unproblematic assumption that when true justice and temporal justice conflict it is true justice that takes precedence, this means that in a limited way true justice then is practically as well as ideally normative for human affairs. It does not tell us in all cases what we ought to do, but it does tell us conclusively in some cases what we ought not to do.[54]

One would expect, for that reason, that it would at least be a necessary condition of the conduct of soldiers being truly just, and (assuming they are under the command of a legitimate authority) a sufficient condition of their being temporally just, that they not be acting from an identifiably evil motive. And indeed one can read at least one well-known passage in Augustine's reply to Faustus as consistent with this. He says:

> What is the evil in war? Is it the death of some who will soon die in any case, that others may live in peaceful subjection? This is merely cowardly dislike, not any religious feeling. The real evils in war are love of violence, revengeful cruelty, fierce and implacable enmity, wild resistance, and the lust of power, and such like; and it is generally to punish these things, when force is required to inflict the punishment, that, in obedience to God or some lawful authority, good men undertake wars.[55]

What this suggests is that, in the broader context of Augustine's views, what is important in war, if one is being realistic, is not that we act from love, since we cannot do that without divine grace and cannot in any event ever know for certain that we are doing it but that we be certain we not act from love of violence, revengeful cruelty, lust

---

[54]   It does not follow from this, of course, that acting from *all* motives other than love entails acting contrary to the requirements of true justice. Whether that is so depends upon whether those requirements demand perfection of us, motivationally.
[55]   *Contra Faustum* 22.74.

of power, and the like. For whatever the obstacles to minimizing the power of these motives, we can at least know when we are consciously acting from them. Thus, in addition to the two interpretations of the precept to love, we need to recognize another precept of more limited scope, applicable to the conduct of warfare:

3. Do as commanded (by a legitimate authority), but do it without cruelty, enmity, love of violence, lust for power, and so forth.

By this, to minimize the evils of war, we should purge ourselves as nearly as possible of those elements of sin that can readily be identified. Death and suffering there will be. But their infliction considered outwardly is neither right nor wrong by itself. The determinant of what they are lies in our motivation.

So I suggest that Augustine's full account of the moral equality of soldiers requires that soldiers not kill for the love of it. If one cannot be certain he is ever acting from right love, that can only be because he cannot be certain that, even when he believes he is acting from love, he is not acting from some base motive like revengeful cruelty, lust of power, and the like in disguise. Whether or not we are capable of fully removing these motives, or at least of preventing them from controlling our conduct, it makes sense to view their removal as a requirement of nonculpable participation in war, hence as a condition of the moral equality of soldiers.

As for rulers their legitimacy need have no more warrant by earthly standards than the power by which they enforce order. For that is what is necessary to avoid the even greater evils of license and disorder.[56] Since rulers have no more privileged access to what constitutes true justice than anyone else and arguably have even less if they are non-Christian, they can be guided at best by temporal justice. If they do not have sole moral discretion to do as they please, they at least have, as we have noted, sole discretion to decide what temporal justice requires of the state. Their judgments to that effect will be fallible and can always fall short of true justice. But the standards of temporal justice to which they appeal are constraints nonetheless, fragile though they may be. Given that opposing rulers in war are both seeking peace as they conceive it, and given that each may believe he acts justly, it can easily happen, and indeed may usually happen, that wars are fought by sides equally convinced of their justice. And the killing that results is done by soldiers who, whatever they think of the justice of the cause they serve, enjoy legal and (temporal) moral immunity for their actions. But there is, I suggest, contrary to what some have maintained,[57] no reason to suppose that Augustine believes that both sides in war can in fact be just, even from the standpoint of temporal justice. If not, then nothing in this aspect of Augustine's account is a bar to considering his account of the moral reality of war as fully coherent and consistent.

---

[56] It is the Pauline spirit speaking here, best represented in Paul's epistle to the Romans: "Every person must submit to the supreme authorities. There is no authority but by act of God, and the existing authorities are instituted by him, consequently anyone who rebels against authority is resisting a divine institution, and those who so resist punishment have themselves to thank for the punishment they will receive. . . . You wish to have no fear of the authorities? Then continue to do right and you will have their approval, for they are God's agents working for your good" (Romans 13:1–4; New English Bible).

[57] See, for example, Stevenson, *Christian Love and Just War*, 44–5. Paul Ramsey contends that, to be consistent, Augustine should have denied that one side only can be just in war, in *War and Christian Conscience*, 28.

The second ground for bridging the gap between true justice and temporal justice in war relates to Augustine's denial of the right of self-defense. Properly understood, love can only be for that which we cannot lose against our will.[58] To cling to such things—earthly possessions, even our mortal lives—is the way of sin; it is trying to sustain ourselves other than in and through God. Because we can have no assurance of saving our own lives, we may not kill in defense of them.[59] But we can no more be assured of saving our neighbor's than our own. And thus—although Augustine does not expressly preclude defense of others in the way he precludes self-defense—it would seem we ought not to cling to their lives (or the preservation thereof) either, at least not when to do so would involve killing. Just as assailants can assault or kill us against our will but cannot thereby truly harm us (unless we allow fear or hatred to corrupt our wills as we try to cling to life or bodily integrity), they can do the same to others without thereby truly harming them either. Our intervening on their behalf does not change that. If an attacker cannot harm others by his act alone, then we cannot, by ours alone, preserve them.[60]

The only ground for love's inflicting pain, suffering, or even death upon another, as it may justifiably do for Augustine, is for the other's sake. Punishment can only be inflicted to chasten the offender. An enemy is confronted, Augustine says, always as the brother he may become, not as the enemy he now is. It is only what he does that one may hate, not the person himself. And if you truly love him, you act on his behalf, even to the point of inflicting pain or death.[61]

From all Augustine says, however, love is hardly the motive governing the conduct of most persons, including rulers and soldiers. Even if we thought it were, we could well be mistaken. But we have seen that we can have virtually conclusive evidence of the absence of that motive, namely, when we self-consciously act from sinful motives. And Augustine repeatedly speaks as though he thinks this is so in the case of war. It is greed, rapacity, desire for domination, and conquest that he finds manifest in war. Even a (temporally) just cause provides no assurance that its prosecution is from love.[62] The desire to punish for the sake of punishing, to harm for the sake of harming, to satisfy desires for revenge—and throughout to profit the spoils of war—ensures that even a temporally just war that has these characteristics cannot be truly just and indeed can be known not to be truly just.

If, therefore, there is this bearing of true justice upon judgments of actual wars, then it may be that by a consistent Augustinian analysis (though not by Augustine's own) virtually all of the wars prior to and during Augustine's time[63] will have been

---

58 *De libero arbitrio* I.
59 Not only may we not, in our capacity as private persons, kill another to save our own lives, we also may not even kill ourselves to prevent others from sinning against us, as in the case of threatened torture or rape; *City of God*, 1.24–5.
60 Augustine says: "For whatever man may do to thee, he shall not straiten thee; because thou lovest that which man cannot hurt: God, the brotherhood, the law of God, the church of God. . . . If no man can take from thee that which thou lovest, secure thou sleepest"; *Homilies on the First Epistle to John* 10.6.
61 *City of God*, 19.17. It is but a short step from this, of course, to justify the thinking behind the inquisition.
62 See, for example, *City of God*, 5.17.
63 Counting as wars, for this purpose, the sack of Rome by the Visigoths in 410 and the Vandal incursion into Africa that had Carthage under siege at the time of Augustine's death in 430.

unjust. This may partly explain why warfare under Christianity, particularly during the crusades, came increasingly to be justified on expressly religious grounds,[64] for such grounds would help minimize the influence of self-consciously base motives. What later Christians seem to have given insufficient attention to is the Augustinian skepticism regarding our ability to certify love as a motive in our own conduct. It may even be—if one gives credence to the more skeptical and pessimistic passages in Augustine—that no actual wars are in fact just; and that, whether or not Augustine was a personal pacifist, he should have been and, to be consistent, should perhaps even have been a universal pacifist as well.

Conclusion

If the preceding is correct, the problem of war is of the first importance to Augustine's thought, not because he identifies it as such and not because he expressly devotes extensive attention to it. It is important because what is of concern in his thought, and of paramount concern in his later thought, namely, to define the implications of Christianity for life in the earthly city,[65] turns upon the understanding of war, the social and political forces that bring it into existence, and the divine purposes that allow it to endure. For no human practice flies more directly in the face of what seem to be the teachings of Christ than the organized, deliberate, and systematic infliction of death and destruction.

Thus there is much in Augustine's philosophy that is important to understanding war, but most of it is directly relevant to understanding the philosophy of war in general rather than the just war in particular. For insofar as the just war theory is understood as a theory in applied ethics, meant to provide practical guidance in deciding when to go to war and how to conduct war when in it, there is, as I have said, little in Augustine of such a theory; and such as there is shows limited concern with the complexities that have concerned subsequent just war theorists. There is more in the way of a theoretical account of the conditions that make for true justice in war. But even much of that is only implicit and in any event—unless developed beyond Augustine's treatment—of limited relevance to providing practical guidance to civil magistrates and individuals contemplating soldierhood.

When one looks at the practical import of Augustine's account, on the other hand, as opposed to his philosophy and theology of war, one finds an acceptance of war, with only the frailest of constraints against entering into it, constraints that even optimists regarding human nature could hardly expect not to provide rulers with a rationale to go to war practically whenever they want. And one finds virtually no constraints against individuals participating in war, provided only that they do so without

---

[64] See Frederick H. Russell, *The Just War in the Middle Ages* (Cambridge: Cambridge University Press, 1975), ch. 1.

[65] As Peter Brown, puts it, "So the *City of God*, far from being a book about flight from the world, is a book whose recurrent theme is 'our business within this common mortal life'; it is a book about being otherworldly in the world"; *Augustine of Hippo*, 324.

otherwise forsaking God and without feelings of revenge, cruelty, and so forth. The way is then prepared for Christians to lament the horrors of war and at the same time actively to support war's perpetuation. Power on the part of rulers and submissive obedience on the part of subjects enable the state to run roughshod over the teachings of the Sermon on the Mount. In its practical import, then, as opposed to its theoretical and philosophical import, Augustine's account sets the stage more nearly for Hobbes, Machiavelli and twentieth-century political realists (some of the most prominent of whom have been Christians) than for just war theorists.

One suspects that Augustine's desire to counteract Christianity's critics was so great that, when it brought him into conflict not only with Christ's injunctions but also with the implications of his own interpretation of those injunctions, he chose to let the latter yield. In this way the self-confessed weaknesses of one of the great thinkers of the Western world may, in the end, have influenced his thought in ways he never suspected, leading him to presume to redirect Christianity's moral course from pacifism to militarism. And this, paradoxically, may at the same time be the greatest compliment to his analysis of the unrelenting power of pride in human nature—that it found confirmation in the very account by which he warned against it.[66]

---

[66] Previously published in *The Augustinian Tradition*, ed. Gareth B. Matthews (Berkeley, CA: University of California Press, 1999), 323–45.

9

War, Power, and Nonviolence

This is a developed version of an essay previously published as "The Sleep of Reason Brings Forth Monsters." With an ingenious idea—speaking from the point of view of an imaginary intelligent alien visitor—Holmes demonstrates the immorality, irrationality, and absurdity of war. Someone who would not take for granted—as we all do—the omnipresence of war, violence, and destruction, who would be genuinely puzzled by the amount of effort normal, decent, and kind human beings put into training people to kill, someone like that would be able to bring to our attention the absurdity of the perpetuation of the war system by virtually every nation. A person of a sound mind would alert us to start thinking about alternatives to the monstrosities such war systems have brought about. As we are finally beginning to explore alternative sources of energy, the time has also come to awaken vast resources of power that lie trapped within the people of every country. The time has come to turn around and organize our lives around nonviolence.

If a visitor from outer space were to come to know human beings on this earth, but to know them only in their personal lives, at work and play, and without knowledge of human history or international affairs, what would he conclude? No doubt that virtually everyone values friendship, peace and happiness; that most persons desire basic creature comforts, love their families, and seek neither to suffer nor to cause pain to others; that they rarely harm one another, and then do so mainly under duress or in fits of anger directed against friends or loved ones and regretted soon after; that while they all can be insensitive, and a few of them cruel, they for the most part treat those they know best with friendly feeling and others with civility; and that most of them wish nothing more than to be left alone to work out their life plans according to their lights, which they do with varying degrees of success when given the chance.

If having observed all of this the visitor were then told that a scheme had been proposed by which to improve the world—not in the foreseeable future or in any future the proposer could identify—but which for the present would require that people pour their wealth into the production of weapons of destruction, organize vast authoritarian bureaucracies called armies, train their sons and daughters to kill and periodically send them off to slaughter and be slaughtered by other sons and daughters similarly organized by their governments, under conditions so brutal that even the survivors often return physically or emotionally incapacitated; if the visitor were told that humans could improve their lot provided only that they do all of these things, he would ridicule the scheme as having not the slightest chance of success, and even less of being accepted by rational beings.

Yet this is precisely what humankind has been led to accept in the case of war.

It has proven willing to abandon virtually everything worth living for, to do things all agree are abhorrent, for reasons few understand, and for ends (such as peace) that history shows cannot be secured by these means.

How have we let it come to this?

Perhaps because at no time did any one generation have to confront the choice of the whole of this state of affairs. Successive generations simply responded to the perceived threats of their day without regard for the cumulative effect of such responses over the course of history. In the process most societies became transformed into war systems, geared socially, politically, and economically to the maintenance and often the glorification of their capacity for organized violence.

As a result we today have inherited a world deeply committed to war as the ultimate means of settling disputes. Not that people think war is a good thing. Most do not. But they see no alternative. They view war as a problem so large and complex as to be incapable of resolution by the efforts of the individual. One can only accept it, they feel, as though it were part of the nature of things. And thus, portending the defeat of the human imagination and spirit, they resign themselves to being swept along to whatever end chance or fate decrees.

But it needn't be this way. War is a problem of our own creation. It can be solved by our own effort. But to do that requires courage, determination, and the resolve to effect a revolution in our moral thinking, which has been left behind with the acceleration of civilization down the path of technological development. The very security long thought to dictate the need for armaments now dictates that we surpass the war system.

People say, treaties have failed to prevent wars so let us be done with treaties; they don't say, war has failed to prevent wars so let us be done with war. Yet this is what they must say if they are to be serious about war's abolition.

And to be done with war means being done with the war system. For that system has a force that will pull apart the best intentioned of agreements.

Train dogs to kill, accustom them to the savagery of the pit, the shouts of spectators, the crunch of bones, and the smell of blood; then put them face to face under the lights and expect them not to fight. "Unrealistic," skeptics will scoff. "It's in their nature to tear each other to pieces."

And the skeptics are right—if, that is, one grants the whole system of values and practices that leads up to the dogs being placed in the ring in the first place. What isn't in their nature is that system itself, the institution of dog fighting. Dismantle it and organized dogfights will stop. Occasional dogs will still scrap, but the bloody, systematic brutalization of dogs and men entailed by that practice will cease.

So with war. The problem isn't so much a lack of desire for peace as it is a commitment to institutions that make peace impossible.

Consider the United States. Thousands earn their livelihood in military industries; forty percent of scientists and engineers work at military-related jobs; colleges train officers for the military (ROTC) and appoint military officers to professorships to instruct them; corporations seat retired military officers on their boards of directors; Congress regularly votes billions for military expenditures; and the highest officials, to a person, whether Republican or Democrat, accept violence as a means of resolving international disputes. In countless ways nonmilitary institutions and practices serve military ends—as though Adam Smith's invisible hand were at work to maximize human destructive potential. When this happens a society becomes hostage to military values as surely, if less conspicuously, as by military takeover. There remain, to be sure, those who wear uniforms and those who don't. But they simply serve the war system in different ways.

Little wonder then that violence erupts when nations—virtually all of which are committed in one degree or another to the perpetuation of their war systems—confront one another angrily in the ring of international conflict. To expect the signing of documents outlawing war to change that is naive.

This state of affairs can be changed only by reconstituting societies. And we must begin with our own. We need to make peace education a priority; to make development of alternatives to violence a priority; to begin to take seriously the values we profess to cherish. Not least of all we need to convert our economy to peaceful ends.

Many who agree basically with this feel that although it would be fine if everyone renounced war in one grand gesture, the consequences could be grievous if some do so while others do not.

But the alternative to war's renunciation isn't passive acceptance of evil. It's resistance and defense, but of a nonviolent sort. This requires not only conversion to a peace-oriented economy, but also the development of alternative means of social defense.

This thought occasions smiles from some people. They want to know how you stop an enemy tank by going limp or melt the heart of a Hitler by turning the other cheek. Fair enough questions. At least as fair as asking them how you defend yourself against a twenty-megaton nuclear bomb about to explode overhead.

The answer is that you cannot do so. Hypothesize situations in which a nonviolentist confronts someone armed and committed maniacally to violence, and the outcome can abstractly always be made to favor the violentist. Let that be conceded. Still, such questions betray a lack of imagination about the potential of nonviolence. Just as it is a mistake to adhere to concepts of defense and security derived from simple models of interpersonal relations, so it is a mistake to evaluate nonviolence solely on the basis of hypothetical cases of the sort presupposed by these questions.

To see this requires attention to the concept of power. For this is the key to understanding both the potential of nonviolence and the failure of the war system.

Power, from a social standpoint, is the ability to achieve one's objectives. And although capacity to use violence is one measure of power and may be effective in some contexts, it's demonstrably ineffective in others. That virtually every war has at least one loser attests to this. Destructive force doesn't automatically add up to social power.

Moreover, beyond a certain point, increments in the capacity for violence cease to yield increases in power. Beyond that point, in fact, one's power may decrease, however much destructive force one commands.

We discovered this in Vietnam—as did the Russians in Afghanistan—where we proved incapable of attaining our objectives despite overwhelming superiority in weaponry. With sufficient superiority one can always annihilate one's opponent. But that only rarely constitutes power in the sense at hand. The objectives of power rarely consist simply of destruction. They consist in securing benefits and advantages for oneself or those one cares about; or, often, in bringing about what one believes would be a better world (as distorted as his conception of a better world was, this was even true of Hitler). It is as means to these ends, or because they are perceived as obstacles to the attainment of the ends, that human beings are usually killed.

But attainment of the objectives for which people wage wars is incompatible with destruction that exceeds certain limits. We could have destroyed North Vietnam in a matter of hours with nuclear weapons. But that wouldn't have deterred the Vietcong in the south (though it would have reduced the scale of their struggle and protracted the war). And though we could have similarly destroyed the Vietcong as well, we couldn't have done so without annihilating South Vietnam in the process. That, however, would have defeated the very objective of creating a showcase anticommunist government in Southeast Asia for which we were fighting. As it was, the destruction of village life, the ravaging of the countryside with bombs and defoliants, and the alienation of the people made the attainment of that objective virtually impossible anyway. When the U.S. officer at Ben Tri immortalized the words, "We had to destroy the town to save it," he not only unwittingly epitomized the thinking that had come to govern our Vietnam policy, he also revealed the absurdity of thinking that you can ultimately achieve your objectives by mere destruction. Years later, the same thinking remained alive and well in the war in Afghanistan. When, during its surge against the Taliban, the U.S. began demolishing vacated homes—and sometimes whole villages—because many of them had been booby-trapped, the district governor allied with the U.S. said, "We had to destroy them to make them safe."[1]

That American power is diminishing in the world isn't, as militarists argue, because we're becoming militarily weaker. It's because we have misidentified power with the capacity to cause destruction. Even theorists of war like Clausewitz, and more recently Mao and Giap, have seen this better than we, in their emphasis upon the social and human dimensions in the attainment of one's objectives. Ever increasing military spending won't solve the problem because there is a basic misunderstanding of what the problem is in the first place.

Nonviolent power, on the other hand, increases in proportion to increases in the instruments of power—namely, the nonviolent actions of individuals—to the point where, as even critics of nonviolence concede, such power would transform the world for the better if everyone were nonviolent.

As one moves from contrived cases, such as that of a solitary Gandhi assuming the lotus position before an attacking Nazi panzer division, to cases in which millions

---

[1] *New York Times,* November 17, 2010.

of persons are hypothesized as confronting an actual adversary pursuing credible objectives, new sources of power can be seen to come into being. They are generated by an increase in the number of persons committed to nonviolence.

Consider a population of more than 300 million persons committed to nonviolent resistance against an invading army bent upon ruling the country. A large industrialized society like ours cannot be run—much less be run with the efficiency necessary to make it worthwhile to try to do so—without the cooperation of its population. People are needed to run factories, grow food, direct traffic, collect trash, and to perform thousands of other essential tasks. In fact, it's difficult enough to run the country *with* the cooperation of the people. Deny to an invading army that support—as one can through passive resistance, strikes, boycotts, civil disobedience, and nonviolent direct action—and you render it virtually incapable of attaining its objectives.

A people who have sought security in arms alone are defenseless once their military forces have been defeated. They are a conquered people. A people committed to nonviolence may be deprived of their government, their liberties, their material wealth. But they cannot be conquered.

True, nonviolence could be effective on such a scale only with the concerted effort of tens of thousands of well-trained persons willing to sacrifice and perhaps die for what they believe in. But no less is true of violence, which is why we now put millions of people in uniform. It's also true that nonviolence is no guarantee against bloodshed, for there are no such guarantees in any system. But the use of violence not only allows situations to develop in which bloodshed is inevitable, it entails the shedding of blood. And if we are to use considerations such as these as a criterion of adequacy in the one case, we must use them in the other as well.

The comparison should not be of nonviolence with some ideal of conflict resolution in an ideal world, but with our present methods in the actual world. Nor should it be of nonviolence in its still relatively early stage of development with a system of violence that is in an advanced stage of development, deeply entrenched in the socio-economic fabric of the major societies of the world. This would be as though one had said at the time of the Wright brothers, "Look, we have only two pilots, no airports, and one plane that can fly a few hundred feet; but we have thousands of miles of railroads, trained engineers, and a nation accustomed to rail travel"; and then argued on that basis against the development of the airplane. It's the potential of nonviolence that must command our attention, and the comparison should be of our present system of violence with nonviolence as it might realistically be developed. Nonviolence may not only be a better way of getting along in the world; it may in the end be the only way.

In short, vast resources of power lie untapped within the people of a country. These resources remain to be explored with all the determination that presently goes into the study of war and the refinement of techniques for waging it. Just as we need alternative sources of energy for the future, we need alternative sources of national power, and we should be developing the one as sedulously as the other.

Is the effort worth undertaking? Here is where our moral thinking must be brought up to speed with our thinking in science and technology.

We have too long conceptualized war as a problem of "us" against "them"; as something we engage in because of the bad conduct of others, rather than as an affliction of all humankind. By overlooking that we are precisely that "other" to others, our behavior as threatening to them as theirs is to us, we maintain a climate of suspicion and mistrust that elicits from all of us the very conduct that others then take as confirming their worst fears.

The problem isn't, as cocktail party wisdom would have it, with human nature. Human nature isn't corrupt. But it can be tricked by the subtleties of complex social, political, and international systems. The problem is with the misdirection of loyalties, with too much rather than too little willingness to sacrifice at the behest of others.

Like men pulling oars from the hold of a ship from which they cannot see an approaching waterfall, good people can, by their corporate effort, loyalty, and devotion to country sometimes ease themselves unwittingly toward catastrophe. All that is required is a few false beliefs about the motives and intentions of others and a willingness to follow political leaders unquestioningly.

From Nuremberg we should know that the key to understanding the horrors nations perpetrate isn't the evil of the occasional Hitlers of this world. It is rather the dedication of functionaries who serve them, and of the millions of ordinary persons like ourselves whose cooperation is essential to the success of their enterprises. Recognition of this fact is central to nonviolence. Unlike violence, which seeks to prevail over the physical manifestations of power—the weaponry and soldiers—nonviolence deals directly with the ultimate source of governmental power, the people themselves.

What is needed is a new perspective that sees the people of the world as arrayed, not basically against one another, but against the deceit and arrogance of governments and the ways of thinking, rooted in a global culture of violence, that have produced that deceit and arrogance. What is needed is a new respect for the preciousness and inviolability of the person. This doesn't require changing human nature or transforming the world into a community of saints. It does require recognizing that if we don't cherish the human person there is no point to the many other activities and strivings that consume our time; no point to saving the environment unless we value the beings that inhabit it; no virtue in self-sacrifice when it is at the expense of the lives and happiness of others. It does require a massive commitment of time, energy, and moral and financial resources to explore nonviolent ways of getting along in the world.

With the development of nonviolent means of social defense a nation could unilaterally disarm without having to acquiesce in the depredations of possible aggressors. It may indeed be only through a commitment to nonviolent defense that disarmament will ever come about. And while to bring it about requires the best in scientific and technical expertise, it requires first and foremost a moral decision that the effort is worth making. And faith that it can be made to succeed.

William James once wrote that faith in certain facts may help to bring those facts into existence. So, we might say, with the power of nonviolence.[2]

---

[2]   Previously published in *Nonviolence in Theory and Practice*, ed. Robert L. Holmes and Barry L. Gan, 3rd edn (Long Grove, IL: Waveland Press, 2012), 233–8.

10

Violence and Nonviolence

This essay, together with the one that follows it, is of central significance for Holmes' ethics of nonviolence. Here he delineates in an exemplary manner the distinctions crucial for understanding the respective natures and roles of violence and nonviolence. Both terms are just the abbreviations for the clusters of concepts. For example, violence can be understood only in connection with concepts like force and power. Holmes also carefully elaborates the similarities and the differences between physical and psychological violence. He follows it with detailed examination of various modes and aspects of nonviolence, with the prohibition to kill, the distinction between nonviolence as a tactic and as a way of life, the relationship of nonviolence and pacifism, and then finally discusses the thorny issue of the effectiveness of violence and nonviolence. A network of connecting notions is examined, as well as a variety of possible scenarios. At least one conclusion emerges from this sophisticated and multidimensional discussion: "It is that we simply do not know whether there is a viable practical alternative to violence, and will not and cannot know unless we are willing to make an effort, comparable to the multibillion-dollar-a-year-effort currently made to produce means of destruction and train young people in their use, to explore the potential of nonviolent action; to explore the possibility of educating ourselves and others to a whole new way of getting along in the world, a way which people now hear of chiefly in the form of piously eloquent Sunday morning ineffectualities which rarely filter down to the springs of conduct." Despite our lack of cognitive certainty, such an effort should be made because, considering the destructiveness of war and the spread of an epidemic of violence in the contemporary world, tomorrow it may already be too late.

It is one of the ironies of history that the issues most in need of cool and dispassionate thinking for their resolution emerge during the course of human events at just those times when this is most difficult to achieve; notably during times of crisis, when emotions are running high and the fires of irrationalism are most likely to have been kindled. So it is with the problem of violence. Not having had the wisdom to come to grips with it during those occasional respites we have enjoyed from the blood and thunder that has characterized so much of human history, we today find ourselves confronting it in the volatile atmosphere of increasing racial tensions, student disorders, and a potentially explosive international scene. The stakes by all accounts are immeasurably higher, and the margin for error less, than ever before.

In a sense the problem has crept up on us. There has always been violence, of course, but with modern technology it has metamorphosed into new and frightening forms, some of which we scarcely comprehend and most of which we are incapable of controlling with any justifiable confidence. Napalm, radiation, and biological agents cannot render a man any more dead than the broadsword or the crossbow, but they have added a new dimension of horror to warfare. And they have done so at just the time that mechanization and bureaucracy have desensitized us to that horror.[1] If men could ever have seriously maintained with Hegel that wars preserve the "ethical health" of nations, that time is past. The heroic spectacle of brave men contending on a darkened plain has given way to the prosaic impersonality of modern industrial society, in which the efforts of millions of ordinary persons—from taxpayers and defense workers to comfortably isolated functionaries in air-conditioned missile silos—conspire to promote and sustain a system for which everyone, and yet no one, is directly responsible. A multitude of loyalties are so arrayed as to generate a potential evil far greater than the goods they severally constitute.

Moreover, the problem of violence once seemed of manageable size. Wars could be waged full tilt, so to speak, with all of the zest and enthusiasm that dangerous adventures inspire; but when they were over the world went on pretty much as before—scarred and shaken sometimes, but always with hope of a better future, or at least of some kind of future. Now all of that has changed. The nuclear age has done more than just enlarge our capacity for violence; it has transformed the whole context in which our reasoning and judging about it must take place. Whereas previously violence could be used rationally in the service of human aims, at least in the sense of providing a means to certain clearly attainable ends (whether or not these in turn were rational), its character today threatens the very conditions essential to the attainment of *any* ends, good or bad. Modern weapons are so awesome that, as Hannah Arendt says, "no political goal could conceivably correspond to their destructive potential."[2] And this is a new problem. To suppose that it can be met short of a full review of the whole social, political, and moral perspective which has informed our current attitudes about violence, and without a reassessment of the repertoire of responses by which we are accustomed to getting along in the world, would be to perpetuate the worst strains in the thinking that has led us to where we are today.

Where one begins on a problem of such magnitude is perhaps less important than that he begin somewhere, for whatever the starting point one eventually encounters all of the relevant complexities. We shall, however, focus on the moral dimension. If concern for humanity, for one's children and loved ones as well as for one's own personal well-being, is of importance—and values of any sort must finally have their roots in some such soil—then

---

[1] As Konrad Lorenz puts it, "The man who presses the releasing button [of modern remote control weapons] is so completely screened against seeing, hearing, or otherwise emotionally realizing the consequences of his action, that he can commit it with impunity . . . Only thus can it be explained that perfectly good-natured men, who would not even smack a naughty child, proved to be perfectly able to release rockets or to lay carpets of incendiary bombs on sleeping cities, thereby committing hundreds and thousands of children to a horrible death in the flames. The fact that it is good, normal men who did this, is as eerie as any fiendish atrocity of war!" *On Aggression* (San Diego, CA: Harcourt, Brace & World, 1963), 242–3.

[2] "Reflections on Violence," *New York Review of Books*, February 27, 1969, 19.

this must ultimately be our paramount concern. Were we indifferent to whether violence was right or wrong, the other aspects of the problem—the scientific, social, political, and technological—would scarcely engage us as they do. At some point, of course, one must attend to the question of the "causes" of war. But he should proceed cautiously in so doing. There one quickly encounters an almost limitless profusion of theories possessing some measure of truth, but each being for the most part unprovable. We simply do not know how to decide whether man is inherently good or bad, whether he is impelled by a death instinct, whether wars are the product of dialectical laws of history, or whether violence has the therapeutic function of curing colonial neuroses.[3] Even when stated coherently, such theories tend either to take flight on the capricious winds of metaphysics or to become mired in the bog of bad psychology. We do know, however, with as much certainty as can be had in such matters, that modern wars cannot be waged without weapons of violence. And we know with equal certainty how to dismantle, destroy, and cease production of such weapons; in short, what must be done to make violence in the form of modern warfare technically impossible. What is needed now is an understanding of violence and the moral issues it raises without which there is unlikely ever to be the impetus for realistic action to achieve what is demonstrably within our grasp.

We shall take our cue from the old Socratic maxim that before one can make headway on a problem he must first understand clearly what he is talking about. This need not mean, as it did for Socrates and Plato after him, that one must proceed by searching for definitions. It may mean, as we shall take it, that complex problems are best handled by first sorting out the myriad issues they typically conceal and which, when left undisclosed, make it tempting to settle for simplistic and dogmatic solutions. Accordingly, we shall try first to clarify the complementary notions of violence and nonviolence, and then to distinguish and place in perspective the ethical issues to which they give rise. This will not resolve the problem of violence for us. That, in its practical aspect at least, can be accomplished only by appropriate action. But it will, if successful, both provide us with the necessary conceptual framework to deal with the problem and disentangle a nest of problems—constituting an almost inexhaustible source of confusion—which hitherto have been largely neglected by all sides concerned with the moral issues. We shall then, in conclusion, make a start at clarifying the specific problem of violence at the international level.

Violence and force

A prominent conservative who is fond of recounting his cocktail party expostulations with liberals tells of one liberal who was earnestly inveighing against the use of violence, particularly as represented by the war in Vietnam. With a sure eye for principle, the conservative confidently asked the latter whether he would be willing to use force to push a child out of the way of an onrushing car. Having to concede that he would, the liberal was reported to have retreated, hopelessly ensnarled in the manifest

---

[3] The latter being maintained by Sartre and Fanon. See Frantz Fanon, *The Wretched of the Earth* (New York: Grove Press, 1968), esp. Chapter 2 and Preface by Jean-Paul Sartre.

inconsistency of his position. The point being, of course, that one cannot consistently sanction force in one case and oppose it in the other.[4]

There are two assumptions here. One embodies a serious confusion, the other a difficult philosophical problem. Both are important to clarifying the concept of violence.

Force, violence, and power

The confusion is the tacit assumption that force and violence are the same. While violence typically involves the use of force, and we often use "force" and "violence" interchangeably, the two cannot be equated. We can use force (such as to lift a heavy object), do things forcefully (like arguing a point of logic), or force others to do certain things (like moving their king in a game of chess), without in any way involving violence. This is because force in its broadest sense is the effecting of change (or the capacity to effect change), and this may be done violently or nonviolently. Indeed, Gandhi in his concept of *satyagraha* or Truth Force and Martin Luther King, Jr, in his philosophy of Soul Force expressly utilize the concept of force to designate nonviolent ways of effecting change.

The second assumption, like the first, is characteristic of much of our common sense thinking. It is that a readiness to use violence in one situation commits one to a readiness to use it in another; or, more specifically, that to judge that violence is morally justifiable (or unjustifiable) in one situation commits one, upon pain of inconsistency, to a similar assessment of similar situations. Kant held it to be central to morality that only judgments based upon rules which are consistently applicable to all actions of the sort under consideration and which, moreover, are valid for all rational beings similarly situated, can be certified as sound. The part of this which requires that all similar actions be judged similarly has come to be called the thesis of universalizability.

The immediate bearing of universalizability upon the problem of violence can be seen by altering our above example slightly. Suppose that instead of pushing the child out of the way of an oncoming car (using force), the question is whether you would defend him (or your wife or grandmother) against an assault by a madman. If you consider violence justifiable in this case to what does it commit you? To being willing to kill in defense of your country? Or in defense of another country? Or at the command of a superior officer? Answers to questions like these are often assumed by both parties to moral disputes, but usually without any clear understanding of whether, or how, one could justify the answers. Yet we must seek to distinguish between consistency (which we all prize) and dogmatism (which we all deplore), for the line between the two is often difficult to draw.

We shall want to return to this problem later, but for the moment let us proceed by noting that not only can violence and force not be equated with one another, but

---

[4] The essentials of this line of reasoning were for many years built into the process for screening conscientious objectors in the US Selective Service Form 150 required of all applicants for CO (Conscientious Objector) status that they indicate under what circumstances, if any, they believed in the use of force, obviously with a view to determining whether they were ingenuous, or at least consistent, in their renunciation of killing.

neither of them can be equated with power. The measure of power is the effectiveness of the force at one's disposal. And just as force may be physical or nonphysical, violent or nonviolent, so the power one wields may be violent or nonviolent. We speak, for example, of the armed forces when referring to agents of violent power, but also and with equal appropriateness of the power of truth or of love.

There is, for all of this, an intimate connection between force and violence. Certainly the paradigm cases of acts of violence against persons (murder, rape, muggings), which is the mode of violence that mainly concerns us rather than that of violence against things or property, do involve physical force; so conspicuously, in fact, that we can take the notion of physical force to be partly definitive of the concept of physical violence. Characteristic acts of physical violence involve the intentional use of physical force to cause harm, injury, suffering, or death to persons against their will. But upon occasion certain of these elements may be missing. For example, the clear presence of an intention to cause harm may compensate for the lack of success; the terrorist who throws a bomb into a crowd performs an act of violence even if the device fails to explode. Similarly, an act may be violent even when there is no contravention of the will of another, as in suicide or the taking of another's life at his behest (e.g., euthanasia). We should also add that the vehemence, passion, or rage that is often associated with acts of violence is not essential to physical violence. The professional killer uses violence in coolly dispatching his victim even if the act itself is not violently executed.

"Do violence to no man"[5]

Another form of violence, which may have nothing to do with physical force or even with physical violence, is the *doing of violence*. This notion is not as close to the surface of our common sense thinking as is that of physical violence, but it is important to assessing the overall ethical question. Consider the debilitating effects of prolonged and intensive brainwashing, or of ghetto schools upon young children, or of the continual humiliation and debasement of a child by his parents. In none of these cases need physical violence be used, but in each case violence is done, and of a sort that may be far more injurious than physical violence.[6]

---

[5] Luke 3:14.

[6] Violence was seen in the Old Testament to be bound up in pride (Psalms 73:6), wealth (Micah 6:12), and in leading others astray (Proverbs 16:29). And the Stoic Marcus Aurelius catalogued a variety of ways in which a man might "do violence" to himself, from becoming vexed to being insincere and threatening harm to others; *Meditations* (Pleasant Valley, PA: Gateway, 1956), 18. Eastern philosophies often expressly distinguish mental from physical harms and associate violence with both. The second Yama, or restraint, of Yoga Ethics requires that "if we adhere to the principle of nonviolence we shall have to give up falsehood, because if we are not truthful and thus deceive others we shall cause them mental injury"; I. C. Sharma, *Ethical Philosophies of India* (Lincoln, NB: Johnsen, 1965), 209. Gandhi clearly intends the same when he says that "under violence I include corruption, falsehood, hypocrisy, deceit and the like"; *Non-Violent Resistance* (New York: Schocken Books, 1961), 294. Tolstoy makes much of this aspect of violence, which he takes to be the heart of the New Testament law of love, even though he does not always distinguish it carefully from physical violence. See, for example, his *A Confession, The Gospel in Brief & What I Believe* (New York: Oxford University Press, 1961), 321 and 351.

Violence in this sense has a closer kinship with the notion of violation than it does with physical force.[7] We may violate laws, rules, orders, good manners, or the spirit of an agreement; and we speak of the violation of persons in at least one type of physical violence, namely, rape. Similarly one can do violence to a wide range of things: language, facts, the truth, an author's intentions, the memory of a deceased, and to persons, including oneself. In each case something having value, integrity, dignity, sacredness, or generally some claim to respect is treated in a manner that is contemptuous of this claim. Persons are preeminently worth of respect, and each person has a claim upon those whose conduct may affect him to be treated in ways which do not diminish him. To deprive him of his freedom, degrade him, or destroy his confidence are all ways of doing the latter and are all accomplishable without resort to physical violence. Indeed, most of them can be effected through the subtlest forms of personal and social interaction, inasmuch as it is in these areas that people are often the most vulnerable. The insidiousness of racism consists largely in the fact that some of its most damaging effects are essentially invisible ones, wrought upon the psyche of a whole people through prolonged oppression.[8]

This reveals the importance of distinguishing between physical and mental (or psychological) harms. The former tend to be conspicuous and come most readily to mind when one thinks of harm. The latter are often inconspicuous and for that reason discounted or insufficiently attended to in our assessment of ways of treating people. Philosophers have, however, at various times showed an awareness of such harms and occasionally even provided the rudiments of a theory for understanding them. Plato, for example, holds that to harm a person is to make him less perfect, where this means disrupting the inner harmony of the soul which enables one to function effectively as a rational being. He may even have thought, as his mentor apparently did, that this is the only way to harm a person, and that what we are calling physical harms cannot really harm a virtuous man and might (in the form of punishment) even benefit one who is not virtuous. Other philosophers like Kant, Dewey, and the existentialists, by stressing the importance of human freedom and the value of the person, explicitly or implicitly direct attention to the fact that one can be harmed in other than physical ways. Marx does the same thing in characterizing the forms of alienation under capitalism which he believes dehumanize and ultimately reduce men to the level of animals. While it is not possible to sum up this mode of violence in anything like a neat formula or definition, let us say that to do violence to someone in any of these ways is to diminish him as a person, where what is central to this notion is the inflicting of mental harms.

The differences between physical violence and this "psychological violence" are sufficiently great as to warrant our treating them as separate concepts. Accordingly, we

---

[7] See Newton Garver, "What Violence Is," *Nation*, June 24, 1968, 819–22; and William Robert Miller, *Nonviolence: A Christian Interpretation* (New York: Association Press, 1964), Chapter 1. The latter provides a good outline of some of the key distinctions discussed above. Gandhi is interpreted by Erik H. Erikson as grounding his opposition to nonphysical harms in the injunction never to violate another person's essence; *Gandhi's Truth: On the Origins of Militant Nonviolence* (New York: W. W. Norton, 1969), 412.

[8] For a discussion of the "official violation of Negroes' humanity" through institutionalized racism, see Harvey Wheeler's "A Moral Equivalent for Riots," *Saturday Review*, May 11, 1968, 19–22, 51.

shall refer to them respectively as "violence$_1$" and "violence$_2$." It is clear from what we have said that one may do violence$_2$, without using violence$_1$, but it is less clear whether the reverse is true. Although the vagueness of these concepts makes it impossible to determine this without more analysis, we shall assume that in principle there may be situations in which one might use violence$_1$ without doing violence$_2$. It might be argued, for example, that suicide or euthanasia, to free oneself or another from a slow and torturous death from an incurable illness, need not entail the doing of violence$_2$, though it may involve using violence$_1$. If so, then physical violence need not always result in violence$_2$. Far from necessarily diminishing one, the willingness to suffer violence in one's own person might sometimes be the mark of one's stature as a person.

Alternatives to violence

The principled alternatives to violence are nonresistance, passive resistance, and militant nonviolence. Since both critics and advocates alike of these positions have not always been clear about what they mean by them, we shall take each one in its most literal sense: nonresistance as signifying a purely negative, noncoercive attitude which willingly suffers evil without resistance of any sort;[9] passive resistance as signifying a mode of opposition (e.g., noncooperation) which stops short of mounting a counteroffensive against evil; and militant nonviolence, or nonviolent direct action, which takes the offensive against evil rather than merely reacting to it.

Each of these can in turn be interpreted as either a tactic, a way of life, or a philosophy. As a tactic they presumably are utilized only so far as they are effective and abandoned when they are ineffective. On this interpretation each one would be fully compatible with any outlook which relies ultimately upon violence.[10] As a way of life, however, each of these is not merely, or even primarily, a means to an end but is

[9] Niebuhr takes this to be the letter of Christ's teaching when he says that "there is nothing in the teachings of Jesus that justifies a distinction between violent and nonviolent forms of resistance. The perfectionist ethics of the Christian Gospels teach complete nonresistance and therefore establish a contrast not between violence and nonviolence but between any prudential and pragmatic effort to establish justice and maintain peace by resistance, coercion, and the balance of power, and the millennial and anarchistic ideal of a completely uncoerced and voluntary social peace and cooperation"; Reinhold Niebuhr, *Love and Justice* (New York: Meridian Books, 1967), 262. Tolstoy, on the other hand, while interpreting nonviolence as nonresistance, views it as a means of resisting violence on a higher level. One does not, that is, suffer evil just for the sake of suffering it: "Christ does not command us to present the cheek and to give up the cloak in order to suffer, but commands us not to resist him that is evil, and adds that this may involve having to suffer"; *A Confession,* 318.

[10] Gandhi distinguishes *satyagraha* from passive resistance, if the latter is interpreted merely as a tactic one is prepared to renounce if it fails. Martin Luther King, Jr, similarly stressed that nonviolence is a way of life and not a tactic. Still, it is as a tactic, at least a necessary expedient, that nonviolence is often interpreted by critics. Herbert Marcuse, for example, says that "nonviolence is normally not only preached to but exacted from the weak—it is a necessity rather than a virtue"; "Repressive Tolerance," in *A Critique of Pure Tolerance,* ed. R. P. Wolff, B. Moore, Jr, and H. Marcuse (Boston: Beacon Press. 1965), 102; and Karl Jaspers says that "this renunciation [of force], into which pacifists would like to coax the nations, is born of fear and the lassitude of wanting just to be happy. It is not an inner renunciation of violence as such, only of its hazards"; *The Future of Mankind* (Chicago: University of Chicago Press, 1961), 36.

the end itself, or at least a part of it. A nonviolent way of life, that is, may be thought worthwhile independently of its success in attaining other goals. Philosophies of nonviolence, finally, in the sense of reasonably systematic statements of the principles of nonviolence, should be distinguished from both the tactics and the ways of life, even though the latter may (but need not) have nonviolent philosophies underlying them.[11] Since the significance of nonviolence lies principally in what it contrasts with, we can distinguish two different concepts of nonviolence: one contrasting with violence$_1$ and the other with violence$_2$. Let us call them respectively nonviolence$_1$ and nonviolence$_2$. They have in common their opposition to violence in either or both of its forms. What distinguishes them is whether they take the form of nonresistance, passive resistance, or militant nonviolence, where each of these may in turn be interpreted as a tactic, a way of life, or a philosophy. There emerge therefore the following basic positions.

	Nonviolence$_1$	Nonviolence$_2$
Nonresistance		
Passive resistance		
Militant nonviolence		

Clearly one can advocate nonviolence$_1$ (opposition to physical violence) without thereby advocating nonviolence$_2$. For this reason many advocates of nonviolence caution against degrading or humiliating one's opponents in nonviolent$_1$ confrontations lest one, in our terminology, do them violence$_2$. It seems equally clear that one cannot generally practice nonviolence$_2$ without also practicing nonviolence$_1$; whether one can ever do so depends upon whether it is possible to use violence$_1$ without doing violence$_2$.

The moral issue

We have not yet said anything to qualify the various forms of nonviolence as ethical positions. Whether an ethical outlook is represented by one's refusal to use violence in either of its basic forms (or to oppose violence in the ways outlined) depends upon whether one's position is a principled one and upon what sorts of reasons, if any, one appeals to in support of it. Let us try to clarify the relevant moral considerations by distinguishing four possible ethical rules or principles:

1. One ought not to kill.
2. One ought not to wage war.

[11] Gandhi, for example, actually had little in the way of a theoretical philosophy of nonviolence (though one speaks of the "philosophy" of *satyagraha*), in keeping with his view that nonviolence is a quality of the heart and "cannot come by an appeal to the brain."

3. One ought not to use violence$_1$.
4. One ought not to do violence$_2$.

Each of these, if taken to express a moral rule, can play a variety of roles within an overall moral position. We cannot explore all of these in detail, but it will be helpful to sketch briefly the interrelationships among these four so as to highlight the relevant distinctions. For this purpose let us interpret each of them as relating specifically to conduct *vis-à-vis* other persons.[12] Thus we shall take (1) to relate only to the taking of human life and (3) to physical violence against persons; (2) and (4) clearly enough relate principally to persons.

To hold (1) on this interpretation, would commit one only to (2) among the others, since a person might oppose killing but not object to forms of violence which do not involve killing. Thus a person could consistently accept (1) but reject (3) and (4). To hold (2), on the other hand, would be consistent with either asserting or denying any of the others, since one could be morally opposed to war but not to all killing (e.g., capital punishment) or to the using or doing of violence as proscribed by (3) and (4). A commitment to (3) clearly involves a commitment to (1) (on the assumption that to kill a person is to use violence$_1$ against him) and to (2) but not necessarily to (4) since, as we have seen, one might oppose violence$_1$ without also opposing violence$_2$. The relationship of (4) to the others is the most difficult to establish, and we can say confidently only that a commitment to (4) involves a commitment to (2), since it seems clear that whatever is involved in the doing of violence to persons it is manifestly done by warfare. But it is less clear whether the respect for persons which is at the heart of nonviolence$_2$ clearly rules out all cases of taking human life or using violence$_1$. One might argue, as suggested earlier, that suicide or euthanasia in certain circumstances are actually consistent with—perhaps even required by—a commitment to nonviolence$_2$; or that the forcible and even physically violent restraint of a deranged person to prevent harm to himself or others is justified by the principle of nonviolence$_2$ represented by (4).[13]

Pacifism is the holding (with qualifications to be noted later) of either (1) or (2) or both. It is first and foremost an opposition to war and killing, and as such it does not commit one to either (3) or (4), though it would preclude such physical and psychological violence as is entailed by warfare. Nonviolence as an ethical position (again with qualifications to be noted) is the assertion of (3) or (4) or both. It will be useful to coin the word 'nonviolentist', corresponding to 'pacifist', to stand for an advocate of nonviolence in either of our senses. A nonviolentist will be a pacifist because he will subscribe to (2) and probably (1), but a pacifist need not (though of course he may) be a nonviolentist.

---

[12] Which, of course, restricts their scope far beyond what it would be, say, for someone like Schweitzer (or for the eastern philosophies) in which the injunction against killing applies to all forms of life. See Albert Schweitzer, *Reverence for Life* (New York: Philosophical Library, 1965).

[13] This possibility seems to have occurred to Gandhi when he wrote: "I have come to see, what I did not so clearly before, that there is nonviolence in violence . . . I had not fully realized the duty of restraining a drunkard from doing evil, of killing a dog in agony or one infected with rabies. In all these instances, violence is in fact nonviolence"; *The Collected Works of Gandhi* (Delhi: Government of India, Ministry of Information and Broadcasting, The Publications Division, 1958), Vol. 14, 505; quoted in Erikson, *Gandhi's Truth*, 374. The apparent paradox here is removed if one recasts the point in terms of the enlisting of violence$_1$ in the service of nonviolence$_2$.

The character of moral justification

It remains to consider how one would go about trying to justify any of the preceding rules.

Notice first that each of these rules can be viewed as either basic or derivative and as expressing either prima facie, actual, or absolute obligations. A rule is derivative if it requires for its justification an appeal to a higher rule or principle, and basic if it is nonderivative. We shall call an obligation prima facie if it tells us what we ought to do all things considered (i.e., if there are no other overriding moral considerations); actual if it tells us, in addition to what we ought to do, that there are no overriding considerations; and absolute if it tells us, not only what we ought to do and that there are in fact no overriding considerations, but also that there could not be any overriding considerations.[14] If, for example, when called upon to justify rule (1) a pacifist appeals to a higher principle, such as that killing is prohibited by his religion or that it always has worse consequences than not killing, then he holds (1) as a derivative principle; whereas if he says that (1) neither needs nor can be given any higher justification, then he holds it as a basic principle. Relatedly, if one says that it is wrong to kill unless there are compelling moral considerations to the contrary, then (1) expresses for him a prima facie obligation. If in a particular case there are in fact no such overriding considerations, then to refrain from killing is one's actual obligation even if in principle there could be such considerations—as it seems there could if (1) is derivative, since then it may conflict with and be overridden by whatever more basic obligation provides its justification.[15] If, finally, one maintains that there are no qualifications whatsoever to (1)—in short, that it cannot even in principle be overridden by another rule—then (1) expresses for him an absolute obligation. So interpreted, (1) is the position of "absolute pacifism."

Because the absolute pacifist holds that there are no *conceivable* circumstances in which killing (or waging war) is justified, his position is clearly untenable. One can easily hypothesize situations, however far-fetched, in which it would scarcely be rational to insist that it is wrong to take human life (as, for example, if by taking a particular person's life, and only by so doing, one could secure for all mankind including that person an eternal existence of creative and happy human society as against one of eternal suffering).[16] This means that only nonabsolutistic interpretations of (1) (and, by similar reasoning, (2), (3), and (4) as well) have initial plausibility; and hence that only "conditional pacifism" (or conditional nonviolence) is defensible.

This alerts us to the further point that the validity of any moral rule or principle is relative to *some* broad set of conditions or circumstances. Indeed, this is characteristic

---

[14] This follows roughly W. D. Ross's explication of prima facie and actual obligations but adds to it the further category of absolute obligations. Cf. *The Right and the Good* (Oxford: Clarendon Press, 1930), Chapter 2.

[15] If a rule or principle is basic, however, it can be overridden (morally) only if it conflicts with an equally basic rule or principle. Both (1) and the rule that one ought to defend the innocent might, for example, be taken to be basic; in which case conflicts between them would have to be settled by appeal to other, possibly nonmoral, considerations.

[16] That one could never know that this would be the result of killing, and hence might never be justified in killing on these grounds, is correct but beside the point since we are here talking only about logically possible situations.

of normative rules generally, since their function is to guide conduct and what is sound in the way of conduct depends partly upon context and circumstances. This can be put, if oversimply, by distinguishing four categories of states of affairs and their interrelationships:

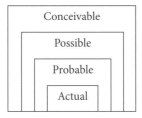

The actual states of affairs are those obtaining at the present, the probable those likely to come about in the future, the possible all of those (including the actual, probable, and improbable) whose realization would be consistent with the laws of nature, and the conceivable those (including the possible and impossible, probable and improbable, existent and nonexistent) whose realization would be logically possible (or non-self-contradictory).

In these terms, the absolutist relativizes his principle to the broadest possible consistent state of affairs—the logically conceivable; this is the consequence of his saying that he is opposed to killing under any and all circumstances. And it is this which renders his position untenable by making it easy prey to counterexamples, especially when the latter presuppose conditions which are neither actual, probable, nor causally possible. But one can relativize his principle to a narrower range of conditions, like the probable or the actual (or within the latter category to more specific conditions defined, say, by reference to time or location[17]), and claim that its validity as an action-guide presupposes that these conditions obtain. He can then consistently acknowledge that there are wildly imaginative hypothetical situations, drawn from categories of conceivable experience which require denying these conditions, in which one ought to violate his principle, and at the same time hold that his principle is valid for conduct, say, in the world as it is now or is likely to be in the foreseeable future. *The point is that putative counterexamples are relevant only framed within the same perspective as the one for which the rule or principle in question is held to be valid.*

This has important practical significance. Consider the applicant for CO status who is asked by his draft board whether he opposes all wars or only a particular war. How he should respond depends upon whether "all wars" is interpreted to mean all conceivable wars, all possible wars, all likely or all actual wars, and also upon the range of conditions for which he holds his ethical position to be valid. If he is an absolutist, of course, he has no problem and can answer flatly that he opposes all wars without

---

[17] Though, of course, if one carries relativization to an extreme, he renders rules and principles pointless by making their scope so narrow as to prevent them from providing the general guidance that is their primary function.

qualification. But if he is a conditional pacifist or nonviolentist he can answer this question affirmatively only by taking "all wars" to be elliptical for something like "all wars of a certain type" or "all wars under certain conditions." What is important is that if one opposes war under specific conditions, such as those obtaining in the nuclear age, but does not necessarily think that all previous wars were wrong, then to elicit from him an admission that he would have fought against Hitler but will not fight, say, in Vietnam, does not signify any inconsistency on his part. To insist that it does, and that the only credible defense in such a situation is to oppose war unconditionally, is to say that the only credible form of pacifism is the least tenable form, absolute pacifism.

This sheds light, moreover, on the problem of universalizability raised earlier. For it means that even if one accepts the principle of universalizability, he is committed at most to judging similarly only those cases which fall within the scope of the conditions to which he relativizes his basic moral principles. Consistency, in this sense, is a relative matter. But, in any event, what we said about conditions and consequences makes it doubtful that the principle of universalizability is a very plausible one if taken other than in the trivial sense of requiring that we judge exactly similar cases similarly. For the same act performed at different times, even if in generally "similar" circumstances, may have different consequences and hence require a different moral assessment. This means that anyone who takes seriously the bearing of conditions and consequences upon morality must always be willing to reconsider and possibly revise both the particular moral judgments he makes and his more general rules and principles.

It is obvious that there is a marked difference between the absolute pacifist, on the one hand, and both the conditional pacifist and the nonpacifist on the other. But one might well wonder what distinguishes the conditional pacifist from the nonpacifist (and the conditional nonviolentist from his counterpart), since nearly everyone subscribes to (1) and (2) on some interpretation, and probably (3) and (4) as well.

Let us explore this further, using rule (1) for purposes of illustration. Rule (1), we have seen, can be interpreted to imply either:

A. Killing never (in principle).
B. Killing sometimes (in principle).

To appreciate the full import of these two interpretations would require that one distinguish among the different modes of killing the kinds of circumstances in which killing might take place (self-defense, capital punishment, warfare, etc.), and the consequences of killing of the various types under the different circumstances—where such consequences would depend upon the two preceding factors. The absolutist, interpreting (1) so as to entail (A), says that all types of killing are wrong no matter what the circumstances and consequences. Both the conditional pacifist and the nonpacifist, whether they hold (1) as basic or derivative, interpret it to imply (B), which means that conditions and consequences—in short, context—are always relevant to moral assessment and that *some* conceivable entries under these headings would render killing permissible and perhaps obligatory. What conditions are relevant and to what moral evaluation they lead depends, as we have seen, upon the scope of conditions to which one has relativized his principle. They depend also upon whether one takes considerations of value, that is, of goodness and badness, to be relevant to moral assessment. For if we distinguish between judgments about what is good, bad, desirable, and the like, on the one hand, and judgments about what is right, wrong, obligatory, and prohibited, on the other hand, we see that one might or might not take judgments of the latter sort (which are the ones of primary interest in ethics since they deal most explicitly with guiding conduct) to be based upon the former. Thus where the conditional pacifist and the nonpacifist differ is in the type of killing they regard as permissible and/or in the sorts of circumstances in which they allow any of the types to be permissible. Beyond this there is no way of stating once and for all where the line between the two is to be drawn, for it will be a shifting one depending upon the perspectives of the persons involved. There will be clear pacifists (e.g., those who say that war and killing are wrong under all existing and probable conditions) and clear nonpacifists (e.g., those who say that killing is permissible in self-defense, to defend one's country, to protect the innocent, etc.). But there will be others (e.g., those who say that war, but not all killing, is wrong) who will be in the borderline area between the two and whose positions defy final classification according to these distinctions.

What leads the pacifist of this variety and the nonpacifist to their different assessments? To answer this requires two final sets of distinctions: the first between those who hold and those who deny that consequences alone determine rightness and wrongness; the second between those who hold and those who deny that it is the value (goodness) actualized by actions (and/or their consequences) which determines rightness or wrongness. Let us mark the first distinction as that between consequentialist and nonconsequentialist moral theories, the second as that between axiological and deontological theories.[18] Now if the pacifist and nonpacifist subscribe to (1) interpreted as entailing (B), then they both take conditions or consequences or both to be relevant to moral evaluation. They may differ with regard to which of these they take to be central and, relatedly, in the importance they attach to value, but they need not. For each of the positions definable by reference to these two sets of distinctions (the most plausible of which are consequentialist-axiological and nonconsequentialist-deontological, or more simply, teleological and deontological) may provide the basis for either pacifism or nonpacifism. For example, both the pacifist and nonpacifist could be teleologists and subscribe to the same basic moral principle: that one ought always to maximize the balance of good over evil in the consequences of his actions. They would then differ either in their judgments about what is good and bad or simply in their estimate of the consequences of killing in different circumstances. In the latter case their disagreement would be strictly factual, not moral, and would in principle be resolvable if both sides had sufficient knowledge about the consequences of actions. In any event, the difference between them may simply be one of degree. Not

[18] Seen in this light, the absolutist will most likely be a nonconsequentialist and a deontologist, because he denies the relevance of consequences and value produced to the moral assessment of killing (though he could theoretically be an axiologist if he maintained that it is logically impossible that killing ever brings about more good than not killing). But neither the nonconsequentialist nor the deontologist need be absolutists. They can both allow that various aspects of context are relevant, such as (for the deontologist) that an act would violate personality or (for the nonconsequentialist who is an axiologist) that the motive of the action or the action itself (or both) actualize value.

only can they accept the same rule, like (1), but they can accept the same fundamental principle by which it is justified, and even agree on the criteria for evaluating goodness and badness in the consequences of actions. But given this common theoretical basis they will still come out with conflicting moral judgments about specific actions if they differ enough in their factual beliefs. So, while there are many levels at which the pacifist and nonpacifist may disagree, the common ground between them can be far more substantial than is generally realized.

To summarize, we may say that to justify any of the rules in question requires clarifying the range of conditions for which the rule is alleged to hold, clarifying whether the rule is basic or derivative and whether it expresses a prima facie or unconditional obligation, and finally whether circumstances and consequences, and particularly considerations of value, figure in the overall assessment of conduct by reference to the rule.

The effectiveness of nonviolence

It should be clear from the foregoing that there is no one problem of violence but rather a whole constellation of problems. Violence can be practiced at different levels, and the practical and theoretical difficulties in arriving at a moral evaluation vary as one moves from one level to the next. Thus it invites confusion to draw conclusions at one level (say, the interpersonal) and to apply them unqualifiedly to another (like the international). This is why one cannot conclude *simpliciter* that because one might be willing to use violence to defend his assaulted grandmother, he must be willing to support preparations for nuclear war. And the type of violence, physical or psychological, may vary within these levels and take institutional and noninstitutional (as well as legal and extralegal) forms. If, as we concluded, only nonabsolutistic positions with regard to violence and nonviolence are defensible, then differences in mode and level of violence will necessitate separate analyses of the ethical problems they raise, and may require different conclusions concerning them. Nonetheless, because the paradigms of violence are also paradigms of how human beings ought (prima facie) not to be treated, violence in either form always requires justification. The burden morally is not upon those who oppose violence to show that it is wrong, though they should for various reasons be prepared to do this. It is first and foremost upon those who advocate it to show that it is right.[19]

---

[19] That there is a felt need to justify violence tends to be confirmed by the fact that most of its practitioners try to provide a rationale for its use. Lenin, for example, while advocating violent revolution, protested that "we set ourselves the ultimate aim of abolishing . . . all organized and systematic violence, all use of violence against man in general"; V. I. Lenin, *The State and Revolution* (Peking: Foreign Languages Press, 1965), 97. Every modern nation tries to justify its participation in war, and no war in recent history has been fought without high ideals being invoked on all sides. Even overtly illegal forms of violence, such as characterized the vigilante movement in the United States, recognized the need for justification and appealed to everything from the right of revolution to that of self-preservation for that purpose. See Richard Maxwell Brown, "The American Vigilante Tradition," in *Violence in America: Historical and Comparative Perspectives,*

If this is correct, can one in fact justify violence? To answer this would require making and defending judgments on all of the fundamental issues raised in connection with the theory of justification. While we cannot hope to do this in the brief compass of this discussion, we can make a start on a problem of more manageable size by observing that the standard rationale for violence is that it sometimes is the only effective means of preventing evil or redressing wrongs. Nonviolence, it is reasoned, is fine as an ideal, but in an imperfect world we must be realistic, and reluctantly but resolutely take up the sword when it is forced upon us. Thus at the same time that people profess to abhor violence they perpetuate whole systems of institutions, roles, and responsibilities geared to preparation for its use and, for the most part, if they are male and young enough, become its willing purveyors first-hand—all on the ground that we must be "realistic."

What is to be made of this argument? First we should note that "effectiveness" has no meaning in the abstract; it is always effectiveness in achieving some purpose, end, or goal, and as such is always in part a function of existing conditions. Thus from a moral standpoint one must ask not only whether what is adjudged to be effective is in fact so, but also whether, if it is, the ends or goals to whose realization it is a means are morally defensible. This means that one must ask further whether in comparing violence and nonviolence with regard to effectiveness the two are presumed to have the same ends. If they are, the matter of effectiveness can be considered decisive and the issue resolvable at least in part on empirical grounds. If not, then attention must be shifted to the moral assessment of their respective ends.

These ends may overlap, but unless nonviolence is considered only a tactic they will diverge at some point; and certainly the basic ends of violence and nonviolence will differ radically. The easy comparison of violence and nonviolence as tactics has contributed to the gradual erosion of support for nonviolence in racial matters, since the philosophy of nonviolence, as preached by Martin Luther King, Jr, failed to achieve many of its specific short-range goals, whereas violence, especially in the form of riots, sometimes elicited a more prompt and constructive response from the white community.[20]

If nonviolence is thought of as a way of life, however, then as we have seen its end is not a far-off state of affairs but an ongoing process of infusing a certain quality into one's day-to-day engagement with the world. To live nonviolently and to encourage others to do the same *is* the end, and the question is not whether nonviolence is effective

ed. H. Graham and T. Gurr (New York: New American Library, 1969), 144–219. It is where violence takes its most monstrous forms, however, such as in Nazi Germany, that the felt need for a rationale is perhaps greatest. And in Germany it was given a rationale—indeed a whole philosophy—in the argument of *Mein Kampf* that the German people were in a struggle for their very survival against Jewish-Marxist defilers of the race. It is noteworthy that Hitler recognized, and evidently took seriously, that "the application of force alone, without the impetus of a basic spiritual idea as its starting point, can never lead to the destruction of an idea and its dissemination . . . Any attempt to combat a philosophy with methods of violence will fail in the end, unless the fight takes the form of attack for a new spiritual attitude"; *Mein Kampf* (Boston: Houghton Mifflin, 1962), 170, 172.

20 For a good discussion of the question of the effectiveness of violence in domestic affairs, see Bruce R. Smith, "The Politics of Protest: How Effective is Violence?" in *Urban Riots: Violence and Social Change*, Proceedings of the Academy of Political Science, 29 (July 1968), 111–28. See also *Urban Violence*, ed. Charles U. Daly (Chicago: University of Chicago Press, 1969).

(though one might ask whether it is effective in achieving other ends) but whether this or that person is successful at living nonviolently. Here means and ends collapse into one another, because it is in part the particular means one adopts in pursuing the many short-range ends in life ("ends-in-view" as John Dewey called them) that go to make up the end. Rather than being steps on a ladder to a lofty and remote destination, means on this view are more akin to ingredients in a recipe, the end or final product of which is made up of what is put into it.

If the nonviolentist, as we are calling him, takes this latter line, there will be little ground for further discussion between him and his opponent on the matter of effectiveness. But if he maintains that nonviolence brings about a greater good and more justice in the world, not only in terms of what is actualized immediately in the lives of those who practice it, but also as measured by its consequences for the well-being, freedom, and happiness of others,[21] then there will be a common ground from which he and his opponent can assess their respective moralities. For then one can examine the bearing of their two approaches upon specific problems like racism, capital punishment, war, and so forth, in which case effectiveness in achieving agreed upon goals becomes a relevant—though even here not necessarily a decisive—consideration.

To take effectiveness to be relevant to the assessment of nonviolent versus violent ethical philosophies is to have to come to grips eventually with the problem of Nazi Germany and World War II—the closest thing there is to a "test case" in matters of this sort. For few today would deny that World War II was justified; even many of those who oppose the war in Vietnam say that they would have fought against Hitler. The question is whether anything short of violence could have been effective against as ruthless a tyranny as Hitler's, and if it could not, whether this isn't decisive against nonviolence.

As a preliminary observation we should remember that there need be no inconsistency in holding that the war against Nazi Germany was justified but that war today is unjustified. The nuclear age has added a new dimension to warfare such that we are no longer discussing phenomena of the same magnitude in the two cases. And if conditions and consequences have any bearing upon morality, as they must for anyone but the absolutist, then changes like this are precisely the sorts which may call for a revision of one's moral outlook.

But what of the nonviolentist who, as it were, sticks to his guns and not only condemns war today but says that the war against Nazi Germany was also unjustified? What, if anything, can be said of this position from the standpoint of the relevance of effectiveness? To make a start on this requires, as we have seen, that one specify the relevant ends or goals to whose attainment the war against Hitler is said to have been instrumental. What were they? To halt Nazi aggression? To eradicate fascism? To secure world peace? Defenders of the war usually do not make clear what it was that

---

[21] Tolstoy at times seems to justify nonviolence in such teleological terms. He says, for example, that "Christ did not think of calling us to sacrifice; on the contrary, he teaches us not to do what is worst but to do what is better for us here in this life . . . He says that men, if they live without resisting others and without property, will be happier"; *A Confession*, 482. Elsewhere, however, he stresses almost exclusively the attainment of inner purity in one's life without apparent regard for consequences; *The Kingdom of God* (New York: Noonday, 1961), 102.

the war was effective in accomplishing, but it usually has something vaguely to do with "stopping Hitler."

Now it seems clear that nonviolence could not have stopped Hitler once the war began. Only military action could have done that. But notice that temporal considerations are paramount here. The nonviolentist may reply that had enough German citizens acted responsibly, with or without a commitment to nonviolence but particularly with it, say, in the 1920s and early 1930s, fascism could never have advanced to the stage where its progress was reversible only by military means. Had German industrialists not financed Hitler's rise to power; had German youth refused to serve in the military; had conservatives not supported him and communists not deluded themselves that anything would be better than the liberal democratic Weimar regime, Hitler might have remained the frustrated and ineffectual Austrian painter that he was in his early years—and indeed very nearly remained despite all.[22] While nonviolence obviously could not have pushed back German armor on the battlefield once the institutions of militarism had been allowed to mature and the self-propelling mechanism of a military state put into motion, it might have been effective at an earlier stage in preventing the rise to power of those responsible for all of this. If the historical fact is that military means stopped Hitler once he began to march, it is also an historical fact that reliance upon such means on the part of the world's nations did not prevent his rise to power in the first place. The point here is that both sides to this dispute must acknowledge the relevance of timing, for there may be a point in the course of events beyond which neither approach has much chance of succeeding. Just as the nonviolentist must concede that after a certain point nonviolence could not have stopped Hitler, so the advocate of military means must concede that had military action not been taken, say, until 1943 (or if Germany had not invaded Russia or had perfected the atom bomb first), it is unlikely that Hitler could have been stopped this way either.

The defender of the war is likely to reply that it would have been all well and good if people had stopped fascism nonviolently years earlier, but the fact is that they did not. They were neither ready nor willing in sufficient numbers to act, and it is precisely this fact (which the nonviolentist himself has to acknowledge) that led to the crisis which called eventually for a military solution.

This cuts both ways, however, and calls attention to another consideration in addition to timing. This has to do with the conditions necessary for success of the respective approaches. The advocate of military violence cannot make a plausible case for its effectiveness unless it is presumed that there are tens of thousands of well-trained and equipped persons willing to make the ultimate sacrifice in the service of the cause for which the action is undertaken; not to mention millions more in the

---

[22] Hitler was considered washed up in 1923 following an attempted putsch, his imprisonment, and the crushing of the German Workers Party which he headed; again in 1928 when the growing prosperity of the Weimar Republic temporarily deprived the Nazis of much of the discontent they fed upon; and still again as late as 1932—the year prior to his rise to power—following setbacks at the polls and the loss of much needed financial backing. Despite the strong-arm methods and street violence we usually associate with his rise to power, Hitler worked primarily through the legal institutional channels of the country, and his future hung precariously in the balance on more than one occasion. Compared with what it took to stop him years later, he could relatively easily have been denied power in the first place by concerted nonviolent (particularly political) action.

society at large who are willing to support this effort financially and often through direct participation in the maintenance of the machinery necessary to war. Military action cannot, in other words, hope to succeed without armies, guns, and equipment. By the same token nonviolence cannot be imagined to have any prospect of succeeding when the basic conditions necessary to its success are similarly absent. And these may well include, at least if it is contemplated on a grand scale, a willingness to sacrifice and a degree of discipline and training on the part of tens of thousands comparable to that required in the military; as well as extensive background research into techniques of nonviolence against various forms of aggression.[23] In short, one cannot make a case for the effectiveness of nonviolence any more than for that of violence in hypothetical situations in which certain obviously necessary conditions of any prospect of success are presumed absent. To point out, therefore, that nonviolence would not have succeeded if tried in a context in which these conditions were absent may suffice to refute simplistic versions of the theory, but it will not tell against versions which hold, among other things, that these conditions ought to be promoted.[24]

We have been assuming, of course, that nonviolence could not have been effective against Hitler, at least at the time war broke out, and that violence was successful. The former assumption, while probably true, does require qualification. Some of the most effective forms of nonviolent resistance in the twentieth century were undertaken, mostly spontaneously and without advance preparation and coordination, against the Germans in World War II[25]—a fact which those who reply to the examples of Gandhi and King by saying that they could not have done it against the Nazis consistently overlook. One could profitably speculate on what might have been the consequences if whole nations had been geared in advance for such action. Any attempt to conquer and rule a modern nation must in the long run be a multifaceted one of which what takes place on the battlefield is but one aspect, for only by enlisting the support or cooperation (willing or coerced) of whole populations can dictators remain in power. There are obvious responses like mass strikes and boycotts which can cripple the administration of a country far more quickly and effectively than all but the most devastating of military actions. The key lies in concerted action by large numbers. It is with regard to the prospect of devising ways of withholding necessary support and making such concerted action possible that nonviolence must make its case with respect to effectiveness.

The second assumption, however, is doubtful. That Hitler was stopped is true, and if among the possible aims of the war this were the only relevant one, then the war

[23] On this, see Commander Stephen King-Hall, *Defense in the Nuclear Age* (Fellowship, 1959); American Friends Service Committee, *In Place of War: An Inquiry into Nonviolent National Defense* (New York: Grossman, 1967); and A. Roberts, ed., *Civilian Resistance As a National Defense* (New Orleans, LA: Pelican, 1969).

[24] This means that we must distinguish the questions (a) whether nonviolence could be effective given existing conditions; (b) whether it could be effective under optimal conditions; and (c) whether the latter conditions can be brought about? Only if the first and either the second or the third of these can be answered conclusively in the negative is it clear that there is no point to nonviolence as a practical alternative to international violence.

[25] For an account of these actions, see A. K. Jameson and Gene Sharp, "Non-Violent Resistance and the Nazis: The Case of Norway," in *Quiet Battle*, ed. Mulford Q. Sibley (New York: Anchor, 1963), 156–86.

succeeded. But considering some of the other ends mentioned, it is either questionable that they were accomplished or clear that they were not accomplished. It is arguable, for instance, particularly in light of the emergence of the neo-Nazi National Democratic Party, with recent election successes comparing favorably with those of the Nazis in the pre-Hitler era, that fascism in Germany was not eradicated but merely temporarily suppressed; or in light of the postwar resurrection of an impressive military that German military might was hardly put to rest. And it is incontrovertible that, with regard to the broader aim of securing lasting peace, World War II failed abysmally. Power has been redistributed and enemies redefined, but injustice and oppression remain, and the ominous clouds of nuclear war forebode a possible devastation of mankind scarcely imaginable in times past.

The foregoing are among the sorts of problems which must be explored as part of any thorough assessment of these issues. While we have confined ourselves in this last section chiefly to violence at the international level, the same needs to be done, and in greater detail, for all of the various levels of violence, and indeed for all of the modes human conflict.

Can any conclusions be drawn from this part of our discussion? There is at least one that stands out. It is that we simply do not *know* whether there is a viable practical alternative to violence, and will not and cannot know unless we are willing to make an effort, comparable to the multibillion-dollar-a-year-effort currently made to produce means of destruction and train young people in their use, to explore the potential of nonviolent action; to explore the possibility of educating ourselves and others to a whole new way of getting along in the world, a way which people now hear of chiefly in the form of piously eloquent Sunday morning ineffectualities which rarely filter down to the springs of conduct.

Why should such an effort be made? It may be that we have no choice. For we have reached the point at which mankind can no longer hope, as it may once have, to muddle interminably through war after war. The potential destructiveness of war has increased to the point where there is no longer any rational end conceivably attainable by the full-scale nuclear war for which the major powers have prepared themselves. Kant laid it down as one of the tenets of rationality that to desire an end is to desire the indispensable means to its attainment. If the ends which we now desire (including peace and a future for our children) cannot conceivably be secured by the means we have traditionally relied upon, then it is at the risk of forsaking our claim to rationality—not to say our lives and well-being—that we fail to make a massive commitment of our moral, intellectual, and financial resources to devising new means. To wait until others do the same, or until that nonexistent future when nations are miraculously "ready" to lay down their arms, is visionary beyond anything proposed by those who today are called idealists.[26]

---

[26] Previously published in *Violence*, ed. Jerome A. Schaffer (New York: David McKay Company 1971), 103–35.

11

The Morality of Nonviolence

*Encouraged by the fact that the past hundred years have witnessed a gradual
awakening to the power of nonviolence, Holmes attempts to set grounding for
an ethics of nonviolence. Following his analysis of various models of nonviolent
commitment that have emerged in different parts of the world, he proposes an ethics
of principled nonviolence, which is normative and impersonal in nature and which
resembles the ancient ethics of virtue. Inspired by one of the original and most radical
proponents of nonviolence—the Jains of India—Holmes argues for nonviolence in
conduct, speech, and thought: in short, for nonviolence as a way of life. By replying
to various criticism traditionally made against nonviolence (and pacifism), he
eliminates the charges of a rational untenability of approaching nonviolence as a way
of life. Holmes' ethics of nonviolence goes further than the ancient ethics of virtue
insofar as it is an ethics not only of individual but of collective aspirations as well: it
projects a vision of a nonviolent and peaceful world. It asks us to search for new and
creative ways of relating to others, by overcoming the differences that separate us, and
encourages each one of us to join in trying to create this new world.*

The past century has witnessed a gradual awakening to the power of nonviolence.
Models of nonviolent commitment have emerged in disparate parts of the world.
These include Tolstoy in Russia, Gandhi in India, Martin Luther King, Jr, in the
United States, and, more recently, Mubarak Awad in the Middle East and the Dalai
Lama in the Far East. But this awakening has not been confined to a few remarkable
individuals. Thousands of ordinary persons have turned to nonviolent action as well:
in Scandinavia during World War II, the U.S. during the civil rights era, the Philippines
during its revolution, and in Poland, China, Czechoslovakia, the West Bank, the Baltic
republics, and the Ukraine in the dramatic events of the 1980s and early 1990s.

Some of this nonviolence has been spontaneous. Some of it has been expedient.
And some of it has been tainted with violence. But all of it is part of the historical
unfolding of an empowering way of dealing with conflict, and beyond that, of living
and being in the modern world.

Viewed in one light, nonviolent action—particularly concerted action by large numbers
of people—is simply the exercise of power. It is power that employs different means than are
involved in the use of force. Rather than trying to prevail by marshalling greater force than
one's opponent, it seeks to undermine the bases of an opponent's power. Governments,
armies, occupying forces and institutions of any sort that control and regulate people's

lives require the cooperation, or at least the acquiescence, of large numbers of people. Withdraw that cooperation and the foundations of such power crumble. Nonviolence studies techniques by which to do that. These techniques require studying with as much care as traditionally has gone into the study of violence and warfare.

As important as it is to understand the practical side of nonviolence, however, it is important to understand the theoretical dimensions as well. This is needed in the interests of clarity. It is also needed to understand whether nonviolence can be justified, and if so, in what ways. It is enough for some that nonviolence often works as a tactic. It is enough for others that it can be used when weapons are unavailable. It is enough for still others that it makes a useful supplement to the standard methods of violence. But for some, nonviolence represents a deeper commitment. It represents a commitment to remain nonviolent even when this or that tactic fails, and even when weapons of violence are available. It is nonviolence in this sense that I propose to examine. My aim will be primarily clarificatory. I shall map out the different ways of understanding nonviolence. But I shall also try to show how I believe nonviolence can most plausibly be defended as a moral position.

Let me begin by locating the moral concern within the broader perspective of a philosophy of nonviolence.

The philosophy of nonviolence

A philosophy of nonviolence may simply describe and elucidate nonviolence. Or it may instead, or in addition, propose and defend its adoption. That is, it may be normative or non-normative. I shall examine nonviolence understood to be normative in this sense.

Nonviolentists (as I shall call advocates of nonviolence) sometimes say that while *they* ought to be nonviolent, others must choose for themselves. Thus they refrain from prescribing nonviolence for others. This represents a common and important position. But it is not the one I want to examine. I want to examine nonviolence understood to be a moral position with an interpersonal character to it—that is, as a position meant for others as well as oneself.[1]

Moreover, nonviolence as an interpersonal position may be held on either moral or nonmoral grounds. I shall call the former, *principled nonviolence,* the latter, *pragmatic nonviolence.* Moreover, principled nonviolence may tell us either to *be* certain sorts of persons, or to act certain sorts of ways, or both. It may tell us, in short, to be nonviolent and/or to act nonviolently. In the first case, it belongs to the ethics of virtue; in the second, to the ethics of conduct. These distinctions can be represented as follows:

---

[1] It is important at the outset to distinguish nonviolence from pacifism. Pacifism is opposition to war, nonviolence opposition to violence. While one cannot be a nonviolentist without being a pacifist, one can be a pacifist without being a nonviolentist. One can, that is, oppose warfare without necessarily opposing other modes of violence (such as in personal self-defense, or by the police, or in the form of capital punishment).

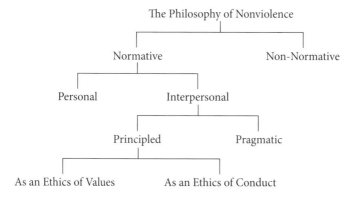

What are the implications of the differences between principled and pragmatic nonviolence?

It is tempting to say that pragmatic nonviolence stresses consequences, whereas principled nonviolence does not. But this is not necessarily so. Just as morality may emphasize consequences (as in utilitarianism), so may principled nonviolence. Whether it does so depends upon the overall moral position of which it is a part. If that position is consequentialist, it will assign as much weight to consequences as does pragmatic nonviolence; if it is nonconsequentialist, it will not.

It is also tempting to say that pragmatic nonviolence values effectiveness in achieving social and political ends, whereas principled nonviolence does not. But this, too, need not be so. To be concerned with effectiveness is to be concerned with achieving ends, goals, and purposes. And this concern typically characterizes principled nonviolence as well as pragmatic nonviolence. Any of the ends of pragmatic nonviolence can become ends of principled nonviolence, provided they have a moral justification. This was the case with some of the better-known uses of principled nonviolence by Gandhi and King.

Finally, it is tempting to say that principled nonviolence renounces violence in all conceivable circumstances, whereas pragmatic nonviolence does not. But once again, this is not necessarily so. *Absolute* nonviolence renounces violence in all conceivable circumstances.[2] But conditional nonviolence does not. It allows there are conceivable circumstances—whether ever realized in the world or not—in which it would be permissible to use violence. Pragmatic nonviolence is conditional in this sense. It advocates nonviolence to the extent that it "works." It may consider violence permissible or even necessary when nonviolence fails. On the other hand, principled nonviolence, held conditionally, concedes there may be hypothetical circumstances in which violence would be justified. But it contends these are rarely, if ever, actually realized.[3] This reflects a difference in the ends or goals of the approaches. Pragmatic nonviolence typically has social, political or national goals. Principled nonviolence may have, either in addition to or instead of these, broader moral ends, like promoting

---

[2] The ancient Jains came as close as anyone to holding nonviolence in this absolutistic way.
[3] Gandhi clearly was a conditional nonviolentist of this sort. He maintained that if the choice were between violence and cowardice, one might better choose violence.

a certain way of life, maximizing value, or showing reverence for life. Its concern, we might say, is with moral effectiveness rather than merely practical effectiveness.

There is, clearly, a sharp distinction between absolute and conditional nonviolence. Hence there will be a sharp distinction between principled and pragmatic nonviolence when the former is held absolutistically. But when principled nonviolence is held conditionally, the difference between it and pragmatic nonviolence will be one of degree (just as the difference between a conditional nonviolentist and someone who rejects nonviolence but thinks violence is justified in only a narrow range of cases will also be one of degree). In practice, principled nonviolence opposes violence in a boarder range of (actual and hypothetical) cases than does pragmatic nonviolence. And it opposes them on moral and not simply on social or political grounds.

Both will maintain that nonviolence has a justification. But for principled nonviolence that justification will be moral, whereas for pragmatic nonviolence it will be social, political, economic, nationalistic, etc. For principled nonviolence, it is necessary and sufficient for the final justification of nonviolence that it be justified from the moral point of view. For pragmatic nonviolence it is not. An important consequence follows from this. It is that whereas principled nonviolence cannot (knowingly, at least) be used for immoral ends,[4] pragmatic nonviolence can. It is an instrument which is neutral in and of itself. It can be used by the wicked as well as by the good.

This latter consideration brings us, however, to the question of what exactly nonviolence says. The first task here is to locate it in the broader context of types of normative theory.

Interactive and reactive conduct

Two areas of conduct are of concern to ethical theory. The first is the normal interactions among people in everyday life. The second is people's response to wrongdoing, either against themselves or against others. The first we may call interactive conduct, the second reactive.

Nonviolence in its interpersonal dimension tends to be concerned with reactive conduct. It proposes an alternative to violence when one confronts those who threaten violence, or who engage in wrongdoing of a more general nature. It may also say something about how we should act in the normal course of our lives—when, that is, we are engaged in interactive conduct. But this will be only when it takes the form of principled nonviolence. Pragmatic nonviolence, as I understand that term, does not presume to tell people what constitutes good or proper conduct in their everyday lives. It presumes only to show them a practical alternative to violence when confronted by violence, injustice, or oppression. Nonviolence held only as a purely personal commitment, which makes no claim that others should be nonviolent as well, may govern either interactive or reactive conduct, or both.

---

[4]   As Gandhi said of his nonviolent method, *satyagraha*, "There can be no *satyagraha* in an unjust cause." M. K. Gandhi, *Non-Violent Resistance* (New York: Schocken Books, 1961), 56.

I shall in what follows confine my attention to nonviolence as a moral position with an interpersonal character, that is, to principled nonviolence. Specifically, I want to ask whether it is possible to formulate a morality of nonviolence that is clear, coherent and plausible.

The scope of nonviolence in governing conduct

Notice at the outset that virtually any moral theory, if it describes normal conduct in an ideal world, would describe it as nonviolent. With the exception of those few who extol violence for its own sake, everyone believes the world would be better off if individuals and nations renounced violence.

This suggests that nonviolence is problematic only in a world in which some people are violent and others are not. Does nonviolence remain plausible for such a world (which, of course, fits the description of the actual world)? There are several possible objections to supposing that it does. The first is largely theoretical, the others substantive.

The theoretical objection holds that because nonviolence is negative in character, it cannot provide a positive guide to conduct in general. And if it fails to do that, it cannot provide an adequate moral position.

The point here is that nonviolence is defined negatively by reference to what it rejects rather than by reference to anything it is for. So, even if we should accept nonviolence, it would at most provide us with only limited guidance. It would tell us only to refrain from violence in circumstances in which we might otherwise be tempted to resort to it. But most of our interactions with others occur in circumstances in which violence would be pointless and counterproductive. Therefore no decision need be made about whether to use it. Nonviolence provides us with no guidance in these circumstances, which make up by far the largest part of ordinary lives.

It may be, of course, that nonviolence is held as a rule or principle. If it is held as one principle among others, or as a rule which presupposes a more basic principle, it would not presume to cover the whole of morality. It would apply only to the area of conduct involving conflict or dispute. Hence this objection would merely point out what is conceded in advance.

But the objection has some force against certain ways of understanding nonviolence. Even if nonviolence is presumed to govern the whole of conduct, if it is understood simply as the principled renunciation of physical violence, it would indeed leave unspecified how we should act throughout most of our lives. It would not preclude the possibility that we could be nonviolent and still treat people badly. This is because physical violence is only one mode of violence. There is psychological violence as well. We can insult, humiliate, degrade, demean, and oppress people; treat them unkindly, unfairly and unjustly; and cause them untold physical and psychological harm—without resorting to physical violence against them. A theory which prohibits only physical violence could claim at best to represent only a part, not the whole, of a plausible moral position.

A fuller conception of nonviolence, however, extends to these other sorts of conduct as well. Even if we understand nonviolence negatively as opposition to violence, we still need to distinguish psychological violence from physical violence. To commit oneself to nonviolence in this fuller sense is to commit oneself to renouncing all of the subtle as well as the overt ways of causing mental harm. Racism and sexism often cause their greatest harms not through physical violence, but through the systematic destruction of self-esteem through subtle psychological devices that are not fully understood or even consciously adopted by those who use them. The sort of fuller commitment to nonviolence of which I am speaking requires cultivating a sensitivity to the countless ways in which language, practices, and social institutions can *do violence* to people even while not using physical violence against them.

More than that, nonviolence may, as I mentioned earlier, ask that we strive to *be* certain sorts of persons as well as that we act certain ways. The Jains maintain that we should be nonviolent not only in action and speech, but in thought as well. One can fail to do this if one is committed only to nonviolence in the narrow sense, which renounces physical violence alone. For without ever using physical violence one can still be judgmental, manipulative, unfair and unkind. And one can harbor ill-will toward others, and think unkindly of them, even if one does not outwardly treat them in these ways. In this way nonviolence may be understood to be, at least in part, an *ethics of virtue* as well as an ethics of conduct.

It will be useful, in light of this, to distinguish two different forms of principled nonviolence: *Minimal Nonviolence,* which renounces only physical violence; and *Maximal Nonviolence,* which renounces all violence, physical and psychological. Although either form could advocate the development of the appropriate traits of character as well as the performance of the appropriate actions, Maximal Nonviolence lends itself most readily to becoming an ethics of virtue. It will be either an ethics of conduct or an ethics of virtue depending upon whether it requires only that we be nonviolent in our conduct, or requires also that we be nonviolent persons.

Now, the objection that nonviolence is inadequate as a comprehensive moral position because it does not provide guidance for the whole of life is valid against Minimal Nonviolence. But it is not, I suggest, valid against Maximal Nonviolence. For the nonviolentist can maintain that if we remain nonviolent in *all* that we do (in situations pertaining to psychological as well as to physical violence), and particularly if we strive to be nonviolent in thought and speech as well as conduct, then whatever we otherwise do in our interactions with others will be permissible. Nonviolence in this maximalist sense does govern all of our life. Once we satisfy its requirements, we may in other respects act as we choose toward others. Even though I have stated it negatively, it has, for all practical purposes, a positive content. It tells us to be *nonviolent.*

This, I suggest, answers the theoretical objection. But another objection needs considering, even against nonviolence understood in this fuller sense. It grows out of the ambivalence some people feel toward nonviolence and pacifism.

Nonviolence and the defense of the innocent

On the one hand, many people regard nonviolence as admirable. That some people should never resort to violence strikes them as extraordinary. Such people are often regarded as saintly. It also strikes many people as admirable, if a little strange, that some people should not only refrain from using violence to get their way with others, but should also refuse to use it even in self-defense; that they should be willing to suffer ill-treatment, harm and even death rather than do unto others what others do unto them.

On the other hand, many people consider it contemptible that anyone would stand by while innocent persons are attacked, beaten and perhaps killed, refusing to assist them merely because that would be to resort to violence. And on a larger scale, it is considered contemptible to refuse to sanction the use of violence by oppressed peoples to resist or overthrow oppressive colonial or totalitarian regimes, even if one does not engage in the violence oneself. It is one thing, they say, to refuse to defend yourself if attacked; it is another to refuse to defend others, particularly the innocent, or to disapprove the use of violence in national defense or for national liberation.

I consider this a serious objection. Before responding to it, however, I want to examine a closely related third objection.

Keeping one's hands clean

Sometimes this objection is put in the following way: The nonviolentist—and the pacifist, for as I say, this objection is frequently brought against pacifists as well—does not want to dirty his hands. He is more concerned with his own moral purity than with the lives and well-being of others. So long as *he* refuses to kill or use violence, he is satisfied, even if this means letting others suffer and die. He keeps his hands clean at their expense.

This objection may be understood in either of two ways. It may mean that to refuse to use violence to help others is wrong, and to do this simply out of revulsion at killing or using violence is cowardly. If this is how the objection is understood, then it is just another way of making the first objection, and it will be covered by what I say later. But the objection can be taken in another way. It may mean that the nonviolentist keeps his hands clean in the sense of refusing to do anything wrong. On this understanding, the objection *concedes* it is wrong to kill and use violence even in defense of others. At the same time it implicitly maintains that sometimes one must do what is wrong; in some situations it is necessary. To keep one's hands morally clean by refusing to do wrong even to help others betrays a self-righteous preoccupation with one's own moral purity.

Understood in this way, the objection is either incoherent or it advocates immorality. If the point is that sometimes it is morally right to do what, by hypothesis, is morally wrong, then the objection is incoherent. If it is wrong ever to resort to violence, and one does so in defense of others, it cannot at the same time be right to do so. If, however, the point is that it is wrong to kill even in defense of the innocent, but sometimes one should do so anyway, then the position expressly advocates wrongdoing, hence arguably is immoral. Theoretically, of course, one might contend that violence in these cases is necessitated by other considerations (the justifiers of violence, at least since the time of Augustine, appeal to an unexplicated conception of "necessity" allegedly operating here). These considerations might be those of self-interest or national interest. But they might also be such considerations as those of sympathy, compassion, caring and love. The claim would then be that, when considerations of these sorts conflict with what morality prescribes, they override morality. This represents a problematic metaethical claim. Whether it can be rendered plausible there is no space to examine here. The objection still reduces to the judgment that in these situations we should act immorally. And so it does not constitute an objection to nonviolence understood as claiming that the morally correct thing to do is to refrain from violence.

Consistency and the defense of the innocent

So let us return to the second objection. It does not concede that it is wrong to use violence on behalf of the innocent. To the contrary, it says it is wrong *not* to do so. Nonviolentists do not keep their hands morally clean by refusing to use violence; they keep their hands clean only by aiding the innocent, even if that means dirtying their hands with the blood of the guilty and sometimes that of the innocent as well. This objection lies at the heart of the assessment of nonviolence as a moral position. To respond to it fully would require a more comprehensive explication and defense of nonviolence than I am able to undertake here. But we may take note of several points relevant to assessing the objection.

Sometimes it is said in support of the view expressed in the objection that the very concerns which prohibit violence sometimes mandate it, such as when it is necessary to protect the innocent.

This is maintained by Jan Narveson and Paul Ramsey, and is at least implied, in somewhat different form, more recently by Nel Noddings.[5] Ramsey argues from a Christian perspective. He contends that the very love which prohibits killing requires that in some circumstances one be prepared to kill lest many more innocent persons die. Narveson argues that the pacifist's very opposition to violence (he characterizes the nonviolentist as a pacifist) should compel him to resort to violence when it is the only way to prevent the violation of rights. Noddings contends that caring for persons may require killing in defense of self or others so long as caring itself is not endangered.

[5] See Jan Narveson, "Pacifism: A Philosophical Analysis," *Ethics* Vol. 75, 1965, 259–71; and "Violence and War," in Tom Regan ed., *Matters of Life and Death: New Introductory Essays in Moral Philosophy* (New York: Random House, 1980), 117–28; Nel Noddings, *Caring: A Feminine Approach to Ethics and Moral Education* (Berkeley, CA: University of California Press, 1984), 100–1; Paul Ramsey, *The Just War: Force and Political Responsibility* (Lanham MD: University Press of America, 1983), 150–1.

Narveson's argument in particular is complex, and there is not space to do justice to it here. I merely want to note that all three positions have one thing in common: they maintain (Ramsey and Noddings implicitly, Narveson explicitly) that the strength of one's commitment to something (love, caring, or nonviolence) should lead one to do the very thing normally prohibited by that commitment in circumstances in which that is the only way to prevent those things from being done by others. Ramsey and Noddings accept this as part of the understanding of love and caring respectively. Narveson contends it shows why pacifism (nonviolence) is incoherent, since it reveals the manner in which pacifists' opposition to violence commits them to using it in certain circumstances.

But this is implausible. If I am a teetotaler, it is not a test of the strength of my commitment to abstain from alcohol that I be prepared to drink some in order to prevent others from drinking. And if I am a vegetarian, my commitment to refrain from eating meat does not require that I be prepared to eat some if that is the only way to prevent others from doing so. The measure of my commitment not to do something (whether it is to refrain from drinking alcohol, eating meat, killing, or using violence) is whether I consistently refrain from doing it. If, in addition, I believe others should do likewise—that is, if I hold this as interpersonally binding and not merely as a personal commitment—then my initial commitment (to refrain *personally* from doing these things) limits what I may do to oppose the doing of those things by others. Although it is true that if my commitment to renounce violence compelled me to engage in it in certain circumstances, my position would be inconsistent, it is false that such a commitment in fact compels me to engage in such conduct.

This, however, even if correct, does not altogether meet the original objection. It does not show that there is not something reprehensible about refraining from saving the innocent when one does so because saving them would require using violence. What it shows is that the preceding attempts to explain why it is wrong fail.

It should be noted before proceeding that we need not stand passively by while innocent people are assaulted or the nation attacked. It is always open to them to resist nonviolently. Gandhi's followers at times insinuated themselves between assailant and victim in the bloodshed between Muslims and Hindus, absorbing the blows themselves. And on a national scale, there is a growing movement in various countries today to promote the idea of nonviolent national defense (or Civilian-Based Defense, as it is sometimes called). It is not my aim here to detail the various techniques one might use at the personal, social, or international levels to try to defuse the threat of violence or to minimize harm once it has commenced; this has been admirably done by Gene Sharp and others. My aim is only to point out that nonviolence as understood by most of its recent practitioners is active. It cannot simply be assumed that in the many cases in which one might be positioned to prevent innocents from being harmed, nonviolent methods would not be as effective, or more effective than, violent methods. That is a factual question answered empirically.

Supposedly, however, we confine ourselves to cases in which, by hypothesis, violence would save the innocent and nonviolence would not. It is easy to conceive of such cases. And critics of nonviolence can focus directly upon them.

The problem with hypothetical cases of this sort is that they distill out certain salient features of a situation and selectively exclude others. Unless one is able to assess all of the relevant features, it is difficult to say with justifiable confidence what the morally correct course would be.

Take the case of an assailant and an innocent child. To stipulate that the child is innocent is to say only that it is free of wrongdoing. It is not to say that it would remain so forever. It does not preclude the possibility that it might grow up to be a mass murderer, a serial rapist, or another Hitler. From a consequentialist or utilitarian perspective, these are relevant considerations. By the same token, those who advance cases like this presume that the assailant is guilty. But need that be so? What if the assailant has been confronted with the choice of either killing this one innocent child or allowing 10 or 100 or 1,000 innocent children to die? Perhaps as a good utilitarian he has concluded with great regret that he must kill the child. To rule this out we would need to specify that he is not a utilitarian, or that utilitarianism does not have this consequence, or that the agent is not confronted with a choice of that sort. Or, to introduce some deontological considerations, perhaps there is a God, and the assailant believes that whatever God commands is right. And perhaps further, as with Abraham, the child is the potential assailant's son, and the assailant has been commanded by God to sacrifice his son.

To extract the conclusion the critic wants would require tailoring the example so that virtually all considerations that would support anything other than violent intervention have been expressly excluded. The potential assailant might have to be described as not only innocent, but destined to remain so. Countervailing consequentialist and deontological considerations would have to be eliminated.

Now, one can do this. One can stipulate anything one wants in hypothetical examples. But to do this risks designing question-begging assumptions into the example which virtually entail the conclusion one wants. If one characterizes the example in such a way as to leave no *conceivable* circumstances in which it would be right to refrain from violence to save the innocent, one refutes at most only those nonviolentists who hold their position in absolutistic form. (I say "at most," because even this will not refute absolutists who doggedly insist that killing is wrong in all conceivable circumstances, for they will simply disregard all the additional considerations the critic brings to bear, no matter what they are.)

If, on the other hand, one leaves some conceptual space in which it would be right to use violence, and constructs an example to conform to the assumptions defining that space, conditional nonviolentists will concede the example. They will simply contend that there are no such cases in the actual world, or so few as not to undermine a general commitment to nonviolence. And they will insist that they subscribe to nonviolence as a guide to conduct in the world as we know it, not as it might be in philosophers' imagination. The question then will be whether cases of that sort are ever in fact encountered, or are at all likely to be encountered, in ordinary life.

This is not to say that hypothetical counter-examples cannot sometimes be effective. They can. If they remain faithful to the assumptions framing the nonviolentist's commitment to nonviolence, and at the same time highlight a dimension of that commitment he has overlooked—whether in the way of possible consequences, or in the way of what he is prepared to concede are relevant deontological considerations—they may lead him to reconsider or even abandon his position. They can, in other words, be effective against a position that is inconsistent or ill-thought-out. But otherwise they cannot.

The commitment to conditional nonviolence

It is a conditional nonviolence that I want to propose as the most plausible candidate for a moral position. Expressed as a principle, it says: *One ought always to act nonviolently*. This will be understood to preclude both physical and psychological violence. But it may also be understood to require that we strive to be nonviolent persons, meaning that we strive to incorporate nonviolence into thought and speech as well as action, to make it a part of our very character. Aristotle says that virtue requires not only performing the right acts, but choosing them in knowledge for themselves, and in such a way that the choice proceeds from a firm and unchanging character. So, we may say, *being nonviolent* requires not just performing nonviolent actions, but doing so because they are nonviolent (and not just out of expediency) and in a way that naturally flows from a nonviolent character. In other words, nonviolence as a principle belonging to the ethics of conduct may prescribe the cultivation of the kind of character belonging to an ethics of virtue.

The distinguishing feature of nonviolence understood in this way lies in its recognition of the limitations of our knowledge in situations of conflict. This is a point stressed by Gandhi, in his method of *satyagraha*. The resort to violence presumes that one knows one is dealing with willful wrongdoers and that one's own position is righteous. We rarely know this in complex social, political and international situations involving large numbers of people. We can only make estimates of varying degrees of probability regarding where the truth lies. Given the limited nature of our knowledge of right and wrong in such situations, we have two choices. On the one hand, we can assume that because we cannot be certain where the truth lies, we should act on the presumption that the best course lies in following conventional morality. We should then abide by the laws of the state or by the customs and practices of peoples. This, in effect, is the course taken by St. Augustine. He recognizes that since sin is a corruption of the soul, and we can never be certain from a person's actions alone whether he or she sins (only God can know that), we do best to abide by the rules that preserve the social and political order. This is a conservative position which favors the status quo. Gandhi, on the other hand, and in certain respects Tolstoy before him and Martin Luther King, Jr, after him, see this epistemological condition as requiring a new *methodology*. We need a manner of dealing with others which enables us to stand by our own convictions regarding what is best in the situation, while at the same time acknowledging that we may be mistaken; which enables us to stand by our belief in the injustice of our adversary, while allowing that we may be mistaken about that as well.

The aim, then, becomes to find the truth. Prevailing over the other is not the objective. Nothing morally worthwhile is gained if you prevail but were wrong to do so. One strives to engage the other in a way that maximizes the possibility that the truth will eventually emerge, whatever it may be, and whomever it may favor.

It is this which, on the view I am proposing, dictates the commitment to nonviolence. For you cannot justifiably kill other people at the same time you acknowledge that they may be acting with a significant measure of the truth whose realization it is your aim to foster. Killing closes off the possibilities for such realization. You must engage opponents only in ways sanctioned by the search for truth. This represents a different way for the nonviolentist from the one chosen by Augustine and most Christians since his time. It means that one must often go, not only against custom and practice, but against law itself. This inevitably brings the nonviolentist into conflict with the state. It is not surprising that Tolstoy, as thoroughgoing a nonviolentist as one finds in Western thought, is led to anarchism, and that Gandhi moves decidedly in that direction. For the state by its nature regulates conduct by force and violence. It holds the threat of punishment over its citizens for failing to do what it decrees or for doing what it prohibits. And when its conflicts with other states are severe enough, it resorts to war. Typically it coerces its citizenry to do the killing and dying which that entails. The consistent and thoroughgoing nonviolentist, as Tolstoy saw, will be an anarchist.

Finally, one further aspect of nonviolence needs emphasizing. It requires asking what the harm is we seek to avoid when acting nonviolently. What harm does violence cause that leads the nonviolentist to oppose it by others (including its manifestations in social, political and economic systems) and to renounce it in one's own conduct?

There are, of course, the harms of physical and psychological violence already mentioned. Perhaps equally important is the moral harm suffered by wrongdoers in oppressing others, killing them, or destroying their possessions. Nonviolence seeks to engage wrongdoers in a way which shows a regard for their victims. When Gandhi followers stepped between assailants and their victims, they attempted to prevent these assailants from becoming murderers as much as they did to protect the victims. There is a long philosophical tradition, from Socrates and the Stoics through Augustine and Kant, which holds that the only real harm (or in Kant's case, the worst harm) that can befall one is corruption of the will. Others can deprive you of possessions and even life. But only you can make yourself morally corrupt. And that is a worse harm than anything others can inflict upon you.

Thus, when we rightly condemn the injustice of Apartheid in South Africa, perhaps we should do so as much because of its effects upon the oppressing white minority as because of its more conspicuous effects upon the oppressed black majority. Or when we express concern about Israeli treatment of Palestinians in the occupied territories, perhaps we should do so as much because of its brutalizing effect upon young Israeli soldiers as upon the Palestinians injured or killed in the process. When we deplore the tragedies of Vietnam and Afghanistan, perhaps we should do so because of the effects upon the surviving American and Soviet soldiers as well as because of the suffering of the Vietnamese and Afghan people. Violence can sometimes put a stop to wrongdoing. It can kill or disable the wrongdoer. Or drive him off in fear. But it rarely produces the conditions under which he confronts the true nature of his acts and freely chooses to turn away from them (and when it does so, it usually does so incidentally, and not as part of one's intention in dealing with him). Principled nonviolence can do that. It does not always succeed. But in seeking the best solution in each situation of conflict, it weighs into the scales the physical, psychological, and moral well-being of all of the persons involved.

Understood in this way, principled nonviolence differs from most of the standard ethical theories in one important respect. Most of them (Kantianism, Utilitarianism, Egoism, etc.) leave largely unchallenged the basic structures of society: the police, courts, prisons, economies, armies and war systems of modern states. Nonviolence asks us to reconsider all of these. It asks us to reflect upon whether they hinder rather than help us to move to a higher plane of moral conduct than humankind has previously achieved. It asks us to seek new and creative ways to relate to others; to consider that the capacities for good and moral growth that we share with all peoples are ultimately of more importance than the divisions of race, sex, class, religion and nationality that separate us. In short, it projects a vision of a new world and asks us to join in trying to create it.[6]

---

[6] Previously published in *Just War, Nonviolence and Nuclear Deterrence: Philosophers on War and Peace*, ed. Duane L. Cady and Richard Werner (Wakefield, NH: Longwood Academic, 1991), 131–50.

12

Terrorism, Violence, and Nonviolence

September 11 has sparked a variety of discussions on terrorism. Holmes approaches terrorism in terms of his discussion of violence and nonviolence. He defines terrorism as "installing extreme fear to achieve one's ends, typically by the use or threat of violence, often against innocent persons." Viewed in this way, Holmes points out that it is unjustifiable to separate the terrorism of individuals or small groups from state terrorism; there is nothing in the definition of terrorism that shows that state terrorism—that is, terrorizing one's own citizens or the citizens of other countries—is any less morally troubling or justified, than that of various Arab and Muslim groups that receive the entire attention of the media. Furthermore, there is no reason to think that the terror inflicted by various individuals dressed in civilian clothes is any less damaging or horrifying than the terror inflicted by soldiers in uniforms. Holmes' conclusion is that, despite the endless proclamations of our politicians and the media to the contrary, terrorism is not clearly worse than many conventionally accepted forms of violence. And like those accepted forms of violence, there is an important alternative to terrorism that has not received sufficient attention—that of nonviolence. To approach terrorism in a constructive way, we should start thinking of it as a criminal rather than as a military offense. And we should also create opportunities for a dialogue, in the spirit of Kant's respect for all human beings as ends in themselves. As Holmes puts it, "Violence is for the morally infallible. Nonviolence is for those who recognize their own limitations and the possibility that others, with whom they are in disagreement, have hold of certain parts of the truth, and are willing to put forth the effort to uncover and cultivate that truth in the interests of nonviolent conciliation."

The September 11, 2001, attack on the World Trade Center and the Pentagon is widely regarded as having changed the world forever. It is seen as inaugurating a new era in which the United States is threatened perhaps as never before, a threat that can only be met by an open-ended war against terrorism.[1] President Bush has said 9/11 was "a day of decision for our country. As a united and resolute people, America declared, 'We'll start the war from here.'"[2] It is also seen as having brought the country together, making it into one family.

---

[1] In these respects, 9/11 arguably had much the same effect that many experts believed would follow only from a terrorist attack using weapons of mass destruction. See Ashton Carter, John Deutch, and Philip Zelikow, "Catastrophic Terrorism: Tackling the New Danger," *Foreign Affairs*, Vol. 77, No. 6, November–December 1998, 80–94.

[2] From an August 26, 2003, speech to the American Legion Convention in St. Louis, Missouri. http://nytimes.com/2003/08/26/politics/26TEXT-BUSH.

There is a measure of truth to some of these claims. But that measure is less easy to assess than current commentary and government pronouncements would suggest. What is perhaps most startling is that people were surprised at the targeting of the United States in the way symbolized by September 11. That targeting was predictable in the broader context of the US role in the world, particularly since the collapse of the Soviet Union and the Gulf crisis of the early 1990s. There is no simple answer to how to respond to this development. But a constructive response must begin by trying to understand terrorism itself.

Maurice Merleau-Ponty once wrote that history itself is terror, and that the common assumption of all revolutionaries is that "the contingency of the future and the role of human decisions in history make political divergences irreducible and cunning, deceit and violence inevitable."[3] This association of terror with cunning, deceit, and violence is overly broad, of course. But it highlights the fact that violence is at the heart of terrorism. And by implication it suggests that violence in human affairs is widespread and widely accepted.

This latter claim is not altered by the fact that most of us do not use violence ourselves. That is done for us by others. Nor is it altered by the fact we deplore violence at some level of our thinking. Our social life has so institutionalized violence that, despite ourselves, we support and sustain its use through government, taxation, the economy, and even the educational system, which at many top universities trains officers for the military through ROTC and profits from military-related research. Internationally, we deplore the threat of nuclear war but support preparations for conventional war, as though it were somehow a respectable compromise. Talk of "regime change"—a euphemism for the conquest of another country—flows freely from the mouths of politicians and government leaders, with scarcely a murmur of concern from the general public.

Violence that maintains the status quo (whether in the way of police action or war) tends to be approved by those who are its beneficiaries; that which threatens the status quo is condemned. But the mode of violence that is almost universally condemned is terrorism. Although at the other end of the scale of destructiveness from nuclear war, it rivals nuclear war in the dread it inspires. When the fear of nuclear war and the fear of terrorism are joined together, they are an explosive mix. When focused on one country—and more specifically, on one person, as in the case of Iraq and Saddam Hussein—they generate powerful motives to turn to violence to remove those threats.

What is terrorism?

What is terrorism? More and more the term is used emotively, to stand for virtually any use of political violence of which we disapprove. One and the same person becomes a terrorist or a freedom fighter, depending upon whether we approve or disapprove his cause.

But terrorism has an underlying descriptive meaning. To terrorize is to instill extreme fear. This can, of course, have a pathological motivation. It can also be

---

[3] Maurice Merleau-Ponty, *Humanism and Terror* (Boston: Beacon Press, 1969), 96.

rationally directed, and then it becomes of moral interest. Terrorism is the calculated creation and manipulation of such fear. It can be defined as the following:

Terrorism: *Instilling extreme fear to achieve one's ends, typically by the use or threat of violence, often against innocent persons.*

Who does the terrorizing does not matter. What counts is what is done and for what reasons. Individuals acting alone can terrorize. So can governments or armies. And *what* the ends are does not matter. They may be social, political, religious, or moral. What makes one a terrorist are the means by which ends are pursued, not the ends themselves. One can terrorize in the service of just as well as unjust causes.

Terrorism presents the greatest challenge when undertaken for a cause. For then it often represents a rationally chosen means to an end. However much we deplore terrorism, it is not necessarily a less rational choice—purely in the sense of being a perceived means to an end—than many conventionally accepted modes of violence.[4] Trotsky perceived this when writing of the Russian revolution. A victorious war, he observed, usually "destroys only an insignificant part of the conquered army, intimidating the remainder and breaking their will. The revolution works in the same way: it kills individuals, and intimidates thousands."[5] Although he was describing the terror of the revolutionary class, what he said applies to terrorism of any sort. Terrorism typically kills few people by comparison with warfare. That remains true, despite September 11th. It will change as terrorists eventually come into the possession of nuclear and/or chemical-biological weapons.[6] Terrorism seeks to achieve its ends by breaking the will of the thousands who learn of it. That is why publicity is important to its success. Whereas conventional war intimidates by inflicting losses, terrorism intimidates by instilling fear.

Conventional war, however, *may* be terroristic. Its rationale then is usually military necessity. This was put with remarkable honesty by the Kaiser during World War I. He said:

> My soul is torn, but everything must be put to fire and sword; men, women, and children and old men must be slaughtered and not a tree or house be left standing. With these methods of terrorism, which are alone capable of affecting a people as degenerate as the French, the war will be over in two months, whereas if I admit considerations of humanity it will be prolonged for years.[7]

---

[4] Not that terrorism has a good track record at achieving its ends. As Walter Laqueur writes, "the decision to use terrorist violence is not always a rational one; if it were, there would be much less terrorism, since terrorist activity seldom achieves its aims." "Post Modern Terrorism," *Foreign Affairs*, Vol. 75, No. 5, September–October 1996, 31.

[5] Leon Trotsky, *Terrorism and Communism* (Ann Arbor, MI: University of Michigan Press, 1963), 58.

[6] Daniel Benjamin and Steven Simon observe in this regard that the "combination of terrorists and weapons of mass destruction is the stuff of countless movies and television shows. The reality is otherwise: very, very few groups have ever seriously tried to acquire such weapons. Almost all of those that have—the Japanese cult Aum Shinrikyo is the most notable exception—have sought them primarily for purposes of blackmail . . . Its forays into procuring unconventional arms are an unmistakable sign that al-Qaeda is prepared to cross a threshold never before approached and kill in a way unlike that of any earlier terrorists." See their *The Age of Sacred Terror* (New York: Random House, 2002), 129.

[7] Quoted in *Crimes of War*, ed. Richard A. Falk, Gabriel Kolka, and Robert Jay Lifton (New York: Vintage Books, 1971), 135.

Much the same rationale, though never stated as bluntly, underlay the fire-bombings of Tokyo and Dresden and the atomic bombings of Hiroshima and Nagasaki during World War II. Those, too, were acts of terrorism. They employed massive, indiscriminate violence against mostly innocent persons. The aim, in each case, was to destroy the morale of the whole country. It has been said that the use of 15,000-pound bombs (euphemistically called "daisy-cutters") in Afghanistan was in part to terrorize the Taliban.

Because of the resources at a government's command, state terror is often the most systematic kind. Some believe that governments lie behind most of international terrorism. When governments terrorize openly, they have a propaganda apparatus to justify what they do. When they terrorize surreptitiously, they can recruit, train, equip, and finance operatives beyond the reach of public and international scrutiny. And they can direct terror against their own people. Stalin did this in the 1930s, as did South Africa and many Latin American governments in the past. Governments like those in Columbia, Indonesia, and Uzbekistan do so today. But whereas many governments operate through torture and death squads, some enlist the country's legal system in the service of terrorism. Stalin worked through the Soviet Union's legal institutions. There was no gunfire in the night, no bodies on Moscow's outskirts in the morning. Yet through trial, conviction, and execution perceived enemies were eliminated as effectively as though they had been gunned down.[8] In the process, countless others were terrified into submission.

Stereotyping Arabs and Muslims

Terrorism is commonly represented as primarily Arab and Muslim. When a toy manufacturer produced a doll representing a terrorist, the doll was named Nomad, dressed in Arab garb, and, according to the company's description, engaged in "terrorist assaults on innocent villages."[9] Political cartoonists often depict terrorists as grizzled and wearing keffiyehs. Some of the most dramatic acts of terrorism, from the Munich Olympics in 1972 to September 11 attacks, were indeed by Arabs. But it is misleading to represent even Middle East terrorism as exclusively the work of Arabs. The Jewish underground used terrorism against the British in Palestine. Both Yitzhak Shamir and Menachem Begin, destined to become Israeli prime ministers, led such groups.[10] Iran, which is high on the US list of terrorist governments, is not even an

---

[8] Thousands were executed by Stalin's regime, of course, but emerging evidence is that they were executed in secret and buried far from Moscow.
[9] *Christian Science Monitor*, December 10, 1986.
[10] Begin's Irgun was responsible for the 1946 bombing of the King David Hotel in Jerusalem. Shamir was one of the leaders of the Lehi (Fighters for the Freedom of Israel) responsible for the assassination in 1944 of Lord Moyne, Britain's minister of state for the Middle East and in 1948 of Sweden's Count Folke Benadotte, the UN representative to the Middle East. Although Shamir claims to have had no direct knowledge of the Bernadotte assassination, Israeli scholars disagree. Interestingly, Geula Cohen, former Knesset member who worked with Lehi at the time, reportedly says the assassination "was no less moral than other wartime actions." *Jerusalem Post International Edition*, Week Ending, October 10, 1998. James Bennet says that after ignoring a British plea to him and other prisoners to renounce their terrorist activities, Yitzhak Shamir "later escaped and returned to the underground, to a campaign of assassination, bombing and arms smuggling, with bank robbery thrown in to finance the effort." "How Ben-Gurion Did It: Is Everyone Listening?" *New York Times,* August 13, 2003.

Arab country. Nor is Arab terrorism all the work of Muslims. The Phalangists who massacred Palestinians in the Sabra and Shatila refugee camps of Lebanon in 1982 were Christian. Ariel Sharon, the Israeli commander whose troops oversaw the massacre is, of course, Jewish and currently prime minister of Israel. Also Christian are the founders of the two principal PLO factions after Fatah: George Habash[11] of the Popular Front for the Liberation of Palestine and Nawef Hawatmeh of the Democratic Front for the Liberation of Palestine. Nor was terrorism (before 9/11) by any means confined to the Middle East or those acting in Middle Eastern interests. The Pol Pot regime undertook a campaign of genocidal terror in Cambodia exceeded in recent history only by the Nazis' extermination of Jews. Terror was used by the IRA in Northern Ireland, the Basques in Spain, and the African National Congress in South Africa.[12]

The point is that it is a simplistic representation of terrorism as a struggle between good and evil. Any people desperate enough are capable of engaging in it, any government unscrupulous enough capable of using it.

Terrorism and conventional violence

Terrorism is not clearly worse than many conventionally accepted forms of violence. True, terrorism is probably intentionally directed against civilians more often than is standard warfare. But, as the preceding quotation from the Kaiser attests, warfare can and does target civilians. The terror bombings of Dresden, Hiroshima, and Nagasaki probably killed more civilians than have been killed by terrorists throughout the world in all the years since.[13] The majority of the 50 million or so killed in World War II were civilians, as most likely would be the majority of persons killed in any sizable war in the future. And while most of them were not targeted as civilians, many of their deaths were foreseeable from the military actions that caused them. US fighter pilots reportedly were ordered to shoot down Flight 93 if necessary to prevent it from reaching Washington on September 11. They were prepared to kill the innocents on board to prevent the plane from reaching its objective. The hijackers were prepared to kill those very same people in the course of achieving *their* objective.[14] This says nothing of the broader context of the two actions or their intended objectives or of the justifiability of either. It is meant only to say that the deliberate killing of innocents does not suffice to distinguish terrorism from much of conventionally accepted military violence.

---

[11] George Habash, trained as a pediatrician, retired as head of the PFLP in 2000. He had been living in Syria. His successor, Ali Mustafa, who was living in the West Bank city of Ramallah, was assassinated soon after by the Israelis.

[12] "Necklacing," burning to death by a gasoline-filled tire around the neck, was a particularly ghastly form of terrorism used by black South Africans against other black South Africans.

[13] This excludes the genocidal slaughters of the Pol Pot regime in Cambodia and of Tutsi's in Rwanda. Genocide is meant to eradicate a people, not to terrorize them into submission. The case of Cambodia was complex, of course. It arguably was the elimination of a particular class (the educated and well-to-do) that was intended to terrorize others into submission. Thus it combined terrorism and genocide.

[14] It is also reported that two mid-level generals are authorized to order the destruction of US and other passenger planes in the future if it is believed that they constitute a comparable threat to the United States.

It would take a casuist of exceeding skill to make much of the moral difference between killing innocents intentionally and killing them foreseeably.

Is it that the pilots, had they felt compelled to shoot the plane down, would not have intended to kill the civilians, even though they knew that they would do so? The Pentagon routinely maintains, after killing civilians in Afghanistan, that it is not its policy intentionally to target civilians. In so doing, it makes use of the same reasoning that underlies the so-called principle of double effect. That principle holds that, *ceteris paribus*, it is permissible to perform an act foreseen to have bad consequences so long as one's intention in performing it is good. But such reasoning is available to terrorists as well. The hijackers of Flight 93 might not have intended to kill those particular civilians either. But they were willing to do so in pursuit of their objective (believed to be to hit a target in Washington). In fact, all of the hijackers of the four planes on September 11 probably would have preferred to fly empty planes that day, if only because it would have simplified their task (rebellious passengers, after all, are believed to have caused the premature crash of Flight 43). Moreover, with a dash of the same ingenuity with which just war theorists manipulate the principle of double effect, they might have argued that their objective wasn't to kill civilians at all. It was, rather, to destroy symbols of US military and economic power. Had those 3,000-plus innocents been assembled in an open field and the hijackers been forced to choose between killing them and attacking an empty World Trade Center (and Pentagon), they might well have chosen to destroy the buildings.

In the case of the hijackers, most people would be quick to say that such reasoning is not good enough; that if the hijackers could foresee that they would kill innocents, they are culpable. But if we say that, then we must say the same when military power is used in ways that will foreseeably kill innocents—as, for example, in the July 23, 2002, Israeli dropping of a 2,000-pound bomb in a Gaza neighborhood that killed not only the targeted Hamas leader but 15 others as well, including 9 children.[15] It is unclear why the same logic thought to justify the killing of civilians in wartime—namely that so doing is believed useful, necessary, or unavoidable in the pursuit of chosen objectives—does not equally justify killing them in terroristic warfare.

It is also unclear why the terrorist as a person is necessarily any worse than the soldier in uniform. If the one uses unconventional means, that is because they are all he has at his disposal. Are we to say to terrorists that if they had an army and an air force at their disposal, it would be all right to use them; but as they do not, they may not use the homemade bombs or boxcutters they do have? The terrorist, in fact, may more often be a person of deep conviction than the ordinary soldier. Rank and file soldiers do what they do because they are told to. Often as not, they have been pressed into service and have little understanding of the issues for which they are required to kill. The terrorist typically does what he does knowledgeably and with conviction of the rightness of his cause. He often thinks of himself as engaged in a legitimate military struggle. When Palestinian Georges Abdalla was convicted of terrorist activities in

---

[15]   When US forces bombed Afghan villages in July of 2002, killing 48 civilians and wounding 117, mostly women and children (according to Afghan government figures; the Pentagon claims they killed only 34 and wounded 50), they denied targeting them, and blamed the Taliban for "placing women and children near valid military targets." *New York Times*, September 7, 2002.

France, he claimed that he was a "Palestinian fighter," not a terrorist.[16] When former Jewish terrorists gathered to reminisce about their bombing of the King David Hotel that left 91 dead, one said, "I am very proud of the operation militarily. I felt myself like a soldier of these Jewish forces." As Algerian-born suspected terrorist Kamel Daoudi awaits trial in Paris, he writes: "I accept the name of terrorist if it is used to mean that I terrorize a one-sided system of iniquitous power and a perversity that comes in many forms. I have never terrorized innocent individuals and I will never do so. But I will fight any form of injustice and those who support it."[17] Aimal Khan Kasi, in a death row interview before his execution, for killing two CIA employees, said, "What I did was in retaliation against the US government" for its Middle Eastern policy and support of Israel. "It had nothing to do with terrorism," he said, adding that he opposed the killing of American citizens in the 9/11 attack.[18] To all appearances, these are people who freely commit themselves to a cause and pursue it with conviction. It is precisely because their conviction is stronger than that of the average person—at least as measured by their willingness to sacrifice and kill—that they are willing to do things ordinary persons consider abhorrent.

During the Vietnam War, a US officer who had commented upon the gloomy prospects of success in operations in the delta area was asked what the answer was.

> "Terror," he said pleasantly. "The Vietcong have terrorized the peasants to get their cooperation . . . We must terrorize the villagers even more, so they see that their real self-interest lies with us. We've got to start bombing and strafing the villages that aren't friendly to the Government." He then added, "Of course we won't do it. That's not our way of doing things . . . But terror is what it takes."[19]

It was reported soon after: "U.S. and allied forces are adopting a program of destroying homes and crops in areas which feed and shield the communist forces. For years, Americans have refused to participate in 'scorched earth' efforts, leaving them to the Vietnamese. Now Americans are directly involved."[20]

Washington Post correspondent John T. Wheeler reported on one such operation on March 30, 1967:

> The Vietnamese woman ignored the crying baby in her arms. She stared in hatred as the American infantrymen with shotguns blasted away at chickens and ducks. Others shot a water buffalo and the family dog. While her husband, father and young son were led away, the torch was put to the hut that still contained the family belongings. The flames consumed everything—including the shrine to the family ancestors.

[16] *New York Times*, September 26, 1981.
[17] *New York Times*, September 22, 2002. Notice that, unlike the Palestinian and Jewish terrorists quoted, Daoudi accepts the label "terrorist" if (and presumably only if) it represents a struggle against iniquity. By implication—at least as it applies to himself—it precludes attacks upon innocents. Most who discuss terrorism accept the emotively pejorative force the term has, and then apply the term only to those of whom they strongly disapprove. Daoudi, on the other hand, tacitly redefines the term in such a way that it acquires a descriptive meaning that most people would find unobjectionable, provided that they do not object in principle to the use of violence.
[18] *New York Times*, November 8, 2002.
[19] Jack Langguth, *New York Times Magazine*, September 19, 1965.
[20] *Rochester Times-Union*, January 6, 1966.

The GIs didn't have much stomach for the job, but orders were orders . . . "God, my wife would faint if she could see what I'm doing now," an infantryman said. "Killing [Vietcong] is one thing, but killing puppies and baby ducks and stuff like that—it's something else, man."

Men the world over readily become killers if compelled to by their governments or, as with terrorists, if they believe strongly enough in their cause. And there is not that much difference among them. Americans, Russians, Afghans, Israelis, Palestinians, Iraqis, Indonesians, Columbians, and so on do or have done comparable things in varying degrees according to the means at their disposal. There may be, as psychologist David Grossman argues, an inborn reluctance to kill one's fellow humans.[21] But the techniques have been nearly perfected by which to overcome that reluctance in most people.

Militarization of the campaign against terrorism

Then FBI Director William H. Webster announced in 1986 that the agency had achieved "extraordinary success" in combating terrorism in the preceding six years by lawful techniques. He said those same principles could be applied internationally as well.[22] He added that "[t]he more we increase our ability to deal with terrorism as a criminal activity, the more successful we will be." Others at the same American Bar Association Convention at which Webster spoke—including then attorney general Edwin Meese—applauded the American attack on Libya in April of that year following the bombing of a discotheque in Germany as a deterrent to terrorism.[23] Implied was the thought that tough military retaliation was the answer to terrorism.[24]

Though not represented as such at the time, there were represented here two perspectives on how to deal with terrorism. The first was to treat it as a form of criminal activity and to respond by refining and expanding the lawful investigative techniques to locate, apprehend, and bring to justice those responsible for such acts. This approach implied intelligence sharing, international cooperation, compliance with domestic and international law. The second was to militarize the campaign against terrorism by visiting swift retribution on offenders with a view to deterring such acts in the future. This approach implied reliance upon military power, unilateralism, and little more than lip-service to law. The declaration of "war" on terrorism and the October 7, 2001,

[21] David Grossman, *On Killing: The Psychological Cost of Learning to Kill in War and Society* (Boston: Little, Brown, 1996).
[22] *New York Times*, August 12, 1986.
[23] Fifteen years later, when convictions for the disco bombing were handed down in a German court, it was still far from clear precisely what connection the attack had with Libya beyond its connection with a few persons in the East Berlin Libyan embassy; *Christian Science Monitor*, November 2, 2001.
[24] A thoughtful article that same year argued that "[t]he law has a poor record in dealing with international terrorism . . . What good is the law in fighting international terrorism? Why has it failed?" See Abraham D. Sofaer, "Terrorism and the Law," *Foreign Affairs*, Vol. 64, Summer 1986, 901–22.

attack on Afghanistan symbolized the final stage in the installment of this second perspective as the dominant approach to terrorism by the United States.[25]

This militarization of the campaign against terrorism has been a gradual process. And it has been two-pronged. One prong has been highly secretive. The details are sketchy even today. Arguably it began when the Defense Department created secret elite units to combat terrorism and engage in covert operations in Central America, Africa, and Asia.[26] As reported by the *New York Times*, the units were established in 1980 following the abortive attempt to rescue the US hostages in Iran. As distinguished from the traditional Special Forces, these units are so secret they are not even officially acknowledged by the government. Referred to as Delta Force and Seal Team 6, many of them wear beards, do not have identifying insignia, and, in Afghanistan, dress like Afghans. They identify themselves only by first name and on more than one occasion have turned journalists back at gunpoint from covering controversial stories. Then Defense Secretary Donald H. Rumsfeld reportedly favors sending them anywhere in the world, with or without the knowledge of local governments, to capture or kill Al Qaeda.[27] Operations of this sort have brought the United States into tension with European countries. In February 2003, for example, the United States reportedly abducted a suspect in Italy without the knowledge or permission of the Italian government, and transferred him to Egypt for interrogation, a process known as "rendition." The Italians, in response, sought the arrest of 13 suspected CIA agents involved in the abduction.[28] Whereas the United States has militarized the campaign against terrorism, the Europeans tend to regard it as a problem for criminal justice.

The other prong has been high profile, including the bombing of Libya in April of 1986 and the cruise missile attacks on Sudan and Afghanistan on August 20, 1998, in retaliation for the US embassy bombings in East Africa. The culmination of the process came in the 2001 attack on the Taliban, in which both massive military power and elite secret units combined to devastate the Taliban as a conventional fighting force.

Whether by initial design or through later realization of its potential in this regard the militarization of the campaign against terrorism has now dove-tailed with a radical transformation of US military policy. Whereas containment and deterrence characterized the years of the Cold War, the Bush administration has seized upon

---

[25] It is arguable that, at least where Libya was concerned, the United States retreated to legal rather than military methods. "After the Libyan role in the bombing [Pan Am Flight 103 in 1988] was confirmed . . . the Bush administration decided that the existing strategy of military retaliation was futile. 'We thought that we weren't likely to get anywhere with another bombing raid and that you couldn't rule out that indeed the Pan Am 103 shoot-down was a consequence of the last bombing raid', Brent Scowcroft, Bush's national security adviser, recalled. Weary of the cycle of killing, President Bush decided to seek a legal solution. The White House redirected its energies into backing UN sanctions against Tripoli in the conviction that the United States did not have an interest in waging an all-out war against Libya and that concerted international pressure provided a better way to change its behavior." Daniel Benjamin and Steven Simon, *The Age of Sacred Terror*, 223. The quotation from Scowcroft is from John Lancaster, "Compromising Positions," *Washington Post Magazine*, July 9, 2000, 10.

[26] *New York Times*, "The U.S. Military Creates Secret Units for Use in Sensitive Tasks Abroad," June 8, 1984.

[27] *New York Times*, August 12, 2002.

[28] As reported in the *Christian Science Monitor*, June 29, 2005.

preemption as the keystone of policy.[29] It appears that this new policy will involve a willingness on the part of the United States to act unilaterally virtually in any place in the world that it believes there are serious threats. Both the aforementioned elite units and the massive use of conventional and perhaps nuclear power presumably will be the chosen means. The so-called war on terrorism[30] needs only to have tacked onto it "and tyrants" to expand its scope. Needless to say, this conjunctive escalation of policy admits of tacking on virtually any other descriptive term (such as "and threats to American interests") to give it limitless scope. After the collapse of the Soviet Union, theorists speculated about whether the end to the Cold War would bring a unipolar world, with the United States as the dominant figure, or a multipolar world, with power distributed among various units, or something altogether different. In 2002 the Bush administration appears to have decided the issue conclusively. The United States will reign as the sole superpower and supreme state, determined to nip in the bud attempts by any other power to rival it militarily.

There is one final step before this logic has run its course. This is the extension of this supposed right to virtually unrestricted use of force to the domestic scene as well. This implies the gradual militarization of the government's control over its own citizens as well. Congress obligingly facilitated the move in this direction with the Patriot Act. The administration is incrementally arrogating more and more power to itself with readiness to put religious and other groups under surveillance, encouraging Americans to become informers on one another, and a readiness to remove any person from virtually all protection of any laws by attaching to them the label "enemy combatant." Appropriating the term "war" for the campaign on terrorism serves this purpose well. It readies people for extreme measures; and it makes available to the government all of the language of war to keep emotions running high. With the enemy ill-defined (those associated with so-called Al Qaeda reportedly do not call themselves by that name, and it is difficult to find more than passing reference to Al Qaeda prior to 9/11), with 5,000 of them and their sympathizers alleged to be in the United States and multiples of that number conspiring abroad, all the boundaries are down; this "war" can be carried on at the discretion of the administration anywhere of its choosing and against virtually anyone of its choosing.

The language of war has been superimposed upon the effort to combat one type of criminal activity and exploited to expand governmental powers almost without limit.

---

[29] Although speaking about conventional war and not terrorism, Franklin Roosevelt had set the stage for such thinking. He said in May of 1941: "Some people seem to think that we are not attacked until bombs actually drop on New York or San Francisco or New Orleans or Chicago . . . The attack on the United States can begin with the domination of any base which menaces our security— north or south . . . Old-fashioned common sense calls for the use of a strategy which will prevent such an enemy from gaining a foothold in the first place." Arthur L. Funk, *Roosevelt's Foreign Policy, 1933–1941*, 399f. Quoted from Charles A. Beard, "'In Case of Attack' in the Atlantic," in Robert A. Divine, ed., *Causes and Consequences of World War II* (Chicago: Quadrangle Books, 1969), 101.

[30] Americans accustomed to "war" on drugs, "war" on poverty, "war" on crime, and so on have scarcely noticed that what arguably is a war only in a metaphorical sense is being treated by the administration, when it serves its purposes, as a literal war. As Susan Sontag writes, "When a president of the United States declares war on cancer or poverty or drugs, we know that 'war' is a metaphor. Does anyone think that this war—the war the America has declared on terrorism—is a metaphor? But it is, and one with powerful consequences." Op ed, *New York Times,* September 10, 2002.

Evidence becomes secondary.[31] Ronald Reagan took ten days to attack Libya after the La Belle disco bombing in 1986. It was not until 15 years later that sufficient evidence was gathered to convict four persons (two Palestinians, a German, and a Libyan) of the crime in a German court; and even then, though the Libyan and one of the Palestinians worked in the East Berlin Libyan embassy, it had not yet been shown conclusively that Quaddafi and the higher levels of the Libyan government were involved. Bill Clinton took 13 days to launch retaliatory cruise missile strikes against Sudan and Afghanistan after the August 7, 1998, attacks on US embassies in Kenya and Tanzania, even though Osama bin Laden had not been shown to be behind the attacks and neither he nor anyone else was under indictment for the crime in any US court.[32] George W. Bush dismissed requests from the Taliban to produce evidence of Osama bin Laden's role in 9/11 attacks before turning him over and began bombing on October 7, less than four weeks after the attack.[33] The logic of this spiraling government power risks treating lack of evidence as itself evidence. If an adversary is highly secretive, then you expect there to be little evidence of his activity before he strikes. So the fact that there is little evidence connecting a given suspect with terrorism is what one would expect. The estimate of a person's cunning and deceit begins to vary inversely with the evidence against him. With the 1996 antiterrorism legislation being so broad as to implicate anyone who so much as lends support to terrorists, the net is cast so wide as to dampen dissent and criticism of government. An antiwar speech, an Op ed piece, or an article like this could be considered suspect.

A nonviolent orientation toward terrorism

If the violence of terrorism is arguably no worse morally than that of much of warfare, the violence of warfare is arguably no less terrible than that of terrorism. We have

[31] Author Bob Woodward writes that the Bush administration discussed "whether to issue a white paper, designed to prove that bin Laden and al Qaeda were behind the September 11 attacks," an idea that was rejected. "The danger of issuing a white paper that presented evidence," Woodward writes, "was that it could condition people to view the war on terror as a law enforcement operation, within the model of the judicial system with its evidentiary standards, burden of proof on the government and proof beyond a reasonable doubt—things that could not possibly be met." Bob Woodward, *Bush at War* (New York: Simon & Schuster, 2002), 135f.

[32] Osama bin Laden was subsequently indicted in a US court for the attack. On September 17, 2003, a Spanish judge specifically charged him, along with nine others, of committing the 9/11 attack; *New York Times*, September 18, 2003. Polls show that a majority of Americans believe that Saddam Hussein was involved in the 9/11 attack. "I think it's not surprising that people make that connection," Vice President Cheney said on NBC-TV's "Meet the Press." Although the administration has repeatedly affirmed that Saddam Hussein had Al Qaeda ties, it has not asserted that he was responsible for 9/11, and President Bush, following the Cheney statement, reportedly said that he had seen no evidence of such involvement; *New York Times*, September 18, 2003. Yet the president has repeatedly encouraged people to make a connection between Saddam and terrorists, such as in his statement, the month before, that "Al Qaida and the other global terror networks recognize that the defeat of Saddam Hussein's regime is a defeat for them"; http://nytimes.com/2003/08/26/politics/26TEXT-BUSH.

[33] Some experts in the area believed the Taliban were willing to hand over bin Laden, or have him expelled to another country, if only because he was believed to have become a liability in their quest for international recognition.

compartmentalized our thinking so as to think of the one as respectable, the other vile. Common to the violence of the terrorist and the soldier alike is the treatment of human beings as objects to be destroyed when seen as obstacles to the attainment of one's ends. Once you accept that violence is a permissible means by which to pursue ends, and that one may do virtually anything to achieve those ends,[34] you need only accustom people to overcome their natural revulsion to killing to turn them to your purposes. The techniques are there. The armies of the world specialize in them.

It is this feature of violence that highlights the central fact in its moral assessment. Kant captured the idea in his second formulation of the categorical imperative: "Act so that you treat humanity, whether in your own person or in that of another, always as an end and never as a means only." To allow oneself to be used by others to do their killing is to allow yourself to become a means. This is as true of the soldier as of the suicide-bomber. To kill others to promote your own ends is to use the others as means. The alternative is simple to state. Rediscover the humanity of all persons, friends and adversaries alike. Accord them the respect owed to all persons. But what that means in the concrete is less easy to state. What are people to do who suffer persecution and injustice? What should European Jews have done who fled the Holocaust and sought a homeland in Palestine only to be turned back by the British? What are Palestinians to do who seek recovery of their homeland only to be turned by the Israelis? Should European Jews have folded their hands and waited for the world to offer them security? Should Palestinians resign themselves to refugee camps until the Israelis invite them back? And what should American have done in the wake of September 11? There are no easy answers to these questions.

A beginning would be to open communication with terrorists rather than, as now, refusing to deal with them at all, or worse yet, expanding their putative ranks by labeling—for political reasons—as terrorists those who may simply be involved in rebellion against what they see as a repressive state. Terrorism does not exist in the abstract. People do not just decide to become terrorists and then conspire with others to go about their deadly business. "We are people," one of the women said at the aforementioned gathering at the King David Hotel. "We know how to love, we know how to hate. We know how to kiss. We have all the emotions of everybody else."[35] We need to recognize terrorists as, for the most part, persons like ourselves, who take into their own hands the violence most of us leave to others. They are not subhuman monsters, to be fought with all the righteous fury that civilized people can muster. Part of our responsibility is to try to understand what leads them to perform such acts and what measure of justice their cause may embody.[36]

In 1985 when the hijackers of a TWA airliner reportedly shouted the words "New Jersey" in the aisles of the plane, most Americans, if they heard of it at all, would

---

[34] President Bush asked Congress for authority to use "all means he determines to be appropriate" to overthrow Saddam Hussein; *New York Times*, September 20, 2002.

[35] *New York Times*, September 26, 1981.

[36] We need also to see the humanity in those who do their killing "legitimately," as part of an established military unit. A journalist reported on an interview with a teenage Israeli soldier on duty in Bethlehem: "'I know I look like a monster in all this,' he said, tapping his helmet, then his vest, then his rifle. 'I'm not a monster,' he said. 'I don't like this. I'm a human being just like you'"; *New York Times,* May 10, 2002.

scarcely have been aware that the reference was to the battleship New Jersey, which had in 1983 turned its 16-inch guns upon Shiite Muslim villages in Lebanon following a suicide bombing of a Marine barracks. The guns hurtled 2,000-pound shells into the homes of those who could not possibly have been responsible for the bombing.[37] Nor were the more than 80 people killed responsible when a US-organized covert Lebanese unit acted on its own to try to assassinate Hezbullah leader Mohammad Fedlallah. It is decent, well-dressed men in Washington—family men, churchgoers, no doubt good neighbors and friends—who ultimately bear responsibility for such actions. With the unprecedented military power at their command, they need only issue a command, and a sequence of events is set in motion that results in bombs exploding thousands of miles away in Afghanistan or Iraq. Those who burn to avenge such actions, or to redress what they perceive as wrongs wrought by the policies of such men, have only guns or explosives and their own strength and wit with which to work. When they commandeer a plane, or plant a bomb, they are terrorists. But what they do is no different in kind from what others do or have done. By no means are any, much less most, of the acts they perform to be presumed justified. Often it is not even known fully what the justification is alleged to be. But sometimes a rationale is set forth. And sometimes it is one that needs to be taken seriously. Such, arguably, is the 1998 document by Osama bin Laden and other leaders of militant Islamist groups, entitled "Declaration of the World Islamic Front for Jihad against the Jews and the Crusaders." Writing in *Foreign Affairs*, Bernard Lewis says: "The statement—a magnificent piece of eloquent, at times even poetic Arabic prose—reveals a version of history that most Westerners will find unfamiliar. Bin Laden's grievances are not quite what many would expect." The document says, in part,

> First—for more than seven years the United States is occupying the lands of Islam in the holiest of its territories, Arabia, plundering its riches, overwhelming its rulers, humiliating its people, threatening its neighbors, and using its bases in the peninsula as a spearhead to fight against the neighboring Islamic peoples . . .

> Second—despite the immense destruction inflicted on the Iraqi people at the hands of the Crusader-Jewish alliance . . . the Americans nevertheless . . . are trying once more to repeat this dreadful slaughter . . . So they come again today to destroy what remains of this people and to humiliate their Muslim neighbors.

> Third—while the purposes of the Americans in these wars are religious and economic, they also serve . . . to divert attention from [Jewish] occupation of Jerusalem and their killing of Muslims in it.[38]

---

[37] As Neil C. Livingstone writes, "the 1983 shelling of the Chouf Mountains in Lebanon by the U.S. battleship *New Jersey* . . . could not reasonably have been expected to punish those specifically responsible for the incidents. Although enemy command and forward observation positions were hit . . . the naval bombardment also inflicted casualties on the civilian population of the region without having a real impact on those who actually carried out the attacks on the marines. Using the *New Jersey* to fight terrorists is rather like employing a sledge hammer to kill a bothersome flea." In Neil C. Livingstone and Terrell E. Arnold, *Fighting Back: Winning the War against Terrorism* (Lexington, MA: Lexington Books, 1986), 122.

[38] Quoted from Bernard Lewis, "License to Kill: Usama bin Laden's Declaration of Jihad," *Foreign Affairs*, Vol. 77, No. 6, November–December 1998, 14–19.

If the challenge is to understand better and appreciate the position of the terrorist, or the revolutionary, or the advocate of violent change, the imperative is to find nonviolent ways of dealing with the problems of injustice, poverty, and oppression that are typically at the root of their actions. As former deputy secretary of state Strobe Talbott has written,

> Disease, overcrowding, undernourishment, political repression, and alienation breed despair, anger, and hatred. These are the raw materials of what we're up against, and they constitute a check on the willingness of Arab and other regimes to take effective action against networks of conspirators . . . [T]here will be a temptation to squeeze down the very programs that will allow us to move from reactive, defensive warfare against the terrorists to a proactive, prolonged offensive against the ugly, intractable realities that terrorists exploit and from which they derive popular support, foot soldiers, and political cover. That's why another phrase from America's political past needs to be dusted off, put back in service, and internationalized: the war on poverty. Only if the long struggle ahead is also fought on that front will it be winnable.[39]

To undertake such a commitment seriously requires that *others*, who are not desperate in the way in which the oppressed or aggrieved are, and who have the means, power, and influence to redirect the course of events, involve themselves cooperatively with all sides in the controversies that lead to violence in an attempt to find creative solutions to them.

Nonviolence, so conceived, must be active, not passive. In a sense, violence—meaning reliance upon violence as the ultimate recourse for resolving problems—is more passive than nonviolence. Violence often waits until situations have deteriorated to the point of no return, doing nothing, or worse yet, doing the wrong things, then flaring up and engulfing those it would help as well as those it opposes. Reliance upon the institutionalized violence of modern war systems did not prevent Hitler from coming to power. While it eventually vanquished him at a horrendous cost, it left in its wake a situation arguably as bad as that which, following World War I, eventually led to World War II, with the world divided between communists and noncommunists; a world that has thus far been lucky to sidestep the calamity of nuclear war. The Vietnam War was ostensibly begun to secure the freedom of the South Vietnamese people. But today the whole of Vietnam is communist. Arab states went to war in 1948 to liberate Palestine, but today Palestinians live by the millions in diaspora, almost certainly never to return to their homeland. Israel relies on military might to preserve itself, yet its security gradually erodes as its margin of superiority over its Arab neighbors diminishes and the second Palestinian Intifada shows no signs of abating. The United States shelled Lebanon in 1983, bombed Libya in 1986, waged war on Iraq in 1991, and bombed Sudan and Afghanistan in 1998 to deter terrorism. But it didn't deter the 9/11 attack.

Nonviolence requires active engagement with the problems of peace and justice, not ignoring them so long as things remain orderly and then sending in troops when

---

[39]   Strobe Talbott, "The Other Evil: The War on Terrorism Won't Succeed without a War on Poverty," *Foreign Policy*, November–December 2001, 75f.

bloodshed finally becomes inevitable. This is what nonviolence meant for leaders like Gandhi and Martin Luther King, Jr.

But can nonviolence "work?" Can it resolve the problems of injustice and oppression? We know that resort to war and violence for all of recorded history has not worked. It has not secured either peace or justice to the world. The most it has brought are brief interludes in which the nations of the world regroup, catch their breath, and prepare for the next war. We know that nonviolence worked in India with Gandhi, in the United States with King, and in Scandinavia against the Nazis in World War II. It worked in the Philippines in the mid-1980s when nonviolent "People Power" averted what might have been a bloody civil war by sitting in front of the government's tanks as the Marcos regime sought to confront rebel commanders in their headquarters. It brought dignity and respect to the Solidarity movement in Poland throughout the 1980s when violence would almost certainly have brought a crushing Soviet response. It worked in the early 1990s when Lithuanians rallied nonviolently in support of independence in the face the overwhelming military superiority of the Soviet Union. Would it work on a larger scale? Who knows? No one can foresee what the results might be if a country like the United States were to spend $300 billion a year in research on techniques of nonviolent resistance and on educating and training people in their use.

What is needed is a new perspective which, in Kantian terms, respects persons as ends in themselves. We need a willingness to cultivate and put into practice an awareness of the humanity in our adversaries, even when they are terrorists; a perspective that approaches conflict in a spirit of seeking the truth in the issues that divide us from our adversaries rather than assuming our own righteousness and trying only to work out the means to our ends. This spirit is captured in a remarkable statement by Mariane Pearl, widow of the American journalist Daniel Pearl, just after confirmation of his death in Pakistan at the hands of terrorists:

> Revenge would be easy, but it is far more valuable in my opinion to address this problem of terrorism with enough honesty to question our own responsibility as nations and as individuals for the rise of terrorism. My . . . hope now—in my seventh month of pregnancy—is that I will be able to tell our son that his father carried the flag to end terrorism, raising an unprecedented demand among people from all countries not for revenge but for the values we all share: love, compassion, friendship and citizenship far transcending the so-called clash of civilizations.[40]

Violence is for the morally infallible. Nonviolence is for those who recognize their own limitations and the possibility that others, with whom they are in disagreement, have hold of certain parts of the truth, and are willing to put forth the effort to uncover and cultivate that truth in the interests of nonviolent conciliation.[41]

[40] Quoted from the Rochester's *Democrat & Chronicle*, February 23, 2002.
[41] Previously unpublished.

13

Understanding Evil from the Perspective of Nonviolence

While acknowledging that evil is a multidimensional phenomenon, Holmes approaches it from a specific angle. He wants to establish a clear conceptual line between badness and evil because, while the existence of badness is indisputable, the existence of evil is for him an open question. Much of Eastern thought contends that human beings are essentially good, and even much of Western philosophy holds the same. There is no evil in the natural order of things, which means that if evil exists, it is produced. And if produced by human beings, then perhaps it can also be eliminated by them. To clarify these issues further, Holmes draws a line between evil acts, evil intentions, evil motives, and evil people. While philosophers from Socrates on often discuss evil (or wrongdoings) in connection with ignorance, Holmes focuses on fear: people who commit evil are guided for the most part by fear, not malice; it is fear that leads people to do horrible things. If this is so, then our usual reactions to evil deeds are simply inadequate. Physical punishments that we inflict on those who commit such deeds—whether they be those of bombing, torture, or imprisonment—simply do not address the source of the problem. They do not remove fear, nor lead to trust, but only intensify that fear into hatred. An ethics of nonviolence aims to remove fear and build trust. If others have no reason to fear us, and if their violence springs from fear, then their fear and their violence can be dispelled only by nonviolence.

The 20th century witnessed the Holocaust, an unparalleled evil in the eyes of most people, as well as attempted genocide in Rwanda. The beginning of the 21st century saw the launching of a so-called "war" against terrorism, proclaimed to be a struggle of good against evil.

But what is evil? If we don't know what we're struggling against we're unlikely to be successful. We can kill plenty of people, of course, but without an understanding of evil we won't know that we're killing evil people or even people who—if they're not themselves evil—are doing evil.

Different understandings of evil emerged historically as religious power gradually receded before secular power. As Tolstoy put it, "Men who were vested with sanctity regarded as evil what men and institutions that were vested with civil power considered to be good, and vice versa, and the struggle became ever more acute."[1] Nietzsche took

---

[1]   Leo Tolstoy, *The Kingdom of God Is within You* (New York: Noonday Press, 1961), 196.

the stakes in the contest to prevail in the defining of evil to be even more momentous. They were at the center of what he saw as an historic struggle between superior and inferior persons. The multitude of inferior persons—those embodying the values of what he called "slave morality"—redefined as *evil* what was by nature good and labeled as "good" what was by nature bad.

What is clear is that without an understanding of evil, the way is open to defining it as one pleases and, in the process, to responding to it as one pleases, typically with violence. Tolstoy, once again, perceived this:

> Previous to Christ's teaching it appeared to men that there was but one way of solving a struggle, and that was by resisting evil with violence, and so they did, each of the contending parties trying to convince himself and others that what each of them considered to be an evil was a real, absolute evil. . . . Men have employed violence against other men and have assured themselves and others that they have employed this violence against the evil which was acknowledged by all men.[2]

In Tolstoy's view, the principle here is that of "defining with authority what is evil and resisting it with violence."[3] While perhaps not recognized and consciously acted upon as a principle, what Tolstoy describes arguably represents the common practice of communities, societies, and states. But, of course, those representing different communities, societies, and states often have different "definitions" of evil. President Reagan called the Soviet Union an evil empire during the Cold War. President Bush later branded Iran, Syria, and North Korea the axis of evil. The U.S. itself has been called the "Great Satan"—a way, for some Muslims, of saying that it epitomizes evil. We can scoff at such accusations against us, but do we understand them? And if we don't understand them, can we justifiably dismiss them at the same time that we make similar accusations against others?

Tolstoy thought this attempt to define evil with authority—in such a way that it would be recognized by all persons—is futile. He therefore concluded that the attempt to resist evil by violence is useless, serving only to perpetuate violence and conflict. Gandhi made a related point when he wrote that *satyagraha* (Truth-Force) "excludes the use of violence because man is not capable of knowing the absolute truth and, therefore, not competent to punish."[4] Both were making an epistemological point, that we lack the requisite knowledge to be justified in resorting to violence. Tolstoy thought this was so because we are incapable of effectively forcing others to accept our own definition of evil as authoritative, and absent such acceptance violence will only beget more violence. Gandhi thought this was so because he believed that absolute truth is required to justify punishment and we lack such truth. Whether the required knowledge is specifically knowledge of evil, as Tolstoy held, is unclear. But much of Gandhi's philosophy suggests that it was.

The Tolstoyan principle contains two claims: the first is that men are unable to define with authority what evil is; the second is that men are unjustified in resisting perceived evil by violence unless they have defined what evil is. I want to focus initially

---

[2] Ibid., 194.
[3] Ibid., 195.
[4] M. K. Gandhi, *Non-Violent Resistance* (New York: Schocken Books, 1961), 1.

upon the first of these claims. But I want to move it away from the question of defining evil authoritatively (which meant for Tolstoy entitling those who hold power to use violence in the service of that definition) to the question of defining evil philosophically, whether or not any such definition is acceptable to all persons. I shall then take up the question of the use of violence to confront evil.

Evil and badness

I want at the outset to emphasize the distinction between what is evil and what is bad. There is kindness, compassion, happiness and joy in the world. These are unquestionably good. There is also pain, suffering, malice, and misery. These are unquestionably bad. Good and bad (along with better and worse and associated terms) are not only part of our ordinary discourse, they are—as Kant saw of causality, space, and time—part of the conceptual and intuitive tools by which we understand the world. We can scarcely go through a day without making at least implicit value judgments of good and bad, better and worse.

Where does evil come in?[5]

Adam and Eve ate forbidden fruit of the Tree of the Knowledge of Good and Evil, not of the Tree of the Knowledge of Good and Bad. A toothache is bad, but it isn't evil. Destructive hurricanes and earthquakes are bad, but they aren't evil. My point is that evil isn't part of the natural order. It's not a force in the natural scheme of things. And I include by the "natural scheme of things" the effects of the actions of nonhuman living things upon other living things. The lion's killing of the lamb is awful. But it's not evil. Nor is the lion herself evil, as she nestles with her cubs with the gentleness of the lamb she has just killed. Plague and pestilence spread misery and death, but bacteria and locusts are not themselves evil, even as they sicken or kill millions.

We do, it is true, sometimes use "evil" interchangeably with *bad*. Thus one might read in an ethics text that utilitarianism calls for maximizing the balance of good over evil or that morality is the study of good and evil. When what is bad rises to a catastrophic scale and magnitude it is sometimes called evil. And sometimes especially catastrophic natural events have been deemed to be evil on theological grounds—that they are the workings of Satan or perhaps of God himself.[6]

This loose way with the term *evil* isn't what interests me. Our ordinary language is sufficiently flexible that we can and sometimes do use the term interchangeably with

---

[5] Theologian Terrence Reynolds reportedly claims that the question "What is evil?" is more interesting than the answer to it, because there is no answer. Neely Tucker, "Giving Evil the Eye," *Washington Post*, July 23, 2007; http://washingtonpost.com/wp-dyn/content/article/200/07/22/AR200/0/220.

[6] See, for example: "And they covet fields, and take *them* by violence, and houses, and take *them* away: so they oppress a man and his house, even a man and his heritage. Therefore thus saith the Lord; Behold, against this family do I devise an evil, from which ye shall not remove your necks; neither shall ye go haughtily: for this time is evil." (*Micah* 2; 2–3). A more recent historical example is the Lisbon earthquake of 1755 that killed 10,000–15,000 people, discussed by Susan Neiman, "Roads to Hell," in *Destined for Evil? The Twentieth-Century Responses*, ed. P. Cicovacki (Rochester, NY: University of Rochester Press), 91–110.

bad.[7] But if we fix upon this use of the term for philosophical purposes, then we will have to distinguish among myriad kinds of evil—that of a tornado, for example, from that of a terrorist bomb. We already have different terms (*bad* and *evil*) readily available for this purpose, and I propose to use them.

Let it also be said that we often use the term *evil* with a pronounced emotive (or expressive) meaning; that is, as a way of expressing certain emotions (say of disapproval or outrage) and of trying to evoke similar emotions in others. Calling the Soviet Union an *evil empire* was Ronald Reagan's way of expressing disdain for the Soviet Union and undoubtedly of trying to encourage the same feeling in others.

The emotive uses of the term also aren't what most interest me. My interest is to try to clarify a descriptive or conceptual meaning of the term, one in which evil and badness are distinguishable. That there are bad things in the world is incontrovertible. Whether there is evil in the world—and if so, in what forms—is an open question. My aim is to try to clarify the nature of evil in such a way as to enable us better to understand this question with a view to making progress toward answering it, and answering it in a way that illuminates its importance for the philosophy of nonviolence. It is this sense I want to explore.

Competing assumptions about the existence of evil in the world

Even when we distinguish between evil and badness, there are two ways of approaching the problem of evil. (1) We can start by assuming that there is such a thing and that we need only to find ways of stamping it out. The only philosophical question of great interest then is how to reconcile the existence of such evil with the existence of a good God, if there be such.[8] (2) On the other hand, we can start by trying to understand *what* evil is, leaving open the question whether anything corresponds to it in the world. Just as we can define the conditions of a just war without assuming in advance that there are any such wars, or define a unicorn even while knowing that there are no such things, so we can clarify the idea of evil while leaving open the question whether there is evil in the world. Given that the first course immediately puts force, threat and violence to the forefront as prime candidates for eliminating evil, the second course is the one I propose to take. It is, I believe, the course counseled by a philosophy of nonviolence. I shall try to clarify the meaning of the term *evil*—not in the sense of what people have before their minds when they use the term, but rather in the sense of what they would have before their minds if they thought the issues through in greater depth.

---

[7] One readily understands Philip Hallie, for example, when he writes: "Nature is the widest drama of good and evil that we can know. When a lioness closes her jaws on a zebra's throat, she is feeding life and destroying life in one and the same action"; *In the Eye of the Hurricane: Tales of Good and Evil, Help and Harm* (New York: Harper Collins, 1997), 83.

[8] Though many people, including politicians and world leaders, speak as though they can readily identify evil, there is still the question of whether it can be given a clear legal definition, for the purposes of law courts. Forensic psychiatrist Michael Welner reportedly thinks that giving a legal definition is important to identifying evil, and that identifying evil is important to eliminating it. See Neely Tucker, "Giving Evil the Eye," *Washington Post*, July 23, 2007.

It might be objected that to start by leaving open whether or not evil exists—or, more particularly, whether or not there are evil people in the world—flies in the face of the obvious. Wasn't the Holocaust evil? Weren't Hitler and Stalin evil? And shouldn't such judgments be the starting point of any discussion of evil? Not necessarily. We should be mindful that much of Eastern philosophy contends, as with Taoism, that people are basically good, that the bad that they do has other explanations than that people are evil. Even much of early Western philosophy holds the same. For Plato (or at least Socrates), we recall, all wrongdoing is from ignorance. Good people often are ignorant; indeed, on Plato's view, most of them are ignorant of the most important things in life. And for Aristotle, wrongdoing owes both to ignorance and to weakness of the will. Basically good people can be weak-willed. For both Plato and Aristotle there are other explanations of wrongdoing than postulating that it is done by evil people.[9] We should not start by assuming that the bad things people do—and in some cases, the horrendous things that they do—are explainable only by assuming that they are evil. Some people cause untold harm to themselves and others, but this is consistent with their being good by nature. We can tell for the most part whether people do bad things by observing their conduct, but I shall argue that we can't tell whether they are evil simply by observing their conduct. There the matter is more complicated.

What is evil?

From a theological perspective it is sometimes said that there is no evil in the natural order because God, being good, and the creator of all things, would not create evil. A popular solution to this "problem of evil" is to locate evil in the doings of humans in their exercise of free will. This seems to me to be essentially correct. But one needn't believe in God to hold that there is no evil in the natural order. One need only recognize that evil presupposes *minds*. Without minds there would be no evil. Mark Twain recognized this when he said satirically: "What, now, do we find the Primal Curse to have been? Plainly what it was in the beginning: the infliction upon man of the Moral Sense; the ability to distinguish good from evil; and with it, necessarily, the ability to do evil; for there can be no evil act without the presence of consciousness of it in the doer of it."[10]

If there is no evil in the natural order, then evil (if it exists) is *produced*. And it takes minds to produce it. This is why—leaving aside religious and supernatural assumptions—there is evil in the world only because there are human beings in the world,[11] or to give it a more Kantian cast, only because there are rational beings in the world.

9   In an insightful essay, Nicholas Wolterstorff writes that "[t]he Stoics would have denied that the two World Wars, the Nazi concentration camps, the Soviet Gulag, and the Chinese 'Great Leap Forward' were evils." See "Identifying Good and Evil," in *Destined for Evil?* ed. P. Cicovacki, 46.
10 Mark Twain, *Letters from the Earth* (New York: Harper and Row, 1942), 181. Whether or not there must be consciousness of evil, as Twain contends, there must be consciousness in order for evil to exist.
11 As our knowledge of nonhuman animals increases, and the evidence for ever-higher levels of intelligence in some of them than previously believed, this judgment may require modification.

What is it about minds that is relevant to the production of evil? Four elements warrant consideration: *beliefs, intentions, motives,* and *feelings.* Without at least the first three of these, I suggest, there would be no evil in the world, but all four are involved in the paradigm cases of evil. Let us see what it is about them that is instrumental to the production of evil.

If we look at much of the harm that people deliberately inflict upon others, we see that it is done in the belief that the harm is deserved. When prison officials strap a person to a gurney and release toxic chemicals into his veins, they *believe* that the person deserves to die. When U.S. troops attack a vehicle in Iraq and mistakenly kill a family inside, they *believe* when they act that they are killing terrorists and that terrorists deserve to die. In the first case, the belief is a moral belief. In the second case, a moral belief combined with a factual belief. The factual belief (that the persons inside the vehicle are terrorists) is incorrect. The moral beliefs in the two cases may or may not be incorrect. But they are widely accepted. We can say further that the intentions in the two cases are, if not good, at least not bad. The prison officials intend to kill the condemned person, to be sure. But beyond that (if we are the least bit charitable) they are intending to carry out an order in keeping with a judicially mandated penalty. The military personnel responsible for the attack on the women and children intend to destroy what they believe is a legitimate military target. They are authorized to do that. On a grander scale, many Christians believe that human beings deserve to suffer because of original sin. Even if some people burn for all eternity in Hell, that too is deserved—if they happen to have been born before Christ and not have had the opportunity to repent.

Evil, in the moral sense I have in mind, isn't simply the result of mistaken beliefs or of misguided good intentions. We sometimes hold people accountable for mistaken beliefs if they should have known better; if, for example, they were negligent in gathering the necessary facts before acting. A whole branch of law (Tort Law) deals with issues of this sort. And we sometimes judge people harshly who act rashly with the best of intentions (the road to hell, remember, is paved with good intentions), but this doesn't warrant saying that they are evil. Carelessness and misguided good intentions are shortcomings, and good people often have shortcomings. We probably all are negligent or act on misguided good intentions at one time or another. Evil is different.

A paradigm evil act is one in which both the intention and the motive are evil. Our intention is that which it is our purpose to bring about by an act. Our motive, on the other hand, is that which explains why we intend to act as we do. A person's intention in turning the key in the ignition is normally to start the car; the motive (let us say) is the desire to get to work on time. Just as there can be good and bad intentions, there can be good and bad motives. Typically good motives are love, compassion, kindness, and benevolence. Typically bad motives are greed, envy, selfishness, and malevolence.

An evil intention, we can now say, is an intention to inflict undeserved pain, harm, suffering, deprivation or death upon others as an end in itself (rather than as a means to a supposedly greater good, moral or non-moral). An evil motive is one of malevolence: a desire to inflict undeserved pain, harm, suffering, deprivation or death upon others, for its own sake. This means that no act by itself—that is, simply considered as a physical event apart from its mental constituents—is evil. Its evil is derivative from the motive and/or intention lying behind it.[12] But this also explains why evil originates in minds. Only minds—or, more exactly, only beings that have minds—have motives and intentions. Since there nothing in the nature of mind (understood as a capacity to reason, make decisions, generalize, make inferences) that is evil, this means that evil, when it exists, is produced by minds. It is not something existing naturally, either in the mental or the physical realm.

There is a fourth element of minds besides beliefs, motives, and intentions that is relevant. That is feelings. When evil is personified, it is often pictured as grinning, enjoying its evil ways. And this certainly is part of the paradigm of evil: the taking of pleasure in the infliction of harm. But it's important to distinguish this element in the paradigm of evil from other notions to which it is closely related, specifically sadism and *Schadenfreude*. Sadism, of course, is taking pleasure in the infliction of pain upon others, but it typically involves being the agent of the pain inflicted (or being in some way responsible for those who are the agent), and, unlike in the case of evil, is sometimes consensual. Masochists enjoy having pain inflicted upon them, just as sadists enjoy inflicting such pain, and they sometimes come together precisely for that purpose. While some evil is sadistic, all sadism need not be evil. *Schadenfreude,* on the other hand, is taking pleasure in the misfortune of others whether or not one is the agent of the misfortune. One may be an observer, even a chance observer. People cheer when the opposing team fumbles the ball, or when the villain in old Western films gets his just deserts. They may be pleased at seeing others embarrassed or suffering accidents or coming to financial ruin. Some feel a little glow of pleasure when they see the car that just passed them at breakneck speed being ticketed a few minutes later down the road.[13] There is a moral element in some of these feelings of satisfaction. Why is this element important? To answer this requires taking account of beliefs once again. In the paradigm case of evil, the suffering one inflicts is underserved and known to be such. This distinguishes evil from the punishment a parent inflicts upon a child for perceived wrongdoing, or that society inflicts upon a criminal for a capital offense, or the violence the military inflicts upon perceived enemies, or that God inflicts in consigning persons to eternal damnation. Indeed, John Stuart Mill says that it is "universally considered just that each person should obtain that (whether good or evil) which he *deserves,* and unjust, that he should obtain a good, or be made to undergo an evil, which he does not deserve."[14] And William James noted that, in the perspective of what he calls

---

[12] One could define actions in such a way that they include motives and intentions. In that case actions having evil motives and intentions would be inherently evil. As I believe it makes sense to speak of one and the same action (type) being performed from different motives and intentions, I don't think this is the best way to understand acts.

[13] John Stuart Mill writes that though "this principle [*lex talionis*, an eye for an eye, a tooth for a tooth] . . . has been generally abandoned in Europe as a practical maxim, there is, I suspect, in most minds, a secret hankering after it and, when retribution accidentally falls on an offender in that precise shape, the general feeling of satisfaction evinced bears witness how natural is the sentiment to which this repayment in kind is acceptable"; ch. 5, *Utilitarianism,* in *Mill's Ethical Writings* (New York: Collier Books, 1965), 331.

[14] Ibid., 318.

subjectivism: "Not the absence of vice, but vice there and virtue holding her by the throat, seems to be the ideal human state."[15]

The suffering of those believed to be condemned to eternal hellfire by God is greater in both kind and quality than could possibly be inflicted on them by all of the evil people that have ever existed. Yet, those who believe in a just God don't think that God is evil for inflicting such suffering. The reason: it is thought to be deserved. Taking pleasure in seeing pain inflicted upon those who are thought to deserve it may not be commendable and may even be bad. But it is distinguishable from evil.

Pulling together these various considerations, let us say that moral evil encompasses evil acts, evil motives and intentions, and evil persons themselves.

Evil Act: An act whose motive and/or intention are evil.

Evil Intention: Having as one's purpose to cause undeserved pain, harm, suffering, deprivation or death to others.

Evil Motive: The desire to inflict undeserved pain, harm, suffering, deprivation or death upon others.

An Evil Person: A person in whom evil motives and intentions predominate or who characteristically takes pleasure in the undeserved pain, suffering, harm, deprivation or death of others.[16]

For the sake of simplicity, I would offer the following general definition of evil: *Intentionally causing or taking pleasure in the undeserved suffering of others.*

Some points of clarification: One's intention might be evil without being accompanied by an evil motive. Some consequentialists might argue, for example, that if a vastly greater good could be achieved by inflicting suffering on some innocent, and therefore undeserving, person, then that should be done. The intention (and the act) in that case would be evil but the motive would not. That one's act will cause underserved suffering can, of course, be known, foreseen or foreseeable without being intended. The principle of double effect trades upon this. Contrary to the principle of double effect, however, which allows that a good (or at least neutral) act may be done if, *inter alia,* its bad consequences aren't intended, I maintain—though I shall not argue it here—that *knowingly* causing undeserved harm suffices to render the act itself wrong (though not necessarily evil), hence to undercut the justification provided by the principle of double effect for the performance of such acts.

If there were a devil and he wanted to maximize undeserved suffering in the world, he could scarcely do better than to contrive to get basically good people to inflict such suffering upon one another—by their own hands, not his—in the belief that by so doing they were combating him. By turning their own basic goodness against them, he would then have legions of unwitting agents doing his work for him. This is the spirit behind Satan's resolve in Milton's characterization:

If then his [God's] providence
Out of our evil seek to bring forth good,

---

[15] William James, "The Dilemma of Determinism," in *Essays in Pragmatism* (New York: Hafner, 1954), 54.
[16] An evil person need not have evil intentions, because the motives might not be acted upon, but it is not unreasonable to assume that typically an evil person will have evil intentions as well as motives.

Our labor must be to pervert that end,
And out of good still to find means of evil.[17]

By the same token, an evil intention may be unattended by evil motivation. One might deliberately target innocent persons in warfare in the belief that only by so doing is one likely to defeat the enemy, an end deemed to be good, and the explanation of that action might be desire to achieve that good. The principle of double effect rules this out, of course, insofar as the suffering of others is deemed a means to the good end, but it doesn't of itself preclude a good motive.

An evil motive might be unattended by either an evil intention or an evil act. Motivation has varying strengths. Some motives might never give rise to an intention or issue into action. But the presence of an evil motive or intention suffices to represent evil in the person having the intention or motive. That, once again, doesn't by itself suffice to make the person evil. That evil might simply be a streak in that person's character or a passing cloud in an otherwise good nature. But it represents evil nonetheless.

An evil person, on the other hand, is one in whom evil motives predominate; in whom the basic traits that make up the person's very character are evil. The paradigm evil person is one in whom evil motives and intentions predominate to the extent of constituting an evil character whose conduct is typically evil and who takes pleasure or satisfaction in the doing of evil.

Typically this would be manifest overtly in one's actions; i.e., typically the evil motivation would be accompanied by evil intentions. This would certainly be true in the paradigm case. But it might not always be true. A person might lack the courage, opportunity, or means to act upon his evil motives. Whether that is so, and to what extent, would depend upon the circumstances in which he finds himself. Racists, anti-Semites and sexists might secretly harbor malice toward members of the relevant groups but conceal this behind outwardly liberal tendencies—though one suspects that their conduct will almost certainly at some points betray signs of evil motivation, even if glaringly bigoted forms of conduct are held in check. If there are unconscious motives, then the biases of racists, sexists and anti-Semites, as well as streaks of evil in some persons' characters, might even be concealed from themselves.

A person may occasionally perform an evil act without being an evil person. Basically good people may occasionally do evil. One doesn't cease to be a good person over a lifetime by occasionally doing something evil, any more than one fails to be a vegetarian by virtue of occasionally eating meat. Perhaps—though this is more problematic—one may even occasionally take pleasure in the doing of something evil and still be basically a good person. To be an evil person, the motivation to do evil—and in the paradigm case, the doing of evil—has to have become a part of one's character. There must be a tendency or predisposition or even a habit of doing evil before one is transformed into an evil person.

[17] From *Paradise Lost* in *The Poetical Works of John Milton* (New York: A. L. Burt, n.d.), 5.

Is there moral evil in the world?

Yes, if we're talking about evil acts. And if we're talking about evil *in* persons—that is, evil motives and intentions—there almost certainly is some such evil, but my guess is that there is much less of it than one might suppose, and such of it as there is, is manifest in relatively minor matters, probably mostly in personal relations. Are there evil persons? Possibly, but there may not be. If there are, my guess is that they are very few, and probably don't account for much of the evil that is done in the world. Most of what we call *evil*—that is, evil acts—is caused by people acting with good intentions and probably from good motives. The greatest suffering and destruction one finds inflicted by persons is in warfare. And almost always, at least in modem warfare, both sides believe they are in the right. Both sides believe they have a just cause. Even when governments act in what they believe is their national interest, they probably believe that it is morally legitimate to do so. They inflict the death and destruction that they do, not for its own sake, but as a means to an end: repelling what they see as aggression or a violation of rights or a threat to their national interest. Often they are motivated by patriotism. And although they take satisfaction in successfully vanquishing enemies, they believe that the suffering they inflict is deserved, brought upon their enemies by their own evil ways.

Consider two horrendous events of the twentieth century, the Holocaust and the atomic bombing of Hiroshima. In each case, innocent civilians were killed; in the Holocaust, by the millions over a period of years, at Hiroshima by the tens of thousands in an instant (and thousands more over the years from the effects of radiation). If we were to catalogue evils these would be near the top of most people's lists. But were they moral evils? In the case of Hiroshima, it seems not. The atomic bombing of Hiroshima (and later, Nagasaki) probably wasn't intended to inflict undeserved suffering, certainly not for its own sake. It was meant to hasten an end to the war and thereby to save lives. Even though the suffering and death of most of the individual persons was almost certainly undeserved, the bombing—viewed as an act, not primarily against them as individuals but against the collectivity to which they belonged, the Japanese nation—was thought by the US government and almost certainly by the majority of the American people to be deserved. It was payback for Pearl Harbor.

The Holocaust is more complex. Both Jews and communists were perceived by Hitler as threats to the German nation. Indeed, he speaks as though it is not only the German nation that is at stake, but also the flourishing of humankind as a whole (which was thought to require the preeminence of the German nation). Only through the defeat of communism and the implementation of proper eugenics could humankind flourish. The philosophy implicit in *Mein Kampf* places race and anti-communism at its center. It's rooted in the long-standing anti-Semitism of Europe, transformed into an ideology by a rabid anti-communism, and combined with eugenics: the attempt to improve the human species by breeding.

The point is that there are grounds for thinking that the terrible death and destruction upon Jews, communists, Gypsies, homosexuals and others by the Nazis at least initially were thought of as means to an end they took to be good. It was a key belief in their thinking. That this belief was egregiously mistaken is beside the point. It needs to be recognized in order to understand the actions to which they contributed. Even if it could be established that those actions were performed for the sake of the suffering they caused rather than as a means to an end, the evidence overwhelmingly points to the conclusion that the suffering was thought to be deserved. Jews and communists were out to corrupt and take over the German nation, the Nazis believed. Even if particular Jews and communists were not guilty, the collectivities to which they belonged were.

Were the Nazis evil persons individually in the sense defined above? Some perhaps. But it's difficult to know for certain. To know that a person is evil requires knowledge of his motives and intentions of a sort that is difficult to come by. Augustine and Kant recognized the difficulty here, as did early Christian theologians like Aquinas, who argued that Divine Law is necessary to cover the inner life of persons that can't be regulated by Human Law. Adultery in the heart is as bad morally as adultery in fact, but human law can't effectively regulate the former. How many of the Nazis were governed by evil motives and intentions, and precisely which ones were so governed, is difficult to know for certain. Some of them were sadistic and took pleasure in humiliating and killing Jews. They obviously displayed some of the ingredients of evil. But whether they combined this with the belief that the suffering they inflicted was undeserved is problematic.

With regard to the so-called "war" on terrorism more recently, the 9/11 attacks are thought of by most Americans as *evil* and Osama bin Laden, their presumed perpetrator, a paradigm of evil. But if we compare bin Laden and George Bush at the time the key events were unfolding, we see that (1) both were millionaires who had especially privileged upbringings; (2) both were devoutly religious, (3) both were convinced that they (and their religion) have the truth with a capital "T"; (4) both were willing to kill and cause destruction (or have others do so on their behalf) in pursuit of what they believed was right. If anything, the suffering unleashed by Bush's attack on Afghanistan and Iraq probably dwarfs anything that can plausibly be attributed to bin Laden. And insofar as willingness to sacrifice personally is a sign of commitment, bin Laden forsook a life of ease and comfort for that of a fugitive and terrorist. Is one man good and the other evil? Possibly, but there's not much in the way of available evidence to say that one is worse than the other or that they are not, in their ways—albeit each misguided in the view of the other—equally good.

There is a paradox here. Call it the Paradox of Evil. It is that the greatest evils in the world are done by basically good people. And that truly evil people—if there be such—are usually hurtful only to a small number of persons with whom they interact closely. The greatest harms, at least of a mental or psychological sort, can often be inflicted only on those one knows well, such as spouses, family members, or children over whom one has control. Vulnerability comes with intimacy, and some people exploit that vulnerability; perhaps a few of them do it from an evil character and take pleasure in it.

Most people probably do evil things from time to time. There may even be some evil people—that is, some in whom evil tendencies predominate—though, as I've said, I suspect that if there are, they are relatively few. The evil that most people do is probably at war with basically good impulses within them. This is reflected in the repeated use of the metaphor of war to characterize the conflict within each person (from Buddhism, to the *Gita*, to Plato, Augustine, *et al*). My guess is that those good impulses are rarely overwhelmed to such an extent as to render the person as a whole evil.

In short, while the infliction of harm, death and destruction abounds in the world, moral evil probably does not, and even where it exists, it is almost certainly difficult to identify with any confidence because it requires knowledge of motivation of a sort we rarely have. So while those who cause great harm and suffering are commonly called "evil," it is probably best to understand that as merely a descriptive, derivative sense. We can't justifiably call them evil in the moral sense unless we know much more about them than simply what their acts have led to. Moral evil is essentially inward and subjective, as Augustine saw. It may even be that some evil is purely subjective, in the sense that some people may harbor malice toward others but never act upon it, at least in ways that resemble violence. In them it may simply fester, rarely receiving outward expression and in the end harming only themselves.

How to respond to evil?

If I am correct, most of the unnecessary suffering, death and destruction caused in the world is a manifestation of descriptive evil, not basic moral evil. It consists of the acts of basically good people operating with various admixtures of false beliefs, misperceptions, biases, bad judgment and outright ignorance. They are governed for the most part not by malice but by fear. By fear, I include insecurity, apprehension, anxiety, worry, suspicion and a host of related notions, at one end, through outright terror at the other extreme. Sometimes people fear for their lives or for the lives of those close to them. Other times they fear for their possessions. Often, they just fear for their future, wanting assurance that it will be secure. At the social and international level, where by far the greatest descriptive evils are found—as measured quantitatively—it is probably more often fear of loss of possessions or political independence or territorial integrity; sometimes, in the case of threatened genocide, it is fear for the survival not only of the state but of a people. Often, however, it is fear on the part of individual leaders for their own political careers. They worry how they will be perceived in times of crisis, whether they will be thought to display weakness. This may lead them to take actions that bring great suffering both to those they would protect and to those whose actions have created their predicament.

Fear can lead people to do terrible things. But it is a different motive from malice. Fear is always of loss of some sort, whether personal, social or political. It is self-referential, in that it represents a concern to preserve something one has or what those have whom one identifies with. Malice is a desire to cause suffering for its own sake. It is other directed. Malice remains unsatisfied unless one is able to cause harm or suffering to those who are its objects.

The central problem is to find ways of dealing with the harm that people do. The typical way is by means of threats of force or violence. But if most evil springs from fear, this won't work—at least other than to the extent that it can eliminate those who are the source of the fear. If those who cause harm to others are motivated ultimately by fear, then threatening them with violence, or trying to inflict pain, suffering and death upon them, won't remove that fear. It will only intensify it. This is at the heart of Gandhi and King's claims that violence begets violence. If those who are violent are governed by fear, using violence in turn against them won't remove that fear; it will only confirm them in their judgments and perceptions from which the fear springs. This is also the key to understanding the contention of Gandhi and King (and Dewey in the philosophical world) that means and ends are intricately related; that the means you adopt affect the very character of the end, meaning in the last analysis that immoral means can't achieve moral ends. On the international scene peace is commonly sought by means of war. But war fails over and over to achieve peace other than temporarily— and then the peace it does achieve is nothing more than the absence of war, not peace with justice and tranquility among peoples. The death, and destruction wrought by violence cannot remove the fear governing those who are perceived as constituting the threat the violence is intended to counteract.

This is why the so-called "war" on terrorism will fail. By having militarized the campaign against terrorism, we have virtually ensured its failure. The very means we have chosen will undercut the attainment of the end. Inflicting pain, suffering, death and destruction on more Muslims will only increase the bitterness that has bred terrorism in the first place. Thousands were killed in Afghanistan and Iraq. Not one of them was shown to have been involved in, or even to have known about, the 9/11 attacks. Tens of thousands of them were civilians.

To deal effectively with evil one must rely upon means that dispel fear in others. Only nonviolence can do that. If those who are violent on the social and international scene are motivated by fear, violence against them can eliminate that fear only by eliminating those who have the fear. But killing them only generates fear in others. When there is no possibility of eliminating all of those who threaten the *evil* one opposes, as in the case of terrorism, one not only spreads the fear to others, one intensifies it in those who survive. When it is intensified to the point where it metastasizes into hatred, the means adopted to combat terrorism succeed instead in increasing it.

Here I am relying upon a theory proposed by one of my students. It is that hatred is simply intensified fear. Marxists point out that in certain areas increasing quantitative changes bring about qualitative changes. Water heated beyond a certain point changes to steam; cooled below a certain point, to ice. So, I would suggest, fear and anger intensified beyond a certain degree become transformed into hatred. And hatred thrives on threats from those who are hated. It is fueled by those threats. Every act of violence simply strengthens the grip of hatred over persons. You can kill such people. To be sure, the hatred embodied in them dies with them. But this only enflames the fear and anger in others that sets the stage for their coming to hate as well. Violence begets violence not because of any exotic metaphysical principle but because of its very nature. It is in the nature of violence to breed violence.

Nonviolence represents an active way of not cooperating with bad and evil that others do, thus undercutting the perpetuation of evil. This may be at the heart of the Taoist thought that if you give evil nothing to oppose, it will disappear by itself. If others have no reason to fear you, and if their violence (and evil, if it involves evil), spring from fear, then this can only be dispelled by nonviolence.

To deal with violence nonviolently requires courage, as Gandhi and King point out. This means that fear is central again. We must overcome the fear within ourselves in order to act nonviolently. Courage is not having no fear; it consists precisely in overcoming fear. To dispel fear in others we must overcome it within ourselves. The practical upshot is that if the preceding analysis is correct, our current repertoire of responses to violence and wrongdoing—by using force and violence—is counterproductive and serves to perpetuate violence and to incite ever more bitterness and hatred than they dispel. If so, the need is for creative nonviolent responses to evil and wrongdoing. To provide these is the challenge to a philosophy of nonviolence.[18]

---

[18]   Previously published in the *Acorn: Journal of the Gandhi-King Society*, Vol. 19, No. 1, Winter–Spring 2010, 5–13.

14

Jallianwala Bagh and the Boston Tea Party

Nonviolent Roots of Indo-American
Anti-Imperialism

In this essay, Holmes discusses two events that played a decisive role in the Indian and American opposition to the British rule: the Jallianwala Bagh massacre of 1919, and the throwing of the heavily taxed British tea into the Boston harbor of 1770. He writes: "In both America and India it was the cost of maintaining the institutionalized violence of the military in British culture that played central roles in the dismantling of British power. And in both cases it was nonviolent actions that were pivotal in unmasking the violent nature of that power." The Jallianwala Bagh massacre changed Gandhi's mind—the home rule and the independence of India cannot be accomplished by a patient collaboration with the British. He thus called for a massive nonviolent resistance against British rule, which became a model of nonviolence for the rest of the world. The situation developed differently in the United States. Although initially nonviolent, the colonists turned to violence to gain their independence. They gradually institutionalized militarization and the organized violence of warfare as the dominant feature of their way of relating to other peoples and nations in the world. From their fear of a standing army they moved to the creation of the most powerful standing army in the world, part of a military force so pervasive that its maintenance and expansion has transformed American society into a virtual "war system."

When General Reginald Dyer ordered his troops to fire on thousands of peaceful protestors that fateful April 13 of 1919, he couldn't have imagined the historical significance of his act. In ten minutes of sustained firing, his troops stripped away the last semblance of justification for 150 years of British domination. More, perhaps, even than the death and suffering that was inflicted, the arrogant cruelty of the act—and of those that soon followed—revealed that for all of its mannered decorum, the ultimate recourse of such an imperium was brute force and violence.

The basic facts are well known. There was widespread peaceful agitation throughout India against the Rowlatt Bills. But unrest developed in the Punjab. A crowd marching to protest the arrest of popular leaders at Amritsar was fired upon. Several people were killed. The killing transformed the crowd into a mob, which in turn attacked and killed several Europeans. A public meeting was subsequently called for April 13. Dyer, summoned to quell the unrest, issued a proclamation prohibiting such meetings. As many as 20,000 persons nonetheless gathered at Jallianwala Bagh. Dyer marched his troops to the site and without warning ordered them to fire. They continued firing until they ran out of ammunition. By one eyewitness estimate, as many as 1,000 people were killed. By official estimates, months later, 379 were killed and well over a 1,000 wounded.[1]

If these are the basic facts, the details are less well known. And the broader significance of the event is yet to be fully explored. So let us fill in some detail and enlarge our perspective.

Massacre of the innocent

The second of Rowlatt Bills—the Criminal Law (Emergency Powers) Bill—was passed on March 18, 1919. It had been recommended by a Sedition Committee appointed by the government of India in 1917 and headed by Justice Sir Sidney Rowlatt. Designed to both counteract and prevent revolutionary activity, in its first part it empowered the government, *inter alia*, to conduct trials with no right of appeal in the case of alleged sedition and to suspend the usual safeguards pertaining to evidence. In its second part, intended to be preventive, it authorized the suspension of suspects' basic civil liberties (prohibiting them from changing address, restricting their travel, and requiring that they periodically report to the police). It also subjected them to arrest without warrant and confinement for up to two years.

A storm of protest ensued. Gandhi had returned to India from South Africa in 1915. He was just emerging as a social and moral leader. He launched a *satyagraha* campaign, with a *hartal* called for April 6, 1919. He asked followers to pledge that "in the event of these Bills becoming law and until they are withdrawn, we shall refuse civilly to obey these laws and such other laws as a Committee to be hereafter appointed may think fit, and we further affirm that in this struggle we will faithfully follow truth and refrain from violence to life, person or property."[2]

The legalistic tone reflecting Gandhi's training as a lawyer is deceptive here. This wasn't just another indignant demand for political justice. Through Gandhi's appeal to truth and nonviolence there shone a light from within the very soul of India. In appealing to some of the deepest values in Indian culture, he arrayed the whole of an inspired and enlightened tradition against the forces of British oppression. Though unnoticed by the British, and at that point perhaps only vaguely sensed by Indians themselves, the spirit of Indian civilization itself had been summoned to stand against a symbol of the British Imperium.

---

[1] There is disagreement as to the exact number of killed and wounded. For example, Romila Thapar, in *A History of India,* Vol. 2 (London: Penguin Books, 1966), 191, gives the figure as 379 killed and more than 1,200 wounded. Lawrence James, in *Raj: The Making and Unmaking of British India* (London: Little, Brown, 1997), 473, gives the figure as 379 dead, 1,500 wounded. The biographer of Gandhi Judith Brown, in *Gandhi: Prisoner of Hope* (New Haven: Yale University Press, 1989), 132, gives the figure as "nearly 400."

[2] *The Congress Punjab Inquiry 1919–1920: Report of the Commissioners Appointed by the Punjab Sub-Committee of the Indian National Congress,* Vol. 1 (Indian National Congress, 1920, republished in 1994 by the director, National Book Trust, India, A-5 Green Park, New Delhi), 24.

True to the integrity of the values he had called forth, Gandhi suspended civil disobedience after violence erupted in Amedhabad, Nadiad, and other towns, calling his effort an "Himalayan miscalculation." That was in April. Because of British censorship, it wasn't until June that he learned of the events in Amritsar. There the government had arrested Dr. Saiffudin Kitchew and Dr. Satya Pal—a Muslim and a Hindu respectively—of the Congress Party. A crowd gathered on April 10 and marched to protest the arrests to the deputy commissioners. It was stopped by armed troops. When the crowd surged forward it was fired upon. Several were killed or wounded. Angered, the crowd went on a rampage against Europeans, killing 3 and assaulting many others, including Marcia Sherwood, as well as looting and destroying property. More shooting later by British troops killed another 20–25 people. Dyer arrived with reinforcements the next day. Accounts differ, but he may have issued his proclamation on April 12, prohibiting—among other things—assembly by more than 3 people and repeated it again on 13. Or he may simply have issued it for the first time on the morning of 13.[3] Either way, it was subsequently confirmed that the proclamation was never read in more than half the city, and that in all probability large numbers of the people who gathered in Jallianwala Bagh in the late afternoon of April 13 had no knowledge of it.[4]

In any event, Dyer arrived at Jallianwala Bagh about 5:00 in the afternoon with 2 armored cars and 90 troops (Gurkhas and Baluchis), 50 of them armed with rifles, the others with daggers. With the armored cars unable to negotiate the narrow entryway to the bagh, he marched the troops in, ordered them into formation, and then immediately commenced the firing. As he was to say months later at an inquiry, it was the thing to do from a "military point of view."[5] When ammunition ran out, he ordered them to withdraw, leaving the 1,000–2,000 dead and wounded where they lay. Had the armored cars' machine guns been available to Dyer, the toll would have been vastly higher. He later confirmed that he would have used them.

For good measure, Dyer officially proclaimed Military Law two days later, on April 15, with sweeping punitive and humiliating provisions. Among them, the street in which Marcia Sherwood had been attacked became a "crawling lane." Those passing through it were forced to crawl on their bellies, subject to flogging if they refused. Public floggings, for a variety of other offenses, including refusal to *Salaam,* had to be done with inordinate precision. There were indiscriminate arrests and trial by special Tribunals, as well as forced servitude of Indian lawyers as constables of the town.[6] With newspapers closed down and censorship tight throughout, the Punjab was for all practical purposes sealed off from the rest of India. A virtual reign of terror ensued under the dictates of martial law.[7]

---

[3] According to *The Congress Punjab Inquiry 1919–1920*, Vol. 1, 49. Dyer entered Amritsar and issued the proclamation, which was read in Urdu and Punjabi at various points in the city over a period of two or three hours, on the morning of April 13. Lawrence James recounts that the proclamation was issued on 13th also; see his *Raj*, 472. Yogesh Chad, in *Gandhi: A Life* (New York: John Wiley & Sons, 1997), 238, reports that the proclamation was issued on 12 and repeated on 13.

[4] Stanley Wolpert reports that of "some 10,000" persons, they were "mostly peasants from neighboring villages who had come for a Hindu festival"; *A New History of India* (New York: Oxford University Press, 1977), 299.

[5] *The Congress Punjab Inquiry 1919–1920*, Vol. 1, 51.

[6] Ibid., 55.

[7] See Madhuri Santanam Sondhi, "Apology for Honour, Not for Revenge," op ed Page, *Asian Age,* September 8, 1997.

Months later, after considerable foot-dragging and the lifting of martial law, a commission of inquiry was appointed by the British, and the following year Dyer was eventually censured and relieved of his command.[8] But the sentiments of many British were clear. A fund, amounting to more than 26,000 pounds, was raised in his support. Even though Winston Churchill spoke strongly against Dyer in the ensuing debate in Commons, according to Lawrence James, "In private, Churchill believed that Dyer had been right to 'shoot hard,' to extricate his force before taking measure for the care of wounded and that the 'crawling order' was a minor issue." What struck in his craw and that of the army's high command was Dyer's repeated assertion that he would liked to have killed more.[9] The problem wasn't that Dyer had massacred defenseless human beings. Or that he had turned his back on the suffering of the wounded. Or even that he had then humiliated the broader population with punitive and demeaning measures under martial law. The problem was that he said he would like to have killed even more. That was bad form. It was a personal failing in Dyer as an officer and a gentleman that offended, not the magnitude of the atrocity he had committed. In the eyes of many Britons, he had saved India.[10]

He hadn't, of course. The bullets that cut down the innocents at Jallianwala Bagh struck straight to the heart of the British Empire as well. But that wasn't yet to be apparent. Better to understand how that happened, and to provide some historical perspective, let us enlarge our view still further, to take in some events in another part of the world 146 years earlier.

The sons of liberty

I refer to the Boston Tea Party arranged by the American colonists in 1773 and to which the British were uninvited—and, I might add, of which they were unappreciative.

It's easy to forget that America was also once under British dominion, and that it, too, had to wrest its independence from the Crown. To be sure, there were striking differences between the case of India and North America. In America, the colonies were populated for the most part by Britishers who had voluntarily left their homeland. It was they who rebelled against the Crown. In India, it was another people—more properly, a constellation of peoples—over whom the British had dominion, and who eventually threw off British rule. Moreover, overshadowing the mistreatment of the colonists in North America, the British (and later, and even more ruthlessly, the Americans themselves) ran roughshod over the rights of the indigenous population—the native Americans, or, if you like, the "American Indians." More shameful still was

[8] The seven-member Hunter Commission, consisting of four British and three Indian members, under Lord Hunter, was appointed several months later. The Congress boycotted the commission, and appointed its own commission consisting of M. K. Gandhi, C. R. Das, Abbas C. Tyabji, and M. R. Jayakar, with K. Santanam as Secretary, which released its findings in two volumes, as *The Congress Punjab Inquiry 1919–1920*.
[9] James, *Raj*, 480.
[10] Ibid., 478–84.

the devastating treatment of the Africans brought to that continent in chains for the purpose of serving European interests. If the exploitation and humiliation of the Indian people was obviously a profounder injury to them than the deprivation of political and economic rights to the colonists, the genocidal destruction of the very culture of native Americans, and the enslavement of millions of Africans, was a far more grievous harm to those peoples than either of the others.

Be that as it may, it was the fortunes of British commercial interests, symbolized by the British East India Company, which played a pivotal role in both cases. Formed in 1600, the Company was the dominant force in British trade in India and the Persian Gulf and in the domestic events within India itself, until after the 1857 uprising. On its last legs financially in 1773, it was hooked up to a government respirator in the form of the Tea Act of May, 1773, which it was hoped would revive the Company sufficiently to enable Britain to continue to profit from its operation in India. Enterprising, if not always law-abiding, the colonists had found they could smuggle in Dutch tea for less than they paid for the East India Company's. This they did on a large scale. To make selling to the colonies profitable again, Parliament allowed the Company to ship and sell the tea directly to the colonies, without having to sell it first at auction to British traders, who would then in turn sell it to the colonies.[11] With the East India Company now able to undersell both the smugglers and legal American importers as well—and the latter included John Hancock—the Tea Act struck an economic blow to American traders. More than that, the colonists feared that similar moves to bolster other British companies could spell financial ruin for American economic interests.

After the passing of the Tea Act half a million pounds of tea were shipped from England to America. Most of the consignees (in New York, Charleston, and Philadelphia) refused to accept the tea. But three of the ships made their way to Boston Harbor in November. There they sat dead in the water as negotiations took place for their return to England. Meanwhile, increasingly restless colonists met repeatedly in the Old South Church to discuss what to do. When, during one of the meetings, a report came that negotiations had broken down, a group of 50 or so men—among the so-called Sons of Liberty—appeared dressed as Mohawk Indians. Reportedly inspired by a final cry from John Hancock, to "Let every man do what is right in his own eyes,"[12] they made for the ships and emptied the tea into the Harbor.

If the Sons of Punjab were deemed responsible for the threat to British rule in twentieth-century India, the Sons of Liberty were seen as the threat to that rule in the eighteenth century colonies. And the British responded swiftly with the punitive Coercive Acts (known to the colonists as the Intolerable Acts) in 1774, directed primarily against the colony of Massachusetts, which was viewed by the British—as they were later to view the Punjab—as the hotbed of unrest. Nip sedition in the bud there, the British reasoned, and you will quell it throughout the colonies. The acts closed down Boston Harbor until the colony paid its check for the tea party. They also severely curtailed town meetings and undermined the colony's charter by replacing

[11] See A. J. Langguth, *Patriots: The Men Who Started the American Revolution* (New York: Simon and Schuster, 1988), 174.
[12] Ibid., 179.

most elective offices with British appointments. Moreover, they provided that British soldiers and officials could now be tried in England rather than in provincial courts (as had the British soldiers charged in the Boston massacre of 1770), and throughout the colonies, and not just in Massachusetts, the Quartering Act required that when deemed necessary food and lodging be provided to British soldiers in people's homes. The details of the ensuing events need not detain us. Suffice it to say that the nonviolence of the Tea Party proved short-lived. After some skirmishes between British troops and colonists at Lexington and Concord in the spring of 1775, both sides resorted to war.

The weakness of institutionalized violence

The events at Jallianwala Bagh and Boston Harbor are important, not merely because they were central to the unraveling of British power in disparate parts of the world, but also because of what is to be learned from them about the attempts of governments to dominate through force and violence.

The Boston Tea Party took place just ten years after the conclusion of the French and Indian War. Britain defeated the French in that war, but in retrospect it was a Pyrrhic victory. It sorely strained the British financially and led them to undertake counterproductive measures *vis-à-vis* the colonies as a way of offsetting their financial losses. As a result, they became convinced of the need of a standing army in the colonies, and came to see the colonies as the key to economic renewal. To help defray the cost of the standing army, they passed the Quartering Act of 1765 requiring colonists to quarter British troops if their barracks were inadequate. Moreover, they passed various revenue-raising measures—most notably the Stamp Act of 1765—to help finance the army. It was opposition to the second of these that gave birth to the Sons of Liberty throughout several of the colonies. But the first measure heightened a longstanding fear colonists had of a standing army, which was seen as a threat to liberty. Its creation among the colonists helped to nurture growing fears that the aim of the British was to deprive the colonists of fundamental human rights, fears that assumed the proportions of a collective paranoia among many of the colonists. It was symptomatic that the Sons of Liberty, who hosted the Boston Tea Party, and who had come into existence years earlier in protest against the Stamp Act, were originally loyal to the Crown. They were led to their nonviolent direct action at Boston only after trust in the King eroded during the intervening years.

In the closing months of World War I, Britain found itself in a similar situation. It had been involved in a long and expensive war, which was now in its final stage, and, once again, it was seeking to shift some of the burden to its colonial possession, in this case India. It did this not only through seeking contributions, but also through active recruitment of Indians for the British army. Indeed, one of the central sources of discontent among Punjabis—who comprised a major part of the Indian component of the British army—was the coercion exerted in recruitment. Sir Michael O'Dwyer had said in 1918 that "No one, of course, dreams of conscripting the whole of

India's manhood for the half million combatants required; and if we can do without conscription in any form no one will be better pleased than I."[13] Yet in documenting the coercive tactics resorted to, the Congress Committee investigating the Jallianwala Bagh massacre said that "though he claimed to regard the others [besides the educated classes] with affection, he estranged them from him and his Government by his methods of recruitment and collection of war contributions."[14] These methods, the Commission said, were in many cases tantamount to conscription.

Just as the Boston Tea Party was the turning point in the relations between the colonists and the British, the Jallianwala Bagh massacre was the turning point in the alienation of Indians from their rulers. Gandhi is illustrative. He had himself in 1918 even supported the Viceroy's call for half a million Indians to strengthen the British army. His recent biographer, Yogesh Chadha, writes that in a speech at Nadiad, "Gandhi called upon people 'to learn the use of arms with the greatest possible dispatch.' Accordingly they must enlist themselves in the army. 'There can be no friendship between the brave and the effeminate', he asserted. 'We are regarded as a cowardly people. If we want to become free from that reproach, we should learn the use of arms.'" Chadha then writes that one of Gandhi's "oft-repeated pleas was that the easiest and straightest way to win *swaraj* was to participate in the defense of the empire."[15] This outlook contrasts dramatically with what Gandhi was to say in the aftermath of Jallianwala Bagh and the subsequent release of the official Hunter Commission report: "The British Empire today represents Satanism and has been guilty of such terrible atrocities that, if it did not apologize for them to God and to the country, it would certainly perish. I will go further and say that, unless it so apologized, it was the duty of every Indian to destroy it."[16]

In both America and India it was the cost of maintaining the institutionalized violence of the military in British culture that played central roles in the dismantling of British power. And in both cases it was nonviolent actions that were pivotal in unmasking the violent nature of that power. The Boston Tea Party, though not an act of principled nonviolence—by which I mean one that grew out of a spiritual or moral commitment to nonviolence—was nonetheless in fact nonviolent in its execution, as was the boycott of British tea by importers in other colonies. In a letter Paul Revere carried to New York, it was asserted that "[n]ot a Tory in the whole community can find the least fault with the proceedings." Of this A. J. Langguth writes in his account of those events, that "[t]he account that Paul Revere carried south had been correct. Boston's Tories did admit that the whole affair had been conducted as correctly as a crime could be. Anonymous Mohawks even sent a lock the next day to one of the ship captains as a replacement for one they had broken."[17]

But in India Gandhi's *satyagraha* was from the first nonviolent to its core, as a matter of principle. And, though this was never to be his primary focus, it reflected a global

[13] Quoted in *The Congress Punjab Inquiry 1919–1920,* Vol. 1, 15.
[14] Ibid., 14.
[15] Chadha, *Gandhi,* 230.
[16] This is attributed to Gandhi in a 1920 speech, otherwise unidentified; Chadha, *Gandhi,* 247.
[17] Langguth, *Patriots,* 184.

vision that extended beyond the issues of Indian independence. Of it he was later to write:

> This doctrine of *satyagraha* is not new; it is merely an extension of the rule of domestic life to the political. Family disputes and differences are generally settled according to the law of love. The injured member has so much regard for the others, that he suffers injury for the sake of his principles without retaliating and without being angry with those who differ from him. And as repression of anger and self-suffering are difficult processes, he does not dignify trifles into principles, but, in all non-essentials, readily agrees with the rest of the family, and thus contrives to gain the maximum of peace for himself without disturbing that of the others. Thus his action, whether he resists or resigns, is always calculated to promote the common welfare of the family. It is this law of love which, silently but surely, governs the family for the most part throughout the civilized world . . . I feel that nations cannot be one in reality, nor can their activities be conducive to the common good of the whole humanity, unless there is this definite recognition and acceptance of the law of the family in national and international affairs . . . It has however been objected that *satyagraha* . . . can be practiced only by a select few. My experience proves the contrary. Once its simple principles—adherence to truth and insistence upon it by self-suffering—are understood, anybody can practice it. It is as difficult or as easy to practice as any other virtue.[18]

Here Gandhi gives us a glimpse of a vision that extends far beyond the events at Jallianwala Bagh and, for that matter, beyond India itself. It's a universal vision, for victims and victimizers, oppressors and oppressed, alike. Blending the central values of truth and nonviolence with the conception of familial love, Gandhi projects a vision for the whole world; one that, as he conceives it, is practical in its bearing, and indeed already finds expression—perhaps largely unnoticed and certainly unappreciated—in some of the most common experiences of millions of people. In his view, it needs only to be recognized and extended to larger spheres. My aim at present isn't to evaluate this conception of *satyagraha*;[19] it received many statements and much elucidation by Gandhi throughout his lifetime, and a full understanding of it would require close examination of its many formulations. The point is that it was thoroughgoing in its commitment to nonviolence, and clear in its conviction of its practical efficacy.

---

[18] From a statement Gandhi prepared for the Congress committee of which he was a member, quoted in *The Congress Punjab Inquiry 1919–1920*, Vol. 1, 35–6.

[19] This Commission, in the text following Gandhi's statement, observed cautiously that "[t]he doctrine of *satyagraha* as explained by Mr. Gandhi seems to be clear and intelligible as a theoretical proposition. But, we think that it is not easy, as it may appear at first sight, to reduce it to practice in every walk of life. For the practice of such *satyagraha* a large amount of discipline in patience and self-control is necessary. And these are the qualities that are in practice found to be most lacking, when they are most needed . . . the average man is more prone to resort to violence than to sacrifice himself, when he is chafing under a sense of wrong"; *The Congress Punjab Inquiry 1919–1920*, Vol. 1, 37–8.

Gandhi's nonviolent experiment in truth

Let us, finally, now enlarge our perspective still further to take in key features of the subsequent history to the present, as well as more of the philosophical and moral outlooks they reflect.

On the philosophical side, the dominant outlook among the American colonists was decidedly European (more specifically, English) and individualistic in orientation. The Western natural law tradition had spawned the idea of natural rights, these being specifically *human* rights, thought to attach to individual persons simply by virtue of their being human. It was these rights and their associated liberties—soon to figure prominently in Jefferson's penning of the Declaration of Independence—that the colonists believed to be threatened by British rule. As expressed in a statement by the Boston Town Meeting to its Assembly Representatives in 1770,

> A series of occurrences, many recent events . . . afford great reason to believe that a deep-laid and desperate plan of imperial despotism has been laid, and partly executed, for the extinction of all civil liberty . . . The August and once revered fortress of English freedom—the admirable work of ages—the British Constitution seems fast tottering into fatal and inevitable ruin. The dreadful catastrophe threatens universal havoc, and presents an awful warning to hazard all if, peradventure, we in these distant confines of the earth may prevent being totally overwhelmed and buried under the ruins of our most established rights.[20]

Conspiratorial thinking abounded among the colonists—probably beyond anything justified by the evidence. But it swirled around real or imagined threats to human rights. Not only were the rights of individuals paramount and inviolable, the right—indeed, the obligation—of each person to decide for himself where the right lay was proclaimed. Recall John Hancock's alleged cry the night of the Boston Tea Party, "Let every man do what is right in his own eyes."[21] Henry David Thoreau, that paradigm of individualism in American history, was in the next century to elevate this sentiment to the status of a moral principle. "The only obligation which I have a right to assume," he wrote, "is to do at any time what I think is right."[22]

To be sure, strains of such thinking were found in Indian thought as well. Even the Congress Commission, in its report, said: "Nor can any sense of duty toward the Empire be allowed to disregard the sacredness of individual liberty."[23] And Gandhi had, of course, been influenced by Thoreau. In his written statement on *satyagraha* for the Commission, he said: "No one disputes the necessity of insisting on truth as one sees it"[24]—a view he often reiterated. But, as I have said, the defining character of the movement was Indian, with some coloration from Christianity. Truth and nonviolence

---

[20] Quoted in Bernard Baylin, *The Ideological Origins of the American Revolution,* enl. ed. (Cambridge, MA: Harvard University Press, 1992), 94.
[21] Langguth, *Patriots,* 179.
[22] Thoreau, "Civil Disobedience," in Carl Bode, ed., *The Portable Thoreau* (New York: Viking, 1964), 111.
[23] *The Congress Punjab Inquiry 1919–1920,* Vol. 1, 14.
[24] Ibid., 36.

were central. The notion of *ahimsa*, as it arose in the *Rig Veda*, has been reshaped by Jainism and Buddhism and finally transformed by Gandhi into an active force for modern India and, at least in some of his thinking, for the world at large.[25]

Beyond this, set against the individualism of the colonists' thinking was a broader perspective in which a greater good was centered. Again, as Gandhi said in his statement for the Congress Commission, "I feel that nations cannot be one in reality, nor can their activities be conducive to the common good of the whole humanity, unless there is this definite recognition and acceptance of the law of the family in national and international affairs."[26] A transcendent good—beyond that of the individual—becomes the end in view.[27]

I've said that there was a nonviolent element, albeit unarticulated, and unsubscribed to as a matter of principle, in the American experience. It contrasted with a strong and central expression of principled nonviolence in the Indian experience. Not surprisingly, these threadlike roots of nonviolence in American thought were insufficient to nourish a full-fledged blossoming of the nonviolent philosophy as a social movement before the twentieth century. And even when this eventually occurred under Martin Luther King, Jr, the influence—other than from Thoreau—came principally from India in the person of Gandhi. The colonists turned to violence to gain their independence and later, in a devastating Civil War, to hold together the resultant union of states. They gradually institutionalized militarization, conscription, and the organized violence of warfare as the dominant feature of their way of relating to other peoples and nations in the world. From their fear of a standing army they moved to the creation of the most powerful standing army in the world, part of a military force so pervasive that its maintenance and expansion has transformed American society into a virtual "war system." It is today a society based on a capacity to inflict death and destruction upon other human beings, which it is prepared to do to the extent thought necessary to maintain (in the jargon of contemporary theorists) its transoceanic power projection strategy. It might well have been just such an extraordinary expansion of military power that Thoreau had in mind when he wrote, "Wile objections which have been brought against a standing army, and they are many and weighty, and deserve to prevail, may also at last be brought against a standing government."[28]

India, on the other hand, pursued its independence nonviolently and with unparalleled dignity, patiently and inexorably winning that independence in fewer than 30 years. That the nonviolent power that served it so well against the British has

[25] On the origins of *ahimsa* in Indian thought, see Unto Tahtinen, *Non-Violence as an Ethical Principle: With Special Reference to the Views of Mahatma Gandhi* (Turku: Turun Yliopisto, 1964).
[26] *The Congress Punjab Inquiry 1919–1920*, Vol. 1, 35.
[27] For a perceptive discussion of the complex interplay of individualistic and collectivistic strains in modernity's impact upon modern India, see Madhuri Santanam Sondhi, *Modernity, Morality, and the Mahatma* (New Delhi: Haranand, 1998), esp. Chapter 1.
[28] Thoreau, "Civil Disobedience," 109. See, for example, Robert W. Chandler, with John R. Backschies, *The New Face of War: Weapons of Mass Destruction and the Revitalization of America's Transoceanic Military Strategy* (Mclean, VA: Amcoda Press, 1998). Along the way to its position as the world's leading military power, the United States had its own "Jallianwala Bagh" in March of 1968, when US soldiers massacred 400–500 unarmed Vietnamese civilians at My Lai during the Vietnam War, an event that has conveniently been all but forgotten in the American consciousness.

receded in the wake of recent increased militarization, symbolized by the nuclear tremors of Pokharan, doesn't alter the fact of the singularity in historical terms of what India achieved. Were history written not, as it typically is now, around the convulsions of war and violence but rather around the examples of what is best in humankind; if there were, that is, a moral history of the world, highlighting the finest expressions of the human spirit in moral achievement, India's would be a towering example. It would be studied and taught everywhere in the attempt to learn from it, to understand the principles which underlay it and to fashion those principles to other times and places so as to actualize in the rest of the world the values it embodied.

Gandhi spoke of his work in nonviolence as an experiment, an experiment in Truth. And he was prepared to reconsider, rethink, and modify his course of action when the experiment seemed not to be bearing the results he hoped. The problem, of course, is that in human affairs—particularly when talking about the social or national or international scene—we cannot conduct experiments in the same way we can in the science laboratory. We cannot try out different social, political, economic, and moral philosophies in virtually identical societies under virtually identical conditions, and then compare the results after 50 or 100 or 1,000 years. Instead we act with limited knowledge and limited understanding of the thinking of others who take a different course from us. The temptation is to cling to our favored social, political, religious, ideological, or moral view come what may, blaming its failures, not on the outlook itself, or upon ourselves, but always upon others, those who don't share that view. This, of course, enables us to preserve the conviction of our own righteousness. In so doing, we fail to see that the refusal—or perhaps worse yet, the inability—to see the evidence of the unworkability of one's favored outlook and to accept responsibility for its failures is the mark of fanaticism.

But while we can't conduct experiments with anything like the rigor of the science laboratory, in the Indo-American histories we perhaps have as close an approximation to it as we may find on the historical scale. Two peoples confronting the oppression of imperialism, one turning away from a nonviolent beginning and resorting to violence, the other persisting in history's most sustained and successful example of nonviolence. Both India and America won their independence. Insofar as that is the sole objective we look at, both violence and nonviolence succeeded. But if we look at the broader picture, the one country has organized and institutionalized its capacity for violence on a scale unprecedented in the history of the world; and is now, arguably—despite its often good intentions and commitment to democracy—one of the greatest threats to peace in the world today. If the longer term objective is to achieve world peace, the violence around which it has framed its society and designed its policies has failed, and failed about as convincingly as one can ever expect in such matters. The other has shifted away from the nonviolence that was part of its heritage and that proved so effective in winning its independence. But it has not moved so far away as to lose sight of that vision or to be free of its gravitational pull. Whether it turns again to that moral light to guide its course in the future or succumbs completely to the allure of militarization, remains to be seen. But play themselves out these two experiments will. The one, I fear, is destined to fail. The outcome of the other remains to be determined. Unlike with laboratory experiments in which we can only sit back and await the results, the outcome of the experiment in nonviolence is up to us. It can and will succeed if enough people resolve to make it succeed. And it is those of us here and now that have a role to play in determining whether that happens.[29]

---

[29] Previously unpublished.

15

Toward a Nonviolent American Revolution

Holmes maintains that a nonviolent revolution is needed and outlines some of the key elements of a possible transition from a dominant idolatry of violence to a culture of nonviolence. Perhaps more than in any of the other essays included in this collection, he focuses here on a gradual militarization of America, with its drift toward imperialism. Given such a set of circumstances and conditions, nonviolence seems both impractical and inefficient. Yet why not change a given set of conditions? And why not change them not as a mere reaction to such a militarization, but with a vision of what human life can and should be like? Holmes quotes the ancient Buddhist insight that "Our life is shaped by our mind; we become what we think." This profound truth, Holmes states, "must be a starting point of any philosophy of nonviolence." This is so because much of our world consists of the physical and social embodiment of human thought. A nonviolent revolution requires changing how we think of ourselves and of our position and role in the world. A new culture of nonviolence demands a nonviolent social defense, an economy of nonviolence, and, perhaps most important of all, education in nonviolence.

Revolutions are typically thought of as violent; the bringing down of a government that is believed to be tyrannical or, perhaps at best, ineffectual. As the American Declaration of Independence would have it, people are widely held to have an inalienable right to effect such a revolution when the conditions under which they live become intolerable. Such revolutions invariably hold the promise of a better society or—in the case of Marxists and some Islamists—a better world. At least that is the hope of their advocates. Such hopes, if they are not quickly dashed, often dissipate over time, as the outcomes of violent revolutions come increasingly to resemble the states of affairs they replaced; not in points of detail—the furniture in the palace gets rearranged and different names attach to those occupying positions of power—but in terms of the basic structures of society: the reliance upon force and the threat of force to compel obedience. This entails the use of police, surveillance, law courts, and prisons to apprehend and punish those who would disturb the order of things. Those institutions and their underlying values remain in place. This is why, in the revolutions unfolding in the Middle East, concern is repeatedly expressed over who is going to fill the power vacuum created by the overthrow of the existing regimes, as though the mechanisms of state power are going to remain intact, and the only question is who is going to control them. It is as though the state were a speeding car, and a violent revolution simply puts a different person in the driver's seat. The vast majority of people—even if, as in a popular revolution, they are the ones who put the new driver behind the wheel—are carried along, often in much the same direction as before they changed drivers, and often with as little real control as they had before. For all states, whether autocratic or democratic, rely upon power, understood as the capacity to instill fear through the use or threat of violence. Indeed, Thomas Hobbes, the 17th century philosopher who wrote the textbook for modern political theory, put it starkly when he wrote that, "the laws of nature, as *justice, equity, modesty, mercy*, and, in sum, *doing to others, as we would be done to*, of themselves, without the terror of some power, to cause them to be observed, are contrary to our natural passions, that carry us to partiality, pride, revenge, and the like."[1]

It is ironic, but worth noting, that in international law, as enshrined in Chapter One of the UN Charter, states are not only enjoined to "settle their international disputes by peaceful means," they are also required "to refrain in their international relations from the threat or use of force against the territorial integrity or political independence of any state. . ." But, though unstated, it is almost universally assumed that standard political power *within* a state rests upon the threat or use of force. States may use against their own people the very means they are prohibited from using against other states, and which if they do use them (other than in self-defense or as part of UN action under Chapter Seven) constitute—at least according to the Nuremberg Laws, that other major component of international law—crimes against peace, and possibly war crimes and even crimes against humanity as well.

This attempt to manipulate fear—practiced in various ways and in varying degrees by democratic as well as autocratic regimes—helps to explain how nonviolent revolutions are possible. For power dissolves when people lose their fear. You can still kill people who no longer fear you, but you cannot control them. You cannot control dead people. Walk through a cemetery with a bullhorn, if you like. Command people to rise up, clean the streets, pay taxes, report for military duty, and they will ignore you. Political power requires obedience, which is fueled by the fear of pain to be inflicted if you refuse to comply with the will of those who control the instruments of violence. That power evaporates when people lose their fear. It was striking how often people were quoted as saying that they had lost their fear in the largely nonviolent revolutions that recently took place in Egypt and Tunisia.

A revolution that leaves in place the instruments of violence, but simply places them in different hands, is a superficial revolution, even if it is nonviolent in the means it uses to bring down a government. In that sense, the "nonviolent" revolutions that swept Eastern Europe after the collapse of the Soviet Union, and that we are witnessing today in the Middle East, are superficial revolutions. They represent changes that do not fundamentally alter society.

By a nonviolent revolution I mean one that brings about a pervasive transformation of society, one that alters the basic assumptions, practices, and values that typically characterize modern nation-states; that, if you like, brings into being a different social mindset about the use of violence, and more fundamentally, about the potential of human beings to relate to one another—and not only to one another, but to animals and

---

[1] Thomas Hobbes, *Leviathan*, selected and with an introduction by Richard S. Peters, ed. Michael Oakeshott (New York: Collier Books, 1966), 129.

the environment as well—in ways that are compassionate and respectful. A nonviolent revolution of the sort I have in mind seeks to foster the best in every person. It seeks nothing less than a transition from a culture of violence to a culture of nonviolence.

A violent revolution can be brought about in days or weeks; sometimes a single bullet will do it. A nonviolent transformation of society requires years, maybe hundreds or thousands of years. It is the work of generations. But it must begin sometime. We can wait for some future generation to begin it, and if every generation does that it will never happen. Or we can begin it ourselves, here and now. If we remain immersed in our own self-interest—or, as Americans, even more broadly committed to the self-interest of America above all else—we will never embark on such a revolution. We will see no commitment to anyone beyond ourselves, either as individuals or collectively as a people or nation or state. Tolstoy once wrote that ". . . from the day of our birth to our death, we are overwhelmingly in debt to others, to those who lived before us, those now living, and those who will live, and to that which was, is, and will be—the source of all things. . . . That only is true life which carries on the life of the past, promotes the welfare of the present, and prepares the welfare of the future."[2]

If it is true that we are indebted to our predecessors, as indeed we indisputably are—each of us is here only because of our parents; each of us enjoys whatever measure of comfort we have because of the efforts of millions of people who preceded us—and if it is true that this creates in us an obligation to try our best to provide a good life for those who follow us, then our concerns must extend beyond ourselves, individually and as a people. I start with America because that is where we now find ourselves. But ultimately the aim is global nonviolence, a transition to a nonviolent world. Not only must the means of such a revolution be nonviolent; the end itself must be *nonviolence*, the pervasive realization of nonviolence in the world. I emphasize this, because the nonviolent revolutions and successes we have witnessed in recent history have been nonviolent only in the sense of not using violent means to effect the changes they have brought about. The ends have not been nonviolent. Their societies remain committed to the use and threat of force. India, the classic example of successful nonviolence in overthrowing British colonial rule, has become a nuclear power; Lithuania, the first of the Soviet Republics to declare its independence from the Soviet Union, and which resisted Soviet rule nonviolently, is joining NATO; civil rights in America have left the country's commitment to force intact, and Martin Luther King, Jr, was excoriated for speaking out against the Vietnam War.

Means and ends, as Gandhi and King saw, are interconnected. A lasting good cannot be achieved by violent means; the means will taint the end, as spoiled food will taint the stew it is used to help create. But also, I would add, nonviolent means are capable of producing nonviolent ends. Ends—contrary to the usual way of thinking, in which ends are projected or supposedly fixed by God or nature in advance—often evolve from means, without having been defined in detail in advance. But such ends will have the character of what produced them, much as the meal you prepare will have the quality and character of the ingredients used in preparing it. A cook can have an

---

[2] Leo Tolstoy, "What I Believe," in *A Confession, the Gospel in Brief, and What I Believe*, trans. Aylmer Maude (London: Oxford University Press, 1961), 432.

end in mind and then go out and buy the food, the means by which to achieve it. But a creative cook can look in the refrigerator and cupboard, assess what is available, then put them together imaginatively to produce a meal. The end, so to speak, grows out of the means through the creative effort of the cook. No one can provide a blueprint of what American society would look like 100 or 1000 years from now if we begin the process of transforming ourselves into a nonviolent people. We must have faith that the end will evolve from our nonviolent efforts. If we demand guarantees in advance that a nonviolent society—and eventually a nonviolent world—will be the outcome, we shall never have it. We can only act upon faith. For some, that will be faith in a God who will make all things come out right in the end; for others it will be faith in the potential of the human spirit to prevail against adversity and to offset the effects of the missteps it has taken historically. In more cosmic terms, it will be faith in the universe itself to produce an inestimable good. For our world might be thought of as a kind of experiment on the part of the universe; a trying-out, if you like, of the potential not only of reason, but of sympathy, compassion and love. It may in the end all come to naught. Humankind may yet destroy itself. But that is not foreordained. It is up to us. We can continue to allow ourselves to be swept along, as though by a giant tsunami created by history's upheavals of war and violence. Or we can as individuals take command of our lives and, as nearly as possible, shape the future for ourselves and generations to come.

Some will say that this is unrealistic; that we must seek betterment of our world by dealing with it as we find it; by accepting the conditions that define it today. This is partly correct, but partly incorrect. Surely we must deal with our world as it is and not as we wish it were. That is the measure of truth in so-called "realism." And it is a point of departure for nonviolent realism. But to deal with the world as it is means to deal with the potential that is within it; that is part of the reality we confront. To ignore that potential, and deal only with the actualized facts of the world and call that "realism," is naive. We need not accept conditions as they are, and define what is possible only within the parameters of those conditions. If you ask what is realistically possible *given* a set of conditions, you get one answer. If you ask what is realistically possible if you change those conditions, you get a different answer. And, as Emma Goldman once wrote, a practical scheme—by which she presumably meant one that is considered realistic—"is either one already in existence, or a scheme that could be carried out under the existing conditions; but it is exactly the existing conditions that one objects to, and any scheme that could accept these conditions is wrong and foolish."[3] The point is that if the existing conditions render possible only policies and practices that are morally indefensible, then one must ask what is possible if one changes those conditions, and then set about to find ways to change them. If the only "realistic" option is to wear gas masks given that the air is dangerously polluted, then stop polluting the air; change the conditions whose continuing existence make that the only realistic option. That is the more realistic solution. Or if you want to get from A to B but a river blocks your path, if you accept the impassibility of the river as a given, then you have no choice but to

---

[3]   Emma Goldman, *Anarchism and Other Essays* (Port Washington, NY: Kennikat Press, 1969), 55. Goldman is citing Oscar Wilde in this passage.

turn back or stay where you are. But if you ask what is possible if you learn to swim or build a raft or construct a bridge, the answer to the question "What is possible?" is different. You find a way to alter the conditions that are obstructing you, that changes what is possible. This is what nonviolence would have us do. It would urge us to have the imagination, creativity and courage to ask, not merely what is possible if we accept as given the conditions that define what we see as an increasingly intolerable world, but to ask what is possible if we change those conditions. If the conditions sustaining a culture of violence make possible only a continuation of violence, militarism, and exploitation in the world, then we must seek to change those conditions. It is the conditions limiting what is now possible that are the problem.

Why should such a nonviolent revolution begin with America? Isn't America the democracy, a light to the rest of the world? Partly, in answer to that, I would respond that, as the most powerful nation in the world, economically and militarily, America is in a unique position to provide world leadership in showing the way to a better world. As Gandhi emphasized, nonviolence needs to be practiced from a position of strength, not weakness. One's motives aren't suspect if one deliberately takes measures that seem to others to increase one's vulnerability. The same is true of America's chief ally, Israel, the nuclear superpower of the Middle East, which could, if it chose, from its position of strength, show respect and compassion for the Palestinians—and help secure its own long-term peace—by withdrawing voluntarily from the lands it occupied during war, rather than waiting until it is forced to do so from a position of weakness.

But this is only part of my response to the question "Why America?" The more important point I will state bluntly: contrary to what most people believe, America is a failed democracy. It retains the external trappings of democracy to be sure, and may do so indefinitely. There are political parties, regular elections, an ebb and flow of Republicans and Democrats in Congress and the White House, TV newscasts, dozens of newspapers, and biting commentary on political and social events. But I predict that without a dramatic change in the course of events, within 50 years—100 at the most—this will be seen to be a sham democracy, in which the vast majority of people have been disempowered by a minority. The form of democracy will remain, but the substance will have drained from it.

Certain aspects of American society today indicate the magnitude of the problem.

First, much of the power in the country is in the hands of the wealthy. As Michael Moore said in a March 5, 2011 speech in Madison, Wisconsin: "Today 400 Americans *have more wealth* than half of all Americans combined." He then added, "For us to admit that we have let a small group of men abscond with and hoard the bulk of the wealth that runs our economy would mean that we'd have to accept the humiliating acknowledgement that we have indeed surrendered our precious Democracy to the moneyed elite. Wall Street, the Banks and the Fortune 500 were running this Republic."[4]

---

[4] "America is Not Broke," by Michael Moore, speech delivered at Wisconsin Capitol in Madison, March 5, 2011. Published on Monday March 7, 2011; *CommonDreams.Org*, www.commondreams.org/view/2011/03/07-5. It is unfortunate that popular figures like Michael Moore, and humorists like Stephen Colbert and Jon Stewart, are left to raise issues that our leaders do not.

Second, and more importantly, it is not merely the vast disparities in wealth that characterizes our country. Disparities in wealth are not in and of themselves of great moral consequence. Few would begrudge ten percent of the population's enormous wealth if everyone else were wealthy too, only less so. Few would mind if their neighbors owned 3 homes, 4 luxury cars, a yacht and a condo in the Caribbean if they owned 2 homes, 3 ordinary cars, a sailboat and a time-share in Miami. But that isn't what we see in America. 46 million Americans not only are not rich, they live in poverty—even by the government's own standards, which may understate the problem. Moreover, we have what, for all practical purposes, is a permanent underclass of persons who, collectively, will—under present conditions—never emerge from poverty and degradation. Perhaps their descendents will after many generations, but they will not. And many of them are themselves, of course, descendents of the crime of slavery, and the lasting effects of discrimination. Even if every trace of discrimination were removed from a society overnight—as if by the wave of a magic wand—the effects of discrimination would last, permeating almost every aspect of society, legal, political, medical, and educational. That doesn't necessarily signify ill-will on the part of people of privilege; it is just the inertial effect of the inequalities of previous discrimination.

Third, we are witnessing a gradual militarization of the police in America. Beginning with the development of SWAT teams (Special Weapons and Tactical units) in 1966, police departments are looking increasingly like combat units, employing the tactics of the military, often with weaponry and sometimes training from the military, including Army Rangers and Navy SEALS. Before the assault by Federal officers on the Branch Davidian compound in Waco, Texas, in 1993, Federal officers were trained by Special Forces units at Fort Hood. It has been reported that between 1995 and 1997 the Department of Defense "gave police departments 1.2 million pieces of military hardware, including 73 grenade launchers and 112 armored personnel carriers," and that nearly 90 percent of the police departments in cities with populations over 50,000 have such units.[5] Combined with this has been increased surveillance of Americans by the government and increased stop-and-searches on the streets by police, notably in the areas of the urban poor. The militarization of the so-called "war on terrorism" is yet another story, in which what is first and foremost criminal activity has been responded to as though it were a military action. The ongoing war in Afghanistan is but the most conspicuous product of this mindset.

---

[5]   These figures are taken from Diane Cecelia Weber, "Warrior Cops: The Ominous Growth of Paramilitarism in American Police Departments," CATO Institute, Briefing Papers, August 26, 1999. She points out that the Posse Comitatus Act of 1878 set a penalty for use of the Army for law enforcement (except as expressly authorized by Congress or the Constitution). But this has often been ignored or more recently amended, as by the 1981 Military Cooperation with Law Enforcement Officials Act and a 1988 directive by Congress to the National Guard to assist in counter-drug operations. Weber reports that today, "National Guard units in all 50 States fly across America's landscape in dark green helicopters, wearing camouflage uniforms and armed with machine guns, in search of marijuana fields." She also reports that in 1994 the Department of Justice and the Department of Defense signed a "memorandum of understanding, which has enabled the military to transfer technology to state and local police departments. Civilian officers now have at their disposal an array of high-tech military items previously reserved for use during wartime" (5).

Fourth, we are witness to a drift toward imperialism. The end of the Cold War provided an opportunity for the projection of American power (as the analysts like to put it) unimpeded by the Soviet Union. The U.S. has waged war on Iraq, bombed the former Yugoslavia, attacked Afghanistan (a country which bordered the Soviet Union), and unleashed its airpower against Libya. Countries that were once republics of the former Soviet Union are now being absorbed into an American-dominated NATO, a military organization created to constrain Soviet action in Europe, and which should have been disbanded after the collapse of the Soviet Union, but which is now also fighting in Afghanistan (far from the North Atlantic). Even if I am wrong about the failure of democracy in America, that does not alter America's increasingly imperialistic character. Imperialism is not, *per se*, incompatible with democracy. A country can in principle have a flourishing democracy and still conduct itself aggressively in expanding its power and influence on the international scene.

The foregoing are not, however, the main reasons for the failure of American democracy. The main reason is the size of the country and the intractability of the issues it faces in its global economic, political, and military entanglements. The scale and complexity of the issues outstrip the capacity of the ordinary person to grasp and evaluate them effectively. It is virtually impossible, for example, to keep abreast of the issues posed by the country's foreign policy alone, much less to analyze and critique the prevailing rationale for that policy, which is rooted in a philosophy of political realism, an American permutation on the German *realpolitik* of the 19th century.[6] Absent such oversight and critical understanding on the part of ordinary citizens, more and more power devolves to political leaders—not through evil designs on their part, but rather through a situation that has evolved gradually from the early days of the republic. When the country was in its infancy, it was expected that people would know those in their communities well enough to be able to make wise choices of those who represent them. And it was thought, in turn, in the case of the Electoral College, that those persons would be wise enough to choose a good president. There was at least a plausible rationale for not putting the choice of the president directly in the hands of the people. Now we have the worst of both options: the people don't directly choose the president and the Electoral College has become a sham. Democracy, as a political system, can function only with an informed and enlightened electorate. When people get limited and biased information from most of the media, and often false information from their government, as they did from the George W. Bush administration with regard to weapons of mass destruction in Iraq, democracy cannot function. Most ordinary citizens have trouble enough keeping abreast of the complexities of their own lives without having to try to keep up with those of the country and the world. Add to this the draw of keeping up with the latest sports scores, and the endless stream of celebrity gossip that comes their way, and it is understandable that they are easily manipulated. So long as they can vote every four years—or every

---

6   The idea was reportedly introduced by A. L. von Rocheau, in an article, "Grundzuge der Realpolitik," in 1853. See H. W. C. Davis, *The Political Thought of Heinrich von Treitschke* (London: Constable, 1914), 6. Although I shall not argue it here, President Barak Obama's acceptance speech for the Nobel Peace Prize represents a version of political realism.

two or fewer if they are conscientious—they believe we have a democracy. And they will point to the fact that we have a two party system, and that the rascals—whether they be democrats or republicans—can be thrown out when they displease the citizens. But this is all part of what allows the situation to perpetuate itself. Republicans and democrats, while they may whistle in a different key, all whistle the same tune. The differences their empowerment signifies—and I do not deny that they are sometimes significant—do not change the basic practices, values, and institutions of society. It was a Republican president who launched the Gulf War, a Democratic president who bombed Yugoslavia, a Republican president who invaded Iraq and Afghanistan, and a Democratic president who attacked Libya. When did Congress declare war on Iraq or Afghanistan, or before that on North Vietnam or North Korea? Can anyone even remember voting in a national referendum on whether we should attack any of those countries, or more recently Libya?[7]

Some may be concerned that it is unpatriotic to propose a nonviolent American revolution. But true patriotism is love of one's country—the people, the land, and the best of its values. It is not love of one's government or even of a particular political arrangement. A society can continue to exist without any particular government or even any particular form of government. Indeed, there is no reason why a society cannot exist without any government at all—and perhaps should not exist without any government at all, if we mean by government a concentration of power in the hands of a few, which is then used, sometimes for the better, more often for the worse, to control the rest. It is perhaps this that Thoreau had in mind when, having cited the saying, "That government is best which governs least," he added that he also believes what he takes this to amount to, that "That government is best which governs not at all."[8] It is from love of one's country, and for humankind generally, that a nonviolent transformation of society must proceed.

Philosophically, the groundwork for the transformation of a culture of violence to a culture of nonviolence requires attention to the metaphysics of nonviolence. My proposed starting point here is not from a philosopher—at least not an academically certified philosopher—but a writer, at times a philosophical one. I mean Mark Twain. In his recently published *Autobiography* (yes, recently published, because he decreed that it not be published until 100 years after his death), in reflecting upon the idea of an autobiography, he writes that a person's acts and words are but a small part of his life. His "real life" is in his head—the constant stream of *thoughts* running through his mind. Thoughts, in turn, he writes, are but the "mute articulations" of feelings. It is these, Twain writes, "not those other things, that are his history. His *acts* and *words* are merely the visible thin crust of his world. . . The mass of him is hiding—it and its volcanic fires that toss and boil, and never rest, night nor day. *These are his life*, and they are not written, and cannot be written."[9]

---

[7] I refer to all of these as countries. It is arguable that neither North Korea nor North Vietnam were strictly countries when those conflicts broke out, as opposed to supposedly temporary areas demarcated at the end of previous conflicts, World War II in the case of North Korea, the Indo-China War in the case of North Vietnam.

[8] "Civil Disobedience," in *The Portable Thoreau*, ed. Carl Bode (New York: Viking Press, 1964), 109.

[9] *Autobiography of Mark Twain*, ed. Harriet Elinor Smith, The Complete and Authoritative Edition (Berkeley, CA: University of California Press, 2010), Vol. 1, 220.

Much the same, I would say, is true of a nation, a society, or a people. When their histories are written, it is the outward acts that are the focus, particularly their wars and revolutions, their collective enactments. A few of their words expressed in writs, charters, and constitutions, or in the chosen pronouncements of a few leaders, are sprinkled into the account. And that is taken for history. But the life of a people, no less than that of an individual, consists mainly in their thoughts; the thoughts of millions of persons over generations. And if it is true that the history of even a single person is incapable of being written, the history of a collectivity of millions of people is also incapable of being written. That, if correct, means that we can know only little of the true history of any people or country, not to speak of the whole world. Humbling though it may be, that fact should not be cause for despair. What we can learn from it is not to be beguiled into thinking that the accounts of wars and revolutions around which so much of history is framed represents more than a tiny portion of the deeper essence of a people. More importantly, we should not think that they represent patterns that cannot be broken.

In the early Buddhist work, the *Dhammapada*, it is written: "Our life is shaped by our mind; we become what we think."[10] This seems to me to be a profound truth, one which must be the starting point of any philosophy of nonviolence. It suggests a way of dealing with a central problem confronting all of us who try to deal with contemporary issues on a large scale. The novelist, Arthur Koestler, posed the dilemma in the form of the tension between the paradigms of the Yogi and the Commissar. The Commissar seeks to change society from above, so to speak; through social engineering and manipulation of the economy—and, we might add, through the threat and use of military force to secure and even expand upon one's power. The Yogi, on the other hand, counsels looking within, promoting spiritual growth, striving, if you like, for inner perfection. Lenin and Stalin were examples of the Commissar; Gandhi embodied elements of the Yogi, even though his social and political activism removed him from the paradigm that Koestler had in mind.

I want to suggest a new way of thinking about our world; not the natural order that is best understood by science, but the social and moral order. It is to recognize that much of the world that most of us live in consists of embodied thought. The building we occupy as I speak did not grow in nature. It was first conceived in the mind of an architect. Those thoughts were presumably then put down on paper (nowadays they would no doubt be entered into a computer), only later to find their way into the hands of engineers and eventually workmen who physically put the stones or bricks together to complete the building. This building, in other words, is the physical embodiment of the thoughts of probably hundreds and perhaps thousands of persons, as is the university itself, as well as the cars we drive, the highways we speed down, the cities and towns we inhabit. But not only is much of our physical world the embodiment of human thought. The same is true of the practices and conventions of society, both good and bad. Injustice is a product of human thought. The institution of slavery and its aftermath are all embodiments of human thought, as are the wars that the accounts of history are framed around.

---

[10] *Dhammapada*, trans. Eknath Easwaran (Peteluna, CA: Nilgiri Press, 1985), 72.

If much of our world consists of the physical or social embodiment of human thought, then we have a direct connection between the philosophy of the Yogi and that of the Commissar. Social progress, as the Commissar rightly perceives, must involve change in the institutions of society, because they constitute so much of the physical world we inhabit. But the change must begin, as the Yogi understands, with the individual—with human thought. And this is what provides grounds for optimism. If the worst conditions we see about us in the world are the embodiment of human thought, then they can be changed, because human thought can be changed. Not that the thoughts—particularly the values, convictions, prejudices—can be changed easily. We can change our clothes, change jobs, or change where we live relatively easily. But to change how we think in basic ways is difficult. We tend to be Christian or Jew, Catholic or Protestant, Republican or Democrat, not because we have thought through the wisdom of those commitments, but because we were born into them. We took them over from others, usually our parents, or sometimes society as a whole, but now cling to them steadfastly—sometimes even fighting and dying for them—as though they represented absolute truth. But it should dawn on us that they cannot all represent absolute truth, because so many of the beliefs comprising them are incompatible with one another. At least some of us, and perhaps all of us in some measure, have to be mistaken. If we become what we think, then we can change what we are by changing what we think. And not only changing what we think, but changing *how* we think—by opening our minds, and critically reflecting on our most basic beliefs and values; not the least of which have to do with the use of force and violence.

It is possible that there are some people whose thoughts have become so ossified that they are incapable of changing. One suspects this is true of many people in positions of power. It is their thinking—and that of generations before them—that fuels the culture of violence. But those people—every last one of them—will eventually die. Violent revolution would hasten their death by guns and bullets. Nonviolent revolution counsels patience; regarding them with respect and compassion as human beings, even while lamenting some of their beliefs, and wishing them a peaceful end by natural causes, surrounded by friends and family, when their time comes. Even so, we should not give up on the human spirit and its capacity to surprise us. Two of the major events of the late twentieth-century were the peaceful dismantling of Apartheid in South Africa and the liberalization of the Soviet Union (leading unexpectedly to its subsequent disintegration), two events that were considered virtually inconceivable until they unfolded. Two individuals, F. W. de Klerk and Mikhail Gorbachev, were instrumental in those events and deserve far more recognition than they have received. They stand as examples of how positive changes in the thinking of even a few people in positions of leadership can affect the course of events.

No one person can provide a blueprint of how nonviolent revolution should proceed over the many years it would take it to unfold. The plan cannot be set down in advance; not in the detail one might hope for if one were undertaking such a grand experiment in a perfect world. It must grow out of the process itself, each step of which must have its own particular, manageable objective, which, once attained, provides a stepping-stone to the projection of the next objective. In this way, an interconnected network of means and ends can unfold through a process of trial and error, always subject to critical revision.[11]

But three general aims can be cited as commanding attention: the need for nonviolent social defense, the need to develop an economy of nonviolence, and the need for education in nonviolence.

When people hear of nonviolence on a social scale, they right away begin asking questions that begin with "What if . . .?" in which they hypothesize all kind of threats to the country and want to know how one would deal with them nonviolently. This is a legitimate and understandable concern. And to move from a culture of violence to a culture of nonviolence requires addressing it. It requires the development of a capacity for nonviolent social defense. I say "social defense" rather than national defense, because it is people whose well-being and security will be the primary concern in a culture of nonviolence, not that of states. Some of this has already been done by Gene Sharp in his work on nonviolent defense and is being explored by the International Center for Nonviolent Conflict. People need to understand and appreciate the examples of nonviolent power that are before their eyes in the modern world—not only the familiar examples of Gandhi in India and King in the U.S., but the examples of the overthrow of Marcos in the Philippines, Milosevic in Yugoslavia, Mubarak in Egypt, not to mention the largely nonviolent revolutions that swept Eastern Europe during and following the collapse of the Soviet Union. The empirical documentation of much of the success of nonviolent power is set forth by Erica Chenoweth and Maria J. Stephan, in their important article, "Why Civil Resistance Works: The Strategic Logic of Nonviolent Conflict," soon to appear in book form.[12] Humankind has for thousands of years sought communal security through increasing its capacity to cause death and destruction; a quest that has proven to be a never-ending spiral, enveloping millions of people in ever-more destructive conflagrations, most notably the world wars and the holocaust of the twentieth century. I include the holocaust because it is important to see it as more than just an irrational spasm of violence born of hatred of Jewish people. It was an outgrowth and logical extension of a culture of violence shared by the victims as well as the victors in those wars; the belief that when the survival of a people is at stake, then one confronts a "supreme emergency," as Michael Walzer calls it—moral considerations must be set aside.[13] One does whatever one must. The bitter irony is that Hitler and the Nazis saw the Jewish people—not to mention the Roma, homosexuals, and Marxists—as a threat to the German people. If to conspire is to breathe together, the victors and the vanquished in the major wars of the twentieth century may be said to have conspired to produce those wars. The air they breathed together was that of a shared culture of violence. Simply declaring one side a victor, another a loser, following the bloodshed doesn't change things in essential ways. It simply legitimizes an outcome that already has within it the seeds of the next violent upheaval. A fresh wind must blow through the world for this to change.

---

[11]   In this, I am indebted to John Dewey's conception of means and ends. See, for example, his *Human Nature and Conduct.*

[12]   Erica Chnoweth and Maria J. Stephan, "Why Civil Resistance Works: The Strategic Logic of Nonviolent Conflict," *International Security*, Vol. 33, No. 1, 2008. The book by the same title was published by Columbia University Press in 2012.

[13]   See Michael Walzer, *Just and Unjust Wars* (New York: Basic Books, 1977), Chapter 16.

A culture of violence can endure in a complex society only if exemplified in a war system, and a war system requires a permanent war economy.[14] It is naive to talk seriously about peace, much less about a transition to a culture of nonviolence, without addressing the need for an economics of nonviolence. Just as one cannot seriously propose dismantling a system of violent national defense without proposing something in its place, so one can't seriously advocate dismantling a war economy without having something to propose in its place.

Conventional wisdom would have it, of course, that war is good for the economy—and least for a capitalist economy. But that can be seriously questioned. The American Institute for Economic Research, for example, writes in a report entitled, "The Economics of War," that although recent American wars stimulated economic activity in the short term,

> sharp downturns in business activity (and sharp increases in unemployment) followed World War I and World War II, and there were recessions after the Korean and Vietnam Wars. . . . These economic reverses would seem to suggest that wartime economic activity may not necessarily contribute to sustained growth . . . war production *per se* does not contribute to increases in the wealth of the nation. In terms of the domestic economy, demand for war material is artificial. Such demand deploys both human and material resources in ultimately non-productive ways. Unlike products dedicated to civilian enterprises, the war products of capital and labor . . . often are literally blown up, or else consumed in ways not useful to either producers or consumers. However, it is difficult if not impossible to measure the net effect of such contrary factors on long-term aggregate growth trends. In other ways the economic effects of war on capitalist economies are unambiguously detrimental.[15]

The development of an economics of nonviolence would be a major undertaking, one far exceeding our time or my competence to undertake here. But we can make a start on one dimension of the problem, the matter of war. For war is the epitome of violence, and its analysis and evaluation is central to any attempt to transform that culture into a culture of nonviolence. World leaders cannot just snap their fingers, and have military strikes occur thousands of miles away, as President Obama did recently in the case of Libya, unless there are missiles, bombers, aircraft carriers, planes, and hundreds of thousands of trained military personnel at the ready to jump at the snap of these fingers; and their jumping to have effect presupposes the efforts of millions of ordinary citizens whose jobs and livelihoods are dependent upon the production of those instruments of destruction; and millions of others, like most of the rest of us, whose tax money makes the whole thing possible. This is all part, in other words, of an economic system. And just as I was speaking earlier of the ultimate role of thought in the metaphysics of nonviolence, here, too, an economic system is an embodiment of human thought, and can be changed only with changes in thought.

---

[14]   For a trenchant analysis of this concept, see Seymour Melman, *The Permanent War Economy: American Capitalism in Decline* (New York: Simon and Schuster, 1974).
[15]   "The Economics of War," *Research Reports*, Vol. 70, No. 5, March 10, 2003; American Institute for Economic Research.

An economics of nonviolence must deal with how best to turn human resources to nonviolent uses. And to do this requires first recognizing the costs of war. And wars do cost. Every regime in history has had to pay for the wars it fought—or find others to pay for them, as the U.S. did in the case of the Gulf War, financed largely by Saudi Arabia. And when they cannot acquire the wherewithal to cover the cost through plunder or exploitation or imposing reparations on the vanquished after a war is over (as happened most conspicuously with Germany after World War I), they must raise the money through taxation—the forcible separation of citizens from the money they have earned through their labors—or the "printing" of money by the government itself, with the predictable inflationary effects.

In the days before paper money, coins actually had some intrinsic value, according to the gold or silver or other valuable metals they contained. To acquire the money they needed to finance wars, rulers would then debase the coinage, either by making the coins smaller or by decreasing the percentage of precious metal they contained.[16] With paper money, the process is much simpler, since our paper money is no longer convertible to anything of value by the government. The government simply prints up more of the money it needs.[17] With more money chasing a constant quantity of goods, as it is put, prices are driven up and we have inflation. Rampant inflation, as Germany experienced during the 1920s, can be ruinous. The other alternative, or more often a supplement, to taxation and the printing of money is to borrow it, as the U.S. has been doing for years. We see all three of these taking place in America today. Inflation at the moment is relatively low but it will predictably increase. Borrowing, on the other hand, has been at monumental levels, with the national debt approaching 14 trillion dollars, and taxation is generating a backlash. Meanwhile we have a military budget of more than 600 billion dollars and are financing three wars of varying scale. The costs of this aspect of the culture of violence cannot be measured in the dollar value of armaments alone. It includes the cost of treating those men and women who return broken in body and often in spirit, and dealing with the resultant suicides, depression, alcoholism, and homicides. Moral consideration aside, these are not cost free. They are among the economic costs of a war system and the conflicts it predictably eventuates in. An economics of nonviolence must deal with these issues. It must evolve strategies for gradually converting the economy from a war economy to a nonviolent peace economy.

Most important of all, however, is education. Nonviolent education is the prerequisite to security and a nonviolent economy. For the hope, not only for a realistic transition to a culture of nonviolence, but for humankind in general, whatever the culture, lies with children and young people. For humankind is in a constant process of renewal.

---

[16] Thus as Rome was in decline it is reported that the amount of silver in the denarius declined from 100% under Augustus, to 90–95% under Nero, to less than 85% under Trajan, to under 75% under Marcus Aurelius, to 50% under Severus to 5% under Gallienos. See Hans Delbruck, *History of the Art of War*, Vol. 2, *The Barbarian Invasions*, trans. Walter J. Renfroe, Jr (Lincoln, NB: University of Nebraska Press, 1980), 213.

[17] The notion of "printing" money has actually become a metaphor. The process nowadays is more complicated, but the net effect is the same—the virtual creation of money out of thin air. The Federal Reserve Board has refined the attempts to control inflation, but it remains to be seen whether they will be successful.

Newborns don't come into the world eager to kill and exploit. They learn to do that. By the age of 16 or 18 most of them—nearly all of the males, but increasingly many of the females as well—can be turned into trained killers by their various governments. The transition to a culture of nonviolence must be grounded in education about nonviolence, its values, practice, and potential, from the earliest ages through college. Young people must be given the opportunity to open their minds to a different way of thinking about their world and their relations to others in it by being given the opportunity to explore the rich and complex issues of nonviolence. They must be given the opportunity fully to appreciate the fact that some of the most revered figures in history, from the Buddha, Socrates, Jesus, Thoreau, Tolstoy, Gandhi, Schweitzer, Einstein, and King have in their various ways, and to various degrees, exemplified the philosophy of nonviolence. Reverence for them at the very least calls for exploring what it is that they perceived, trying to understand and to build upon their examples and teachings. All of this involves trying to change the way we think—our collective mindset. For this is where a culture of nonviolence must be situated and nurtured. And it must begin with children. We neglect their moral and spiritual growth if we fail to provide them with this opportunity, not only for their sake, but for the sake of those to come. For we neglect our obligation to future generations as well if we fail to prepare our children to do better than we and our predecessors have done in creating a culture of nonviolence.[18]

[18] Previously published in the *Acorn: Journal of the Gandhi-King Society*, Vol. 14, No. 2, Fall–Winter 2011–2012, 5–14.

16

My (Non-)Teaching Philosophy

Holmes presented this speech on the occasion of being granted a teacher of the year award. The previous essay ends with an assertion that the most important aspect of a nonviolent revolution is education. In his various essays he emphasizes that nonviolence should be understood as a way of life. That radically changed way of life must include a different way of educating our students. And if nonviolence is really to be understood as a way of life, then the emphasis cannot be just on what we teach, but on how we do that. This essay provides a wonderful illustration of precisely this aspect of Holmes' ethics of nonviolence. He explains how he had come to teach not by imposing certain instructions on his students (which is akin to violence in some respects), but by leading them to get a deeper appreciation and form their own opinion about crucial ethical issues. Instead of forcing students to read about nonviolence and then memorize it and reproduce it during their exams, learning through dialogue and personal trial and error is precisely teaching something in a nonviolent manner; it demonstrates how teaching and learning can be an integral part of a new nonviolent way of life.

I begin a course by telling students I can't teach philosophy. A few dutifully write that down. Most look puzzled. I then explain what I understand philosophy to be. Conveniently, what that is coincides with the word's etymological meaning, the love of wisdom. I point out that wisdom isn't knowledge. It's not facts, data, information. You can teach knowledge. That is, you can impart it. In fact, a common conception of teaching is that a person with a lot of knowledge stands before students who have relatively little of it and then transmits that knowledge to them. They, in turn, passively receive it, write it down, memorize it for exams, and maybe even learn it. It's a one-way process. If it works, at the end of the process students possess knowledge the professor possessed at the beginning (luckily without any reduction in the professor's stockpile).

But that model doesn't work for wisdom. Wisdom involves judgment, sensitivity, understanding; a capacity to make good use of what you know, not only practically but morally. As such, it has a strong evaluative component. It involves being able to assess what is of value or importance, not only for careers and practical undertakings, but for life itself. And it can't be quantified. You can give objective tests to determine how much students know. Or how skilled they are (say, in doing logical or mathematical proofs). No such test measures wisdom. Wisdom's more like sensitivity to music, or art, or beauty. Its exercise is more art than science. The educated sometimes fail utterly to have it. And the uneducated are sometimes blessed with it. It's as though it were, as Socrates said of virtue, a gift of the gods.

I was slow to come to this conclusion. It required overcoming much of my graduate training and throwing off the cloak of academic professionalism that came with it. It began with uneasiness. I wasn't sure that what I was doing was worthwhile. Then I became unsure even of what I was doing. Student Course Opinion Questionnaires helped a little, but not much. The positive comments were reassuring, but it was the critical ones I had to learn from. "Holmes is boring," one student wrote years ago, "but really nice." If the first part was true, I knew I couldn't do much about it. If the second part was true—and I had to admit it could have been a misperception on the student's part—I knew it didn't make me a good teacher. I would (almost) rather have been an s.o.b. who was a good teacher than a nice guy who wasn't. I felt a little better when another student wrote: "He's no Jesse Jackson, but he sure knows his s…" But only a little. I was sure that knowing your—well, knowing your subject matter—is at least necessary to being a good teacher. But I knew that it wasn't enough either. I was mindful of the *Tao Te Ching's* admonition that the more you know the less you understand. I'm not sure there's an inverse relation there. But I believe it's possible to have your mind so cluttered with useless knowledge that you cease to think. At least about anything important. And if you're not thinking about anything important, you shouldn't be inflicting yourself on students. I would like to have believed the student who wrote, "He is god." But I didn't get carried away. The student might have been on something. And after all, it was a small 'g'. I didn't know what god he or she had in mind.

The defining moment came one morning when I was standing before 150 students in my course on Contemporary Moral Problems. I placed my folder on the lectern, opened it, looked down, and was seized with terror. I'd brought the wrong notes. The adrenalin flowed, and I winged it. I had to. But as the panic gradually subsided, I sensed something was different. Of necessity, I was talking to the students, not lecturing at them. And they were listening to me. I could see it in their faces. Thereafter, I conducted that course without notes. Just to be sure, I didn't bring any with me. I began to appreciate something Tolstoy said—that the key to education lies in the teacher's *relation* to students. That relation involves an interaction. A connection has to be made. It doesn't matter how much you know, or whether you've organized the material to death. If it's dry and lifeless in the presentation, it fails. Not for all students, but for most. You can lead students to the Pierian spring, but you can't make them drink. Much less drink deeply.

With this eventually came the realization that all I can really do that is of much importance is to encourage students to open their minds and develop their potential for wisdom. What would have seemed trite to me when I was fresh out of graduate school now seemed to me to be the central truth about education.

I caution students not to expect that everything they learn will immediately have practical value. This is something the ancient Greeks understood. The use of our intellects to gain understanding of life and the world is valuable *in itself*, apart from its utility. Aristotle saw it as the highest human excellence. This is why it's important to resist the tendency to commodify education, as though it were a product in a commercial transaction. Besides making education a branch of the dismal science, that tendency reduces learning to purely instrumental value. Bread needs to be put on the table, to be sure. Knowledge, training, and skill are needed to do that. But learning is also of value in itself. The most fulfilling lives, if they aren't devoted to learning, at least involve a respect for it. This students can't learn by hearing it said. They have to see it for themselves. They have to get caught up in the excitement of ideas—whether philosophical, scientific, literary, economic, mathematical, or whatever. Especially, I believe, they need to develop an appreciation of the philosophical tapestries that humankind has woven over the centuries. These represent new ways of seeing and understanding the world. As such, they have their own special beauty, an intrinsic value. They can enhance the quality of one's life apart from any other consequences they have, including the deepening of understanding.

Not only is the love of wisdom evaluative, education is pervasively evaluative as well. Every course represents a professor's judgment that this or that is worth learning. Some disciplines aspire to be value-neutral, but education itself cannot be. Nor can the university. This fact, if nothing else, establishes the centrality of ethics to education. Students often fail to grasp this. To many of them, the university is a place exclusively for teaching. And some of them are disgruntled that professors don't do more of it. It's only a partial answer to point out that some institutions are research universities. That may convey the mistaken impression that universities are only partially engaged in what they should be doing, namely educating students. A better view, in my judgment, is that universities are centers of learning. Some of that learning—but only some of it—takes place in the classroom. Professors are engaged in learning as well. As are graduate students. Learning goes on throughout the university. It just takes different forms at different levels.

But there's a dilemma here. It's highlighted by another observation of Tolstoy's: that "education is the tendency toward moral despotism raised to a principle." If the very idea of education is pervasively value-laden, which values should predominate? In public schools, the question is: If schools should teach values, which values should they teach? But in the university the problem I've felt most acutely concerns what to do about my own convictions. Do I set them forth openly and defend them? Or do I keep them under wraps and give a balanced presentation of all sides of issues?

This isn't a problem for much of philosophy. No one gets bothered over whether you defend evidentialism or reliabilism in epistemology, even with passion and conviction. Or realism or nominalism in metaphysics. Even within ethical theory it doesn't raise eye-brows one way or the other which side you take on the question of whether you can logically derive an "ought" from an "is." But when you're talking about abortion, the death penalty, or physician-assisted suicide the matter is different. Here students' emotions are engaged in a way they aren't on the other issues. And if you use the classroom for advocacy, you run the risk—whichever side you're on with regard to these issues—of fostering the moral despotism of which Tolstoy warned.

But maybe the risk is worth taking. A case can be made for saying that it is. It can be argued that by stating where you stand openly, at the beginning of a course, or at the beginning of discussion of the topic at issue, you're treating students as responsible, rational, moral agents. They know what to expect. They're then in a position to accept or reject what you say. Confronted with a thoughtful and reasoned defense of a position on a controversial moral issue, they can see the professor as an engaged person, with views on the same issues that concern them. The corollary, of course, is that you then have to be scrupulously objective in grading and conducting discussion and not expect students to agree with you. That's possible to do. Objectivity doesn't demand neutrality.

On the other side, a case can also be made for a balanced presentation of all sides of controversial issues, one that cites the strengths and weaknesses of the arguments but leaves the professor's own convictions out of the picture. The assessment of where the "truth" lies is then left to students. If you do this, you minimize the possibility that students will be unduly influenced by your views, perhaps tailoring papers and answers to exam questions to what they think will please you. The downside is that your convictions are what they are whether you disclose them or not. And if there is any imbalance in your treatment of views you disagree with, students are unable to be on the lookout for it.

I've wrestled with this issue for years, with no conclusive resolution to the dilemma. The extent to which I had adopted the second approach was brought home to me years ago when, after the last class in a course on the philosophy of religion, two students came up and eagerly asked whether I believed in God. They couldn't tell. They'd thought, perhaps, that I was saving it for the end. I'm still not telling, but I've shifted ground since then. While I think the arguments on each side of these two general approaches are about equally good, I have settled for something of a blend of the two. On some issues (e.g., racism and sexism) I simply pose at the outset the question *why* they are wrong, not whether they are wrong. I then bring in the arguments on the other side and show where they are deficient. Even then, however, I stress that if you're to feel confident in rejecting a position, you have to consider it in its strongest form. Only then can you be on firm ground in rejecting it. So I make the strongest cases I can for racism and sexism and show why they're nonetheless defective. If racists and sexists call to complain, I'll deal with it. With regard to issues like abortion and affirmative action, on the other hand, I step back, analyze the controversy, and put before students what appear to be the strongest arguments on each side. But I leave it entirely to them to decide for themselves which position is more nearly correct.

So, I explain to students that I can teach them a lot *about* philosophy. I can tell them who said what and when. I can assign them good readings. I can define terms, explain theories, and analyze arguments. I can also teach them reasoning skills. Not that they won't get anything out of that. They'll be better educated, if nothing else. But I can't teach them philosophy. I can't teach them to love wisdom, to *want* to understand—and not just know about—the world and their place in it. I can't teach them to want to understand what makes for a good life, and what kind of person that requires one to be. I can't teach them to make sound judgments, to become sensitive and compassionate persons. Only they can do that. But I can help them in the process. I can encourage, coax, nurture, support (and occasionally prod) them. And do my best to provide an intellectually safe and comfortable environment for them to grow in. That's what I see my role to be. But the process requires effort, discipline, and hard work on their part as well. In the end, learning at its best is a cooperative enterprise. Occasionally—or so I'd like to believe—I succeed in teaching that.[1]

---

[1] Previously published in *How I Teach: Essays on Teaching by Winners of the Goergen Award for Excellence in Undergraduate Teaching*, Vol. 4, University of Rochester, 2011, 7–13.

Appendix 1

An Interview with Robert Holmes

Predrag Cicovacki[PC]: Your long-time colleague and my teacher, Lewis White Beck, once wrote an essay, "How I Became Almost a Philosopher." Was Beck being too modest? What does it mean to consider oneself a philosopher? How would you assess your own career?

Robert Holmes[RH]: Lewis, I think, was being too modest. He had become a philosopher—not almost a philosopher—in the experience he recounts; not a card-carrying philosopher, so to speak, because he hadn't yet gotten his PhD, but a philosopher nonetheless. One can consider oneself a philosopher when one is properly certified. That typically means a PhD. But the grinding toil of writing a dissertation, and the hard work of writing articles and books, doesn't necessarily engender any sense of what wisdom is about, much less instill a love of it, which I take philosophy to be. Indeed it may turn one away from it, or worse yet, lead to a supercilious disdain for it. Thoreau wrote in *Walden*:

> There are nowadays professors of philosophy, but not philosophers. Yet it is admirable to profess because it was once admirable to live. To be a philosopher is not merely to have subtle thoughts, nor even to found a school, but so to love wisdom as to live according to its dictates, a life of simplicity, independence, magnanimity, and trust. It is to solve some of the problems of life, not only theoretically, but practically.[1]

That's a tall order for most of us and a little disconcerting to one who has made a living as a philosophy professor. But the central idea of it connects with my own experience. I had to overcome some of the effects of my graduate training (not the fault of my professors, I should say) before it began to dawn on me that some of the wisest people in my life weren't philosophers at all. They didn't necessarily love wisdom, and in some cases probably couldn't have told you what it is. But they possessed it. They were centered, humble, understanding, had good judgment, and were caring and compassionate people. They were the sort you could go to for good counsel and be confident of getting it. In any event, I came to appreciate what wisdom is and why the ancients prized it. But just as one can have wisdom without consciously desiring it, one can desire wisdom without possessing it. In my case, I'm still on the track of it.

PC: What is the role of the university today? What is the future of the university?

RH: Universities today have become overgrown high schools. More importantly, and unfortunately, they have intertwined themselves with the corporate, military world

---

[1] Quoted from *The Portable Thoreau*, ed. Carl Bode (New York: Viking Press, 1964), 270.

(the "military-industrial complex" as Eisenhower called it). Many of them have contracts with the military, open their doors to corporate and military recruiters, and many of their faculty do research for the war system that our society has become. Quite a few of them, in addition, appoint on-duty military personnel to professorships (bypassing the usual standards for such appointments), and train students to become military officers, sometimes drilling them in combat tactics on campus. Equally as important, the academic culture tends to foster careerism rather than learning among faculty. Universities understandably would like to have as faculty professors [those] who have something original to contribute; who write and do research. And such persons are distinguishable from those who just want to teach or who want to do research but not publish. What happens is that, in the effort to get good jobs, tenure, and promotions, young people are drawn into research and publishing for the sake of those ends, rather than for the sake of learning. Advancing one's career becomes no less the objective than in the corporate world. Graduate students often choose dissertation topics, and young faculty choose topics for articles and books, not so much because they yearn to understand those particular topics, but because they are the ones they believe will advance them. This mindset, when extended across the world of higher education, has a dampening, and even degrading, effect upon the spirit of learning.

PC: What inspired you to go into teaching?

RH: In truth, I wasn't inspired to go into teaching. I was inspired to go into philosophy, and most philosophers, wise or not, have to teach to put food on the table, so I taught. It was hard work and took time away from writing. But a part of me liked it. I came to wonder, though, whether what I was doing was worthwhile. I could teach what other philosophers had said and load students up with theories. In the process, I could teach them how to reason. Those things were valuable, but there wasn't much there that diligent students couldn't learn on their own. And without paying an arm and a leg for college tuition.

I eventually came to feel that all I could really do of importance was encourage learning—help open students' minds to the excitement learning brings and the enrichment of life it promises. This transformed [my] teaching, and I became something of a partner with the students. The process was a cooperative one, in which I was learning as well. What had been an ember of satisfaction gradually became a joy. I've always loved philosophy. I only gradually came to love teaching. But in the process—and perhaps most importantly of all—I came to love my students as well.

PC: If you were to meet your former self at the time when that former self was entering Harvard University as a freshman, what advice would you, now, give to that student? To study philosophy? To study ethics? What problems would you advise him to wrestle with?

RH: My advice to my former self at Harvard would be to drop out and found Microsoft. More seriously, it would be to study Greek and Latin and at least have a sporting chance of becoming a well-educated person. More seriously still, I would advise him to do pretty much as he did: study philosophy, do a lot of running, and a little wrestling and boxing, and not look back with regrets.

PC: Many analytic philosophers focus on a few philosophical disciplines in the course of their careers, or they start with one, then switch to another, and so on. In the graduate school, at the University of Michigan, your prevailing interest was metaethics. Why ethics rather than epistemology? Or philosophy of language? Or philosophy of science? Who among your teachers influenced you the most and in what ways?

RH: Actually, I was much taken with aesthetics as an undergraduate, having studied it under Henry Aiken. I also loved Greek philosophy. In fact, I wrote my undergraduate honors thesis on Plato. My oral exam under Rafael Demos and Rogers Albritton was more chastening than my final oral exam for the PhD years later. Albritton raised some questions about the translation of a passage from the *Philebus*, but Demos pressed and pressed until he found a question I couldn't answer (it concerned the precise nature of the "world-soul"), then seemed satisfied. I ended up not pursuing ancient philosophy seriously, as I thought I might, when I got to graduate school in Michigan and became caught up in metaethics. There W. K. Frankena and C. L. Stevenson were the biggest influences on me: Stevenson, for the energy and enthusiasm he brought to the classroom—his lectures were almost performances—Frankena, because of the clarity and precision he brought to philosophy. With him, the excitement came not from high energy, but from being made to feel that philosophical issues, however dry and abstract on the surface, were important and inherently exciting.

PC: Speaking of your nonphilosophical interest in music and sports, how is that you never tried to teach or write about aesthetics or philosophy of sports?

RH: I've never seriously considered writing about sports, although I love sports, and think that ethical issues abound in them, especially in the idea of competition—trying to succeed by prevailing over people rather than by collaborating with them. We're inured to the capitalist ethic, where it's believed that the "invisible hand" (as Adam Smith had it) creates good from unfettered self-interest playing itself out in the economic sphere. But it's far from obvious that competition plays that role, at least in a social context in which one doesn't have a choice of whether or not to play the game. In sports, one does. Engaging in competition is consensual. And when leavened by sportsmanship—which, sadly, many sports, especially at the professional level, are deficient in—competition can be both fun and positive. Where I have the most serious issues with sports is where they involve violence, as some of them clearly do, including some that I like, such as boxing and football. But with rule-changes, and the cultivation of a different mindset toward them, most of the harm—and all of the deliberately inflicted harm—could be eliminated. On another front, were I still teaching, I'd be tempted to offer a course on the philosophy of music. I say the philosophy of music, and not the aesthetics of music, because it is the philosophical importance of music that most intrigues me, as opposed to the experience of music, which I enjoy immensely but don't feel the same need to understand. Burnet, in his *Early Greek Philosophy*, writes that after Pythagoras, "Greek philosophy was . . . to be dominated by the notion of the perfectly tuned string."[2] In various ways, the theory of music entered into much of later philosophy and science. Harmony, of course, was a central concept in understanding virtue for Plato, as was the mean, which was closely associated with music, for Aristotle. Descartes wrote a treatise on music, and it's written that for Newton "music, light,

---

[2]   John Burnet, *Early Greek Philosophy* (New York: Meridian Books, 1961), 112.

and the planets were simply different constituents of one eternal, divine harmony. Why shouldn't the laws of gravity be the same as the laws governing musical strings?"[3]

PC: Metaethics has lost some of its popularity among professional philosophers. Is this statement accurate? If yes, why has this change happened? Should metaethics be renewed? Does it still have an important role to play in normative and applied ethics? Can metaethics be practiced as it was in the middle of the twentieth century? Or must metaethics itself evolve to serve a rapidly changing field of philosophical ethics?

RH: Metaethics gained new life at the end of the twentieth century and into the twenty-first, and will, I think, continue to flourish so long as people approach ethical issues in a philosophical way. If you look back, of course, Socrates was doing metaethics, though it wasn't called such, when he sought definitions as the way into constructive philosophical discourse, and metaethics is laced through the entire history of philosophy. It was practiced with a vengeance in the first half of the twentieth century, and sometimes with an inflated conception of its importance. Unfortunately, much of revivalist metaethics in the twenty-first century is a rerun of the old issues in new terms. The basic positions in metaethics have been staked out, at least with regard to the analysis of moral judgments. When that happens, there's a tendency among academics to invent new terms, or retread existing terms, for what are supposed to be new theories. Accordingly, there has been a proliferation of "isms" in recent metaethics. People will tire of this after a while and move on to other things. The pendulum will then swing away from metaethics once again, as philosophers swarm to what appear to be newer and fresher topics. As others have noted, theories recede into the background, not so much from having been refuted (though occasionally that happens), as from philosophers growing tired of them. They grew tired of metaethics for a while, but are now back at it with renewed vigor.

PC: Kant once said that it is a scandal for philosophy that it has not proved the existence of the external world. Do you see any scandals in the philosophy of today?

RH: The pragmatists would have said that the real scandal for philosophy was to think that you had to prove the existence of an external world in the first place. We are in the world, for better or worse, and have no choice but to make our way. Although I wouldn't be so presumptuous as to call it a scandal, I think it unfortunate that many recent philosophers try to analyze knowledge in terms of true belief. Knowledge and belief (however true, and however hedged about with qualifications) are, in my view, altogether different things, and it's a category mistake to try to analyze the former in terms of the latter. Plato recognized this in the *Meno* but may have lost sight of it in the *Theaetetus*. If I had a second philosophical life to live, I could well devote a part of it to epistemology.

PC: Among your persistent philosophical interests has been American pragmatism, especially the work of John Dewey and William James. How and why did you become interested in Dewey and James? Why has this interest persisted through the decades of your philosophical activity?

RH: I've admired the pragmatists for making their own way in philosophy, without regard to what was considered academically respectable. Doing so probably cost Peirce a career in philosophy, since his ways left him an outsider all of his life, despite the support he got from William James. But his work on the nature

---

[3] Stuart Isacoff, *Temperament: How Music Became a Battleground for the Great Minds of Western Civilization* (New York: Vintage Books, 2001), 194.

of meaning was groundbreaking. While it's true that some of his formulations of the pragmatic theory of meaning—those which anticipate the logical positivist "verificationist criterion"—seem to render much of his own highly speculative philosophy meaningless, attention to the range of his formulations shows the complexity and richness of his thinking about meaning, and open the door to the significance of his own theories as well as to speculative philosophy in general (even Royce had a pragmatist bent to some of his philosophy, most of which was anathema to the pragmatists). James and Dewey broadened the pragmatic enterprise, James by adding to it a theory of truth, and taking seriously the role of faith and religion; Dewey by enlarging the scope of philosophy to take in not only the standard concerns of philosophical ethics, epistemology, logic, aesthetics, etc.—but also the critique of society as a whole, its assumptions, values, customs. No doubt this reflected the influence of his early Hegelian years. Although I had early on encountered this aspect of Dewey, it wasn't until much later—in thinking about issues of violence and nonviolence, war and peace—that I was able to pull myself away from fairly deeply engrained preconceptions of academia regarding the importance of confining oneself to one area of philosophy, and came to realize that some problems of a social, political, and ethical sort cannot be dealt with effectively by confining oneself to any one academic discipline. Such compartmentalization, one might even say, is an obstacle to a constructive engagement with issues. Dewey in his pedestrian, tenacious way, took on whatever issue seemed to be most in need of close examination. I found it liberating to stop worrying about whether all of what I was doing was philosophy as academically practiced, and to let the demands of the topic determine how I would approach it.

PC: Tolstoy and Gandhi, together with the *Gita* and the *Tao-Te-Ching*, have an impact on your thinking. Can you explain your interest in them and the role they play in your thinking? I am asking that with more than one objective in mind, but here is what perhaps interests me the most: in your philosophical thinking, you are trying to be as rational as possible. The sources I mention sometimes (or often, like *Tao-Te-Ching*) seem to invoke paradoxes which cannot be easily reconciled with rational thinking and in which Western philosophers, especially analytic philosophers, are not interested at all. How do you reconcile rational thinking with the tradition which seems to deny the relevance of such thinking?

RH: Some philosophical problems call for a highly rational, even analytical, approach. In ethics, for example, unless you are dismissive of the problem as being too inconsequential to bother with, you can only deal effectively with the question of whether one can derive an "ought" from an "is" by going at it rationally: making distinctions, clarifying concepts, talking about logic. Precision then becomes important. But precision isn't always important or even desirable in philosophy. Accuracy is, but not precision. That having been said, there are differences between Eastern and Western approaches to philosophical thinking. While there are all kinds of exception in both traditions, the Western tradition *tends* to be rationalistic, in the broad sense of having confidence in the potential of reason to answer the most important questions, whereas at least much of Eastern thought *tends*, not to be irrational, but to be nonrational, in the sense of believing that there are limits to what rational though can achieve, and that in the end we have to look to other resources within us—such as meditation—to achieve understanding, peace of mind, or enlightenment. As the *Tao-Te-Ching* puts it, "Can you stand back from your own mind, and thus understand all things?" Some of Western thought recognizes the seriousness of the problem. The ancient skeptics, for example, by defending one thesis one day, its contrary the next, tried to show the seriousness of the problem—as, in their way, did Parmenides and Zeno, and much later, Kant and the absolute idealists. But they used a rational approach that led them to the limits of rational thought. If you can't, in the end, make sense of notions like plurality and motion, or more basically still, as Bradley argued, relation, then you are led either to skepticism or to the conclusion that ultimately reality is One. Eastern thought arrives at the same conclusion, but by different means: by stilling the mind and probing the depths of the subconscious. As the *Tao-Te-Ching* again puts it, "Can you coax your mind from its wandering and keep to the original oneness?" Not that some of them didn't use rational means to show the limits of rationality. In one of my favorite passages, Chuang Tzu reasons:

> Suppose you and I argue. If you beat me instead of my beating you, are you really right and am I really wrong? If I beat you instead of your beating me, am I really right and are you really wrong? Or are we both partly right and partly wrong? Or are we both wholly right and wholly wrong? Since between us neither you nor I know which is right, others are naturally in the dark. Whom shall we ask to arbitrate? If we ask someone who agrees with you, since he has already agreed with you, how can he arbitrate? If we ask someone who agrees with me, since he has already agreed with me, how can he arbitrate? If we ask someone who disagrees with both you and me to arbitrate, since he has already disagreed with you and me, how can he arbitrate? If we ask someone who agrees with both you and me to arbitrate, since he has already agreed with you and me, how can he arbitrate? Thus among you, me, and others, none knows which is right.[4]

But for the most part, the Eastern tradition draws upon other resources than pure intellect. That strand of Western thought that runs through Parmenides, Zeno, and the Stoics, through Kant to Bradley (and, I suspect, quantum physics as well), thus ultimately converges with Eastern thought, despite their radically divergent approaches. I've become convinced that the Eastern approach is the more nearly correct path than the highly rationalistic Western approach. Rational thought obviously has its place. But it can only take us so far. Either we can never understand the ultimate truth about what this life is all about—and I differ with the pragmatists in remaining convinced that there is such an ultimate truth—or we can access it only through meditation. Or, of course, perhaps death.

PC: What is the role of philosophy in today's world? Is philosophy the discipline that should give us a "big picture" of the world in which we live and its present crisis? Can philosophy help people to think and care about what goes on in the world around them? Can philosophy get us out of Plato's cave?

RH: I believe that there is little in this life, other than providing for basic necessities and well-being, that is more important than philosophy. Most people just pass the time between birth and death. By the time they die, their minds are cluttered with a lot of useless knowledge. What passes for understanding is usually little more than uncritical acceptance of what others have thought and would have them believe.

---

[4] *Sourcebook in Chinese Philosophy*, Wing-Tsit Chan, ed. (Princeton, NJ: Princeton University Press, 1963), 189–90.

Those who are convinced that they have the truth with a capital 'T' abound. And they would like the rest of us to accept that Truth as well; either because they think it represents the will of God, and that spreading that word makes them pleasing in the eyes of God; or because it supports the social, political, and economic arrangement they are convinced is correct—whether it be capitalism, socialism, communism, or something else—and which profits them and those they identify with at the expense of others. Philosophy, [no matter] whether it can lead us out of Plato's Cave, teaches us humility in seeking the path, and ultimate recourse to our own resources. In the end, we must seek the way alone. As Elizabeth Cady Stanton once wrote, in a passage that might have been penned by the existentialists,

> Nothing adds such dignity to character as the recognition of one's self-sovereignty; the right to an equal place, everywhere conceded—a place earned by personal merit, not an artificial attainment by inheritance, wealth, family and position . . . In that solemn solitude of self, that links us with the immeasurable and the eternal, each soul lives alone forever . . . there is a solitude which each and every one of us has always carried with him, more inaccessible than the ice-cold mountains, more profound than the midnight sea; the solitude of self. Our inner being which we call ourself, no eye nor touch of man or angel has ever pierced. It is more hidden than the caves of the gnome; the sacred adytum of the oracle; the hidden chamber of Eleusinian mystery, for to it only omniscience is permitted to enter.
>
> Such is individual life. Who, I ask you, can take, dare take on himself the rights, the duties, the responsibilities of another human soul?[5]

PC: Occasionally, you make references to Henry David Thoreau and Martin Luther King, Jr, but they do not seem to have the same impact on your thought as Tolstoy and Gandhi. Can you explain why that is so?

RH: Although it's true I haven't been as influenced by them as by Tolstoy and Gandhi, I admire Thoreau and King immensely. Their essays, "Civil Disobedience," and "Letter from Birmingham Jail," are inspired pieces of writing and compare with anything Tolstoy and Gandhi wrote. They should be included in every curriculum. I feel a surge of inspiration every time I reread them, as I do with much of Tolstoy and Gandhi. Indeed I sometimes reread them when my spirits flag. I also find a wealth of insights in Thoreau's *Walden*, and to a lesser extent, *A Week on the Concord and Merrimack Rivers*, both of which reflect the influence of his reading of Eastern philosophy. Tolstoy was greatly influenced by Eastern thought as well and became something of a Taoist in his later years. King, like Gandhi, was more of an activist than either Tolstoy or Thoreau (despite Thoreau's having spent a night in jail for refusing to pay taxes) and his commitment to nonviolence, though of a principled sort, didn't extend to a way of life as completely as it did, say, for Gandhi and Tolstoy. His most powerful message came through in his speeches. It is hard not to be stirred by them. He wrote that the universe is on the side of justice, and it is almost as though the universe was speaking through him, thundering a message of hope to all of humankind. Remarkably, the whole of King's activist life—his campaigns, speeches, books—were compressed into a little over 12 years; while

---

⁵ *The Elizabeth Cady Stanton-Susan B. Anthony Reader: Correspondence, Writings, Speeches;* Ellen Carol Bubois, ed. (Boston: Northeastern University Press, 1992), 251, 253–4.

Gandhi and Tolstoy lived into their seventies and eighties, King's death at the age of 39 cut short a life that was probably nowhere near realizing its potential for moral leadership. But they are all figures of enormous importance to the evolution of a moral spirit in humankind. Tolstoy was a prophet of biblical proportions, as well as a deep philosophical thinker. Thoreau was a cranky individualist, who by a different path came within a hair's breadth—as did Gandhi by a vastly different route—of the anarchism Tolstoy embraced. Gandhi was the most saintly of the four, but with a political shrewdness that King shared but Tolstoy and Thoreau lacked. Indeed, Tolstoy came—no doubt through the influence of Taoism—to be convinced that large-scale social action was futile. This, over and above his commitment to nonviolence, was part of the reason he sympathized with, but did not support, the revolutionaries of his day. Thoreau, in his way, took much the same position, but more from his particular vision of individual responsibility than from the broad concern of Tolstoy. As he wrote in "Civil Disobedience" (and I've taken the liberty of reversing the order of the sentences): "A man has not everything to do, but something; and because he cannot do *everything*, it is not necessary that he should do *something* wrong . . . What I have to do is to see, at any rate, that I do not lend myself to the wrong which I condemn." Gandhi and King, however, plunged forward in their attempts to effect social change, King with a respect for law that ran deeper than with the others. One could do worse than to put the four of them at the center of every course of learning that one undertakes.

PC: In some of your recent papers the concept of fear has played a prominent role. You connect it with manipulation by the powerful, and also speak about overcoming fear in order to disobey the powerful and resist their pressure by nonviolent means. As you know, this concept of fear has a long tradition. In Buddhism, we are invited to overcome fear and desire. In ancient Greece, the challenge was to find enough courage to know ourselves and become moderate. Have these traditions influenced your interest in fear, or have you come to it in some other way?

RH: I'd never given much thought to the notion of fear until I began thinking about nonviolence and the qualities its cultivation requires. Gandhi says repeatedly that nonviolence requires courage, and courage, of course, requires overcoming fear. One doesn't show courage in the face of adversity, no matter how great that adversity, unless it creates fear. Even risking one's life doesn't require courage unless one values life and fears losing it. But courage is a broader and deeper quality than mere bravery. This, no doubt, is why it was one of the cardinal virtues for the Greeks. Bravery signifies courage in the face of physical danger. We pin medals on men (and women) who show exceptional bravery in achieving unusual distinction in war. But physical bravery in that sense can readily be cultivated in people, as evidenced by the fact that millions upon millions of men can be trained to exhibit it, and are so every day in the armies of the world. Courage, however, requires inner strength; it must come from oneself. Ten thousand men can be conditioned by drill sergeants to march into battle and face horrifying threats; but you cannot drill courage into the human spirit. As Plato saw, it is a quality of the soul when it has achieved a certain harmony, and this can only be the outcome of personal effort. Courage is essential to one of the attributes of nonviolence as a way of life, truthfulness. It takes courage to be consistently and thoroughly truthful. For truthfulness in thought, word, and deed—as the Jains stressed, and Gandhi, following them—requires extraordinary courage. It is difficult for most people to avoid lying—the paradigm example of untruthfulness in speech—even about little things. There is an understandable tendency to want to cover up what one has done as well as to spare others the discomfort and sometimes outright hurt that truthfulness sometimes occasions. But untruthfulness in speech goes well beyond lying; prevarication and equivocation are practices that one can engage in (as politicians know) that are intended to deceive but may not involve telling a single falsehood. Dissembling and dissimulation may be practiced without even using language; one's behavior can, as it were, lie. William Wollaston, the eighteenth-century British philosopher, advanced the theory (that never received its due) that actions express propositions, and are right or wrong according to whether the propositions expressed are true or false. As he says, "whoever acts as if things were so, or not so, doth by his acts declare, that they are so, or not so; as plainly as he could by words, and with more reality."[6] There are signs as well as symbols and indexes, and actions may themselves be regarded as signs (there is some recognition of this in the notion of so-called "body language"), and it's important to factor them into the analysis of truthfulness. The importance of fear runs through courage to the notion of trust, which is important to nonviolence. If you can't overcome fear, you're unlikely to be able to meet the challenge of truthfulness, and if you can't meet the challenge of truthfulness, then you're unlikely to be able to inspire trust. Only those who are truthful can be trusted. And creating trust is essential to nonviolence as a way of life, and probably to most uses of nonviolence as a tactic or strategy as well.

But fear plays another important role in nonviolence, because not only must one learn to overcome one's own fear in facing violence and oppression, one must also strive to dispel fear in others; perhaps fear of you, or of those identified with you, or of the changes you symbolize. As a student wrote in a journal, in which the class was asked to reflect on a passage from the *Dhammapada*,

> I don't believe that there is evil; I think that evil, hate, and anger are just intensified fear. Therefore, the only way to stop evil is to stop fear. Hating someone does not stop fear and therefore cannot stop evil. (Emily Miller, Journal of Philosophy 116Q, Fall 2000)

The idea that hatred is intensified fear is a powerful one. Glenn Gray came close to this idea when he observed of men in combat, in his book, *The Warriors*: "The hatred that arises for the enemy in wartime, whether it be for Nazis, Communists, or Capitalists, for White, Yellow, or Black, is peculiarly one-sided, for it is a fear-filled image." When Americans asked of terrorists following 9/11, "Why do they hate us?" perhaps part of the answer is that they fear us. If that is so, then to deal effectively with terrorism, as well as with some of the more daunting challenges of interpersonal relations, we must find ways to dispel the fear others often have of us, individually and collectively as a people. Violence can't do that. It intensifies fear. Nonviolence can—not invariably and with certainty, but often in a slow and subtle way. As Gandhi once wrote, "even a tiny grain of true nonviolence acts in a silent, subtle, unseen way and leavens the whole society."

PC: Has the concept of human nature been important in your thinking? Do you believe that there is something like human nature? Can philosophy help us understand

---

[6] Selby-Bigge, ed., *British Moralists*, 364.

what it is? Or is the task simply to learn how to become and remain human, even if there is no fixed or stable human nature?

RH: If one writes about war and nonviolence, it's difficult not to give some thought to the idea of human nature, because one encounters references to it all the time; often of the sort: "Until you change human nature, there'll always be wars." The assumption, of course, is that you can't change human nature, hence there'll always be wars, hence—to extrapolate—you can't really change much of anything in the social, political, or economic realm. It's true, of course, that you can't change human nature if by that you mean one's biological nature. We are animals, not plants or fungi or minerals. We can't change that. But if by human nature one means characteristics that supervene upon our physical and biological nature—the predispositions, customs, basic assumptions—then human nature can be changed, because these can be changed. We know that individuals can change. Some people at age 40 or 50 are different persons than they were at age 20. Even criminals sometimes reform in striking ways. Moral growth has transformative powers. If an individual can change, and become virtually a different person, there's no reason why humankind generally can't change. And those changes might be so extensive, and so dramatic, as to warrant being called changes in human nature. A nonviolent world order then becomes a possibility.

PC: Finally, since I know that you are a big fan of the Buffalo Bills, I must ask you this question: Has the time arrived? Is this the year? When are the Bills going to win the Super bowl?

RH: The Bills will rise again and one day win the Super bowl. But not just yet.

Appendix 2

Bibliography of Robert Holmes' Publications

Books

Philosophic Inquiry, 2nd edn with Lewis W. Beck. Upper Saddle River, NJ: Prentice-Hall, 1968.

On War and Morality. Princeton, NJ: Princeton University Press, 1989.

Nonviolence in Theory and Practice (ed.). Belmont, CA: Wadsworth, 1990. Republished 2001 by Waveland Press, Long Grove, IL; 2nd edn (coedited with Barry Gan), 2005; 3rd edn, 2012.

Basic Moral Philosophy. Belmont, CA: Wadsworth, 1993; 2nd edn, 1998; 3rd edn, 2003; 4th edn, 2006.

Articles and reviews

1. "Ultimate Rules in Ethics: A Reply to Mr. Schon," *Philosophy and Phenomenological Research*, Vol. 21, March 1961, 984–7.
2. "Good Reasons in Ethics," *Forum*, University of Houston Quarterly, Vol. 3, Winter 1962–3, 28–31.
3. "On Generalization," *Journal of Philosophy*, Vol. 70, June 1963, 317–23.
4. Review of Paul Tillich, *Morality and Beyond*, in *Union Seminary Quarterly Review*, Vol. 19, March 1964, 265–7.
5. "The Case against Ethical Naturalism," *Mind*, Vol. 83, April 1964, 291–5.
6. "The Development of John Dewey's Ethical Thought," *Monist*, Vol. 48, July 1964, 392–406.
7. "Descriptivism, Supervenience, and Universalizability," *Journal of Philosophy*, Vol. 73, March 1966, 113–19.
8. "Moral Decision in the Nuclear Age," *Bulletin of the Atomic Scientists*, April 1966, 27–9.
9. "Moral Stance and Political Action," *Christian Century*, Vol. 83, June 1966, 776–7.
10. "John Dewey's Moral Philosophy in Contemporary Perspective," *Review of Metaphysics,* Vol. 20, September 1966, 42–70.
11. "Negation and the Logic of Deontic Assertions," *Inquiry*, Vol. 10, Spring 1967, 89–95.
12. Review of Shia Moser, *Absolutism and Relativism in Ethics,* in *Social Science Quarterly*, Vol. 49, No. 4, March 1969, 141–2.

13. "Kim on Kant's Supreme Principle of Morality," *Kant-Studien*, Vol. 61, No. 3, Fall 1970, 393–6.
14. "Some Conceptions of Analysis in Recent Ethical Theory," *Metaphilosophy*, Vol. 2, No. 1, January 1971, 1–28.
15. "Violence and Nonviolence," in *Violence*, J. Shaffer (ed.). New York: David McKay, 1971, 103–35.
16. "University Neutrality and ROTC," *Ethics*, Vol. 83, No. 3, April 1973, 177–95. Republished in *Neutrality and the Academic Ethic*, Robert L. Simon (ed.). Lanham, MD: Rowman & Littlefield, 1995.
17. "On Pacifism," *Monist*, Vol. 57, No. 4, October 1973, 489–506.
18. "The Concept of Physical Violence in Moral and Political Affairs," *Social Theory and Practice*, Vol. 2, No. 4, Fall 1973, 387–408.
19. "John Dewey's Social Ethics," *Journal of Value Inquiry*, Vol. 7, No. 4, Winter 1973, 274–80.
20. "Is Morality a System of Hypothetical Imperatives?" *Analysis*, Vol. 34, No. 3, January 1974, 96–100.
21. "Royce, Pragmatism and the Egocentric Predicament," *Proceedings of the Bicentennial Symposium of Philosophy*, 1976, 19–24. Republished in *Two Centuries of American Philosophy*, Peter Caws (ed.). Oxford: Blackwell, 1980.
22. "Philippa Foot on Hypothetical Imperatives," *Analysis*, Vol. 36, No. 4, June 1976, 199–200.
23. Review of Onora Nell, *Acting on Principle: An Essay in Kantian Ethics,* in *Kant-Studien*, Vol. 68, No. 3, 1977, 369–70.
24. "Nozick on Anarchism," *Political Theory*, Vol. 5, No. 2, May 1977, 247–56. Republished in *Reading Nozick*, J. Paul (ed.). Lanham, MD: Rowman and Littlefield, 1981.
25. Review of Steven M. Cahn (ed.), *New Studies in the Philosophy of John Dewey,* in *Transactions of the Charles S. Peirce Society*, Vol. 14, No. 3, Summer 1978, 215–19.
26. "The Concept of Corporate Responsibility," in *Ethical Theory and Business,* Tom L. Beauchamp and Norman E. Bowie (eds). Upper Saddle River, NJ: Prentice-Hall, 1979, 151–60.
27. "State-Legitimacy and the Obligation to Obey the Law," *Virginia Law Review,* Vol. 67, No. 1, February 1981, 133–41.
28. "Frankena on 'Is' and 'Ought,'" *Monist*, Vol. 64, No. 3, Summer 1981, 394–405.
29. Review of Thomas Regan, *Utilitarianism and Co-Operation*, in *Review of Metaphysics,* Vol. 36, No. 3, 1983, 729–30.
30. "The Sleep of Reason Brings Forth Monsters," *Harvard Magazine*, March–April, 1983, 56A–56G.
31. "Labelling the Mentally Retarded: A Reply to Lawrence McCullough," in *Ethics and Mental Retardation*, L. Kopelman and J. C. Moskop (eds). Dordrecht: D. Reidel, 1984, 119–23.
32. Review of Edward Walter, *The Immorality of Limiting Growth*, in *Idealistic Studies*, Vol. 14, No. 2, May 1984, 173.
33. "Perspectives on Morality and War in American Society: A Symposium," in *While Soldiers Fought: War in American Society*. Lexington, MA: Ginn Press, 1986, Vol. 2, 763–97.
34. "Ethics before Profits," in *Ethics for Modern Life*, Raziel Abelson and Marie-Louise Friquegnon (eds); 3rd edn. New York: St. Martin's Press, 1987, 288–98.

35. Review of Jo Ann Boydston (ed.), *John Dewey: The Later Works, 1925-1953*, Vol. 7: *Ethics*, in *Transactions of the C. S. Peirce Society: A Quarterly Journal of American Philosophy*, Vol. 23, No. 1, Winter 1987, 135-44.

36. Review of Richard De George, *The Nature and Limits of Authority*, in *Ethics*, Vol. 97, No. 2, January 1987, 494-5.

37. "Terrorism," *Acorn: A Gandhian Review*, Vol. 2, No. 2, September 1987, 4-5.

38. Review of Sergio Cotta, *Why Violence: A Philosophical Interpretation*, in *Journal of Social Philosophy*, Vol. 18, No. 2, Summer 1987, 65-6.

39. "Consent and Decisional Authority in Children's Health Care Decisionmaking: A Reply to Dan Brock," in *Children and Health Care: Moral and Social Issues*, L. M. Kopelman and J. C. Moskop (eds). Hingham, MA: Kluwer Academic, 1988, 213-20.

40. "Children and Health Care Decisionmaking: A Reply to Angela Holder," in *Children and Health Care: Moral and Social Issues*, L. M. Kopelman and J. C. Moskop (eds). Hingham, MA: Kluwer Academic, 1988, 173-80.

41. Review of Alan Ryan (ed.), *The Idea of Freedom: Essays in Honor of Isaiah Berlin*, in *Nous*, Vol. 22, No. 2, June 1988, 297-8.

42. "Violence in the Middle East," *Acorn: A Gandhian Review*, Vol. 3, No. 1, March 1988, 6-7.

43. "Progress or Wisdom?" *Free Inquiry*, Vol. 8, No. 3, Summer 1988, 17-18.

44. "Terrorism and Violence: A Moral Perspective," in *Issues in War & Peace: Philosophical Inquiries*, K. Klein and J. Kunkel (eds). Wolfeboro, NH: Longwood Press, 1989, 115-27.

45. "The Moral Irrelevance of the Distinction between Conventional and Nuclear War," in *Building a World Community: Humanism in the 21st Century*, Paul Kurtz (ed.). Buffalo, NY: Prometheus Books, 1989, 98-105.

46. "The Limited Relevance of Analytical Ethics to the Problems of Bioethics," *Journal of Medicine and Philosophy*, Vol. 15, 1990, 143-59.

47. "Absolute Violence and the Idea of War," in *In the Interest of Peace: A Spectrum of Philosophical Views*, K. Klein and J. Kunkel (eds). Wakefield, NH: Longwood Academic, 1990, 25-31.

48. "Commentary on Stephen Darwall's 'Autonomist Internalism and the Justification of Morals,'" *Nous*, Vol. 24, No. 2, April 1990, 283.

49. Review of Fernando R. Tesón, *Humanitarian Intervention: An Inquiry into Law and Morality*, in *Law and Philosophy*, Vol. 9, No. 3, 1990, 319-24.

50. "Nenacilia Kak Moralniz Princip," *Etika Nenacilia* (Philosofiskoia Obshestvo SSSR, 1991), 23-34. ("Nonviolence as a Moral Principle," in *Ethics of Nonviolence*, Moscow, The Philosophical Society of the USSR, 1991, Russian translation by R. G. Apresyan.)

51. "The Morality of Nonviolence," in *Just War, Nonviolence, and Nuclear Deterrence: Philosophers on War and Peace*, D. Cady and R. Werner (eds). Wakefield, NH: Longwood Academic, 1991, 131-48. Reprinted as "The Morality of Nonviolence," *Concerned Philosophers for Peace Newsletter*, Vol. 15, No. 2, Fall 1995, 5-16.

52. "Emotivity and Elusiveness in Definitions of Violence," in *Justice, Law and Violence*, J. Brady and N. Garver (eds). Philadelphia: Temple University Press, 1991, 48-53.

53. "On War and Morality," selections from my book by that title, in *Taking Sides: Clashing Views on Controversial Moral Issues*, Stephen Satis (ed.), 3rd edn. Guildford, CT: Dushkin, 1992, 363-71.

54. Review of Peter Brock, *Freedom from War: Nonsectarian Pacifism 1814–1914,* in *Journal of Church and State,* Vol. 34, No. 1, 1992, 160–2.
55. Review of Peter Brock, *Freedom from Violence: Sectarian Nonresistance from the Middle Ages to the Great War,* in *International History Review,* Vol. 14, No. 2, May 1992, 348–9.
56. "Can War Be Morally Justified?" in *Just War Theory,* Jean Bethke Elshtain (ed.). New York: New York University Press, 1992, 212–15. Republication of chapter of Holmes, *On War and Morality,* by that same title.
57. Review of Janna Thompson, *Justice and World Order: A Political Inquiry,* in *Ethics,* Vol. 104, No. 1, October 1993, 203.
58. Review of G. Runyon (ed.), *Theology, Politics, and Peace,* in *Critical Review of Books in Religion,* Vol. 5, 1993, 455–6.
59. "Entries: 'Peace' and 'Nonviolence'" (trans. into Polish), in *Prawda Moralna-Dobro Moralne.* Lodz: Wydawnictwo Uniwersystev Lodzkiego, 1993, 141. (Volume in honor of Polish philosopher Ija Lazari-Powlowskiej.)
60. "Bosnia: Resurgent Nationalism and the Need for Nonviolent Responses," *Concerned Philosophers for Peace Newsletter,* Vol. 13, No. 1, Spring 1993, 3–4.
61. "Nenacilia Kak Moralniz Princip" ("Nonviolence as a Moral Principle," trans. into Russian by R. G. Apresyan), in *Ninacelia: Philosophia Etika Nenacilia.* Moskva: Nayuka, 1993, 23–35.
62. Review of Walter Wink, *Engaging the Powers: Discernment and Resistance in a World of Domination,* in *Fellowship,* Vol. 60, No. 1–2, January–February, 1994, 24–5.
63. "Pacifism and Wartime Innocence: A Response," *Social Theory and Practice,* Vol. 20, No. 2, Summer 1994, 193–202.
64. "The Challenge of Nonviolence in the New World Order," in *The Military in New Times: Adapting Armed Forces to a Turbulent World,* James Burk (ed.). Boulder, CO: Westview Press, 1994. Appears also in second edition of this book entitled *The Adaptive Military: Armed Forces in a Turbulent World.* New Brunswick, NJ: Transaction, 1998, 201–20.
65. "From Lenin to Gandhi," in *World Without Violence: Can Gandhi's Vision Become a Reality?* Arun Gandhi (ed.). New Delhi: Wiley Eastern—New Age International, 1994, 125–6.
66. Five entries: "Pacifism," "Violence," "Nonviolence," "Just War Theory," and "Gandhi," in *The Cambridge Dictionary of Philosophy;* Cambridge: Cambridge University Press, 1995; 2nd edn, 1999.
67. "Bosnia: Resurgent Nationalism and the Need for Nonviolent Responses," in *In the Eye of the Storm: Philosophers Reflect on Militarism and Regional Conflicts,* Laura Kaplan and Laurence Bove (eds). Amsterdam-Atlanta: Rodopi, 1995, 293–7.
68. "Privacy: Philosophical Foundations and Moral Dilemmas," in *Privacy Disputed,* Pieter Ippel, Guus de Heij, and Bart Crouwers (eds). The Hague: Registratiekamer, 1995, 15–30.
69. "Morality and Social Good," in *Moralnia E Razionalnosta* (*Morality and Rationality*), trans. into Russian by R. Apresyan. Moscow: Institute of Philosophy of the Russian Academy of Sciences, 1995, 64–79.
70. "Death Be Not Proud," *UR Voice* (student publication of the University of Rochester), Vol. 3, No. 1, 1995, 3, 10.
71. "The Challenge of Nonviolence in Eastern Europe," in *Nonviolence and Tolerance in Changing Eastern and Central Europe.* Vilnius: The Baltic Institute and the

Lithuanian Institute of Philosophy and Sociology, 1996, 119–26. (Volume published simultaneously in Lithuanian.) This essay was also published in 1995 in *Reports and Abstracts: From Nonviolent Liberation to Tolerance: The Development of Civil Society in Eastern Central Europe* (Vilnius, 1995), 21–8.

72. "Nonviolence and the Intifada," in *In the Eye of the Storm: Philosophers Reflect on Militarism and Regional Conflicts*, Laura Kaplan and Laurence Bove (eds). Amsterdam-Atlanta: Rodopi, 1996, 209–23.

73. "Justice, Can Both Sides Have?" in *An Encyclopedia of War and Ethics*, Donald A. Wells (ed.). Westport, CN: Greenwood Press, 1996, 252–5.

74. "Sexual Harassment and the University," *Monist*, Vol. 79, No. 4, October 1996, 499–519.

75. Review of Richard Norman, *Ethics, Killing and War*, in *American Political Science Review*, Vol. 90, No. 2, 1996, 412.

76. Review of Jennifer Welchman, *Dewey's Ethical Thought*, in *Transactions of the Charles S. Peirce Society*, Vol. 32, No. 4, Fall, 1996, 684–9.

77. "The Limited Relevance of Just War Theory to International Violence," in *Morals and Might: Ethics and the Use of Force in Modern International Affairs*, George Lopez and Drew Christiansen (eds). Boulder, CO: Westview Press, 1996.

78. "Beyond Justice and Rights: Competing Israeli and Palestinian Claims," in *Philosophical Perspectives on the Israeli-Palestinian Conflict*, Tomis Kapitan (ed.). Armonk, NY: M. E. Sharpe, 1997, 297–309.

79. "Pacifizm: Pravo na zivot," *Filozofska Istrazivanja*, Zagreb (Croatia), Vol. 1, 1997, 61–70; "Pacifism and the Right to Life," *Synthesis Philosophica*, Zagreb Vol. 12, No. 1, 1997, 255–65; English language version published simultaneously.

80. Review of Richard J. Regan, *Just War: Principles and Cases*, in *International Philosophical Quarterly*, Vol. 37, No. 4, 1997, 483–4.

81. Review of Madhuri Sondhi, *Modernity, Morality and the Mahatma*, in *Acorn: Journal of the Gandhi-King Society*, Vol. 10, No. 1, Fall 1999, 43–5.

82. "Pacifism for Nonpacifists," *Journal of Social Philosophy*, Vol. 30, No. 3, Winter, 1999, 387–401. Republished in *Social and Political Philosophy: Contemporary Perspectives*, James P. Sterba (ed.). New York: Routledge, 2001, 391–407.

83. Forward, *Essays by Lewis White Beck: Five Decades as a Philosopher*, Predrag Cicovacki (ed.). Rochester, NY: University of Rochester Press, 1999, xl–xv.

84. "Kantianism," in *Conduct & Character: Readings in Moral Theory*, Mark Timmons (ed.); 3rd edn. Belmont, CA: Wadsworth, 1999. (From Chapter 8 of *Basic Moral Philosophy*, 3rd edn.)

85. Entry on "Morality," *Dictionary of Existentialism,* Haim Gordon (ed.). Westbrook, CN: Greenwood Press, 1999.

86. "St. Augustine and the Just War Theory," in *The Augustinian Tradition*, Gareth B. Matthews (ed.). Berkeley, CA: University of California Press, 1999, 323–45.

87. "How Good Christians Can Be Good Citizens," *Christian History*, Vol. 19, No. 3, 2000, 38–9.

88. "Consequentialism and Its Consequences," in *Kant's Legacy: Essays in Honor of Lewis White Beck,* Predrag Cicovacki (ed.). Rochester, NY: University of Rochester Press, 2001, 227–45.

89. "A Western Perspective on the Problem of Violence," *The Proceedings of the Twentieth World Congress of Philosophy,* Vol. 11, *Social and Political Philosophy*, David M. Rasmussen (ed.). Boston, MA: Boston College, 2001, 193–205.

90. Review of Glenn D. Paige, *Nonkilling Global Political Science*, in *Fellowship* (magazine of the Fellowship of Reconciliation), March–April 2003, 23–4.
91. Review of Mark Timmons, *Moral Theory: An Introduction*, in *Philosophical Books*, Vol. 44, No. 4, Fall 2003, 371–2.
92. Review of Deen Chatterjee and Don Scheid, *Ethics and Foreign Intervention*, in *Notre Dame Philosophical Reviews*, December 7, 2003; http://ndpr.nd.edu/news/23475-ethics-and-foreign-intervention/.
93. Memorial notice for Richard Taylor, *Proceedings of the American Philosophical Association*, Vol. 77, No. 5. Reprinted in *Philosophy Now*, Vol. 4, 2004.
94. "Pacifism and Weapons of Mass Destruction," in *Ethics and Weapons of Mass Destruction*, Sohail H. Hashmi and Steven P. Lee (eds). Cambridge: Cambridge University Press, 2004, 451–70.
95. Critical Review of David Rodin, *War and Self-Defense*, in *Philosophical Books,* Vol 46, No. 3, July 2005, 254–60.
96. Addendum to entry on "Peace, War, and Philosophy," in *Encyclopedia of Philosophy*; 2nd edn. Detroit: Macmillan, 2006.
97. "Pacifism, Just War and Humanitarian Intervention," in *Pazifismus: Ideengeschichte, Theorie und Praxis*, Barbara Bleisch and Jean-Daniel Strub (eds). Bern, Stuttgart, Wien: Haupt Verlag, 2006, 145–62.
98. "NATO Intervention in Kosovo," in *Rising India: Friends and Foes*, Prakash Nanda ed. New Delhi: Lancer, 2007, 190–207.
99. Entries on "Nonviolence" and "Nonviolence in South Asia," in *Oxford Encyclopedia of the Modern World: 1750–Present*. New York: Oxford University Press, 2008.
100. Review of Henrik Syse and Gregory M. Reichberg (eds), *Ethics, Nationalism, and Just War: Medieval and Contemporary Perspectives*, in *International Review of History*, Vol. 30, No. 4, December 2008, 822–3.
101. Review of C. A. J. Coady, *Morality and Political Violence*, in *Analysis Reviews*, Vol. 69, No. 2, April 2009, 390–2.
102. "My (Non-)Teaching Philosophy," How I Teach: Essays on Teaching by Winners of the Goergen Award for Excellence in Undergraduate Teaching, Vol. 4, University of Rochester, 2011, 7–13.
103. "Toward a Nonviolent American Revolution," *Acorn: Journal of the Gandhi-King Society*, Vol. 14, No. 2, Fall–Winter, 2011–12, 5–15.
104. "Affirmative Action, Diversity and Reparations: How Best to Deal with Social Inequality?" *Hamline Review,* Vol. 31, 2012, 45–76.

Index